ORDER AND ADVENTURE
IN POST-ROMANTIC FRENCH POETRY

C. A. HACKETT

ORDER AND ADVENTURE
IN POST-ROMANTIC
FRENCH POETRY

Essays presented to C. A. Hackett

Edited by
E. M. Beaumont, J. M. Cocking
and
J. Cruickshank

BOOKS
10 East 53d St., New York 10022
(a division of Harper & Row Publishers, Inc.)

Published in the U.S.A. 1973 by HARPER & ROW PUBLISHERS, INC., BARNES
& NOBLE IMPORT DIVISION

ISBN: 06–490334–6

Printed in Great Britain

EDITORS' NOTE

A few days before this volume went to press news came of Ernest Beaumont's sudden death at the age of fifty-seven. His was the moving spirit of the editorial committee. In spite of the difficulties of a professional life shared between Southampton and Dublin he shouldered the main responsibility throughout, with characteristic efficiency and quiet good humour. His fellow editors wish to record their gratitude and their deep sense of loss.

J. M. C.
J. C.

ACKNOWLEDGEMENTS

The editors wish to express their thanks to the University of Southampton for the financial guarantee which it offered in connection with the publication of this volume.

CONTENTS

PLATES

PROFESSOR C. A. HACKETT: THE EARLIER YEARS

Cecil Arthur Hackett entered Birmingham University with a science scholarship. There he escaped into Honours English, with French, Latin and Philosophy as subsidiary subjects. His choice was confirmed by success; fired with enthusiasm by Ernest de Sélincourt on Wordsworth and A. M. D. Hughes on Shelley, he came out top of his first year. In the meantime he had decided to try for Cambridge, and when he moved to Emmanuel College was exposed to the quite different but no doubt equally powerful stimulus of F. R. Leavis. It was not until Part II of the Tripos that he shifted his main interest to French, and again succeeded brilliantly, leaving with a First, a scholarship and a college prize in 1931.

After a brief spell teaching at Coatham School in Yorkshire he came to London as resident tutor at the Mary Ward Settlement, teaching at the same time at Trinity County, a mixed school at Wood Green. At that time he heard someone read *Le Bateau ivre* and decided that the research he wanted to do in French poetry must be first on Rimbaud. Then, in 1934, to Paris, Louis-le-Grand, and later a thesis with a Freudian approach to Rimbaud; this was supervised by Fortunat Strowski, and published by Nizet in 1938. The author was soon acknowledged as an authority and a pioneer in the interpretation of Rimbaud's work; his reputation was consolidated by *Rimbaud l'enfant* in 1948.

We who knew him at that time were aware of his unusual maturity. He seemed to have come to terms with himself and with life; and if he had any *enfer*, it was certainly not *les autres*. I wondered vaguely then why 'Sam' Hackett had the initials C. A. We all knew of his academic success at Emmanuel, but not about the human side of his undergraduate career; that he was identified by his friends with the burglar in an Edgar Wallace thriller, played in Cambridge while he was there—hence 'Sam Hackett'; that he swam and played tennis, soccer and water-polo for his college; that wherever he went he made friends. We were aware of a kind of quiet radiance in his personality, but if we learned anything of his social success it was always from others; and what one heard spelled always respect and affection for a man who never found it difficult to get on with people.

Small wonder, then, that when the war took him into the Field Security and Psychological Warfare Branch of the Intelligence Corps he got to know personally so many of the French writers he already knew well through their work. In Tunis he met Gide, Amrouche, Saint-Exupéry and Philippe Soupault. After the landings in the south of France he met Aragon and Elsa Triolet in Grenoble. Later, in Paris after the liberation, Camus, Éluard, Char and Frénaud. So when, after a year as Education Representative with the British Council in Paris, he came back to academic life as Lecturer, then Senior Lecturer at Glasgow, nobody was better qualified in all respects to provide an introduction to modern French poetry. There must be many specialists teaching French poetry now whose interest was first stirred either by his teaching or by the critical anthology which appeared in 1952, and again, in a revised and enlarged edition, in 1964.

In 1952 he was elected to the Southampton chair, and there I must hand the story on to a colleague who was close to him at the time. It is good to know that his retirement is nominal; that students in Western Australia will have had the benefits of his teaching and that we can look forward to reading yet more of his work, not only on Rimbaud, but on Baudelaire, Villiers, Valéry, Jarry and Michaux. His *New French Poetry: an Anthology* includes twenty-two poets born since 1924 and will no doubt have appeared before the present volume.

J. M. C.

THE LATER YEARS

Sam Hackett came to us in Southampton at a critical juncture in the development of the University and therefore of the French Department. The University had just achieved independent status. One of the new professor's first objects was to devise a syllabus that allowed for a more detailed textual study than had been possible under the tutelage of London. Poetry was ever his prime concern and the first casualty of his coming was the poem, offered for translation into English, as an alternative to a prose passage, in the London paper. That such an irreplaceable work of art should be subject to the multifold mutilations inflicted by students often of indifferent aesthetic discernment as well as inadequate linguistic achievement he could not tolerate. Indeed, what Professor Hackett brought to his Department, staff and students, of inestimable value was his own acute aesthetic sensitivity, his own fine, discriminating, indeed unerring, sense of literary judgment and his own exacting standard of accurate and fully documented scholarship. His stringent tongue did not spare those who failed at times to live up to these desiderata. It was always a delight to wait for, and usually to hear, the telling phrase that came in a vote of thanks to a visiting speaker which, without causing offence, nevertheless elegantly and lightheartedly highlighted some disquieting shortcoming. He was a Head of Department of uncompromising integrity, concerned only with academic issues. Under his guidance the Department grew from a total of six members in 1952 to a total of thirteen when he retired in 1970. The undergraduate course was radically revised when the Arts Faculty decided in the early 1960s to replace General Degrees by Combined Honours Degrees. The French Department of Southampton was among the first to insist on a full year abroad for students of French. Professor Hackett was not deterred by Faculty opposition from insisting on a Part 1 examination after two years and a Part 2 examination after four years.

Under Professor Hackett, the French Department of Southampton developed a strong literary orientation, particularly in the modern period, but without sacrificing language work. Professor Hackett's own concern for the spoken language was shown by his award each year of a personal prize for spoken French. He was always well aware of new developments and tried early to secure the interest of the

Faculty in Linguistics; however, he had to content himself with the appointment of a linguist in his own Department. He was also very much concerned with the development of Fine Arts and played for many years a dominant role on the Fine Arts Committee. After serving on the Library Committee for many years, he became Curator and eventually Senior Curator. He was also for many years a member of the Committee for Advanced Studies and was Chairman of the B.Ed. Committee. His most distinguished service to the University was, however, as Dean of the Faculty of Arts from 1956 to 1959, a period of vital expansion. He was a good Dean, patient, yet firm, imperturbable and businesslike. It was during his term of office as Dean that he was made *Chevalier de la Légion d'Honneur*. He was at different times President of the Southampton Branch of the Alliance Française and of the Modern Languages Society. In the last few years he has been a member of the Editorial Board of *French Studies*.

The eighteen years that Professor Hackett spent in Southampton were for his colleagues precious years in which they could fulfil their own potentialities without irksome pressures. He was not anxious to reserve all aspects of administration for himself, taking small pleasure in these unscholarly and aesthetically unproductive pursuits. The Department worked smoothly with a general sharing of various burdens. His charm of manner, his liveliness of wit, his urbanity and his courtesy were qualities, by no means the universal heritage of the academically distinguished, which endeared him to many. He was an excellent host, as his wife Hazel was an unsurpassable hostess, warmly welcoming and efficiently discreet.

One can say truly of Sam Hackett that to have worked with him closely was an experience that was both pleasurable and profitable; the keen edge of his mind sharpened one's own. That in itself is sufficient tribute to the enduring quality of his influence. He was much in demand and had to refuse many invitations. Among those he accepted were a year's Visiting Professorship at Brown University in Rhode Island in 1962–63 and a shorter term as Visiting Professor at Dalhousie University in 1967–68. His retirement allows him to accept more of these invitations as well as to put to paper the many essays in discernment that he alone can provide. His former colleagues are happy in the knowledge that he has chosen to live in retirement within easy reach of Southampton.

E. M. B.

BIBLIOGRAPHY OF THE WRITINGS
OF C. A. HACKETT

BOOKS

Le Lyrisme de Rimbaud, Paris, Nizet et Bastard, 1938.

Rimbaud l'enfant (with a Preface by Gaston Bachelard), Paris, Corti, 1948.

An Anthology of Modern French Poetry. From Baudelaire to the Present Day, Oxford, Basil Blackwell, 1952. (Second enlarged edition, 1964, third revised edition, 1970.)

Rimbaud, London, Bowes and Bowes, 1957.

Autour de Rimbaud, Paris, Klincksieck, 1967.

New French Poetry: an Anthology with Introduction and Notes, Oxford, Basil Blackwell, 1973.

ARTICLES

'Mallarmé "Poète sans Œuvre"', *French Studies*, IV, no. 2 (April 1950), pp. 179–87.

'Rimbaud et Balzac', *Revue des Sciences humaines* (1955), N.S. fasc. 78, pp. 263–6.

'Some Aspects of Contemporary French Poetry', *Second Wessex*, IX, no. 2 (Summer 1955), pp. 4–9.

'Verlaine's Influence on Rimbaud', in *Studies in Modern French Literature presented to P. Mansell Jones by pupils, colleagues and friends*, Manchester University Press, 1961, pp. 163–80.

'Michaux and Plume', *French Studies*, XVII, no. 1 (January 1963), pp. 40–9.

'La Lumière dans l'œuvre de René Char', *L'Arc*, VI, no. 22 (Summer 1963), pp. 70–5.

'A Note on the *Album de Monsieur Teste*', *French Studies*, XVIII, no. 1 (January 1964), pp. 33–5.

'*Being Beauteous*: Rimbaud et Longfellow', *Revue d'Histoire littéraire de la France*, LXV, no. 1 (January–March 1965), pp. 109–12.

'Rimbaud's "Poetic Practice" and "Design"', *Modern Philology*, LXII, no. 4 (May 1965), pp. 348–52.

'Rimbaud and Apollinaire', *French Studies*, XIX, no. 3 (July 1965), pp. 266–77.

'An Introduction to the Poetry of René Char', *Forum for Modern Language Studies*, II, no. 4 (October 1966), pp. 347–55.

'Teste and *La Soirée avec Monsieur Teste*', *French Studies*, XXI, no. 2 (April 1967), pp. 111–24.

'Rimbaud and the "splendides villes"', *L'Esprit créateur*, IX, no. 1 (Spring 1969), pp. 46–53.

'Seven Young French Poets, A New Trend in French Poetry', *Mosaic*, II, no. 4 (Summer 1969), pp. 95–111.

'Rimbaud, *Illuminations: Aube*', in *The Art of Criticism, Essays in French Literary Analysis*, ed. Peter H. Nurse, Edinburgh University Press, 1969, pp. 217–23.

'André Frénaud and the Theme of the Quest', in *Modern Miscellany presented to Eugène Vinaver, by pupils, colleagues and friends*, Manchester University Press, 1969, pp. 126–36.

'Baudelaire and Samuel Cramer', in *Studies in Honour of A. R. Chisholm*, ed. Wallace Kirsop, Melbourne, The Hawthorne Press, 1969, pp. 179–87.

'Valéry and the Swans', *Yale French Studies*, no. 44 (1970), pp. 148–56.

'Image et figure, du Surréalisme au Formalisme', *L'Information littéraire*, XXII, no. 5 (November–December 1970), pp. 230–3.

Professor Hackett has also written numerous reviews.

ORDRE ET AVENTURE DANS
AURÉLIA
Sur quelques passages obscurs des *Mémorables*

Gérard de Nerval a déclaré que ses *Chimères* avaient été composées dans un état de 'rêverie surnaturaliste' et qu'il ne fallait pas trop se préoccuper d'y découvrir un sens. Cette déclaration ne s'applique sans doute pas à la suite des cinq sonnets dont se compose 'Le Christ aux Oliviers', ni à la poésie gnomique des *Vers dorés*. Mais les pièces les plus célèbres, 'El Desdichado', 'Artémis', sont placées sous le signe de l'hermétisme.

Tout autre fut son dessein dans *Aurélia*. D'emblée, le narrateur prend ses distances avec le rêveur dont il transcrit les impressions. Son intention didactique est explicitement affirmée : 'Si je ne pensais que la mission d'un écrivain est d'analyser sincèrement ce qu'il éprouve dans les graves circonstances de la vie, et si je ne me proposais un but que je crois utile, je m'arrêterais ici, et je n'essayerais pas de décrire ce que j'éprouvai ensuite dans une série de visions insensées peut-être, ou vulgairement maladives' (I, 3); 'Je croirai avoir fait quelque chose de bon et d'utile en énonçant naïvement la succession des idées par lesquelles j'ai retrouvé le repos et une force nouvelle à opposer aux malheurs futurs de la vie' (II, 4). Aussi a-t-il cherché la clarté : 'Cela est devenu clair, c'est le principal', écrivait-il le 25 Juin 1854 au Dr Blanche. Il a voulu mettre en évidence la logique de ses rêves, afin d'en dégager une signification.

Des difficultés d'exégèse subsistent certes. On ne saurait s'étonner d'en rencontrer surtout dans les *Mémorables* (II, 6), puisque le narrateur note sans les commenter une succession de rêves dont l'étrangeté est la loi. Mais ces rêves, comme tous les précédents, possèdent un pouvoir signifiant. Ils s'inscrivent dans l'œuvre à une place bien déterminée : 'Je crois que c'est ici', indiquait-il sur une épreuve au directeur de la *Revue de Paris*, Louis Ulbach, 'que se placent naturellement les rêves *Sur un pic élancé de l'Auvergne . . .* et les rêves qui suivent'; il ajoutait, songeant à l'enchaînement avec les passages voisins, que 'le sens suit très bien'.

Essayer de retrouver une logique interne dans les *Mémorables*, c'est donc être fidèle au dessein de l'écrivain qui, loin de tendre aucun piège, aurait été plus clair encore, s'il l'avait pu. Notre analyse portera sur quelques passages qui posent encore des problèmes.

I. LA PREMIÈRE OCTAVE

Le premier mouvement des *Mémorables* s'éclaire presque tout entier grâce à deux textes que M. Jean Richer rappelle dans son édition critique d'*Aurélia*. De l'un, qui se trouve dans le Carnet de Notes du *Voyage en Orient*, il suffit de citer quatre mots: 'Auvergne—Montagnes—Harmonie première' et de l'autre, dans une lettre de 1841 à Cavé, cette phrase: 'Le Cantal d'Auvergne correspond au Cantal des Monts Himalaya', qui illustre toute une audacieuse théorie sur l'origine commune des races humaines. Le passage sur la chevauchée triomphale accomplie par le héros, grâce à la médiation de Saturnin, en compagnie du Christ et de la 'Grande Amie', ne présente pas non plus d'obscurités majeures.

Mais le mouvement suivant comporte des détails d'une interprétation beaucoup plus délicate, que les commentateurs ne se sont guère risqués à expliquer. Il sera précieux de recourir à une comparaison avec le manuscrit, fort heureusement conservé pour ce fragment (les différences apparaissent en italiques):

Texte imprimé	*Manuscrit*
Une étoile a brillé tout à coup et m'a révélé le secret du Monde et des mondes. Hosannah! paix à la Terre et gloire aux Cieux.	*Savez-vous, mes enfants, le secret du Monde et de tous les mondes, c'est Harmonie épouse de Cadmus qui vous l'apprendra:*
Du sein des ténèbres muettes deux notes ont résonné—l'une grave, l'autre aiguë,—et l'orbe éternel s'est mis à tourner aussitôt. Sois bénie, ô première octave qui commenças l'hymne *divin*! Du dimanche au dimanche, enlace tous les jours dans ton réseau magique: les monts *te* chantent aux vallées, les sources aux rivières,—les rivières aux fleuves, et les fleuves à l'Océan [. . . .]	Du sein des ténèbres muettes, deux notes ont résonné,—l'une grave, l'autre aiguë,—et l'orbe éternel s'est mis à tourner aussitôt. Sois bénie, ô première octave qui commenças l'hymne *éternel*! Du dimanche au dimanche, enlace tous les jours dans ton réseau magique: les monts *le* chantent aux vallées, les sources aux rivières,—les rivières aux fleuves, et les fleuves à l'Océan [. . . .]

Le texte des *Mémorables* a été livré par Nerval à Ulbach au dernier moment; il n'a pas eu le temps d'en lire une épreuve. Toute la dernière partie d'*Aurélia* ayant été publiée après sa mort, rien ne permet donc d'affirmer qu'il ait lui-même indiqué les variantes livrées pour ce passage par la *Revue de Paris*. Les leçons du manuscrit appellent donc une attention particulière. Attachons-nous à celle qui est fournie par le premier paragraphe.

Dans le texte imprimé, 'le secret du Monde et des mondes' est révélé par 'une étoile' qui 'a brillé tout à coup': indication vague et peu significative. En désignant 'Harmonie', le manuscrit aide à retrouver la continuité vraisemblable de l'inspiration. Cette 'fille de Cadmus' est la figure mythologique de l'Ordre et de la Beauté. 'Harmonie' a donné la première impulsion au Cosmos, à 'l'orbe éternel' dont le globe terrestre est l'image, en lançant les deux première notes de l'hymne qui en règle le mouvement.

Quelles sont ces deux notes, 'l'une grave, l'autre aiguë'? Apparemment celles de l'octave fondamentale ou première (du *do* au *do*) où s'inscrit l'accord parfait (*do–mi–sol–do*). Mais le syncrétisme religieux de Nerval associe la tradition du christianisme aux légendes du paganisme. 'Du dimanche au dimanche' (*do*minica dies, jour du Seigneur), le calendrier chrétien définit une autre octave, celle où s'inscrivent les jours de la semaine.

'L'hymne éternel' se déroule ainsi à travers le temps, d'une semaine à une autre, comme à travers l'espace, des monts aux vallées, des sources aux rivières, des rivières aux fleuves et des fleuves à la mer: commandé par le pouvoir céleste, il anime d'abord les hauteurs et résonne de proche en proche, dans le monde entier, en un hosannah perpétuel.

II. LE DIEU DU NORD ET LA PERLE ROSE

Malheur à toi, dieu du Nord,—qui brisas d'un coup de marteau la sainte table composée des sept métaux les plus précieux! car tu n'as pu briser la *Perle rose* qui reposait au centre. Elle a rebondi sous le fer,—et voici que nous nous sommes armés pour elle. . . . Hosannah!

Le *macrocosme*, ou grand monde, a été construit par art cabalistique; le *microcosme*, ou petit monde, est son image réfléchie dans tous les coeurs. La perle rose a été teinte du sang royal des Walkyries. Malheur à toi, dieu-forgeron qui as voulu briser un monde!

Cependant, le pardon du Christ a été aussi prononcé pour toi!

Sois donc béni toi-même, ô Thor, le géant—le plus puissant des fils d'Odin! Sois béni dans Héla ta mère, car souvent le trépas est doux,—et dans ton frère Loki, et dans ton chien Garnur!

Le serpent qui entoure le Monde est béni lui-même, car il relâche ses anneaux, et sa gueule béante aspire la fleur d'anxoka, la fleur soufrée,—la fleur éclatante du soleil!

Que Dieu préserve le divin Balder, le fils d'Odin, et Freya la belle!

Ce second fragment des *Mémorables* a longtemps été mal compris, car l'érudition mythologique en masque l'unité profonde. L'allusion au 'dieu-forgeron' paraît avoir égaré les commentateurs, qui se souvenaient de Tubal-Kaïn, ancêtre des forgerons, évoqué dans la partie du *Voyage en Orient* intitulée *Histoire de la Reine du Matin et de Soliman, prince des génies*. Selon ce texte, Tubal-Kaïn guidait son descendant Adoniram, l'architecte, dans les profondeurs où s'entretenait le culte du Feu. Grâce à lui, Adoniram pénétrait les secrets des théogonies disparues, retrouvait les merveilles du génie primitif et ressuscitait le rêve orgueilleux de Caïn.

D'après certaines gloses, l'apostrophe des *Mémorables* au 'dieu du Nord', d'abord maudit, puis pardonné, signifierait la condamnation, puis la rédemption du caïnisme. Mais le caïnisme ne nous paraît aucunement mis en question dans ce passage, entièrement consacré aux légendes de la mythologie germanique et scandinave.

Tout devient clair si l'on s'avise que Thor, fils d'Odin, est traditionnellement armé d'un marteau d'or. Nerval et Gautier l'ont vu figuré avec cet attribut dans les dessins composés par leur ami Paul Chenavard en vue de la décoration du Panthéon. Des articles sur ce projet, parus dans *La Presse* en 1848 et signés de Théophile Gautier, mais rédigés avec le concours de Nerval, comme l'a montré M. Richer, l'évoquent en compagnie de Balder et de Freya. Or l'idée de Chenavard était d'associer en une frise les dieux de toutes les religions. Il avait d'autre part dessiné, pour la mosaïque centrale du pavement, 'les trois vertus théologales, la Foi, l'Espérance et la Charité', conduisant 'les dieux du Nord, Odin [. . . .] et Thor, le fils d'Odin'. Tout l'esprit réconciliateur des *Mémorables* est déjà dans cette composition.

Le mouvement général de ce rêve, ou plutôt de cette méditation religieuse, est donc le suivant: 'Malheur à toi, Thor, fils d'Odin, qui as voulu briser un monde. Sois béni cependant, avec ta mère [Héla ou la Mort, reine des enfers], avec ton frère et ton chien, puisque le Christ t'a enveloppé dans son pardon universel. Que Dieu te préserve, avec tes compagnons de légende!'

Quelques détails obscurs demeurent à expliquer. Quelle est cette 'sainte Table composée des sept métaux les plus précieux', que le Dieu-forgeron des fables nordiques a brisée de son marteau d'or? Deux autres textes de Nerval concourent à éclairer cette énigme. Dans la première partie d'*Aurélia* (chapitre VII), le narrateur racontait comment, dans une crise mystique, il avait tâché 'de réunir les pierres de la Table sacrée'. Dans le Carnet de Notes du *Voyage en Orient*, d'autre part, l'écrivain évoquait 'la Table d'émeraude bordée de pierres précieuses de Salomon', monument biblique signalé dans la *Revue britannique* de décembre 1840, dont il fournissait la référence. Salomon, dépositaire des pouvoirs de son maître, le dieu juif Adonaï, réunit dans sa main les prestiges symbolisés par cette Table où figurent les sept pierres précieuses, dotées chacune des propriétés talismaniques correspondant à l'une des sept planètes.

Au centre de la Table, une Perle rose, attribut familier de la reine de Saba, la bien-aimée du roi Salomon. 'Un collier de perles roses entoure son col', lisait-on dans la version primitive d'*Aurélia*. Le symbolisme des *Mémorables* est mis ainsi en plein évidence. Suscitées par Thor, fils d'Odin, les Walkyries de la mythologie germanique ont répandu leur sang pour lutter contre la civilisation judéochrétienne; elles se sont attaquées à la tradition de Salomon; mais elles n'ont pu vaincre la magique inspiration qui anima la sagesse du fils de David. La Perle rose a 'rebondi sous le fer'; le message oriental a survécu aux atteintes des envahisseurs barbares et trouvé de nouveaux protecteurs, prêts à la défendre. Mais au delà de la lutte est déjà affirmée la certitude de la victoire et, au delà de la victoire, celle du pardon.

Signe suprême de ce pardon: la bénédiction du serpent qui entoure le monde, image de l'Esprit des Ténèbres. Selon la version primitive d'*Aurélia*, il tentait de saisir la mystérieuse 'fleur d'anxoka', le pavot solaire, que balance dans ses mains la reine de Saba (ou du Matin, ou du Midi); selon les *Mémorables*, il aspire cette fleur de feu et s'irradie lui-même de la lumière qui doit régner de nouveau sur un monde réconcilié.

III. LA PAIX EUROPÉENNE

Nourri des souvenirs d'un voyage en Hollande, le rêve suivant (celui de la petite fille et de la chatte maigre, rencontrées par temps de neige à Zaandam) ne soulève aucune difficulté d'interprétation littérale, en dépit de sa bizarrerie. Une leçon de sagesse cosmique semble s'en dégager, parfaitement accordée avec l'inspiration générale des *Mémorables*. 'Un chat, c'est quelque chose': le plus humble des êtres vivants a sa place et tient son rôle dans la création.

Plus déroutant apparaît le dernier rêve, si on n'en distingue les éléments constitutifs, associés non sans quelque artifice par la fantaisie de l'écrivain. En les mettant en lumière, nous pourrons montrer comment se composent des souvenirs rattachés à des épisodes bien distincts de son expérience.

'Cette nuit', écrit le narrateur, 'mon rêve s'est transporté d'abord à Vienne'. En fait, Gérard de Nerval réutilise un souvenir de 1839, noté dans le *Voyage en Orient* (*Œuvres complètes*, Pléiade, II, 54):

Aurélia	*Voyage en Orient*
On sait que sur chacune des places de cette ville sont élevées de grandes *colonnes* qu'on appelle 'pardons.' Des *nuages* de marbre s'accumulent en figurant l'*ordre salomonique* et supportent des *globes* où président assises des divinités.	Au milieu [du Graben] se trouve une *colonne* monumentale ressemblant à un bilboquet. La *boule* est formée de *nuages* sculptés qui supportent des anges dorés. La colonne elle-même, torse, comme celles de l'*ordre salomonique*.

La description d'*Aurélia* est plus ample: il est question, non plus d'une colonne au milieu d'une place, mais d'un ensemble de colonnes élevées sur chacune des places de la ville. Elle est plus homogène: la comparaison presque burlesque d'une colonne avec un bilboquet disparaît. Elle est plus majestueuse: l'écrivain ne note plus le simple ornement des 'anges dorés', mais évoque la présidence de divinités assises. La référence à l'ordre salomonique est soigneusement conservée, car elle assure au tableau une dimension légendaire.

Voici, cependant, un nouveau recoupement et, cette fois, avec un souvenir de 1850, noté dans *Lorely* (*Œuvres complètes*, Pléiade II, 835), à propos d'une visite au palais archiducal de Weimar:

Aurélia	*Lorely*
Tout à coup, ô merveille! je me mis à songer à cette auguste sœur de l'empereur de Russie, dont j'ai vu le palais impérial à Weimar. Une mélancolie pleine de douceur me fit voir les *brumes* colorées d'*un paysage de Norvège éclairé d'un jour gris et doux*. Les nuages devinrent transparents, et je vis se creuser devant moi un abîme profond où s'engouffraient tumultueusement les flots de la Baltique glacée. Il semblait que le fleuve entier de la Néva, aux eaux bleues, dût s'engloutir dans cette fissure du globe. Les vaisseaux de Cronstadt et de Saint-Pétersbourg s'agitaient sur leurs ancres, prêts à se détacher et à disparaître dans le gouffre. . . .	On admire encore, dans les appartements des princes, de fort beaux paysages de M. Heller, dont la teinte *brumeuse et mélancolique* rappelle les Ruysdaël. Ce sont des *paysages de Norvège éclairés d'un jour gris et doux*, des scènes d'hiver et de naufrage, des contours de rochers majestueux, de beaux mouvements de vagues, une nature qui fait frémir et qui fait rêver. . . .

Le narrateur présente comme une 'merveille' de son rêve l'ingénieuse idée qui lui est venue d'associer au souvenir du séjour à Vienne celui du passage plus récent à Weimar. Le voyageur de *Lorely* se rappelait les tableaux qui se trouvent dans le palais et qui représentent des paysages norvégiens. Mais l'auteur d'*Aurélia* feint d'avoir été transporté en Norvège par un élan de son imagination : il déclare avoir vu, non pas des œuvres d'art dans une salle de musée, mais un paysage naturel, un paysage agité, où se déroulent des scènes d'hiver et de naufrage. Ce naufrage, on le pressent, on le redoute. C'est celui de la flotte russe qui risque de s'engloutir dans la Mer Baltique.

En se remémorant les 'marines' septentrionales réunies au musée de Weimar par la grande-duchesse Amélie, sœur du tsar, l'auteur d'*Aurélia*, dans un même mouvement, évoque deux pays : la Norvège et la Russie. Ainsi s'explique un nouveau transfert du rêve, qui s'achève à Saint-Pétersbourg :

> Sous le vif rayon qui perçait la brume, je vis apparaître aussitôt le rocher qui supporte la statue de Pierre le Grand. Au-dessus de ce solide piédestal vinrent se grouper des nuages qui s'élevaient jusqu'au zénith. Ils étaient chargés de figures radieuses et divines, parmi lesquelles on distinguait les deux Catherine et l'impératrice sainte Hélène, accompagnées des plus grandes princesses de Moscovie et de Pologne. Leurs doux regards, dirigés vers la France, rapprochaient l'espace au moyen de longs télescopes de cristal. Je vis par là que notre patrie devenait l'arbitre de la querelle orientale, et qu'elles en attendaient la solution. Mon rêve se termina par le doux espoir que la paix nous serait enfin donnée.

Nous voilà ainsi amenés par le narrateur d'*Aurélia* à l'actualité de 1854. Le rêve des *Mémorables* date, en effet, de l'époque critique où s'annonçaient la guerre de Crimée et l'expédition de la Baltique. Nerval veut croire à la possibilité d'une démarche pacifique de la Russie et d'une médiation de la diplomatie française pour le règlement de la question d'Orient. D'où la vision de Saint-Pétersbourg. Sur de nouveaux 'nuages' sculptés, semblables à ceux de Vienne, sont rassemblées les deux Catherine, symboles historiques de la grandeur russe, avec l'impératrice Hélène, mère de Constantin, qui fit ériger la basilique du Saint-Sepulcre, et en compagnie 'des plus grandes princesses de Moscovie et de Pologne' : tous les prestiges de l'Histoire sont mis en œuvre pour suggérer l'idée d'un règlement pacifique de la crise orientale. Les images qui se sont succédées dans ce dernier rêve sont donc agencées avec une lucidité subtile par un écrivain pleinement conscient de ses fins.

Toute la suite des *Mémorables* témoigne de la même vigilance. Au terme de l'aventure décrite dans *Aurélia*, le narrateur veut donner à entendre qu'il a conquis le salut en retrouvant sa place au sein de l'universelle harmonie, idéalement restituée. Peu soucieux d'une fidélité littérale à ses souvenirs, il les ordonne dans le double dessein de composer une œuvre d'art et de formuler un message spirituel.

Paris   PIERRE-GEORGES CASTEX

BAUDELAIRE AND JOUVE

Dear 'Sam',

Thanks for your article on *La Fanfarlo*. Yes, I do indeed share your admiration for this story, and am delighted to find it is a favourite with you too. Of course, your 'Baudelaire and Samuel Cramer' (*AJFS*, 1969) explains much better than I could how Baudelaire went on to 'achieve a more profound and cruel lucidity', and with it (as you say) a poetic liberation very different from that which he has ascribed to his creature, Cramer.

My own affection for the story is founded more on the way in which it can supply an illuminating key to much which must at first sight baffle the young reader of *Les Fleurs du Mal*. The series of conversations between Cramer and Madame Cosmelly and between him and La Fanfarlo herself do give us the best introduction to many of the violently ambivalent 'love-poems' such as 'Le Vampire', 'Le Flacon', 'A une Madone', 'La Béatrice' or even 'Héauton-timorouménos'. Nor am I thinking only of passages like Cramer's speech to Madame Cosmelly: 'Figurez-vous qu'au moment où vous vous appuyez sur l'être de votre choix et que vous lui dites: Envolons-nous ensemble et cherchons le fond du ciel—une voix implacable et sérieuse penche à votre oreille pour vous dire que nos passions sont des menteuses . . .,' for there Samuel is playing his comedian's role. There are others where Baudelaire stands back and *explains* his own hero in whom 'love was less a matter of the senses than *le discernement*'.

La Fanfarlo résumait donc pour lui la ligne et l'attrait et quand . . . il la regardait il semblait voir l'infini derrière les yeux clairs de cette beauté. . . . Du reste, comme il arrive aux hommes exceptionnels, il était souvent seul dans son paradis, nul ne pouvant l'habiter que lui . . . aussi dans le ciel où il régnait, son amour commençait à être triste et malade de la mélancolie du bleu, comme un royal solitaire. . . . .

Or finally, and still more appositely: 'il est probable que la Fanfarlo a aimé Samuel, mais de cet amour que connaissent peu d'âmes, avec une rancune au fond.' It is curious that in each of these instances Baudelaire visibly asks us to take his creation, his caricature, Samuel, for more singular than he may appear. Who hasn't heard at some time that 'voix implacable et sérieuse?' Does it only happen to 'des hommes exceptionnels' that have a suspicion they are 'seuls dans

leur paradis?' That love, 'avec une rancune au fond', is it so un-
common, alas!, even if not pushed, as Baudelaire at once indicates, to
the extreme of exemplifying 'l'amour maladif des courtisanes.'

Thus the texture of this beautifully written story is for me the best
of all introductions to the paradoxes of Baudelaire's psychology. The
self-caricature is carefully shaded to render Cramer less singular than
he thinks, or than Baudelaire was to become; and even if, as Jean
Prévost claimed, 'comme Stendhal, Baudelaire a élaboré son esthétique et ses dogmes avant son œuvre,' this tale of his twenty-fifth year
deserves a privileged place as introduction.

It is perhaps time to admit that *à son défaut* I have a preference—an
anti-professorial one which perhaps dates me—for the short-essay as
an introduction to most poets, and, best of all, the essays of other
poets, that *critique des créateurs* of the inter-war period which Valéry
and Claudel (among others) practised, and whose monument was, I
suppose, the NRF *Tableau de la littérature française*, edited by Gide
and of which only the first part ever was collected, but where more
than a dozen brilliant essays on authors from Corneille to Chénier
by writers from Alain to André Malraux show how valuable it is to
have a sharp view-point to stir a student's imagination, instead of
blunting the sharp impact of the chef d'œuvre with a safely padded
mattress of historical information.

Thus in the case of Baudelaire the famous *Situation de Baudelaire*
of Valéry remains the most stimulating panoramic view of its subject,
above all because Valéry, like his subject, saw in Poe the great mid-
century landmark in poetics. Against a still wider perspective one
could claim this, too, for the opening chapter of Marcel Raymond's
De Baudelaire au surréalisme. Yet I think that Raymond himself
might agree that an essay, originally dedicated in fact to him, P.-J.
Jouve's *Tombeau de Baudelaire*, is of quite peculiar interest both for
what it succeeds and does not succeed in doing.[1]

There are a number of ways in which Jouve's own poetry cannot
fail to remind us of Baudelaire (as has often been remarked). Unlike
Baudelaire though, whose whole aesthetic and dominant traits were
defined when he was still a young man, Jouve has suppressed all that
he wrote before he was thirty-seven years of age, on the ground that it
lacks any genuine inner tension. This contrast between the two poets
certainly leads Jouve to insist all the more on the essential unity of
Baudelaire's brief career. His essay is quite specifically a *tombeau*
since—Mallarmé-wise—his concern is Baudelaire:

> Tel qu'en lui-même l'éternité le change.

Jouve's *conversion* or *vita nuova* (as he describes it) appears to have lain in his discovery, at a moment of personal crisis, of Freudian psychoanalysis, for the disavowed *Tragiques* amply show the permanence of his *nature d'écorché* and of his acute sense of sin. These are (in Starobinski's phrase) elaborated into a new source of highly condensed inspiration, a *force poétisante* where the effort to reconcile erotic impulse and desire for self-destruction has produced a somewhat abstruse poetical mysticism (in the fullest sense of that term).

All these factors are turned to advantage in *Le Tombeau de Baudelaire*. In the first place, they forbid him to discuss Baudelaire's 'Satanism' as merely a piece of juvenile exhibitionism of which he was unable to rid himself. For Jouve this Satanism is one of the masks of Baudelaire. *La beauté du Mal* is claimed as the *recherche de l'Inconscient*, as being central to his motivation *qua* poet—'sous l'impulsion d'une curiosité intense et quelque peu perverse . . .' An analysis of *Les Litanies de Satan* serves to show that a Satan who can be invoked as full of pity for the outcast is indeed God 'ayant dû subir un déguisement'. It also shows us how this mask has become part of Baudelaire's very nature, an instrument of his self-knowledge, of his painful dualism and his taste for blasphemy and horror.

This is not Baudelaire's only mask, of course. Indeed Jouve's emphasis on the necessary self-contradictions, the defence mechanisms of Baudelaire are part of an almost Pirandellian way of saving some relic of self-respect and, indeed, Jouve's comprehension of his poetic conscience is a welcome relief from the sterile indictment of Sartre, whose demonstration that the author of *Les Fleurs du Mal* chose deliberately his tragic lot seems so futile a performance precisely because it is wholly irrelevant to that masterpiece.

There is also the dandy's mask, *le masque esthétique*, which leads Baudelaire to push to the limit Poe's aesthetic pretension to an ultra-lucid, wholly calculated art. In theory at least, if not in practice, for the function of this mask too is to hide from the world his own suffering; it is only for himself that he admits: 'j'ai cultivé mon hystérie avec jouissance et terreur'. But it is *à propos de* Poe that Jouve is one of those perspicacious enough to discern the influence of the *Tales* on *Spleen de Paris*—*histoires en raccourci*, and this leads him to note that, while it is here that Baudelaire insists on the memory of simple, daily happenings which only indirectly acquire the value of symbols, it is also here that he escapes from the mechanism of the mask, and as a result the poetic tension is singularly diminished. Yet, strangely enough, while dream inspiration figures increasingly in the list of projected but unwritten *poèmes en prose*, those written never constitute, as one might have expected, a prefiguration of surrealism. Indeed, the most moving sentence of what is an unfinished work is the invocation which explodes in 'A une heure du matin . . . Ames de ceux que j'ai aimés, de ceux que j'ai chantés, fortifiez-moi'—or more unexpectedly the prayer which ends the strange *Mademoiselle Bistouri:* 'Seigneur . . . vous qui avez peut-être mis dans mon esprit le goût de l'horreur pour convertir mon cœur, comme la guérison au bout d'une lance, Seigneur, ayez pitié des fous et des folles . . .'

Finally, to turn to the Baudelairian paradoxes on the theme of Prostitution, that complex which may well have its roots far deeper than the disastrous consequences of the *liaison* with *Sara la louchette* away back in 1840, but which eventually acquires the philosophical generality of the much quoted declarations of *Mon Cœur mis à nu*, on this topic Jouve is certainly both succinct and illuminating. 'Tout son système de pensée à cet égard, orienté en vue d'une liberté cynique, tendait à renouveler en lui une honte dont il avait besoin,' he says, giving what I have called a Pirandellian interpretation. He continues: 'La Prostitution reçoit le caractère sacré. A travers son affection sensuelle de la fille, Baudelaire s'identifie à la fille même, il est prostitué comme elle, et par cet abandon il trouve sa propre résolution . . . en vient à donner de la Prostitution une version spirituelle, à rêver une prostitution idéale, à faire de la prostitution le masque nécessaire à l'adoration.' And Jouve quotes the surprising declaration of *Fusées*: 'L'Amour, c'est le goût de la Prostitution. Il n'est même pas de plaisir noble qui ne puisse être ramené à la Prostitution.' The key to such a view is, of course, that any *lending* of oneself, any sacrifice of one's total independence (regardless of motive), is regarded as 'prostitution', all of a piece with the earlier Dandy code dating from the days of the Hôtel Pimodan. It is thus that we reach the final paradox—some eleven years after *Fusées*, in *Mon Cœur mis à nu* which Jouve also quotes—'L'être le plus prostitué, c'est Dieu, puisqu'il est l'ami suprême pour chaque individu, puisqu'il est le réservoir commun, inépuisable de l'amour.'

Perhaps Jouve's most interesting suggestion here is one relating this preoccupation to *Spleen de Paris*, in which he sees the nostalgia of a full self-confession.

No doubt there is great danger in identifying some of the views and complexes of Jouve with those of Baudelaire, a subject which would lead us far afield. It is, however, in this context that he indicates a group of poems—most of them well-known,[2] and undertakes an analysis of 'Le Cygne'.

The performance is a curious one, and indicates the limitations of the essay examined. What is unique about 'Le Cygne' is that it deals with the creation of a poem, its creation by the fusion of two recollected glimpses of the past. In fact, 'Le Cygne' gets as close as any poem I know to the famous *souvenir involontaire* of Proust. The plain sense of Baudelaire's admirable stanzas is wholly clear, I am sure you would agree. '... Comme je traversais le nouveau Carrousel', it is *then*—whether it is the 'wide esplanade' (as I see you hold) or the new bridge, as our friend Frank Scarfe maintains—it is *then* that the thought of Andromache and the Virgilian phrase suddenly occurred to him, the phrase that sums up the whole tonality of the evocation— *Falsi Simoëntis ad undam*—on which he adds his comment: it is the mean trickle, mirroring the noble figure of the mourning widow, which has 'fécondé ma mémoire'. What is given is the *telescoped* moment of emotion which explains its pungency or depth, as he finds, and relates the explanation to a moment long ago when Paris was so different yet so like in the still colder light of 'Le Crépuscule du Matin'. The 'Paris . . . vieillard laborieux' in the one, the 'Travail . . . où la voirie pousse son ouragan' are almost phrases out of the same mould. The moment of the inconsequential vision of the swan escaped from its menagerie cage merely into that vast building yard which the place du Carrousel had temporarily become. Myth or emblem whose clumsy, pathetic gestures have their full connotation stated only in the 'ridicules mais sublimes' which links bird and tragic heroine in that second modulation, or recapitulation which opens out to embrace life's victims, whoever they are, in a gesture of heart-rending fraternity.

To revert now to Jouve's remarks, he will have it that 'Le petit fleuve est la première image de la chose qui va vivre . . . comme miroir des pleurs de la souffrance d'une telle mère'. This seems a curious aberration since, *quite naturally* in the context, it is Andromache and not her son nor even, in the first part of the poem, either her first or her second husband who is evoked. The other key terms, according to Jouve, are le *vieux* Paris ('puissantes images ancestrales', etc.) and *le travail*. In fact, again in the context, it is simply the disappearance in the last twenty years of the whole *quartier* between Louvre and Tuileries, the construction of the two wings joining the palaces, the blotting out of little houses where friends like Gautier and Nerval had lived: these are the changes which supply the background of the poor swan, as once seen. As for *le travail*, it seems clear that Jouve has quite failed to see that this is an allusion to the early morning stint of the street-sweepers. What seems significant to him is that, among material *bric à brac*, appears 'la chose animale . . . une ménagerie'. According to him, we are thus led step by step to the swan 'symbole de la voix, de l'inspiration. Mais il est dans la malédiction', and so on. It is surely clear that the whole pattern of discovery has been missed.

The commentary on the second part is not as perverse, yet it hardly shows the perspicacity one would expect from a poet. The 'Paris change! mais rien dans ma mélancolie n'a bougé', this *reprise* is ample confirmation of those recent changes of the city which I have enumerated. They serve to reassert that the memory of the swan remains before his mind's eye, confirms his melancholy and constitutes a symbol (or 'allegory' as he calls it) which is amplified right to the end of the poem, since all these exiles are impaired by their inappropriate if not absurd settings: the swan, but also an Andromache, not only the victim of Pyrrhus but reconciled to a later marriage one would rather forget, the negress in the fog, and the enumeration goes on to the pitiful lot of not only *captifs* or *vaincus*, but those half-reconciled to a life of tears or to unhappy children who do not even understand what has befallen them. We can agree with Jouve when he claims that 'la catharsis se produit dans la mesure où le poème a obtenu l'amour pour eux'.

This commentary, aberrant as it is, is worth lingering over, perhaps, for what it is able to tell us about Jouve himself, who was clearly conscious of how strange it might well appear to his readers.[3]

The search for a symbolic meaning beyond the compelling logic of Baudelaire's own text where the potency of a *Vieux Souvenir* brings reconciliation, resignation or, as Jouve will have it, *catharsis*, is a compelling reminder that, if he shares with Baudelaire an intensely ambivalent attitude to any sexual relationship, this is coupled in his case with a mistrust of memory.

> Tués parmi nos souvenirs vivent nos corps

(he once wrote)

> Coupables du désir coupables du néant
> Coupables de mémoire, nous vivons morts.

From this infernal cycle which is the character of Life itself, the sequences of mechanical repetition, of memory, nostalgia, guilt seemed to impose themselves ineluctably. However, in the heroine of *Matière céleste* and of *Dans les années profondes* we find indeed his attempt to regard as an admissible passion the hypothesis of an Hélène whose death in her lover's arms appears somehow to reconcile the erotic urge and the self-destructive death-wish. Although the Hélène poems and the story are among the most compelling of the poet's achievements, it is worth noticing that, as the years have passed, Jouve's attitude has changed. He has become clearly more willing to recognize memory as a liberation from the present, and to do so partly through the figure who appears in some of his later poetry as Yannick or *L'Étrangère*, who certainly illustrates the survival of an ultra-Baudelairian preoccupation with the figure of the prostitute.

In the valuable autobiographical notes, *En Miroir*, he writes of Yannick ... 'Et cet être me paraît pourtant précieux, précieux comme le dernier animal d'une société qui n'a plus rien de la nature, employé à faire jouer constamment autour de lui le drame fondamental.' [It is here that Jouve betrays how deeply he is committed to a Freudian view which may appear dubious in the light of the reactions of a more permissive society.] 'En regard de cette fonction d'animal sacré, entouré de la réprobation générale, que pèse l'argent et qu'importent les acteurs?'[4]

In *Ode*, the figure of Yannick *L'Étrangère* is defined, indeed, as she who is *la page blanche*, whose fascination lies in her whole existence within the trivial day-to-day, and whose story will never be written, who is without memory, for she is still wholly turned towards the future of *sa vingtième année*.

Fifteen years later in *Ténèbre* (1962), Jouve's reflexions, no less intense, no less intricately interwoven, turn more to the admission that it is poetry alone which can somehow construct a reconciled image of the poet after his death:

> ... une île
> Au fronton de Pallas en mirages d'argent

to admit how by 'mélancolie mortelle ... tu parviens à ranimer ... De si anciennes choses, ... Qu'elles passent du feu à la divine vie ...', to admit, ' ... le sel dans les larmes'.

Glasgow   ALAN BOASE

NOTES

1 This essay, originally written during the War, was first published in the volume entitled *Défense et Illustration* and in revised version with the same group of essays in *Le Tombeau de Baudelaire* (1957).

2 They include—predictably—'Les Bijoux', 'La Chevelure', 'Le Balcon', 'Chant d'Automne', 'L'Amour du mensonge'. 'Recueillement', as well as the early 'Crépuscule du matin', the mysterious 'Yeux de Berthe', and 'L'Ennemi'.

3 *'Je ferai*, he says, *une analyse des symboles qui pourra paraître surprenante'* (loc. cit.).

4 *En Miroir*, p. 110.

'MÈNE-T-ON LA FOULE DANS LES ATELIERS?'—SOME REMARKS ON BAUDELAIRE'S VARIANTS

Montre-t-on au public [. . .] le mécanisme des trucs? Lui explique-t-on les retouches et les variantes improvisées aux répétitions, et jusqu'à quelle dose l'instinct et la sincérité sont mêlées [*sic*] aux rubriques et au charlatanisme indispensable dans l'amalgame de l'œuvre? (*CBP* 370)[1]

How dearly Baudelaire would have liked to do just this. He never completed the projected 'grande préface où j'expliquerai mes trucs et ma méthode et où j'enseignerai à chacun *l'art d'en faire autant*' (*Corr.* IV, 105); but if the pose of weary disdain and the sincerity of deep difficulty alike make him repeatedly put aside[2] this 'sérieuse bouffonnerie' as being useless to the vulgar throng, he would still have wished to 'amuser les esprits amoureux de la rhétorique profonde', whose number he sardonically estimates as requiring a modest 'dizaine d'exemplaires' (*CBP* 369).

For these few, to whom technique is not automatically equated with triviality, or worth with spontaneity,[3] he would have analysed the need for exact command of every detail of rhyme, of rhythm, of syntax, of suggestion (*CBP* 364, 366), would have anatomised that 'série d'efforts' which is the terror and the triumph of the artist:

Les loques, les fards, les poulies, les chaînes, les repentirs, les épreuves barbouillées, bref toutes les horreurs qui composent le sanctuaire de l'art (*CBP* 370).

We have only fragments of that analysis, scattered throughout letters and critical works; but, increasingly, we are able ourselves to look at some of the detailed evidence from which it would have been drawn: the variants to the poems. All too few remain; the rare poems where we do have a rich harvest of successive versions, and also Baudelaire's own famous protestations ('Facilité à concevoir? ou facilité à exprimer? Je n'ai jamais eu ni l'une ni l'autre, et il doit sauter aux yeux que le peu que j'ai fait est le résultat d'un travail très douloureux' (*Corr.* V, 36)),[4] sufficiently suggest how many must have been the stages of correction, now lost, to other poems. But simply to look as a whole at what we do have, now so splendidly presented by Claude Pichois in the Corti edition, is to be amazed by the quantity, the range and the value of Baudelaire's meticulous alterations. Some of the most important, of course, have long been familiar, and have been tellingly commented on here and there in general critical works on the poetry;[5] there have also been occasional studies on particular aspects of the variants as such.[6] A whole book would be needed for this rich subject. In the present brief article I hope simply to suggest further, from a deliberately limited choice of examples, how, as an ancillary method, the close study of variants may offer one of the most stimulating and revealing means to a full delight in that specially subtle simultaneity of effects which the final poems so firmly and so finely achieve.[7]

It is only on rare, if important, occasions that the central meaning of a poem has been changed—and then usually in succinct alterations to a final stanza. The evocation of an experience, with its divers potentialities, stands as it was throughout the poem; in the clinching last lines the poet chooses a different emphasis for his flash of personal retrospect. The outstanding example here is 'Un Fantôme', where in the manuscript the last three lines of the fourth sonnet continue the image of Time as destroyer of that delicacy which the poem has recalled with mingled sorrow and delight:

> Comme un manant ivre, ou comme un soudard
> Qui bat les murs, et salit et coudoie
> Une beauté frêle, en robe de soie.

The very fineness of this initial end, evoking conquering crudity and defenceless, evanescent grace, and moving to a dying fall like that of 'Le Cygne', suggests the importance of the change from sad and lovely lament to challenging and bitter victory:

> Noir assassin de la Vie et de l'Art,
> Tu ne tueras jamais dans ma mémoire
> Celle qui fut mon plaisir et ma gloire!

The placing of the poem at the culmination of the Jeanne cycle, immediately before the magnificent *Exegi monumentum* of 'Je te donne ces vers', may well have determined the change.[8] The final version is no abstract proclamation of Eternal Values; simply, a personal sense of ineradicable and defiant persistence emerges through the ways in which sense and sound unite in disciplined structure. Life and Art are alike threatened by the ravages of Time; the conquest set against them is purely personal: '*ma* mémoire', '*mon* plaisir', '*ma* gloire'. Two sound-patterns interplay: 'n*oir* a*ss*assin . . . *Art* . . . tue*ras* j*a*mais . . .

m*a* mémo*ire* . . . m*a* gl*oire*', and '*Tu* ne t*ue*ras . . . Celle qui f*ut*'. To the vast 'Vie' and 'Art' of the first line correspond, in placing, in sound and in sense, the personal equivalents 'plaisir' and 'gloire' of the end, while the loss from which this bitter conquest is drawn stands in the monosyllabic cut of the past historic 'Celle qui *fut* . . .'

Minor changes of meaning within the poem may of course be important. The implications of one line may be far-reaching, as when

L'orbe mystérieux tracé par le bonheur

around the eyes of Sapho becomes

Le cercle ténébreux tracé par les douleurs (*CBP* 274).

The change of just one letter gives a vitally different tone, as 'Où je traînais mon agonie' becomes 'je traînais mon atonie' (*CBP* 283); and that of one word, in 'Confession' ('cette confidence étrange' becoming 'cette confidence horrible' (*CBP* 99)) gives the full shock of seeing the Ideal reveal a mere plaintive humanity. Or both insinuation and music may be enhanced, as in the line where the sensuously enchanting woman was first destined to 'charmer les loisirs d'un Mécène ou d'un prince', then comes to

. . . charmer les loisirs d'un *p*ontife ou d'un *p*rince (*CBP* 57).[9]

For most of Baudelaire's revisions, whether in manuscript or in proof, are concerned with making each detail of expression still more adequate to the tone and meaning of the whole. And no tiniest detail is irrelevant in his desire for total perfection of material presentation, where spacing, punctuation, capitals, all have their suggestive functions. For each of these, his comments indicate his search for a balance between personal adventure and traditional order, even down to the placing of a comma: as in the two-sided comment: 'est-ce bien ainsi qu'il faut ponctuer? peut-être trouverez-vous que cette ponctuation rend bien la langueur du rythme', concerning the line: 'Suivant un rythme doux, et paresseux, et lent' (*CBP* 110).

His consequent and life-long battles over proofs reveal his vigorous fury at finding his works sometimes published with

autant de fautes d'impression qu'il y a de puces dans la poussière d'un fleuve espagnol (*Corr.* III, 42)

(one remembers how 'Tristesse de la lune' became 'Vitesse . . .' or 'Citadins' turned to 'Italiens', *Corr.* I, 115–16, III, 207); his delight in reading Soulary's Sonnet to a Proof-Reader (*Corr.* III 44); his recurrent conviction that his fundamental honour is at stake in any imperfection (*Corr.* IV, 254, etc.); and his recognition of a factor shared by many others:

Mon infirmité qui ne me permet de juger de la valeur d'une phrase ou d'un mot que typographié (*Corr.* II, 9).[10]

And from his brief comments on proofs, to editors who neglect or contest his corrections, comes a rich sense of the areas of suggestion lying behind the choice of each single word. Of the lines in 'L'Amour du mensonge' where a variant read:

> Le souvenir divin, antique et lourde tour
> La couronne, et son cœur, meurtri comme la pêche,
> Est, comme son corps, mûr pour le savant amour (*CBP* 193),

to become:

> Le souvenir massif, royale et lourde tour
> La couronne, et son cœur, meurtri comme une pêche,
> Est mûr, comme son corps, pour le savant amour,

Baudelaire wrote:

Le mot *royale* facilitera pour le lecteur l'intelligence de cette métaphore qui fait du souvenir une couronne de tours, comme celles qui inclinent le front des déesses de *maturité*, de *fécondité*, et de *sagesse* (*Corr.* III, 71)[11]

—and, if he did not draw attention to the triumphant replacement of the abstract 'divin' by the physically evocative 'massif', to the removal of the over-specific '*la* pêche', or to the change in the last line to give exact balance between 'cœur' and 'corps', yet he commented on the double sense of 'savant amour': 'L'amour (sens et esprit) est niais à 20 ans, et il est savant à 40', adding: 'Tout cela, je vous l'affirme, a été très lentement combiné'. Similarly, when Calonne chose for a line from 'Danse macabre' the wrong set of variants, giving

> Bayadère sans nez, aux yeux pleins d'épouvantes

instead of

> Bayadère sans nez, irrésistible gouge (*CBP* 191),

Baudelaire's reasons for his final version are several. First, since there is a line with 'le gouffre de tes yeux plein d'horribles pensées',

Des yeux pleins d'épouvante font double emploi. J'ai l'air d'être privé d'imagination.

Second, the aptness of the word to the tone of the whole:

Gouge est un excellent mot, mot unique, mot de *vieille* langue, applicable à une *danse macabre*, mot contemporain des *danses macabres.* UNITÉ DE STYLE . . .

(here follow detailed discussions of the sense of the word). Third, its suggestive range:

Or, la Mort n'est-elle pas la Gouge qui suit en tous lieux la *Grande Armée universelle,* et n'est-elle pas une courtisane dont les embrassements sont *positivement irrésistibles?*

and the conclusion, as before, stresses how one change serves several purposes:

Couleur, antithèse, métaphore, tout est exact (*Corr.* II, 265–6).

If one seeks, however roughly, to group the multiple preoccupations that may underlie even the slightest alteration, Baudelaire's famous attack on Musset may provide a starting-point:

Je n'ai jamais pu souffrir [. . .] son impudence d'enfant gâté qui invoque le ciel et l'enfer pour des aventures de table d'hôte, son torrent bourbeux de fautes de grammaire et de prosodie, enfin son impuissance totale à comprendre le travail par lequel une rêverie devient un objet d'art. [. . .] le décousu, la banalité et la négligence (*Corr.* III, 38).

Once again Baudelaire is looking for originality within a disciplined and accepted tradition: avoidance of both the banal and the facile; adherence to the laws of language and versification; concentration of effects; and if he rejects what he sees as inapposite juxtaposition of the lofty and the trivial, it is with a sense of that UNITÉ DE STYLE which figured in capitals in the letter to Calonne.

I leave aside here the many small changes made so as to remove repetition, tautology, over-obvious epithet or potential cliché; though each of these adds its own touch of suggestion, as 'sombres chagrins' becomes 'vastes chagrins', or 'les flèches de l'amour' turn to 'les griffes de l'amour'. Where grammatical purity is concerned, the Baudelaire constantly on the watch for 'des lourdeurs et des violences de style' (*Corr.* III, 66) will remove awkward constructions ('Qu'on dirait que j'emprunte' becoming 'Que j'ai l'air d'emprunter' (*CBP* 54), or 'Et c'est pourquoi l'on peut' turning to 'Et l'on peut pour cela te comparer au vin' (*CBP* 59)), will closely discuss the phrase 'Tel que jamais mortel n'en vit' (*CBP* 199), or the expression 'la couleur noire' ('le noir étant le zéro de la couleur, cela peut-il se dire?' (*CBP* 201)); will find a simple solution, and one that intensifies the tone of longing, to the strange initial error of 'Le Cygne', so that 'Eau quand pleuveras-tu?' becomes 'Eau, quand *donc* pleuvras-tu?'[12] (*CBP* 168).

But one manuscript note is specially significant. On the proof for 'Le Beau Navire' in the first edition, the opening had read:

> Je veux te raconter, pour que tu les connaisses
> Les diverses beautés qui parent ta jeunesse;

corrected by Baudelaire to 'connaisse', with the remark: 'Violons plutôt la grammaire que la rime' (*CBP* 110).[13] The violation was not left, of course; scored out in its turn, it led to the new supple and suggestive opening:

> Je veux te raconter, ô molle enchanteresse. . . .

But the primacy of rhyme and rhythm is certain, and the subtlety of Baudelaire's changes to meet their needs causes some of his finest variants.

It is when working on the proofs of the first edition that he writes to Poulet-Malassis:

> Si vous pouvez dénicher, dans vos greniers ou armoires un ou deux dictionnaires de rimes, apportez-les-moi. Je n'en ai jamais eu.—Mais ce doit être une chose excellente dans le cas d'épreuves (*Corr.* II, 13).

He has not, then, needed the rhyming dictionary as stimulus, stand-by or stop-gap in the act of composition;[14] and his assurance over rhythm emerges in the angry remark on hiatus:

> 'e suis incapable de faire un hémistiche tel que celui-ci: "*Pourquoi, heureuse enfant* . . .? Ce ne peut être que: "pourquoi, l'heureuse enfant . . . ?' (*Corr.* V, 158),

or in the still more justifiable fury with which he finds ('voilà une faute sans cesse répétée') the spelling 'encor' ruins the resonance of the tremendous line from 'Le Reniement de Saint Pierre'

> Les cieux ne s'en sont point encore rassasiés! (*CBP* 238)

But the hesitations on which he wishes to check are often concerned with tricky traditions of diphthongs, in words where the dictionary indicates whether they count as one, two or more syllables; one of his most effective changes, both broadening the sense and prolonging the sound, is in the line from 'Un Voyage à Cythère', originally reading

> Le long fleuve de fiel de mes douleurs anciennes

and finally becoming

Le long fleuve de fiel des douleurs anciennes (*CBP* 233)[15].

Tiny changes give new sound-patterns: sometimes onomatopœic, as the replacement of 'pleurs' by 'cris' gives the echo of

Ses cr*is* me déch*i*raient la f*i*bre (*CBP* 212),

or 'les violons mourant' becomes

Les v*i*olons v*i*brant derrière les coll*i*nes (*CBP* 129);

sometimes simply serving to hold a line more tautly together, as 'Cherchant la jouissance avec férocité' changes to

Épr*i*se du plais*i*r jusqu'à l'atrocité (*CBP* 180);[16]

and just as often moving away from initial imitative harmony, to affect the tone of the whole in a subtler or deeper way: the famous penultimate line of 'Les Phares' at first began 'Que ce cri renaissant', then tried the physically more intense 'Que ce long hurlement', before achieving:

Que cet ardent sanglot qui roule d'âge en âge . . . (*CBP* 40).

But it is especially in the play of mute 'e's, evoking often the rocking waves of the sea, the skimming flight of birds, or the graceful walk of woman, that the slightest variant tells. The astonishing dance of 'e' mutes in stanzas three and four of 'A celle qui est trop gaie' is heralded when the opening line moves from 'Ta tête, ton geste et ton air' to 'Ta tête, ton geste, ton air' (*CBP* 283); the stress and movement are completely different when in 'Que diras-tu . . .' the line 'Son fantôme en dansant marche comme un flambeau' becomes

Son fantôm*e* dans l'air dans*e* comme un flambeau (*CBP* 93).

Jean Pommier has finely indicated[17] how in 'La Vie antérieure' the change from

Au milieu de l'azur, des flots et des splendeurs

to

Au milieu de l'azur, des vagues, des splendeurs (*CBP* 47)

suggests in the two syllables of 'vagues' (the first, strong; the second half-absent) the crest and the fall of the wave. The poem where Baudelaire's revisions as a whole achieve the subtlest effects of this kind is 'La Musique'. There the second stanza read, in the first edition:

> La poitrine en avant et gonflant mes poumons
>   De toile pesante,
> Je monte et je descends sur le dos des grands monts
>   D'eau ruisselante ['retentissante', in a proof] (*CBP* 136).

The opening image there is awkward, hard to follow; and the rising and falling movement is merely stated. In the final version:

> La poitrine en avant et les poumons gonflés
>   Comme de la toile,
> J'escalade le dos des flots amoncelés
>   Que la nuit me voile

the 'comme' both elucidates the image and sets going a sequence of 'e' sounds, to be echoed in comm*e* d*e*, toil*e*, escalad*e* l*e*, qu*e*, m*e*; instead of the relative ordinariness of 'monte, descends, grands monts', there is the redoubled triumph of 'es*ca*lade', the liquidly echoing sounds of 'le dos des flots amoncelés', and the veiling by night which recalls the 'plafond de brume' and 'pâle étoile' of the opening stanza. For the final stanza, there is a tiny, but a very powerful, change. The poem had ended:

> Le bon vent, la tempête et ses convulsions
>   Sur le sombre gouffre
> Me bercent, et parfois le calme,—grand miroir
>   De mon désespoir!

The new version:

> Sur l'immense gouffre
> Me bercent. D'autres fois, calme plat, grand miroir
>   De mon désespoir!

creates, instead of the quiet and almost imperceptible alternation led into by 'et parfois', an abrupt physical shock. The prolonged sentence which had stretched through four stanzas carrying the delight and terror of the mighty rocking of the waves, is sharply broken off, both at the most unexpected early point of the line (the third syllable) and immediately after the climax of 'Me bercent'—to create, through the pause, the contrast of 'D'autres fois', and the echoing and clinching monosyllable that now follows 'calme': '*ca*lme pl*at*', the sudden fall into blank and motionless impotence.

Even the briefest attempt to examine rhythmical effects will of course show how inseparable they are from central meaning and tone. For the rest of this discussion, I propose to group one or two main aspects which seem to emerge as one examines Baudelaire's variants.

On the one hand, there is the enhancement, by very varied means, of all that contributes to a deliberate dignity and solemnity; on the other, the specially difficult achievement of an apparently effortless, familiar, conversational style—familar but not trivial; seemingly simple, but penetratingly suggestive.

In 'Paysage', poem of his plans for poetry, the 'chants mélodieux' of the bell-towers give way to an expression more telling at once in its meaning, in its sound patterns, and in its contrast with the rest of the line:

> Leurs *hymnes solennels* emportés par le vent (*CBP* 161).

Of Baudelaire's many means of deepening this suggestive solemnity, one notices first, perhaps, how he introduces, when revising, classical or literary reminiscences: superficially suspect to the romantic period as artifice or periphrastic stereotype, these may now come to take up once again their traditional and lasting function of succinctly relating individual insight to a wide range of significance in the stretch of time and space. If this sense of suggestive interaction across the ages is clearly inherent in Baudelaire's approach throughout his works, it emerges yet more strongly through his variants, as the haunting spectre of the eighth sinister figure in 'Les Sept Vieillards' becomes at once a

> Sosie inexorable, ironique et fatal

and a

> Dégoûtant Phénix, fils et père de lui-même (*CBP* 173);

as 'un riche' and 'une catin' in 'L'Imprévu' take the particular and evocative form of Alceste and Célimène dissected in a new light; or, especially, as, in 'Les Litanies de Satan', we follow the threefold transformation from the abstract 'bonheur insolent', through the more specific and contemporary 'un banquier', to an agelong echo enhanced by its placing at the key-point of the line:

> Sur le front du Crésus impitoyable et vil (*CBP* 245).[18]

Such changes extend the bounds of time and space. Of all the effects that most strike home when one looks at Baudelaire's variants as a whole, the strongest is probably that of the alterations which intensify a sense of a vast universe, its enhanced immensity serving to stress in turn man's insatiable appetites, recurrent terrors, and brief, bitter, miraculous conquests. In his minor changes, when Baudelaire removes an over-obvious or tautological epithet, it is very frequently to substitute an adjective of undefined extension:

'sombres chagrins' become 'vastes' (*CBP* 82); 'ces beaux yeux', 'ces grands yeux' (*CBP* 86); while adjectives already evocative are changed to add to the sense of stretching space: 'cette vieille nuit' becomes 'cette immense nuit' (*CBP* 73), and in 'La Musique' 'le pur éther' and 'le sombre gouffre' turn to 'le vaste éther' and 'l'immense gouffre' (*CBP* 136).

This is no mechanical process. Where context demands, adjectives of extension have been replaced by others, as in 'Le Cygne', where 'Comme je traversais *ce vaste* Carrousel' (in itself evocative of the demolitions) has given way to the contrast between progress and memory in '*le nouveau* Carrousel' (*CBP* 166). And in 'Brumes et Pluies' the earlier

D'un linceul vaporeux et d'un *vaste* tombeau (*CBP* 198)

was first subjected to the wish to call up both the title and the first half of the line, by the substitution of 'brumeux tombeau', before culminating in the one word where the sense of misty uncertainty, the extension into undefined space, and the echo of sound are united in:

D'un linceul *vaporeux* et d'un *vague* tombeau (*CBP* 198).

Extensions in space are conveyed of course through much more varied means than mere changes of adjective. 'Projette l'illimité' becomes '*allonge* l'illimité' (*CBP* 106), 'Traversant la forêt' is changed to '*parcourant les* forêts' (*CBP* 124); 'Au travers de l'espace ils galopent' is intensified to '*ils s'enfoncent*' (*CBP* 138). Perhaps most suggestive may be the difference between the positive stress on immensity:

Un triste cimetière *à l'immense horizon*

and the blank, negative sense of infinity:

Le cimetière immense et froid, *sans horizon* (*CBP* 138).

The variants to one of the most deliberately discreet of the poems, 'Je n'ai pas oublié', are perhaps the more significant in that here Baudelaire certainly seeks no rhetorical tone; it is all the more notable that his rewriting of a quiet personal fragment should gently extend personal memories to the breadth and richness of a cosmic background. The first version evokes the separate sunsets of each evening descriptively:

Et les soleils, le soir, orangés et superbes
. . . Semblaient, au fond du ciel, en témoin curieux . . . ;

the second gives lasting generality, richness, and the magnification of the physical image:

> Et le soleil, le soir, ruisselant et superbe,
> . . . Semblait, grand œil ouvert dans le ciel curieux,
> Contempler nos dîners longs et silencieux,

while the original variants ('Et versant doucement', then 'Et versant largement') finally find the expression for the most bountiful sense of stretching space as a benison behind the daily world:

> *Répandant largement* ses beaux reflets de cierge
> Sur la nappe frugale et les rideaux de serge (*CBP* 195).

The sense of time, like that of space, may be intensified, as in 'Un Fantôme', where the generalised opening and the tense of

> De tout ce qui pour nous a flamboyé

move into the brief image, the alliteration, and the cutting off by the past historic:

> De tout le feu qui pour nous flamboya (*CBP* 86),

or in 'Le Reniement de Saint Pierre', where the first version in descriptive imperfect:

> Où tu venais remplir l'éternelle promesse

shifts to separate that past promise ineluctably from the present:

> Où tu vins pour remplir l'éternelle promesse (*CBP* 238)[19]

In these and other lines, variants often stress a sense of inexorability. 'L'homme . . . Porte souvent le châtiment' in 'Les Hiboux' becomes 'Porte *toujours* le châtiment' (*CBP* 134); the endless wastes of *ennui* find, in place of the flat 'sous le premier poids des neigeuses années' a musically and sensuously evocative image for the softly and insidiously irresistible:

> Quand sous *les lourds flocons* des neigeuses années . . . (*CBP* 143);

or the already strong 'irrésistible calenture' of 'Le Vin des amants' takes on a harder and more obsessively echoed compulsion as 'une implacable calenture' (*CBP* 216). Two poems are specially suggestive here.

In 'La Fontaine de sang', the ebbing blood, which at first had flowed in 'tranquilles sanglots', becomes, seeming to beat with the human pulse, a 'fontaine aux *rythmiques* sanglots'; incidental expressions are changed to give greater strength and dignity (*j'ai beau*

me tâter' becoming 'je me tâte *en vain*', and 'le marché' changing to
'la cité'); and finally the lines:

> J'ai demandé souvent à des vins généreux
> D'endormir pour un jour la terreur qui me mine,
> Mais le vin rend la vue et l'oreille plus fine

take on, in the change to highly original adjective, and in the redoubled irony of the last line with its balanced monosyllables, a
stranger and sharper threat:

> J'ai demandé souvent à des vins *captieux*
> D'endormir pour un jour la terreur qui me mine;
> Le *vin rend l'œil plus clair* et l'oreille plus fine.

(We have here Baudelaire's own note on 'captieux': the printer had
tried to correct it to the epithet that would more normally go with
wine: 'capiteux', and he replies:

Mais non! s'il y avait: *captieux*, c'était fort bien. *des vins captieux*, et non pas
capiteux qui d'ailleurs ne rime pas (*CBP* 226 [the rhyme is with
'oublieux'].)

The last stanza of 'Quand le ciel bas et lourd' (*CBP* 147) moves
through a whole sequence of variants, gradually to discover its final
magnificent means of conveying at once endlessly prolonged oppression and the sharp stab of anguish. The opening had read successively

> Et de grands [d'anciens] corbillards sans tambours ni musique,
> Passent en foule au fond de mon âme;

before finding its prolonged and rich dignity:

> Et de *longs* corbillards, sans tambours ni musique,
> *Défilent lentement* dans mon âme.

There had then followed:

> et l'Espoir
> Fuyant vers d'autres cieux [Pleurant comme un
>   vaincu], l'Angoisse despotique
> Sur mon crâne incliné plante son drapeau noir.

The removal of the 'et' and of the long participial phrases, the splitting
up of the lines, the monosyllabic present tense, and the placing of
'atroce' in a stressed position lead up to the sudden piercing movement of the end:

> et l'Espoir,
> Vaincu, pleure, et l' Angoisse atroce, despotique,
> Sur mon crâne incliné plante son drapeau noir.

Solemnity and irrevocability contribute to the growing emergence of ritual invocations, whether in 'Crépuscule du soir', where the conversational early line:

> Oui, voilà bien le Soir, le Soir cher à celui . . .

is strengthened and intoned:

> O soir, aimable soir, désiré par celui . . . (*CBP* 184);

or in 'Les Litanies de Satan', where the already dignified 'Souverain incompris' becomes the still more mighty and litanesque:

> *O Prince de l'exil*, à qui l'on a fait tort.

This last poem, too hastily dismissed by some critics, is a rich example of Baudelaire's close re-writing. The changes sometimes involve only one word, but profoundly affect both sound and sense: the line originally opening 'Et qui toujours vaincu' takes on a different stress and indomitability as it becomes:

> Et qui, vaincu, toujours te redresses plus fort;

Hope becomes not simply the ironically charming daughter of her grim parents ('une fille charmante') but the still more ironically suggestive 'une *folle* charmante'; the treasures hidden in the depths are not just in 'secrets arsenaux' but in '*profonds* arsenaux'; 'l'homme faible' becomes the more suggestive 'l'homme *frêle*'; finally, in the line which at first read

> Bâton des exilés, *soutien* des inventeurs,

after first substituting 'torche', Baudelaire finds his stronger symbol

> Bâton des exilés, *lampe* des inventeurs.

Meantime there have been more extended changes. In the stanza which first read:

> Qui même aux parias, ces animaux maudits,
> Donne[s] avec l'amour le goût du Paradis,[20]

the tautology or padding of the first line has been removed, and the deliberate gift of the second has been strengthened:

> Toi qui, même aux lépreux, aux parias maudits,
> Enseignes par l'amour le goût du Paradis.

The abstract and somewhat flat nobility, and the awkward inversion, in

> Aux nobles malheureux, toi qui donnes l'orgueil,
> Et les fais sans broncher aller jusqu'au cercueil

is given a new strength and dignity:

> Toi qui fais au proscrit ce regard calme et haut
> Qui damne tout un peuple autour d'un échafaud.

The awkward mingling of abstract and concrete in

> Toi qui mets un opprobre éternel et sanglant
> Sur le front mal fardé du bonheur insolent

becomes, after a number of changes, the sinisterly musical and evocative

> Toi qui poses ta marque, ô complice subtil,
> Sur le front du Crésus impitoyable et vil.

An in itself physically suggestive phrase

> Toi qui frottes de baume et d'huile les vieux os

makes way for a more haunting and prolonged musical effect

> Toi qui, magiquement, assouplis les vieux os.

The stanza, initially near to flat sentimentality,

> Toi qui mets dans les yeux et dans le cœur des filles
> Un invincible amour des hommes en guenilles

is changed to recall the bitter pondering on the obsessions of Madamoiselle Bistouri in the *Petits Poèmes en Prose*:

> Toi qui mets dans les yeux et dans le cœur des filles
> *Le culte de la plaie* et l'amour des guenilles.

In the final stanza Baudelaire had first written of 'Du ciel d'où tu tombas' [then of 'Des Cieux spirituels'], and of 'L'Enfer où couché [then 'fécond'] tu peuples le silence' [then 'couves le silence'], before achieving his final expression for lost glory and potential creation:

> Gloire et louange à toi, Satan, dans les hauteurs
> Du Ciel, *où tu régnas*, et dans les profondeurs
> De l'enfer, où, *vaincu, tu rêves* en silence.

But most suggestive perhaps are the changes made in a line from the third stanza, which first read:

> Puissant consolateur des souffrances humaines,

then moves through three stages from the pitch of dignity to the subtlety of the familiar. First the 'souffrances' are intensified to 'angoisses', and, at the same time, instead of 'Puissant consolateur', Baudelaire tries another tone, giving

> Aimable médecin des angoisses humaines.

The discrepancy is over-incongruous, and he then finds instead of 'médecin' the term which will fit his atmosphere of litany: 'Guérisseur tout-puissant'. Finally he discovers the means of at last combining the power and the intimacy:

> Toi qui sais tout, grand roi des choses souterraines,
> Guérisseur familier des angoisses humaines . . .

And in poems where conversational intimacy is the predominating tone, it is the achieving of an effect of quiet and total ease that has required Baudelaire's detailed care. The slight changes in the opening lines to one of the best-known poems:

> La servante au grand cœur dont vous étiez jalouse,
> *Dort-elle* son sommeil sous une humble pelouse?
> Nous *aurions déjà dû* lui porter quelques fleurs

remove the rhetorical question, make for a gentle continuous movement, and increase the immediacy:

> La servante au grand cœur dont vous étiez jalouse,
> *Et qui dort* son sommeil sous une humble pelouse,
> Nous *devrions pourtant* lui porter quelques fleurs.

Later the lofty expression for the infinite passing of time 'Et l'éternité fuir' is made the more telling for its reduction in scope and its stranger physical verb: 'Et le siècle couler'. Finally the unspoken reproach of the end is made again the more immediate by substituting for

> si le soir,
> Calme, dans le fauteuil *elle venait* s'asseoir

the one touch

> Calme, dans le fauteuil *je la voyais* s'asseoir.

Outstanding from this point of view is the sonnet 'Le Rêve d'un Curieux' (*CBP* 254) where, to the mighty theme of death and the life after death, Baudelaire has chosen to give no lofty oratory, but the tone and imagery of the most every-day conversation. The opening, originally

> As-tu connu, dis-moi, la douleur savoureuse,
> Et de toi disait-on [changed to 'De toi dit-on souvent']: 'Quel homme
> singulier!'?

is made less jerky, less dramatic, with the removal of 'Quel', and is
given the immediacy of the present tense:

> Connais-tu, comme moi, la douleur savoureuse,
> Et de toi fais-tu dire: 'Oh! l'homme singulier!'

The final lines, at different stages, had read:

> J'étais comme l'Enfance, avide du spectacle,
> Et qui hait le rideau comme on hait un obstacle
> Et puis la vérité froide se révéla

[*Or* Mais voilà qu'une idée étrange me glaça]

> J'étais mort, ô miracle, et la fameuse [terrible] aurore
> Avait lui! 'Quoi! me dis je alors, ce n'est que ça?'

The abstract 'Enfance' is removed, the present participle 'Haïssant'
adds to the immediacy, the 'mais' or 'puis' becomes the cry of
'Enfin'; instead of 'une idée étrange' and the emphatic 'me glaça',
there is simply the blank revelation. Further emphatic stresses are
removed—'ô miracle!' and 'avait lui', and so is the diluting: 'me
dis je alors'; meantime instead of 'avait lui' the stretching verb in the
imperfect has already imperceptibly and completely spread around
him. The terror and the simplicity of the realisation have been fully
fused:

> J'étais comme l'enfant avide du spectacle,
> Haïssant le rideau comme on hait un obstacle . . .
> Enfin la vérité froide se révéla:

> J'étais mort sans surprise, et la terrible aurore
> M'enveloppait.—Eh quoi! n'est-ce donc que cela?
> La toile était levée et j'attendais encore.

　This limited paper has touched on only a few of the many sides
where every detail counts. At one end of the scale are changes in one
apparently insignificant word: from 'à' to 'vers' in

> Et cependant je sens ma bouche aller vers toi (*CBP* 278);

at the other, broad questions concerning Baudelaire's images: how
far are his corrections concerned simply with developing his initial
discovery, or how far does he discard or change images once found,
as in the first half of 'La Mort des Artistes', with the completely

different strength and subtlety of its final version, or in the intriguing case of 'Spleen' (Pluviôse, irrité') (*CBP* 142) which earlier read

> Mon *chien* sur le carreau cherchant une litière

but substitutes the mangy and wretched cat indoors to lead on to the phantom cry from the roof-top. Above all, the increasingly strong or delicate ways of conveying certain sense-impressions, and effects of rhythm and sound, would need much further investigation, closely related to their context as a whole, than I have been able to give them here.[21]

But I should like to end with a stanza from 'Au Lecteur'. The early version was already very strong in its vocabulary and its effects:

> Dans nos cerveaux malsains, comme un million d'helminthes,
> Grouille, chante et ripaille un peuple de démons,
> Et, quand nous respirons, la mort dans nos poumons
> S'engouffre, comme un fleuve, avec de sourdes plaintes.

But its slow-moving opening lacks the 'attack' of previous stanzas, its 'malsains' is weak by the side of other adjectives and images of condemnation, and 'chante' even in the ironical feasting context, risks being too pleasant in its associations. The final version has a quite different concentration:

> Serré, fourmillant, comme un million d'helminthes,
> Dans nos cerveaux ribote un peuple de Démons,
> Et, quand nous respirons, la Mort dans nos poumons
> Descend, fleuve invisible, avec de sourdes plaintes (*CBP* 22).

Where the first had moved through a regularly divided alexandrine, there is now the unusual division 5/7, isolating 'serré, fourmillant' so that the seething pressures are intensified by the very fact of these words being crammed together in shortened space; and lengthening the effect of the loathly worm-image. The swarming and devouring lead up to the one fierce, colloquial word 'ribote' at the place of strongest stress in the line. And whereas the early version had moved in logical sequence, its opening phrase showing that all is within the brain, the variant first creates the intense sense-impressions of pressure, pullulation, filth and carousal, holding them in suspense until the elucidation of 'un peuple de Démons'.[22]

The last line shows intensification of a different kind. Here, the strongest word was used in the first version: 'S'engouffre, comme un fleuve'. The 'comme' is removed, perhaps so as to avoid a repetition of the first line: then the full terror is suggested, not by the resounding verb, but by the quiet statement of 'Descend', and by the insidious sense of the adjective and its echo in the sound pattern.

Descend, fleuve invisible, avec de sourdes plaintes.

Here indeed is brought out the force of Baudelaire's own meditation on 'La décence du langage qui augmente la profondeur de l'horreur'. 'Au Lecteur' opened the volume. Among the variants of 'Le Voyage' which so majestically closes it, there is one which may serve as a symbol. Baudelaire began by writing 'Il est, hélas! des âmes sans répit', changed it to 'des Ennuis' and then to 'des martyrs', moving from the over-abstract through the over-romantic or pathetic before reaching the word which discreetly and physically evokes the sense and tone which his stanza, the whole poem and indeed the volume, need:

'Il est, hélas, des *coureurs* sans répit'

To Soulary he wrote:

Vous savez imiter les élans de l'âme, la musique de la méditation; *vous aimez l'ordre*; vous dramatisez le sonnet et vous lui donnez un dénouement; vous connaissez la puissance da la réticence (*Corr.* III, 45).

Imagination, music, structure, art of discreet suggestion: he has here defined some of the central qualities behind his own tireless perfecting of a creative balance between Adventure and Order.

Cambridge   ALISON FAIRLIE

NOTES

1 The following abbreviations will be used:

   CBP: Charles Baudelaire: *Les Fleurs du Mal*, édition critique Jacques Crépet—Georges Blin, refondue par Georges Blin et Claude Pichois, I, Paris, Corti, 1968.
   CB: Les Fleurs du Mal, édition critique établie par Jacques Crépet et Georges Blin, Paris, Corti, 1942.
   Corr.: Correspondance générale, recueillie, classée et annotée par Jacques Crépet [and Cl. Pichois for Vol. VI], Paris, Conard, 1947–53, 6 vols.
   Pl. Œuvres complètes, texte établi par Y.-G. Le Dantec, édition révisée, complétée et présentée par Claude Pichois, Paris, Gallimard (Editions de la Pléiade), 1961.

2 See the four Projets de Préfaces, *CBP* 361–71. The pose (especially p. 370) deliberately recalls Gautier.

3 Cf. (*Pl.* 609) Baudelaire's comments on Dupont's work for the Academy Dictionary and the immense value of the 'gymnastics' involved in discussing grammar, rhetoric, and the 'mot propre': 'Ceci paraîtra peut-être puéril à beaucoup de gens, mais ceux-là ne se sont pas rendu compte du

travail successif qui se fait dans l'esprit des écrivains, et de la série des circonstances nécessaires pour créer un poète.' Cf. also *Pl.* 722: 'Parmi les innombrables préjugés dont la France est si fière notons cette idée qui court les rues, et qui naturellement est écrite en tête des préceptes de la critique vulgaire à savoir qu'un ouvrage trop bien écrit *doit* manquer de sentiment', *Pl.* 746: 'J'ai entendu dire à beaucoup de personnes, fort compétentes d'ailleurs, que le fini, le précieux, la perfection enfin, les rebutaient et les empêchaient d'avoir, pour ainsi dire, *confiance* dans le poète. Cette opinion (singulière pour moi) . . .'; and the outstanding passage on 'les rhétoriques et les prosodies' from the *Salon de 1859, Pl.* 1043.

4 Cf. also *Corr.* II, 256, IV, 324, etc.

5 See especially the basic studies by L. J. Austin, F. W. Leakey, J. Prévost, R. Vivier. H. Peyre, *Connaissance de Baudelaire*, Paris, Corti, 1951, pp. 129 et sqq., pointed out how much needed to be examined; there is a pungent remark in R. Kopp and Cl. Pichois, *Les Années Baudelaire*, Neuchâtel, A la Baconnière (Études baudelairiennes, I), 1969, p. 139, on the value of analysing how Baudelaire re-works his own material as compared with what he does with sources or influences.

6 André Guex, *Aspects de l'Art baudelairien*, Lausanne, Imprimerie Centrale, 1934, gives in a 62-page appendix an 'Étude des variantes'— largely useless, as the 1868 edition is taken as the basis, there is no proper apparatus of references, and the variants are forced to fit the headings of the main thesis. There are some interesting comments in the section on variants (pp. 164–95) in Marc Seguin's *Aux Sources vivantes du symbolisme—Génie des 'Fleurs du Mal'*, Paris, Messein, 1938.

   J. Doucet, 'Quelques variantes de Baudelaire', *Les Études classiques*, 25, 1957, pp. 327–43, somewhat contestable on general points, has some perceptive comments on detail. Alfred Noyer-Weidner, 'Stilempfindung und Stilentwicklung Baudelaires im Spiegel seiner Varianten', *Linguistic and Literary Studies in Honour of Helmut Hatzfeld*, Washington, 1964, pp. 302–27, provides a thorough and scholarly analysis of some interesting examples, with the merit of setting details in their context and seeking to see how lexical and syntactical changes contribute to poetic value. The most stimulating and sensitive treatment of one set of variants which I have read is that comparing the first and second editions, in J. Pommier, *Autour de l'Édition originale des Fleurs du Mal*, Geneva, Slatkine reprints, 1968, pp. 150–69.

7 Some of my examples will be familiar from previous works, though here set in another framework of discussion. I have left aside some aspects ably discussed in the works mentioned above; I have also left to be discussed on another occasion the multiple variants to three poems in particular: 'Le Vin des Chiffonniers', 'Une Gravure fantastique', and 'Sur Le Tasse en Prison'. I am not here concerned with drawing chronological conclusions about developments in Baudelaire's style at given dates (for suggestions here, see F. W. Leakey, *Baudelaire and Nature*, Manchester University Press, 1969; Professor Leakey was able to use *CBP* for his Chronological Index but not for his text). Where I speak of 'initial' or 'first' version, I mean of course the first *extant* version; many others must have existed.

8 Similarly, the change in the last stanza of 'Le Vin des Chiffonniers', where wine, seen first as the gift of God, becomes the invention of man, fits the function of the section *LE VIN* as leading up to the sections on *FLEURS DU MAL* and *RÉVOLTE*.

9 Cf. also 'Pauvre pendu muet' becoming 'Ridicule pendu' in 'Un Voyage à Cythère' (commented on in Fairlie, *Baudelaire: Les Fleurs du Mal*, London, Arnold, 1960, pp. 31–2); 'grand comme le monde' becoming 'laid comme le monde' in 'L'Imprévu'; etc.

10 For his struggle for total perfection in material presentation see especially *Corr.* II, 38 and III, 94. For grammatical correction, he applied to others the same rigorous standards as to himself: Cf. the firm and tactful letter to Soulary, *Corr.* III, 44–5. He once amusingly over-reached himself in his zeal for such helpful amendment, when he set out to correct the language of Barbey d'Aurevilly's *L'Ensorcelée*, thereby removing all the deliberate 'patois normand' (*Corr.* II, 236).

11 For suggested sources of the classical reminiscences here, see *CB* 473; L. J. Austin, op. cit. p. 248, discusses this variant. The comment on 'maturité' and 'fécondité' suggests the closeness to the complete Du Bellay quotation of which Austin gives a portion: 'Telle que dans son char la Bérécynthienne, / Couronnée de tours et joyeuse d'avoir / Enfanté tant d'enfants.'

12 Cf. also the change at the end of 'Je te donne ces vers'. The second-last line had read:

Les stupides mortels qui t'appellent leur frère—

the 'te' depending on 'Etre maudit' from five lines earlier. In a poem to a woman, and immediately preceding 'Statue', 'leur frère' stands out oddly, and was changed to 'Les stupides mortels qui t'ont jugée amère' (*CBP* 88), adding, too, a new echo of sound in the repeated 'u'. For other important grammatical points, see the articles mentioned in footnote 6 above. See also Jacques Crépet, *Propos sur Baudelaire*, pp. 85–9, for hesitations over 'bétail' and 'satyre'.

13 In the almost impeccable *CBP*, there is an error in the note to line 14 of 'L'Examen de minuit'. In the text this line is given as 'Digne vassal des Démons', and in the note is the variant of the third edition 'Digne vassale des Démons', with an appended [*sic*]. Not only would 'vassal' leave the line short of a syllable, but, when one examines the context, 'vassale' is intended to be feminine, in apposition to 'la brute': the lines read: 'Nous avons, pour plaire à la brute, / Digne vassale des Démons, / Insulté ce que nous aimons'.

14 For a different use of rhyming dictionaries see A. Fairlie, 'Nerval et Richelet', *Revue des Sciences Humaines*, 1958, pp. 397–400.

15 See J. Crépet, op. cit. p. 88, for examples of hesitation over dividing syllables. Baudelaire corrects 'viande' in 'Le Reniement de Saint Pierre' where 'Comme un tyran gorgé de vian/des et de vins' becomes 'Comme un tyran gorgé de vi/ande et de vins'; but the opposite takes place in the line from 'Bénédiction'; which was first 'De génuflexions, de vi/ande et de vins' and becomes the more ringing and balanced 'De génuflexions, de vian/des et de vins'.

16 The change from 'avec' to 'jusqu'à' is of course also significant.

17 J. Pommier, op. cit., p. 157.

18 Cf. also, in 'La Mort des artistes', 'N'ont plus qu'un seul espoir qui souvent les console' which becomes 'N'ont qu'un espoir, étrange et sombre Capitole' (*CBP* 252); 'Le Jet d'eau' with its refrain of 'Phoebe réjouie' in place of 'la lune pâlie' (*CBP* 291); 'Le Couvercle' with its 'riche', 'richard', 'Crésus' (*CBP* 345).

19 For other means of intensifying time, cf. the change from 'Le Temps descend sur moi minute par minute' to '*Et le Temps m'engloutit* minute par minute' (*CBP* 149), or from 'ne connaît pas le nom' to '*n'a jamais su le nom*' (*CBP* 257).

20 *CBP* 244 gives 'Donne' as the variant here, without a *sic*. Was this a misprint in the Placard? Scansion and grammar would require 'Donnes'.

21 Among rhythmical questions, it would be interesting to discuss the variants where Baudelaire gives a new movement to the line by placing on the sixth syllable a word to which tradition would not have allowed that stress (a frequent practice in Leconte de Lisle). Cf. the change from 'Car il est fait, amis, de l'immortel péché' (relatively flat and with an effect of padding at the caesura) to the urgency of 'Car il est fait *avec* l'universel Péché (*CBP* 319); or from the regular 'Puisqu'il me trouve belle et qu'il veut m'adorer' to 'Puisqu'il me trouve *assez* belle pour m'adorer' (*CBP* 29).

Among other points there emerges Baudelaire's frequent substitution of the personal for the general: 'l'amour' becomes 'votre amour'; l'argent' becomes 'ton or'; 'ce carquois' becomes 'mon carquois', etc. (Though there are occasional examples of the opposite.) In 'Les Petites Vieilles' the hortatory 'Aimez-les' becomes the shared 'aimons-les'.

22 This technique of intense sense-impressions held in suspense to await a later elucidation of their connection and meaning makes one think ahead to Mallarmé. Cf. L. J. Austin, 'Mallarmé et le Réel', in *Modern Miscellany presented to Eugène Vinaver*, Manchester University Press, 1969, p. 17.

THE ORIGINALITY OF BAUDELAIRE'S 'LE CYGNE': GENESIS AS STRUCTURE AND THEME

'Le Cygne' (1859), with its dedication to Victor Hugo, is among the most widely admired of all Baudelaire's poems; and yet, I feel, its distinctive originality of *structure* still remains to be fully elucidated and explored. In most (perhaps all) previously written poems, including those by Baudelaire himself, what is finally presented to the reader is the *rearrangement* in some form (logical or chronological) of the original ideas, the original experience, from which the poem is fashioned; almost by definition there is a gap, more or less wide, between the original sequence of ideas, and the rearranged sequence ultimately laid before the reader. Baudelaire's unusual achievement and innovation in 'Le Cygne' is to have *closed* this gap, to have made a poem simply by setting down the thoughts that freely came into his mind at the actual moment of composition. In so doing, he not only goes some way towards anticipating certain modern techniques ('free association', 'stream of consciousness', 'automatic writing', and the like); he also affords us the unique privilege of assisting, as it were, at the actual creation of the poem. Theme, structure and genesis are thus no longer distinct but identical; in the ensuing analysis, I shall be concerned mainly and simply to trace out this developing sequence of the poet's thoughts, exactly as he presents it to us in his poem.[1]

> Andromaque, je pense à vous! Ce petit fleuve,
> Pauvre et triste miroir où jadis resplendit
> L'immense majesté de vos douleurs de veuve,
> 4 Ce Simoïs menteur qui par vos pleurs grandit,
>
> A fécondé soudain ma mémoire fertile,
> Comme je traversais le nouveau Carrousel.

In these opening lines, the poet *voices* his thoughts quite literally and directly: he is thinking of Andromache, he sees her in his mind's eye (in a pose remembered, and adapted, from a few lines of Virgil's),[2] therefore he speaks *to* her, and to her he will continue, ostensibly, to address all the ensuing thoughts which in their sequence constitute the poem. But just as, in the mind, one thought leads to another even before the first is fully completed, so within the very syntax and imagery of these opening lines, the succeeding lines (and thoughts) are anticipated and prepared: the 'mock Simoïs' which (in Baudelaire's version) directly receives and is swelled by Andromache's tears, is imagined, as it 'flows' into his mind, to be actually 'nourishing' his already fertile memory—for all the world like some real river flowing through a rich and green valley. What here specifically activates (or reactivates) his memory is his awareness of the *external* scene through which he is passing: the new, transformed square, across which (as he thinks, suddenly, of Andromache) he finds himself walking, and which he now immediately and infallibly recalls as it once was and as he had previously known it. But this substitution of the old for the new, is first presented in more general, even seemingly sententious terms:

> Le vieux Paris n'est plus (la forme d'une ville
> 8 Change plus vite, hélas! que le cœur d'un mortel);

The opening phrase here is clearly something of a *cliché* (like so many phrases that come, unbidden, into one's mind!); Baudelaire is echoing a familiar and predictable reaction to Haussmann's endless 'renovations' of the 1850s and 1860s—a reaction epitomised in a satirical ditty of the time:

> A tout instant le marteau
> Attaque un quartier nouveau . . .[3]

But what distinguishes Baudelaire's 'stock' response from that of other contemporary Parisians, is the qualifying parenthesis he goes on to add, under the guise of a paradox which appears simply to be asserting, in the most general terms, that buildings (supposedly so solid and enduring) change in fact more quickly than human hearts (supposedly so fragile and capricious). And yet in its context the aphorism is unmistakably self-regarding: the involuntary 'hélas!' betrays a deep personal commitment to the past, and the ensuing verses—introduced by the significant phrase: 'Je ne vois qu'*en esprit*' —make fully clear that the unchanging heart is specifically Baudelaire's own. Effectively, this parenthesis not only qualifies the preceding phrase, it undermines and even contradicts it: the old Paris may have disappeared in reality, but in this particular mortal heart at least, *nothing* has changed. And so, in his mind's eye, the

new square is slowly transformed back into the old, the vanished
scene re-creates itself in his memory, detailed and entire:

> Je ne vois qu'en esprit tout ce camp de baraques,
> Ces tas de chapiteaux ébauchés et de fûts,
> Les herbes, les gros blocs verdis par l'eau des flaques,
> 12 Et, brillant aux carreaux, le bric-à-brac confus.

Critics have often remarked on the 'prosaic' realism of these and the
succeeding lines, and on the audacious (albeit successful) contrast
that this presents with the 'classical' nobility of other sections of the
poem. But this is a highly 'literary' comment: if, as I have suggested,
we regard 'Le Cygne' as essentially the poetic transposition of a man's
thoughts—if we *listen* to it (and no purely silent reading can convey its
full resonance) as if to Baudelaire speaking his thoughts aloud to us,
just as they come into his mind—then we may feel this sequence of
descriptive verses to be the obvious and inevitable medium whereby
he builds up for us (and, initially, for himself) the accumulating
picture that has begun to form in his mind. Just as in those other (but
more studied) poems of recollection, 'Parfum exotique' and 'La
Chevelure', Baudelaire's imagination is here fired by an external
stimulus (the newly changed appearance of a familiar part of Paris)
to re-create from memory a past scene, in its fullest and most crowded
detail; here, too, he literally 'transports' himself, in time if not in
place, to a past reality that utterly displaces the present. We must not
forget, however, when noting this seeming obliteration of the present
by the past, this reduction of the present to the one phrase 'le nouveau
Carrousel', without further description of any kind, that Baudelaire
would certainly have assumed in his contemporary reader a prior
familiarity with the present scene; to a Parisian reader of 1860, the
words 'le nouveau Carrousel' would draw the same immediate and
informed response as would, for instance, the words 'new Euston
concourse' to a Londoner (or traveller to London) of 1972. The same
could scarcely be assumed, however, of the *old* Carrousel, already
fully demolished by early 1852 (any more than one could assume, in
today's Londoners, a detailed recollection of the old Euston station
of pre-'reconstruction' days); for the reader to share fully in Baudelaire's re-creation of the past, and 'relive' with him, in the subsequent
verses, an episode that only the poet has truly experienced and
known, the scene must be described to him in its fullest and most
prosaic detail—in short, before he can *feel*, he must first *see*.
    With the succeeding verses, Baudelaire begins to narrow down his

field of vision, to the point where, with the apparition of the swan, we
at last see the reason for the poem's title:

> Là s'étalait jadis une ménagerie;
> Là je vis, un matin, à l'heure où sous les cieux
> Froids et clairs le Travail s'éveille, où la voirie
> 16 Pousse un sombre ouragan dans l'air silencieux,
>
> Un cygne qui s'était évadé de sa cage,
> Et, de ses pieds palmés frottant le pavé sec,
> Sur le sol raboteux traînait son blanc plumage.
> 20 Près d'un ruisseau sans eau la bête ouvrant le bec
>
> Baignait nerveusement ses ailes dans la poudre . . .

There is of course an element of dramatic suspense in the delayed
revelation here of what exactly it *was* that the poet saw on that far-off
morning in Paris: 'Là, je vis . . .'—and then, three lines later, in a
place of exceptional emphasis at the beginning of a new verse, the
completed proposition: 'Un cygne . . .' And, moreover, this is
a device Baudelaire had employed successfully, for specifically
dramatic purposes, in several earlier poems: 'Une Charogne', 'Une
Martyre', 'Un Voyage à Cythère'. And yet, however calculated may
be the stylistic effect (and this is a matter to which I shall return later),
the construction equally corresponds, and with singular appropriateness, to the laborious, almost hesitant processes of mental association,
on those occasions when we allow our minds to wander, and follow
freely yet often gropingly a train of thought leading we know not
whither. Thus now into Baudelaire's mind, as he stands in the new
Carrousel and thinks back to the old, have come successively and in
spontaneous sequence: first, the crowded square, with its chaotic
clutter of huts and junk-shops, its heaps of unused building materials,
its weeds and puddles; next, the menagerie, spreading across a part
of the square; next again, the specific *moment* fixed for us with some
solemnity, with its vague general impression of men going off to
work, and of street-cleaners making their 'hurricane' progress
through the bright, chilly dawn; finally, as the poet's thought reaches
its point of destination and he is at last able to define clearly what it is
that all the time he has had 'at the back of his mind', the single figure
of the swan emerging in all its pitiful (and dramatic) isolation.

With the next line of the poem (and in mid-sentence), a remarkable
transformation occurs in the poet's conception and presentation of
the swan:

20 Près d'un ruisseau sans eau la bête ouvrant le bec

Baignait nerveusement ses ailes dans la poudre,
Et disait, le cœur plein de son beau lac natal:
"Eau, quand donc pleuvras-tu? quand tonneras-tu, foudre?"
24 Je vois ce malheureux, mythe étrange et fatal,

Vers le ciel quelquefois, comme l'homme d'Ovide,
Vers le ciel ironique et cruellement bleu,
Sur son cou convulsif tendant sa tête avide,
28 Comme s'il adressait des reproches à Dieu!

The 'transformation' hinges, it will be seen, on the dual function given to the phrase 'ouvrant le bec'. Initially, when forming part of the realistic description of the swan, this phrase records simply the swan's gesture of distress (a 'nervous' gesture, similar to that noted in the next line: the 'bathing' of wings in the dust); it is only when the sentence is completed, in line 22, that the gesture is interpreted by the poet (and the reader) in anthropomorphic terms: the swan, it now transpires, has opened its beak in order to '*speak*'. It is this anthropomorphic role given to the swan, which constitutes the transformation referred to, and thereby marks an entirely new inflection in the poet's train of thought. The swan is now suddenly endowed with various attributes appropriate only to a human: nostalgic sentiments ('le cœur plein de son beau lac natal'), speech of a highly rhetorical kind ('Eau, quand donc pleuvras-tu? quand tonneras-tu, foudre?'). It is of course very difficult to convey sympathy with, and compassion for, the sufferings of animals, except through anthropomorphic forms of expression—and, indeed, this tendency is already here displayed, in the (marvellously precise) use of the adverb 'nerveusement'. But Baudelaire's 'humanisation' of the swan does not spring from mere sentimentality; the explanation lies rather in the ensuing lines (which conclude the first part of the poem), and especially in the appositive phrase 'mythe étrange et fatal'. From being a mere object of compassion, however deeply felt, the swan has now, through the poet's deepening vision, acquired the status of a *myth*; its new behaviour is entirely appropriate to such a status—for how else should a mythical swan communicate, than through the most gravely rhetorical language? And the new role is extended still further, in the final verse of the first part of the poem: because the swan's neck strains convulsively *upwards*, towards the sky which by its 'cruel' and 'ironic' blueness, its settled promise of fair weather, appears to mock the poor creature's need for rain or water of any kind—*therefore* the gesture is seen as embodying a form of 'reproach' which is almost an act of protest (and not only on the swan's behalf) against an unheeding God.

The break between parts I and II of the poem, represents a *pause* in Baudelaire's thoughts: we can imagine him standing alone in the square, lost in his memories, and then as it were coming to himself again, gathering his thoughts together as he once more becomes aware of the present scene. But even in this renewed awareness, he still remains wholly under the dominance of the past:

> Paris change! mais rien dans ma mélancolie
> N'a bougé! palais neufs, échafaudages, blocs,
> Vieux faubourgs, tout pour moi devient allégorie,
> 32 Et mes chers souvenirs sont plus lourds que des rocs.

With this verse, we are given the full explanation, almost the symmetrical elaboration, of that seeming digression (lines 7-8) which earlier carried us from Andromache to the swan; the cryptic parenthesis which there followed the sententious affirmation: 'Le vieux Paris n'est plus' (a formula here echoed directly in the words 'Paris change!'), and which lamented the impermanence of buildings when set beside the unchanging constancy of the human heart, now takes on a heightened significance, a more explicitly personal application. The outward forms of Paris may change, but the poet's mood remains obstinately rooted, in its melancholy, to the images of the past he has conjured up for himself; his own heart, indeed, *contradicts* the reality of change, since for him nothing has 'moved' or abated, everything stands unchanged. Or rather, as he goes on to explain, everything, whether old or new, has become for him 'allegorical'—and this is as true of the 'new palaces' (i.e. the two new wings of the Louvre?) he sees before him, as of the scaffoldings or blocks of stone that by 1856 had been cleared from this particular site but were still everywhere else to be seen in Paris, or of the old districts now threatened with destruction if not already destroyed.[4] What Baudelaire means by the phrase 'tout pour moi devient allégorie', can be clearly enough inferred from the poem as a whole: anything and everything that he sees in Paris has the power to awaken some image in his mind, and such images, by their inter-connection with others, can serve to crystallise a central emotion or idea. In that sense, all things may be said to 'become'—i.e. to give rise to—allegories (or myths, or images, or symbols);[5] by implication, *any* part of Paris that he might choose to visit, could stir memories no less deep than those at present aroused by the place du Carrousel, and thereby set in motion some further train of 'allegorical' or 'symbolic' associations. As to the adjective 'lourds' ('Et mes chers souvenirs sont plus *lourds* que des rocs'), the next verse shows this to carry, in retrospect, a double meaning: not only does it take up again the paradox of lines 7–8 (mortal hearts are more enduring than cities, cherished memories 'heavier' than rocks; the immaterial outlasts, and outweighs, the material); it also hints at all the dragging sadness that is crystallised in the ensuing verb 'opprime':

> Aussi devant ce Louvre une image m'opprime:
> Je pense à mon grand cygne, avec ses gestes fous,
> Comme les exilés, ridicule et sublime,
> 36 Et rongé d'un désir sans trêve! et puis à vous,
>
> Andromaque, des bras d'un grand époux tombée,
> Vil bétail, sous la main du superbe Pyrrhus,
> Auprès d'un tombeau vide en extase courbée;
> 40 Veuve d'Hector, hélas! et femme d'Hélénus!

The line 'Aussi devant ce Louvre une image m'opprime' is crucial to the development of the poem. Already, in the previous verse, we have begun to see the poet in his role as the 'promeneur solitaire' lost in his *urban* reverie, for whom the past, sadly, is more real than the present. Now, additionally, by the syntax and rhythm of this ensuing line, we gain a vivid sense of approaching climax; suddenly the poet's thoughts have become clear to him in their underlying and wider meaning, and with this line begins the long, slow, majestic unfolding of the *idea* towards which all his associations and memories have been obscurely converging. The words 'une image', which at first glance might seem to be referring merely to the swan which is next evoked, are revealed in retrospect to be of much wider scope: this image that 'oppresses' him as he stands before the new Louvre, becomes in effect a composite of *all* those various 'allegorical' or 'symbolic' images—beginning with Andromache and the swan, but extending far beyond them—that now begin to crowd into his mind. What in fact defines this unfolding image is the long sentence that develops, over the whole of the rest of the poem, from the phrase 'Je pense à . . .'—a phrase that Baudelaire had already used in the very first line of the poem ('Andromaque, je pense à vous!'), and to which he was significantly (if perhaps unconsciously) to recur, in the letter to Victor Hugo (7 December 1859) which accompanied a manuscript copy of the poem: 'Voici des vers faits pour vous et *en pensant à vous*'[6]—a phrase that in itself furnishes the whole structure of the last five verses, acting as the hinge on which all else turns, governing almost every subsequent sentence, whether directly or as an unexpressed antecedent. Here at last, with his renewed and conjoined descriptions of the swan and Andromache,

Baudelaire makes fully explicit to us (and to himself) the link that binds these two figures, and that had remained implicit or purely circumstantial in the first part of the poem. In this second presentation of the two main figures, with its reversed (and more reflectively logical?) order, we note certain significant differences from what has gone before. The two previously separate aspects of the swan are now telescoped into a single impression: the creature is 'ridicule' with its 'gestes fous', just as in the earlier section in which its physical plight was described with such realistic, almost zoological precision; but also, and in the same breath, it is 'sublime', with its endless and tormenting desire ('rongé d'un désir sans trêve' harks back to 'le cœur plein de son beau lac natal')—as befits the humanised 'myth' into which we saw it transformed. A significant interpolation here is the simile which connects the swan to exiles in general—not only (and we must take careful note here of Baudelaire's always deliberate punctuation) because like them it is at once absurd and sublime, but also because, like them, it knows all the torments of longing and nostalgia. In the transition to the next verse, continuity of thought and expression are maintained by the run-on effect, which serves also to throw the name 'Andromaque' into high relief at the beginning of the next verse. In this further tableau, Baudelaire completes the visual impression furnished in the opening verse of the poem, by borrowing one further detail from the *Aeneid* ('Auprès d'un tombeau vide'), and adapting another ('en extase courbée'); he also deepens the tragic identity established for Andromache in the opening verse ('L'immense majesté de vos douleurs de veuve'), by recalling the successive stages of her misfortune: widowed by Hector, made captive by Pyrrhus, 'passed on' by him as wife to Helenus (enslavement to a slave, in Virgil's words: 'Me famulo famulamque Heleno transmisit habendam').[7] But still more striking in its artistry and subtlety, is the way in which, by their pattern, both imagery and sound reproduce or 'echo' the fate of Andromache. I spoke earlier of the 'high relief' into which her name is thrown by its isolation at the beginning of the verse; but this is almost literally true, in that through each successive image we are made to follow, as if with our own eyes, this sad *downward* movement: once great herself (as the initial emphasis twice given to her name implies), she *falls* from the arms of her great consort into subjection under Pyrrhus (whose pride humbles hers), and must now *bow down*, in a transport or 'ecstasy' of grief, beside the simulacrum of Hector's tomb; from being great Hector's widow, she has now sadly *declined* to being the wife of the base-born Helenus. So, too, when speaking this verse, the voice must follow a

similar cadence: pitched high on the opening word 'Andromaque', it
then pursues its continuous downward curve until it reaches the final
and *contemptuous* enunciation of the three syllables 'Hélénus'.[8]

I mentioned earlier, as a particularly significant interpolation, the
phrase 'comme les exilés', which by analogy connects the swan with
exiles in general; and this is tacitly confirmed, at the end of this verse,
by the immediate linkage of the swan with Andromache, evoked in her
place of *exile* in Epirus. But it is only when, in the final verses of the
poem, we discover these two figures to be the first only in a whole long
gallery of 'victims', that we understand exile, in its widest sense, to be
the essential theme of the whole poem, the motive principle determining Baudelaire's whole chain of associations:

> Je pense à la négresse, amaigrie et phthisique,
> Piétinant dans la boue, et cherchant, l'œil hagard,
> Les cocotiers absents de la superbe Afrique
> 44 Derrière la muraille immense du brouillard;
>
> A quiconque a perdu ce qui ne se retrouve
> Jamais, jamais! à ceux qui s'abreuvent de pleurs
> Et tettent la Douleur comme une bonne louve!
> 48 Aux maigres orphelins séchant comme des fleurs!
>
> Ainsi dans la forêt où mon esprit s'exile
> Un vieux Souvenir sonne à plein souffle du cor!
> Je pense aux matelots oubliés dans une île,
> 52 Aux captifs, aux vaincus!... à bien d'autres encor!

Like Andromache, whom she here follows, the negress is a literary
recollection—but one deriving from a youthful poem of Baudelaire's
own, recently revised by him under the new title 'A une Malabaraise'.[9]
Even more felicitously than in those earlier versions, Baudelaire now
contrives to amalgamate past and present, reality and desire, within a
single haunting image; the palm-trees of Africa may in reality be
'absent', but to us as readers (no less than to Baudelaire in his
imagination, or to the girl in her desperate longing) they are made
vividly *present*; the majestic alexandrine of line 43 replaces them
before our eyes, and we feel almost that they are truly *there* within her
reach, if only somehow she could break through the imprisoning wall
of fog. By her demeanour and gestures, her physical wretchedness,
her awkward subjection to the rigours of an alien climate, the
negress reminds us of the swan; what links all three figures, however,
is not merely a common plight (exile from a cherished land), but also
the vain yet pathetic gesture whereby each in turn seeks to assuage a

hopeless longing. Thus Andromache, weeping tears for Hector into the 'false' stream she has renamed in honour of Troy, by the very copiousness of those tears mimics the realisation of her desire, and seems almost to achieve the impossible transformation; the swan, mocked by the arid pavement, lost in its 'dream' of deep, native waters, strains its neck in supplication towards a sky that could bring (but ironically withholds) the desired refreshment and release; the negress, finally, pursues with her haggard gaze what her heart tells her *must* somehow lie behind the vast curtain of fog—as if 'projecting', into the outward scene, those exotic palm-trees she has conjured up, as nostalgic 'ghosts', within her own mind.

At this point, when it might seem that Baudelaire had identified and drawn together all the diverse threads of his poem, its perspectives suddenly broaden: individual figures are succeeded by groups, and at the same time the relationship between these various figures is greatly simplified; a whole gallery of exiles imposes itself on the poet's mind, displacing altogether the Parisian scene from which, in the imaginative and associative sense, they have arisen. But the term 'exile' now itself takes on a wider and more inclusive (and at the same time, more personal) scope; in a formula of marvellous simplicity and poignancy, Baudelaire defines once and for all the wider theme of the poem, the wider range of his compassion: '[Je pense . . .] A quiconque a perdu ce qui ne se retrouve/Jamais, jamais!'—a compassion that is still further deepened in the remaining lines of this verse, with their deeply expressive articulation of that sense of primal loss, of unsatisfied and eternally frustrated yearning, already so movingly rendered by the simple repetition of the adverb 'jamais'. Perhaps we may feel the 'classical' simile of line 47 (Suffering pictured as a 'bonne louve') to be needlessly contrived; yet in the next line, how profound a truth of child nurture (foreshadowing all the discoveries of Freud, Bowlby, et al.) is enshrined in the touching image of the orphans 'withering like flowers'![10]

Exile (in both its literal and extended senses); irrecoverable loss or inconsolable suffering of any kind—to these broadening aspects of his theme Baudelaire in his final verse adds still another: alienation—and in so doing, in effect inserts *himself* within the series; he too becomes a link within the endless chain forged through his reverie. This continuity of thought is not immediately apparent, it is true: the renewed mention of 'Souvenir', the consequential 'Ainsi' (interrupting—and, it would seem, suspending—the long anaphoric sequence which at line 34 had developed from the phrase 'Je pense à . . .')—these might suggest at first some further, interpolated meditation on the processes of memory and change, such as we have twice before encountered (in lines 7–8, 29–32). But the rhyme-word ('s'exile') clearly identifies the poet with all those other *exiles*, of one kind or another, that he has enumerated: Andromache, the swan, the negress, the orphaned, the children of Suffering . . . 'Un vieux Souvenir' (with its 'allegorizing' capital) refers back, of course, to the poet's recollection of the swan— but linked with all the other figures which in a more immediate sense are also memories; we are thus reminded of the composite 'une image' of line 33. As to the horn-call which figures this 'ancient Memory', this suggests (particularly if set in relation with the cognate metaphor from 'Les Phares': 'Un appel de chasseurs perdus dans les grands bois'), a certain *solidarity* of exile and misfortune—betokening as it must another presence in the forest, and thereby, perhaps, some mitigation of solitude, secured through the multiple reverberations of a single 'vieux Souvenir'. But in what way exactly, we are led to ask, does the poet regard himself as 'exiled'? The simplest answer might be to relate this to the feelings of disorientation and *dépaysement*, the implied resistance to change, that have been aroused in him by the transformation and rebuilding of Paris: on walking through the new Carrousel, he feels himself to be an exile simply because he can never (except in memory) return to the old square that once stood there. 'Exile' in this strictly topographical sense may well have been what first brought the image of Andromache into his mind; now, however, at this final stage of the poem, the concept has been extended to embrace every kind of deprivation and suffering, and has moreover passed beyond the purely Parisian scene. Indeed, if we relate the present couplet to the verse immediately preceding, we may feel the poet to be himself enlisting within each and all of these variously deprived groups: he, too, has lost what never can be regained, he too has been nurtured by Suffering, he too has been orphaned. . . . It is certainly significant, in this connexion, that in a line from a companion poem, 'Les Petites Vieilles' (equally dedicated to Victor Hugo, and written only a few months earlier than 'Le Cygne'), Baudelaire should have described himself, in an image identical with that here used for the generality of life's victims, as 'celui que l'austère Infortune allaita'.[11] Equally, of course, if we pay full regard to the reflexive mode of 's'exile', we may feel Baudelaire to be referring simply to that lifelong sense of solitude and 'apartness' attested by so many texts.[12] On either interpretation, the 'forest' must represent the particular 'world' (spiritual as well as material) inhabited by Baudelaire, rather than any more localised setting such as Paris old or new; the horn call, in its turn, would seem to have the particular function of affirming the poet's *kinship* with that whole community of exiles he has brought together in his mind.

The final couplet of the poem brings a still further widening of this community. From a particular category (the shipwrecked and forgotten mariners) the resumed anaphoric sequence takes us to one so broad ('Aux captifs, aux vaincus!') that one might at first think it to be simply the collective designation, the ultimate summing-up, of *all* the figures previously evoked. For are not Andromache, the swan, the negress, the poet himself, the orphans, the children of Suffering—are not *all* these in some way either 'captive', or 'vanquished', or both at once? But Baudelaire does not choose, or is not free, to end his poem on this note; he is not content merely to *sum up*, as might be appropriate in a poem of more logical and conventional structure, but must needs follow his train of thought through to its ultimate conclusion— and in so doing indicate to the reader, by the suspensive (and infinitely suggestive) phrase: 'à bien d'autres encor!', the still wider, indeed infinite possibilities that lie open to the truly compassionate mind. It is this opening-out of perspectives at the poem's close, this suggestion of wider and wider ripples and resonances spreading from one victim of exile to another, that give the poem what is to me its most important quality: that of *universality*. Before arriving, with the poet, at this final stage of his journey, we have travelled far in time and space—from classical times to the present day, from Epirus to Paris (old and new), and thence to all the nameless islands and prisons with their store of anonymous victims. But now, finally, having linked in a single compassion so many different figures of misfortune, Baudelaire generalises this feeling to the point where it embraces *any* person or creature destined or condemned to suffer; transcending the personal past in which it was initially rooted, he now extends his vision timelessly into an eternal future. Viewing the poem from our modern perspective, we may thus feel it, indirectly, to be speaking to us of *our* problems: by implication, or additional resonance, it becomes at will a poem about Vietnam, Biafra, Ulster, Bangladesh—about any time or place where there are orphans, exiles, captives, vanquished . . . The last five verses of the poem form, as we have seen, a single, vast elegiac cadence—but it is a cadence that never quite finds its resolution, since these final words, 'à bien d'autres encor!', still leave us in suspense, continuing the poem, as it were, in our own minds. There is certainly no 'feebleness' here, no 'fading away' or 'dying fall'; on the contrary, the tone is musingly prolonged on the final syllable of 'en*cor*', there is prior stress of a kind on the first syllable of '*d'au*tres', the poet's voice (and the reader's) retains its full sonority to the end.[13] The final phrase, in short, compels attention, challenges and haunts the imagination; no other ending is imaginable, and none could serve to associate the reader more fully with the creative experience in which, from the opening lines, he has been privileged to share.

Baudelaire's transcription of his reverie is of course a highly 'organised' one, both psychologically and aesthetically; however complete may have been his initial surrender to the wayward flow of his associations, in this poetic version he remain continuously and consciously in control, shaping his text not only to the obvious exigencies of rhyme and metre, but also to innumerable other detailed effects of balance, contrast, harmony, suspense, and so on.[14] And yet, on the evidence of the letter to Hugo (aforementioned), Baudelaire would appear to have regarded this first version as having a certain 'unfinished' quality, as being still something of a 'sketch' for the final and fully polished text. Thus he begins by asking Hugo to judge these verses not with a severe but with a 'paternal' eye; he explains that their 'imperfections' will be 'touched up' later, and goes on 'to add:

Ce qui était important pour moi, c'était de dire vite tout ce qu'un accident, une image, peut contenir de suggestions, et comment la vue d'un animal souffrant pousse l'esprit vers tous les êtres que nous aimons, qui sont absents et qui souffrent. . . .[6]

In the event, the poem appeared in print, in *La Causerie*, barely a month after it had been sent to Hugo, in a text very little different from that finally published in the *Fleurs du Mal* of 1861: the few revisions brought by Baudelaire scarcely justify the promises and disclaimers of the letter, and one wonders therefore whether these may not have reflected some doubt or hesitation concerning the novelty of the technique he had adopted—and which, precisely, he so well describes in the formula above-quoted ('Ce qui était important pour moi, c'était de dire *vite*, etc.'). And to confirm such a speculation, one might cite a passage from the essay on *Le Peintre de la vie moderne*, first published in 1863 but written during this very period of his life (November 1859 to February 1860); in a chapter significantly entitled 'L'Art mnémonique', Baudelaire is discussing the specific individuality of technique of the admired draughtsman Constantin Guys:

Ainsi, dans l'exécution de M. G. se montrent deux choses: l'une, une contention de mémoire résurrectionniste, évocatrice, une mémoire qui dit à chaque chose: "Lazare, lève-toi!"; l'autre, un feu, une ivresse de crayon, de pinceau, ressemblant presque à une fureur. C'est la peur de n'aller pas assez vite, de laisser échapper le fantôme avant que la synthèse n'en soit extraite et saisie. . . . M. G. commence par de légères indications au crayon, qui ne marquent guère que la place que les objets doivent tenir dans l'espace. Les plans principaux sont indiqués ensuite par des teintes au lavis, des masses vaguement, légèrement colorées d'abord, mais reprises plus tard et chargées successivement de couleurs plus intenses. Au dernier moment, le contour des objets est définitivement cerné par de l'encre. A moins de les avoir vus, on ne se douterait pas des effets surprenants qu'il peut obtenir par cette méthode si simple et presque élémentaire. Elle a cet incomparable avantage, qu'à n'importe quel point de son progrès, chaque dessin a l'air suffisamment fini; vous nommerez cela une ébauche si vous voulez, mais ébauche parfaite. Toutes les valeurs y sont en pleine harmonie, et s'il les veut pousser plus loin, elles marcheront toujours de front vers le perfectionnement désiré.

(Pléiade, p. 1168)

A few months earlier, in his *Salon de 1859*, Baudelaire had applauded with equal enthusiasm Boudin's sketches of sky and sea (taken, in this case, directly 'from life'), but without quite being able to agree that these 'étonnantes études' could qualify as finished works of art—a contradiction which results (as I have shown elsewhere) from Baudelaire's general theories of art during this period.[15] But to return to the passage from *Le Peintre de la vie moderne*: without seeking to establish any too exact analogy between Guys's technique of draughtsmanship, as described by Baudelaire, and the method of composition followed in 'Le Cygne', I would suggest that in such phrases as 'une contention de mémoire résurrectionniste, évocatrice . . . qui dit à chaque chose: "Lazare, lève-toi!"', or 'C'est la peur de n'aller pas assez vite', or 'vous nommerez cela une ébauche si vous voulez, mais ébauche parfaite', Baudelaire is evincing preoccupations which are equally to be discerned both in the letter to Hugo, and in the specific text and structure of 'Le Cygne'. At the time of writing the letter, Baudelaire may well have felt his newly completed poem to be essentially, by the very method of its composition, a 'sketch' or 'rapid' draft, and therefore have resolved that in a final version the 'imperfections' would need to be refined away; on reflection, however, and no doubt in deference also to the practical need for rapid publication, the 'ébauche' may perhaps have seemed to him after all to be an 'ébauche *parfaite*', sharing with Guys's sketches not only their 'air suffisamment fini', but also a certain distinctive novelty and audacity of technique. Be this as it may, I would certainly maintain, from the evidence of the actual text as I have analysed it above, that the *decisive* factor shaping the poem's structure was more often 'psychological' than aesthetic or stylistic—that, for instance, the abrupt-seeming changes of 'register' or tone, the apparent digressions, the slow and elaborate unwinding of the sentences, the whole culminating 'movement' of the final verses, will have been dictated above all by the accidents and vagaries, the twists and turns, of Baudelaire's processes of thought, as here recorded by him with such close and patient fidelity.

It is difficult to be sure how fully Baudelaire himself was aware of the specific originality of this poem—that 'deep originality' which, as Garnet Rees has remarked, so instantly impresses the reader entering the 'new world of compassionate meditation' created from a simple *fait divers*.[16] A sense of innovation is certainly suggested by the comment, in a letter (also of 1859) to Jean Morel, on the companion poem 'Les Sept Vieillards' (the poet has just described it as forming 'le premier numéro d'une nouvelle série que je veux tenter'): 'je crains bien d'avoir simplement réussi à dépasser les limites assignées à la Poësie'.[17] But perhaps more important for us is to see 'Le Cygne' as the fulfilment—or as *one* fulfilment—of a lyrical ambition cherished by Baudelaire for much of his life. He first defines this ambition in a passage of his article of 1851 on *Les Drames et les romans honnêtes*, when ranging himself ironically among 'tous ces gredins qui ont des dettes et qui croient que le métier de poëte consiste à exprimer les mouvements lyriques de l'âme dans un rythme réglé par la tradition!'; he returns to it over ten years later, in the new (and specifically urban) context of his prose poems, when dedicating a selection of these texts to Arsène Houssaye:

> Quel est celui de nous qui n'a pas, dans ses jours d'ambition, rêvé le miracle d'une prose poétique, musicale sans rythme et sans rime, assez souple et assez heurtée pour s'adapter aux mouvements lyriques de l'âme, aux ondulations de la rêverie, aux soubresauts de la conscience?
>
> C'est surtout de la fréquentation des villes énormes, c'est du croisement de leurs innombrables rapports que naît cet idéal obsédant.[18]

The fixity and persistence of this particular 'obsession' is shown by the recurrence, at some ten years' distance, of the identical phrase 'les mouvements lyriques de l'âme'; such further phrases, in the 1862 *dédicace*, as '[les] ondulations de la rêverie', '[les] soubresauts de la conscience', 'la fréquentation des villes énormes' with its attendant 'croisement de leurs innombrables rapports', describe even more exactly the content and structure of 'Le Cygne'.[19] In its metrical form, admittedly, and for all the freedom and flexibility with which it deploys its alexandrine quatrains, the poem might be thought to be adhering, conservatively, to the model laid down in 1851, with its prescriptive 'rythme réglé par la tradition'. But if structure be considered an aspect of form (as it surely must), then 'Le Cygne', more than any other poem of Baudelaire's, gives the lie to Rimbaud's famous complaint at the older poet's lack of formal inventiveness: '... la forme si vantée en lui est mesquine. Les inventions d'inconnu réclament des formes nouvelles'. One way of 'inventing the unknown', as the Surrealists were to demonstrate, is by exploring the 'vastes et ... étranges domaines' of the human mind, with the aid of such 'formes nouvelles' as 'l'écriture automatique'.[20] In this whole 'adventure' (in Apollinaire's sense), the Baudelaire of 'Le Cygne' may be regarded, I suggest, as the specific if distant precursor of the Surrealists—by his willingness to exploit for poetic purposes the associative mechanisms of the human mind, by his tacit recognition that therein lies a rapid and effective medium for the transcription of 'les mouvements lyriques de l'âme.'

Reading   F. W. LEAKEY

NOTES

1 I reserve for a further article the study of the *composition* of this poem, i.e. of the external influences (personal, literary, philosophical, topographical, etc.) which shaped and determined what is here revealed to us of its immediate genesis. In my comments on Baudelaire's text, I have borrowed on occasion from my contributions to a recorded discussion, with Andrew Macanulty, of four poems by Baudelaire, including 'Le Cygne' (Sussex Tapes, 'French Language and Literature' series F.10, London, 1971)—as also from two other publications of mine: *Baudelaire and Nature*, Manchester University Press, 1969, pp. 256 and n. 2, 318 n. 4; 'Baudelaire and Mortimer', *French Studies*, VII, 2, April 1953, p. 108. All verse citations in the present article are to the critical edition of *Les Fleurs du Mal* by Georges Blin and Claude Pichois (revision of edition by Jacques Crépet and Georges Blin), Paris, Corti, 1968, vol. I; prose texts by Baudelaire (other than letters) are quoted from *Œuvres complètes*, ed. Claude Pichois (revision of edition by Y. G. Le Dantec), Paris, NRF-Gallimard, 'Bibliothèque de la Pléiade', 1966 reprint (hereafter abbreviated: 'Pléiade'). In titles cited hereafter, the place of publication is Paris, unless otherwise stated.

2 *Aeneid*, III, 294–329. A phrase from line 305: 'Falsi Simoëntis ad undam' is cited as epigraph to the first published text of Baudelaire's poem (*La Causerie*, 22 January 1860, p. 3), but this disappears from subsequent versions. For a full discussion of Baudelaire's adaptation of his Virgilian source, see the interesting (if at times over-ingenious) article by Lowry Nelson, Jr., 'Baudelaire and Virgil: A Reading of *Le Cygne*', *Comparative Literature*, XIII, 4, Fall 1961, pp. 332–45.

3 Cit. G. Laronze, *Le Baron Haussmann*, Alcan, 1932, p. 137. The theme of 'changing Paris' goes back, in fact, to the 1830s; cf. the numerous authors cited, for the whole period 1830–62, by P. Citron, *La Poésie de Paris dans la littérature française, de Rousseau à Baudelaire*, Éditions de Minuit, 1961, I, 331–42

4 The phrase 'vieux faubourgs' (line 31) need not necessarily be taken as referring to outlying suburbs. In other poems (e.g. 'Le Soleil', line 1; 'Le Vin des chiffonniers', line 3; 'Spleen: Pluviôse, irrité . . . , line 4; 'Les Sept Vieillards', line 12), Baudelaire uses the term to refer in a general way to the more populous districts of Paris; it in any case continued to be applied also to central districts—the Carrousel area itself being known, before 1852, as the 'faubourg du Doyenné'.

5 In line 24, it will be recalled, Baudelaire had described the swan as a '*mythe* étrange et fatal'; in line 33, he speaks of the composite '*image*' which 'oppresses' him; in his letter to Victor Hugo, finally, (see n. 6, below), he refers to the poem as a whole as 'mon petit *symbole*' (my italics). For the general interchangeability for Baudelaire of these various terms, and of such other expressions as 'emblème' and 'hiéroglyphe', see my book *Baudelaire and Nature*, p. 225 n. 1 (L. J. Austin and M. Gilman cit.).

6 The complete text of this letter (reproduced in part in Baudelaire, *Correspondance générale*, ed. Jacques Crépet and Claude Pichois, Conard, vol. VI, 1953, p. 82 n. 1; see also Pléiade, pp. 1537–8) will be furnished by Claude Pichois in his forthcoming Pléiade edition of this *Correspondance*. My italics, in the phrase 'en pensant à vous'.

7 *Aeneid*, III, 329. For the previous references cited, cf. lines 304 (for the 'tombeau vide') and 307–8 (from which may have derived 'extase', taken in its etymological sense).

8 I have tried to illustrate these various effects in a reading of 'Le Cygne', which precedes the recorded discussion mentioned in note 1, above.

9 *Le Présent*, 15 November 1857; the earlier version, under the title 'A une Indienne', had appeared in *L'Artiste*, 13 December 1846. The poem, though omitted by Baudelaire from both the 1857 and 1861 editions of *Les Fleurs du Mal*, was included by his posthumous editors in the 1868 edition.

10 For a comment on the intimate relation of Baudelaire's work to his childhood, see C. A. Hackett, *Rimbaud*, London, Bowes and Bowes ('Studies in Modern European Literature and Thought'), 1957, p. 16; cf. also L. J. Austin, 'Retrouver la vision de l'enfance', *Les Nouvelles littéraires*, 6 June 1957, and Léon Cellier, 'Baudelaire et l'enfance', in *Baudelaire. Actes du Colloque de Nice (25–27 mai 1967)*, Minard, 1968, pp. 67–77.

11 Line 36 (my italics). A third poem dedicated to Victor Hugo during this same period, was 'Les Sept Vieillards'; see, in this whole connexion, the article by Claude Pichois and myself 'Les Sept versions des *Sept Vieillards*' in *Mélanges baudelairiens offerts à W. T. Bandy*, Neuchâtel, La Baconnière ('Études baudelairiennes', vol. 3), 1973, pp. 262–89, and cf. p. 52 above.

12 Cf. the prose poem 'L'Étranger' (Pléiade, p. 231); *Mon cœur mis à nu*, VII (Pléiade, p. 1275); the letters to his mother of 10 January 1850, 11

January 1858, 5 June 1863 (*Correspondance générale*, ed. J. Crépet, I, p. 122; II, p. 120; IV, p. 168); etc.

13 This also is an effect I have tried to convey in my own reading of the poem, as recorded for Sussex Tapes (see notes 1, 8, above). The comment on the supposed 'feebleness', etc., of the final phrase, is made by P. Mansell Jones, in an otherwise notably perceptive analysis ('Baudelaire's Poem, *Le Cygne*', in *The Assault on French literature, and other Essays*, Manchester University Press, 1963, p. 128); see also J. D. Hubert, *L'Esthétique des 'Fleurs du Mal'*, Geneva, Cailler, 1953, p. 101—but cf., on the other hand, the sensitive comment by Alison Fairlie, *Baudelaire: 'Les Fleurs du Mal'*, Arnold ('Studies in French Literature', 6), 1960, p. 25, on the way in which, in this couplet, Baudelaire 'fade[s] deliberately and penetratingly into the distance of anonymous and forgotten sorrows'.

14 Cf. my comments, above, on the effects of dramatic suspense, emphasis and 'cadence', in lines 13–17 and 34–40. One might also mention, as further examples: the substitution of 'le nouveau Carrousel' for 'ce vaste Carrousel', in the final version of line 6, in order to bring out more strongly the contrast ('*nouveau* Carrousel'—'*vieux* Paris') with the succeeding line; the very choice of 'Le Cygne' as title, for a poem which begins, so arrestingly and mysteriously, by evoking a quite different figure (with a third one interposed between the two, in the person of the dedicatee Hugo!—three figures of exile presented to us within the first six words we read . . .); and so on.

15 See *Baudelaire and Nature*, pp. 134–7; for the passage in question from the *Salon de 1859*, see Pléiade, pp. 1081–2. For the dating of the previous text cited (*Le Peintre de la vie moderne*), see Pléiade, p. 1711.

16 'Baudelaire and the Imagination', in: *Modern Miscellany presented to Eugène Vinaver*, ed. T. E. Lawrenson, F. E. Sutcliffe and G. F. A. Gadoffre, Manchester University Press, 1969, p. 213.

17 *Correspondance générale*, II, p. 324 (letter assigned to June 1859).

18 Pléiade, pp. 618, 229. Cf. also, in another text of this period, *Le Poëme du haschisch* (first published 30 September 1858 in the *Revue contemporaine*), Baudelaire's parenthetical comment on the related word 'rhapsodic', as used by Poe in a passage describing the effects of opium: 'le mot *rapsodique*, qui définit si bien un train de pensées suggéré et commandé par le monde extérieur et le hasard des circonstances' (Pléiade, p. 373).

19 They could also be taken as applying to two others, at least, of Baudelaire's later poems: 'Le Voyage'; 'Danse macabre'; cf. in this connexion my comments in my article 'Baudelaire: The Poet as Moralist', in *Studies in Modern French Literature presented to P. Mansell Jones*, Manchester University Press, 1961, p. 215, and in my book, *Baudelaire and Nature*, p. 294 and n. 1.

20 The phrase 'vastes et . . . étranges domaines' is of course taken from Apollinaire's *La Jolie rousse*; the Rimbaud quotation, from the letter to Demeny (the so-called 'lettre du *Voyant*') of 15 May 1871.

MALLARMÉ'S RESHAPING OF 'LE PITRE CHÂTIÉ'

In February 1865, Mallarmé (then aged twenty-three) declared that he had completely changed his poetic manner since his first schoolboy efforts at the Lycée de Sens.[1] He had replaced 'une prolixité violente et une enthousiaste diffusion' by 'l'amour de la condensation'.[2] But this was only the beginning of a lifelong adventure. Each of Mallarmé's successive achievements became the springboard for a new departure towards a richer and subtler mode of poetic expression. What distinguishes his later works from his earlier is not only a higher degree of condensation and concentration,[3] but also a different technique, that of suggestion rather than statement.[4] This poetry of suggestion is not of course confined to the poems first composed in the latter part of Mallarmé's life. It is also to be found in certain poems which, although first written in the early part of Mallarmé's career, notably in the years at Tournon, were published only twenty years or more later, after being radically revised or totally rewritten. Certainly there is a great difference between the schoolboy's poems written at Sens and the poems written in London or Tournon which appeared in 1866 in the *Parnasse contemporain*.[5] But this difference is slight compared with that between the *Parnasse contemporain* poems and those written by Mallarmé in the full mastery of his maturity. Probably the best example of this radical change is the sonnet 'Le Pitre châtié'. Two versions of it exist: one prior to April 1864; the other, the definitive version, first published in 1887 in the photolithographic edition of the *Poésies*.[6] If there were any intermediate versions, they have not yet been found: the contrast between the two extant versions is all the more striking.

In both versions, the essential theme is the same. But a theme in itself counts for little in literature: expression is what matters. The finest conception has little value until it is embodied in form. True of all art, this is specially true of literature. As Flaubert put it, style is in itself 'une manière absolue de voir les choses.'[7] The two versions of 'Le Pitre châtié' are virtually two different poems, despite their identical theme.[8] In each sonnet, the poet is portrayed as a clown, joyously escaping from the sordid booth where he performs, to plunge into the lakes which are his beloved's eyes and so wash himself clear of the defiling grease-paint, only to realise at last that in washing off the grime and make-up he has lost what was his most sacred possession. Behind the physical images are the abstract implications. The poet has fled from both the outer and inner limitations that stifle the striving artist (the sooty booth of the world in which he is confined, the parodic insufficiency of his own nature as mere clown); he has hoped to find in love a purifying and total renewal; and has finally discovered that the limitations from which he fled were the necessary conditions of his highest worth.[9]

Before examining in detail the two versions, the meaning of the word 'pitre' must be clarified.[10] Properly speaking, a 'pitre' is defined as a 'Bouffon qui fait la parade devant un théâtre forain, un cirque, qui est chargé d'attirer le public, par ses facéties, autour des tréteaux d'un charlatan, d'un saltimbanque.'[11] Such a clown, after attracting the public by his antics outside, would also of course perform inside. The 'pitre' is the lowest form of actor, a mountebank or clown.

LE PITRE CHÂTIÉ
First Version (1864)

Pour ses yeux,—pour nager dans ces lacs, dont les quais
Sont plantés de beaux cils qu'un matin bleu pénètre,
J'ai, Muse,—moi, ton pitre,—enjambé la fenêtre
Et fui notre baraque où fument tes quinquets.

Et d'herbes enivré, j'ai plongé comme un traître
Dans ces lacs défendus, et, quand tu m'appelais,
Baigné mes membres nus dans l'onde aux blancs galets,
Oubliant mon habit de pitre au tronc d'un hêtre.

Le soleil du matin séchait mon corps nouveau
Et je sentais fraîchir loin de ta tyrannie
La neige des glaciers dans ma chair assainie,

Ne sachant pas, hélas! quand s'en allait sur l'eau
Le suif de mes cheveux et le fard de ma peau,
Muse, que cette crasse était tout le génie!

This first version, opposing art and love clearly from the outset, moves slowly and explicitly through syntax and explanation of images, leading straightforwardly into the theme of the escape from the Muse, a traditional figure for the poet's struggle with his art. The conventional, demonstrative structure is held together by the regularly renewed apostrophe to the Muse: 'Muse,—moi, ton pitre', 'notre baraque', 'tes quinquets', 'quand tu m'appelais', 'loin de ta tyrannie', and the climax, 'Muse . . .' of the last line.

The opening quatrain is built up on two metaphors: the beloved's

eyes are lakes; poetry is a performance in a canvas booth where the
poet plays the part of a clown.[12] The metaphors are perfectly explicit,
both terms of each being given ('Pour ses yeux,—pour nager dans ces
lacs'; 'Muse,—moi ton pitre'). The beloved is identified only by the
possessive adjective 'ses', and only her eyes are evoked. An implicit
metaphor ('plantés') transforms her eyelashes into reeds, as in the
lovely stylisation of the last line of 'Las de l'amer repos . . .' ('trois
grands cils, roseaux').[13] The delightful, somewhat precious elaboration of the details also conveys the sensation of the freshness of the
morning air in the world outside, as opposed to the smoky lamps within
the booth.[14] The clown's departure into the morning light is described straightforwardly as a perfectly possible everyday action: 'j'ai
enjambé la fenêtre', the first of several such actions given in a sequence
of narrative verbs ('j'ai plongé', 'j'ai baigné mes membres nus' in the
second quatrain).

This second quatrain develops the metaphor of the purifying
plunge into the lustral waters of the lakes. The clown knows that his
flight is a betrayal (this is conveyed by the open simile 'comme un
traître'), and that human happiness is forbidden him ('ces lacs
défendus'). The conveying of physical delight is strong but relatively
simple here: again the details are specific, precise, and decorative
rather than functional: the white shingle, the clown's clothes left
hanging on the beech-tree ('hêtre,' called up by the rhyme rather than
reason, although pleasing and plausible), or the sensuous 'd'herbes
enivré', only partly related to the theme of the purifying waters.

But it is in the tercets that strong and subtle sense-impressions
(with the elemental force of sun and ice) come more concentratedly
together in the swift collocation of purification, past disgust, and
ironical discovery. Joy at having found a new life, far from the Muse's
tyranny, is followed by the realisation of catastrophic loss. Both
emotions are conveyed in terms at once of sensation and of sound-
patterning: the sunshine drying the clown's new body as he feels, in
his purified flesh, a cool freshness like that of glacial snow; the water
washing away the tallow that stuck down his hair and the grease-
paint that plastered his skin, but taking away with it all genius.[15]
Patterns of [ɛ] and [i] run through the sense of appeasing and cold
purity ('je sentais fraîchir [. . .]/La neige des glaciers dans ma chair
assainie'), while the deliberate beat on [a] or [ɑ] culminates in the
climax of 'crasse', the grime that was also greatness:

> Ne sachant pas, hélas! quand s'en allait sur l'eau
> Le suif de mes cheveux et le fard de ma peau
> Muse, que cette crasse . . .

The poem is perfectly clear from beginning to end. The metaphors are explicit and fully developed. The attempt to escape is related in detail in its various phases, to end in the ironical conclusion. This is a poem of statement, making only slight demands on the reader's imagination and intelligence. As it stood, it could easily have been included in the poems of the first *Parnasse contemporain* series, where Mallarmé had intended to insert it, as another variation on the central theme: the tyranny of the ideal and the inadequacy of the real. Here the form of escape from the ideal is love; and this attempt fails as did all the others.

LE PITRE CHÂTIÉ
Second Version (1887)

Yeux, lacs avec ma simple ivresse de renaître
Autre que l'histrion qui du geste évoquais
Comme plume la suie ignoble des quinquets,
J'ai troué dans le mur de toile une fenêtre.

De ma jambe et des bras limpide nageur traître,
A bonds multipliés, reniant le mauvais
Hamlet! c'est comme si dans l'onde j'innovais
Mille sépulcres pour y vierge disparaître.

Hilare or de cymbale à des poings irrité,
Tout à coup le soleil frappe la nudité
Qui pure s'exhala de ma fraîcheur de nacre,

Rance nuit de la peau quand sur moi vous passiez,
Ne sachant pas, ingrat! que c'était tout mon sacre,
Ce fard noyé dans l'eau perfide des glaciers.

This second version deals with the same theme as the 1864 sonnet, but in a totally different style, compact and suggestive, where every word is charged with meaning and is completely functional, and no irrelevant details are retained.[16] Although the first version is a most welcome aid to interpretation, the final version contains all the necessary hints for the patient and perceptive reader to work out the meaning for himself.[17] The cryptic first quatrain, for example, is explained by the second, a frequent method in Mallarmé's later manner. But the first reading is bound to be baffling, and this is certainly Mallarmé's intention: he invites the reader to 'deviner peu à peu'. Why should the reader accept this challenge? Because the poem makes an immediate impact on his senses by its haunting musical structure and on his mind by its provocation to penetrate the mysterious meaning behind its strange and striking imagery.

In this final version, Mallarmé has completely removed the clear, conventional, demonstrative structure he had given the poem: instead of the regular apostrophe to the Muse, the almost imperceptible address is to 'Yeux, lacs', taken up once only in l.12: 'quand sur moi *vous* passiez'. But it is only after careful study and analysis that this becomes apparent. The initial bold 'attack' of the two monosyllables 'Yeux, lacs' clamped together forces the mind to hold both in suspension, and to cast about for all possible associations in meaning or syntax. Jumping to symbolic conclusions can lead to error and has done so for some critics.[18] The two enigmatic words begin to fall into place only when we reach 'nageur' and 'onde' in the second quatrain. Mallarmé has ruthlessly cut away, despite their delicate and imaginative loveliness, the explicative details of the eyes and lakes, and the developed analogy between them. The 'arithmetic' of the descriptive detail has been replaced by the 'algebra' of the bold equation, juxtaposing the two terms.[19] The striking apposition 'lacs' condenses into one single word the metaphor worked out at length in the first version.[20] Here the development of the metaphor is postponed until the second quatrain, which evokes the action of the swimmer. For the moment, all we know is that the poet feels a 'simple ivresse de renaître' and that this exhilaration is associated with the eyes that are lakes. Here two apparently very ordinary words are given quite special suggestive value by rhythm and meaning in the lines:

> Yeux, lacs avec ma *simple*/ivresse de renaître
> *Autre que* l'histrion . . .

The word 'simple' is stressed by its place at the caesura in a run-on line; it suggests a primal, uncomplicated purity, unhesitant, un-Hamlet-like; but it also has overtones of scarcely perceptible irony, leading on to the end of the poem ('ne sachant pas'). An exceptional intensity—a kind of breath of longing—is placed on 'Autre que', by this very strong enjambement, running right on from 'avec ma simple ivresse de renaître/AUTRE que . . .' For this rebirth completely transforms the poet: he is no longer the actor (designated by the pejorative term 'histrion'),[21] the poor player that he was, who evoked with his gesture the vile soot of the lamps. But neither 'pitre' nor 'baraque' is here: we have to deduce them from the past 'histrion' and the 'mur de toile' (a suggestive metaphor or metonymy conveying a concrete impression in place of a general term or 'label'). The precise meaning of l. 3 is open to discussion. It is most likely that 'Comme plume' refers to the soot: the actor, wishing to evoke a plume, calls up only the soot which rises from the lamps to fall around him in tiny, feathery flakes. Another interpretation takes 'Comme plume' as modifying the subject in 'j'évoquais', and involving an identification between the actor and the writer.[22] But instead of the hoped-for masterpiece, the actor-poet succeeds in evoking only the vile soot of the lamps. In the first version, the smoky lamps were simply a decorative detail for which the clown was not responsible: in the definitive version, he himself evokes soot instead of diffusing light. That is why, disgusted with himself and with his calling, he flees. And here, instead of stepping over an existing window-sill, he violently creates a window by bursting through the canvas wall, like a clown leaping through a paper hoop, or more precisely like the exultant clown in Banville's poem 'Le Saut du tremplin'.[23]

The second quatrain picks up the opening metaphor of 'Yeux, lacs'. But there is no explicit transition from booth to lake, nor even a direct statement of the act of swimming (still less the undressing and hanging up of clothes): the violence and urgency of 'troué' is followed by the compressed nouns and adjectives of intense delight in escape and purification ('jambe', 'bras', 'nageur', 'bonds', 'limpide', 'traître', 'multipliés'), by the comparison 'comme si', and by the absolutism that culminates necessarily in nothingness ('sépulcres', 'vierge', 'disparaître'). The sensations powerfully evoke the intellectual content and its resonance. The poet is a traitor because he has abandoned his calling. He disowns 'le mauvais Hamlet': and there is a double implication here. *Hamlet* is of course for Mallarmé the play *par excellence*, 'le spectacle même pourquoi existent la rampe ainsi que l'espace doré quasi moral qu'elle défend';[24] Hamlet himself is the epitome of the man who, despite intense aspiration, cannot nerve himself to fulfilling his destined role; and the 'histrion' playing the part of Hamlet acts it badly. He therefore leaps towards a new life, a new, virginal existence: this picks up the 'simple ivresse de *renaître*' of the first quatrain, and restates the central theme of *Stirb und werde* which runs through so much of Mallarmé's work.[25] In this definitive version there is an altogether different depth of implications from those in the early poem. The dynamic image of the swimmer powerfully evokes the longing to escape from fumblings, limitations and absurdities into either the ideal or the oblivion of death, pointing forward to the conclusion, which conveys the realisation that limitation and aspiration are the condition of existence and worth.

In this quatrain, patterns of sound run parallel to the illusion of escape. At first discreetly introduced, this sound-patterning in [i] reaches its climax in the last two lines of the quatrain. The stress falls on 'comme si' because of its position at the caesura; then follow the words 'j'innovais/Mille sépulcres pour y vierge disparaître'. The sound of [i] is repeated three times in the following line, and then gradually dies out, to be significantly caught up again at last in 'l'eau perfide des glaciers'.

In the first tercet, there is no longer the mere description of the sun drying the swimmer's body, but an extraordinary evocation, by an anticipated apposition, of the sun's intense heat and light. The radiant apparition of the sun is suggested by the metaphor of cymbals struck by the flailing fists of the percussion man in the orchestra. Characteristically, Mallarmé throws out the words in such a way that their syntax is baffling and deliberately misleading at first: the line:

Hilare or de cymbale à des poings irrité

is a perfect example of that kind of poetic line which for Mallarmé constituted what he called 'un mot total, neuf, étranger à la langue et comme incantatoire'.[26] We are confronted with a set of apparently unrelated words. The first group baffled a Belgian reader, who wrote indignantly, as 'Un vieux et fidèle abonné', to the editor of L'Art Moderne: 'Hilare or de cymbale! Il paraît que c'est beau et que c'est une fanfare. . . . Dans les temps reculés où on demandait aux phrases de signifier quelque chose et aux vers d'être harmonieux, peut-être que: Hilare or (ror!) de cymbale n'eût paru ni bien clair ni bien euphonique.'[27] Immediate clarity and facile euphony were not what Mallarmé was seeking. His challenge to the reader's response continues with the juxtaposition of 'poings' and 'irrité', inviting the interpretation of 'angry fists' until the masculine singular ending makes it clear that 'irrité' qualifies 'or de cymbale'. The cymbals disappear in a golden mirage, expressing intense joy both by the golden colour of brass and by the jubilant clash of the sound, 'hilare' in its sound, sense and strangeness[28] evoking the idea of a sudden outburst of laughter or gaiety. Mallarmé seeks, beneath the commonplace words he had first used ('le soleil du matin'), the sensation they merely indicated, and finds a totally new and exciting expression for this sensation. Once again he portrays 'non la chose, mais l'effet qu'elle produit'; sensation precedes designation.[29] This is precisely how words can be made effective again: through replacing labels, nomenclatures and stock expressions by words that both convey and suggest sensations. After the shock of this sensation, Mallarmé does in fact 'name' the object suggested, stressing the key-word by its position before the caesura: 'Tout à coup le *soleil* frappe la nudité'. But immediately, the sensation is again evoked, in both its literal and figurative connotations. The pearly texture of the skin washed clean and the sensation of the cool water are united: it is as if nakedness were exhaled from the sensation of coolness and freshness itself. In the juxtaposition of 'nudité' and 'fraîcheur' we have an example of what Valéry called 'sensations abstraites', more evocative, perhaps, than the concrete description of the earlier version. In 'ma fraîcheur de nacre', the abstract noun 'fraîcheur' combines, in a strongly sensuous effect, tactile and visual, with the iridescence of 'nacre'.

In the second tercet, the syntax is intricate but perfectly coherent. Once again, Mallarmé first gives the striking metaphor which evokes the sensation in an anticipated apposition, complicated by a fresh apostrophe picking up the initial invocation of the eyes. But 'Rance nuit de la peau' is in double apposition: by anticipation, with 'fard' in the last line, but also, in immediate juxtaposition, with 'fraîcheur de nacre', emphasising the contrast between the new-found cleanness and the grime of old. Given the complexity of the syntactical connexions involved, a paraphrase may help to clarify them. The sun suddenly strikes the nakedness emerging from the pure iridescent freshness of the skin, which had been covered in rancid grease-paint until the cool waters passed over it. Mallarmé has placed the sequence of events in reverse order. The 'fraîcheur de nacre' finally attained had been the 'rance nuit de la peau' when the purifying process began. 'Rance nuit' combines the fetid smell of the rancid grease of make-up with its griminess: 'la peau' brings a note of concrete intelligibility. 'Quand sur moi vous passiez' is of course addressed to the eyes, those lakes whose waters flowed over the poet's body. 'L'eau perfide des glaciers' expresses at once the coldness and purity of this water coming from the melting of glaciers, and the perfidy of the purification. The 'pitre' now realises that the rancid grease-paint he has washed away was in reality the anointing oil of his royal consecration as a poet. Mallarmé recognises the inevitable 'grandeur et misère', or 'servitude et grandeur' of the poet, those limitations which are the inevitable conditions or concomitants of man's finest achievements. 'La poésie, sacre. . . .'[30]

In the definitive version, every word counts, communicating a sensation or an emotion or an idea. The most striking example of how every detail is here woven into the intellectual structure of the poem is the way the grease-paint becomes in itself the symbol at once of all the inadequacy of the poet's calling, and also of its royal splendour and its sacred mission. There is also a subtler rhetoric. In this final tercet, the earlier version led up to a Parnassian climax, with the strongest and most significant word as the final blow—the abstract word 'génie'. In the definitive version, the magnificent crescendo of rich [a] sounds moves to a first pointed climax in 'Ne s*a*chant p*a*s, ingr*a*t!' (Compare the 'hélas!' of the early version: a sigh as opposed to the self-criticism of the later sonnet.) Then the summit of the poem is attained *before* the end: 'Ne s*a*chant p*a*s, ingr*a*t! que c'était tout mon s*a*cre' (with all its physical and symbolic associations of coronation and anointing with oil), in order to allow for the deliberate, subtle and lovely diminuendo of a last line which, after the final summary of sense and echo of sound in 'Ce f*a*rd', tails off into distant space and past time, evoking once again in its own movement and in a dying and whispering fall the royal consecration now washed away to nothingness, 'noyé dans l'eau perfide des glaciers'.[31]

Cambridge   L. J. AUSTIN

NOTES AND EXCURSUSES

1 See Mallarmé's first collection of *juvenilia*, *Entre quatre murs*, in Henri Mondor, *Mallarmé lycéen*, Paris, Gallimard, 1954 ('Vocations', I), pp. 121–225; and L.-J. Austin, 'Les "Années d'apprentissage" de Stéphane Mallarmé', *Revue d'Histoire littéraire de la France* [*RHLF*], LVI (janvier-mars 1956), pp. 65–84.

2 Stéphane Mallarmé, *Correspondance 1862–1871*, recueillie, classée et annotée par Henri Mondor, avec la collaboration de Jean-Pierre Richard, Paris, Gallimard, 1959 [*Corr.* I], p. 155.

3 See the excellent analysis of Mallarmé's art as it was in 1864 by his friend Lefébure, in Henri Mondor, *Eugène Lefébure: sa vie—ses lettres à Mallarmé*, Paris, Gallimard, 1951, p. 176: 'Ce qui me frappe surtout, dans vos vers éclatants et sombres, c'est une singulière puissance de concentration. [. . .] Vous revenez obstinément sur votre impression première, déjà très forte, et vous en faites jaillir ces poèmes tourmentés et sanglotants, pleins de crispations, où, par places, à travers les surcharges des nouvelles idées, se déroulent fièrement des vers du premier jet, des vers pleins et tout d'une pièce. [. . .] Ces vers-là ramènent à temps l'harmonie dans vos strophes gorgées d'images et parfois comme étouffées de pensées. Ce sont des coups d'archet qui donnent le *la*. Si vous pouviez moins bien faire, vous feriez peut-être mieux; mais je crois qu'il faut se prendre comme on est.'

4 See Stéphane Mallarmé, *Œuvres complètes*, texte établi et annoté par Henri Mondor et Georges Jean-Aubry, Paris, Gallimard, rev. ed., 1956 (Bibliothèque de la Pléiade) [*OC*], pp. 368 (rejection of narration, didacticism and description), 400 (evocation), 869 (suggestion).

5 See L.-J. Austin, 'Mallarmé disciple de Baudelaire: *Le Parnasse contemporain*', *RHLF*, LXVII (avril-juin 1967), pp. 437–49.

6 ' "Le Pitre châtié" parut, quoique ancien, la première fois, dans la grande édition de la *Revue Indépendante*' (bibliographical note by Mallarmé, *OC*, p. 77). But the poem which appeared in 1887 in this edition (the photolithographic reproduction of Mallarmé's manuscript, limited to 40 copies) was radically different from the early version, first attested in April 1864 (see H. Mondor, *E. Lefébure*, p. 177). This figured in the little notebook into which Mallarmé transcribed thirteen of his poems written between 1862 and 1864, and which formed the nucleus of his contribution to the first *Parnasse contemporain*. 'Le Pitre châtié' did not, however, appear in that volume: Mallarmé described it and two other omitted poems ('Le Guignon' and 'Le Château de l'Espérance') as forming part of what he called 'L'Œuvre enfantine' (*OC*, p. 1392; see also the text of the thirteen poems in their original form in H. Mondor, *Autres précisions sur Mallarmé et inédits*, Paris, Gallimard, 1961, pp. 43–55). When 'Le Pitre châtié' did appear in 1887 in its definitive¦ form, it was at once singled out by Émile Verhaeren in his review of the *Poésies* in *L'Art Moderne*, 30 octobre 1887, pp. 346–7 (reproduced in *Intentions*, Troisième série, Paris, Mercure de France, 1928, pp. 77–83). This review led to a polemic in *L'Art Moderne*, which Verhaeren closed by a 'Réponse mallarmiste', 20 novembre 1887, pp. 372–4, including a detailed exegesis of the sonnet (this article was not reproduced in *Intentions*). Verhaeren later claimed that Mallarmé had endorsed his exegesis, 'sauf une réflexion sur une incidente' (*Intentions*, 3e série, p. 179). Curiously enough, I have found no significant comment on this poem made between 1887 and 1929, when Dr Bonniot published the early version in his article 'La Genèse poétique de Mallarmé', *Revue de France*, 19 avril 1929. Since then, there have been over twenty studies of the poem, in books and articles. It is obviously impossible to discuss them all fully here. But I have tried in the notes which follow to give some indication of work done and to indicate points of convergence or divergence.

7 Gustave Flaubert, *Correspondance*, nouvelle série augmentée, Paris, Conard, 1926, II, p. 346.

8 Some critics have discerned differences in the fundamental meaning of the two versions. A. R. Chisholm, in *Towards Hérodiade*, Melbourne, Melbourne University Press, 1934, affirmed that Mallarmé 'condenses the whole theory of Will and Representation' into the fourteen lines of the sonnet: 'The actor who bursts through the back-cloth [. . .] of his mediocre stage is none other than the poet escaping from the world of Representation and Illusion into the world of pure will . . .'. In a note he adds: 'I cannot see that the 1864 version of this sonnet [. . .] affects my interpretation. Maurice Levaillant (*Figaro*, 27 avril 1929) seems to imply that Mallarmé, in his final version, merely made the earlier one more difficult and obscure: but I think that he utilised the imagery of the earlier, comparatively banal sonnet, to express his later philosophy' (p. 139, and n. 3). But in his later book, *Mallarmé's 'Grand Œuvre'*, Manchester University Press, 1962, A. R. Chisholm gives a different interpretation of the sonnet as symbolising the conflict between art and love (pp. 25–7). The general consensus of critical opinion endorses this interpretation, formulated by Kurt Wais, *Doppelfassungen französicher Lyrik*, Tübingen, Max Niemeyer Verlag, 2nd ed., 1963 [1st ed. was 1936],

p. 32 as 'die Spannung zwischen der Kunst einerseits, der Liebe und dem Leben anderseits'. See also Kurt Wais's detailed exegeses of the poem in the two editions of his *Mallarmé*, Munich, C. H. Beck, 1938, pp. 60–1; 1952, pp. 106–7 (identical, except for an added reference to *L'Après-midi d'un faune*).—Wallace Fowlie asserts, however: 'It would be false to depend completely on the first version for an understanding of the final form of the sonnet. In tightening the language and developing the initial images, the poet unquestionably discovered new meanings or new aspects of meanings' (*Mallarmé*, Chicago, University of Chicago Press; London, Dobson, 1953, p. 91).

9 This 'punishment' has been variously interpreted or misinterpreted. For example, Edmond Bonniot wrote: 'C'est pour les yeux de sa bien-aimée que le Poëte dépouille sa gangue du fard: le châtiment de son infidélité à la Muse lui est de s'apercevoir alors comme Pitre' (quoted in *OC*, p. 1417). A. R. Chisholm rightly objects: 'But it seems to me, on the contrary, that the poet's punishment consists of forfeiting his status as a "pitre" ' (*Mallarmé's 'Grand Œuvre'*, p. 26). Franz Nobiling, after what I consider to be a basically sound reading of the poem, ends by saying that the Muse punishes the poet for his betrayal by awaking in him an eternal longing for a supreme but unattainable art ('Mallarmés "Le Pitre châtié" ', in *Zeitschrift für französische Sprache und Literatur*, LV, 1931, pp. 325–9, esp. p. 327). Kurt Wais rectifies this view in *Doppelfassungen . . .* (see preceding note). Guy Michaud, *Mallarmé, l'homme et l'œuvre*, Paris, Hatier-Boivin ('Connaissance des Lettres', 39), 1953, pp. 27–30, in a confused and confusing interpretation, seems to me to miss the point entirely, when he suggests that the poet ends with the feeling that 'finalement, la poésie pure n'est peut-être qu'un mirage et une illusion' (p. 29). Michaud's error comes from identifying the 'lacs' with 'l'eau pure du rêve', instead of seeing in them the symbol of love. Sounder readings of the poem are given by Hubert Fabureau, *Stéphane Mallarmé, son œuvre*, Paris, Nouvelle Revue Critique, 1933, pp. 68–9; Pierre Beausire, *Mallarmé. Poésie et Poétique*, [Lausanne], Mermod, 1949, pp. 93–4 and Stéphane Mallarmé, *Poésies. Gloses de Pierre Beausire*, [Lausanne], Mermod, 1945, p. 27; Frederick Chase St. Aubyn, *Stéphane Mallarmé*, New York, Twayne, 1969 (*TWAS* 52), pp. 35–6, and above all, Jean Starobinski, *Portrait de l'artiste en saltimbanque*, Genève, Skira, 1970 ('Les Sentiers de la création'), pp. 40–1 (see n. 23, below).

10 It is curiously misinterpreted by Charles Chadwick, 'Mallarmé et la tentation du lyrisme', *RHLF*, LX, 1960, pp. 188–98, esp. pp. 190–93 (reproduced in *Mallarmé, sa pensée dans sa poésie*, Paris, Corti, 1962, pp. 13–19): '[. . .] le premier sens du mot "pitre" est celui de "renégat" et c'est précisément parce qu'il a, dans 'Les Fleurs', renié sa vraie muse, celle de la poésie cérébrale, en faveur du lyrisme facile que Mallarmé est châtié' (p. 14). Chadwick later recognises that 'le mot "pitre" a aussi un sens théâtral'; he goes on to say: 'Mallarmé est donc puni non seulement pour avoir été un renégat à sa muse mais aussi, dans les derniers vers de la version primitive [. . .], pour avoir abandonné son métier d'acteur fardé, de poète cérébral.' (p. 15). Chadwick, like Michaud, fails to see that the 'lacs' are the antithesis to art of any kind; but whereas Michaud sees in the lakes the symbol of 'la poésie pure',

Chadwick takes them as corresponding to 'le lyrisme facile'. His general thesis seems to me to be radically mistaken, and to lead to misinterpretations of many poems in terms of erroneous initial assumptions. P.-O. Walzer, however, follows Chadwick, as far as the 'tentation du lyrisme' is concerned, in his *Essai sur Mallarmé*, Paris, Seghers, 1963 ('Poètes d'Aujourd'hui', 94), pp. 85–6.

11 Robert, s.v. 'Pitre'. Littré's definition is similar, followed by the metaphorical meaning of 'Bouffon, mauvais plaisant'. Littré gives an interesting example from Champfleury. But neither Littré nor Robert records the meaning of *pitre* as 'renégat' at all.

12 Both these metaphors come from Baudelaire, as several previous critics have noticed: the lake of the eyes from 'Le Poison', the poet as a poor player or clown from 'La Béatrice' ('[. . .] cette caricature/Et cette ombre d'Hamlet imitant sa posture [. . .] Ce gueux, cet histrion en vacances, ce drôle,/Parce qu'il sait artistement jouer son rôle,/Vouloir [. . .]/ Réciter en hurlant ses tirades publiques'), from 'La Muse vénale' ('saltimbanque à jeun'), and of course from the *Petit poème en prose* 'Le Vieux saltimbanque', which Mallarmé could have read in *La Revue fantaisiste*, 1er novembre 1861. Also relevant for the poet's struggles with his art, and his sense of inadequacy, are 'La Beauté' and 'La Mort des artistes', and above all 'Le Fou et la Vénus' (which appeared in *La Presse*, 26 août 1862): we have here several related themes, uniting a sense of desperate and inadequate striving for, or capering before, the ideal Form of Art. The theme of the artist as mountebank has been treated, in a not very illuminating article, by Hannelore Zaubitzer, 'Clownmetaphern bei Baudelaire, Mallarmé und Michaux', *Die neueren Sprachen*, 1966, 10, pp. 445–56, and, on a quite different level of imaginative insight, in the penetrating and profound book by Jean Starobinski, *Portrait de l'artiste en saltimbanque* (see n. 9 above).—Mallarmé described himself as 'moi, idiot saltimbanque' in a letter to Cazalis of 7 July 1862 (*Corr.* I, p. 41, quoted by E. Noulet, *L'Œuvre poétique de Stéphane Mallarmé*, Paris, Droz, 1940, p. 72). He repeatedly uses the metaphor of eyes as lakes: 'ces gouttes du lac Léman, enchassées dans de la candeur et qu'elles [les Anglaises] veulent bien appeler leurs yeux' (letter to Cazalis, 24 May 1862, *Corr.* I, p. 27), '[. . .] des yeux, ces lacs où se fond l'éternel azur d'un jour de bonheur' (*OC*, p. 592), etc. Writing to Marie Gerhard, he asks: 'Du reste qui est coupable de mon amour?' and replies: 'C'est vous, O charmante, et ce sont ces yeux . . .' (26 June 1862, *Corr.* I, p. 33).

13 The plunge into the eyes, and the eyelashes again, are to be found in the last two lines of Baudelaire's 'Semper Eadem': 'Plonger dans vos beaux yeux comme dans un beau songe,/Et sommeiller longtemps à l'ombre de vos cils!' And of course Baudelaire is following Gautier: the plunge into the eyes in 'Cœrulei oculi' ('Ses yeux où le ciel se reflète [. . .] Les teintes glauques de la mer [. . .] Comme dans l'eau bleue et profonde [. . .] à travers l'onde [. . .] ce regard céruléen,/Et mon coeur, sous l'onde perfide,/Se noie et consomme l'hymen.'); the eyelashes both in 'Cœrulei oculi' (but with a different image: 'comme des mouettes [. . .]/Palpitent, ailes inquiètes,/Sur leur azur indéfini') and in 'La fuite' ('Mes cils te feront de l'ombre'). (See *Poésies complètes*, ed. R. Jasinski, Paris, Didot, 1933, II, p. 233, III, pp. 35–7.)

14 These *quinquets*, oil lamps with a cylindrical wick, often appear as theatrical accessories: in Mallarmé's early poem in prose 'Réminiscence', 'l'heure sainte des quinquets' (*OC*, p. 278) means the time when the lamps are lit for the play to begin. É. Noulet points out that this poem describes the kind of *baraque* or canvas booth from which the *pitre* breaks out, and she also identifies the Muse in question as Thalie (*L'Œuvre poétique*, p. 72). But in 'Le Pitre châtié' 'Hamlet' suggests rather Melpomene.—A recent article invokes the slang sense of *quinquets* as 'eyes', but fails to make this convincingly relevant. The author also somewhat ludicrously suggests that the *pitre* is an *unijambiste*, who simply mimes the movement of swimming by standing on one leg and kicking the other, while waving his arms in the air. The article can be recommended for comic relief, if for nothing else (Will L. McLendon, 'A new reading of Mallarmé's "Pitre châtié"', *Symposium*, XXIV, 1, Spring 1970, pp. 36–43).

15 Ernest Lefébure objected to the definite article in 'tout le génie', and said he remembered a version in which Mallarmé had written 'tout *mon* génie' (H. Mondor, *E. Lefébure*, p. 177; *OC*, p. 1417). Mallarmé, however, is not concerned with the 'acquired' aspects of genius, but with the inevitable limitations and inadequacies of the highest human activities; what Baudelaire, in his notes for a preface to *Les Fleurs du Mal* (which Mallarmé could not have known), called 'toutes les horreurs qui composent le sanctuaire de l'art'.—On this point, see Claude Abastado, *Expérience et théorie de la création poétique chez Mallarmé*, Paris, Minard, 1970 (Archives des Lettres Modernes, 119), p. 17: ' "tout *mon* sacre", dit la version définitive: l'anathème, alors personnel, n'exprime plus que le désespoir d'un poète. Cependant l'idée de subterfuge, l'image de l'histrion, demeure au long de l'œuvre mallarméenne.'

16 É. Noulet has admirably summed up some of the essential differences between the two versions: 'En comparant la version de 1864 et le texte définitif, on saisit toute la différence qu'il y a entre la poésie explicative, circonstancielle et qui prend toute sa longueur et la poésie suggestive, essentielle et qui contracte ses parties./Ainsi, se rend-on compte que l'oubli dans lequel le poète se jette, qui le rénove en même temps qu'il le découronne, c'est l'amour? A peine. Car l'idée de la femme, déjà réduite à deux vers dans la première version, et laissant toute la place à l'idée de la trahison, de la joie physique et du châtiment, se trouve ramenée, en 1887, à l'unique symbole des *yeux*, dont la seule raison d'être paraît d'appeler l'apposition *lacs*. Ce qui a tout à fait disparu, c'est l'adresse romantique à la Muse; c'est d'elle, pourtant, que dérivent les accessoires de l'allégorie (l'idée du pitre, des quinquets, de travesti, du fard) [. . .] / En fait, Mallarmé avait raison; le sonnet était inédit et il appartient à sa deuxième manière; modifié profondément non dans sa matière mais dans son style, dont l'hermétisme tient tout entier dans la métamorphose de "le soleil du matin" (première version) en "hilare or de cymbale à des poings . . ." ' (*L'Œuvre poétique*, p. 72).

17 Nevertheless, errors and confusions did arise. Charles Mauron, in *Mallarmé l'obscur*, Paris, Denoël, 1941, wrote, in obvious ignorance of the early version: 'Une obscurité syntaxique sérieuse marque le premier quatrain. La simple opposition "yeux, lacs" est d'une telle condensation

que plusieurs interprétations sont possibles d'où un casse-tête sans grand intérêt. Si les "yeux" sont ceux du pitre, la phrase devient "mes yeux comme des lacs, j'ai troué . . ." (comme on dirait "Les bras en avant, j'ai troué . . ."). Mais les "yeux" peuvent être ceux du public à qui s'adresse le pitre: et toute la pièce deviendrait d'un symbolisme compliqué, mais nullement improbable pour cela—l'artiste se plongeant dans la vision d'autrui, essayant d'y perdre son histrionisme. Le choix entre les deux hypothèses est sans importance: je préfère la première, plus simple et parce que "ma simple ivresse" semble s'exprimer dans "mes yeux".' (p. 102). Later, Mauron came to know of the 1864 version, and his commentary on the poem in the 1951 edition of the volume of translations into English by Roger Fry benefits from it: 'The general idea is thus made plain: the eyes of the beloved are compared with a pure water in which the poet hopes to wash away the effects of his literary barnstorming —but the thing has its dangers, for it is difficult to distinguish between the player and the artist, the disguise and the genius.' (Stéphane Mallarmé, *Poems*, translated by Roger Fry. With commentaries by Charles Mauron, London, Vision Press Ltd., 1951, p. 183.—There is no commentary on this poem in the first edition of this book, London, Chatto and Windus, 1936.) Then, as Mauron developed his method of *psychocritique*, he interpreted the poem 'in depth': 'Leur azur [the pure waters into which the clown dives] est celui des yeux de Marie Gerhard; et l'on a ainsi le sentiment que la fuite devant le mensonge du rêve s'oriente vers une véritable vie. Mais les yeux de Marie sont aussi ceux de Maria [the poet's sister, who died at the age of thirteen] et sournoisement leur eau vive redevient le sépulcre où l'on rêve d'entrer' (*Introduction à la psychanalyse de Mallarmé*, Neuchâtel, A la Baconnière, 1950, p. 164; new ed., 1968, p. 144, with no change). The interpretation of the eyes as being those of the audience goes back to Verhaeren (see n. 6 above) and is continued by Wallace Fowlie, *Mallarmé*, p. 92).

18 For J. Gengoux, in a very muddled commentary, 'les Yeux symbolisent ici la perfection absolue' for which the poet 'a quitté l'Art vulgaire et la Vie' (*Le Symbolisme de Mallarmé*, Paris, Nizet, 1950, p. 70).

19 Valéry frequently compared Mallarmé's poetic method with algebra: see Paul Valéry, *Œuvres*, édition établie et annotée par Jean Hytier, Paris, Gallimard, 1957–1960 (Bibliothèque de la Pléiade), I, pp. 631, 685, 709, and especially 658: 'Il [Mallarmé] rejoignait par là [. . .] l'attitude des hommes qui ont approfondi en algèbre la science des formes et la partie symbolique de l'art mathématique'.

20 The overtone of *lacs* as 'traps' or 'snares' is improbable and such an interpretation is phonetically impossible (it is proposed by Robert Greer Cohn, *Toward the poems of Mallarmé*, Berkeley and Los Angeles, University of California Press, 1965, p. 38, and Will L. McLendon, 'A new reading . . .' (see n. 14 above).

21 Littré definitely states: 'Aujourdhui, comédien, mais avec un sens de mépris', after recalling that in the ancient world it referred to an actor in 'bouffonneries grossières'. Walter Naumann goes too far when he affirms that 'histrion' in Mallarmé *always* has an elevated meaning (see *Der Sprachgebrauch Mallarmé's*, Marburg, Hermann Bauer, 1936, p. 55). For it is surely pejorative here (cf. 'le mauvais Hamlet' in the next quatrain);

and this illustrates the dangers of deducing meanings from other contexts in the author. Where Mallarmé does take 'histrion' in an elevated sense, it is perhaps by way of deliberate contrast with expectations, and with overtones of irony (the limitations of greatness). In 'Le Pitre châtié', Mallarmé almost certainly had in mind Leconte de Lisle's sonnet 'Les Montreurs', especially such lines as:

Je ne danserai pas sur ton tréteau banal
Avec tes histrions et tes prostituées.

22 For Mallarmé, theatre and book are one, and the poet is identified with the actor. Guy Michaud quotes a passage from Baudelaire's translation of E. A. Poe's *Philosophy of Composition* (*La Genèse d'un Poème*) where the poet is described as an 'histrion littéraire' (*Mallarmé*, p. 27). Mallarmé himself affirms that the poet, in his writings, becomes the 'spirituel histrion [. . .] de ses maux ou d'une allégresse' (*OC*, p. 370), and that everyone bears within himself 'un théâtre, inhérent à l'esprit' (*OC*, p. 328). In this poem he perhaps expresses this double notion of the actor-poet by the words 'du geste', for the actor's gestures, and 'comme plume' (that is, 'en tant que plume') for the poet's essential instrument. Littré, s.v. *Plume*, gives: '10. L'auteur même . . . C'est la plus belle plume de son siècle. J.-J. Rousseau.' And Vigny, in 'L'Esprit pur', uses *plume* in a double sense:

J'ai mis sur le cimier doré du gentilhomme
Une plume de fer qui n'est pas sans beauté.

For the symbolism of the feather, see Jean-Pierre Richard, *L'Univers imaginaire de Mallarmé*, Paris, Seuil, 1961, p. 445. Hamlet of course traditionally wears a black feather in his cap: cf. the lines from Banville quoted by Mallarmé in his review of a performance of *Hamlet* at the Comédie Française in October 1886, not long before this revised version of the poem was written:

Le vent qui fait voler ta plume noire
Et te caresse, Hamlet, ô jeune Hamlet! (*OC*, p. 299).

Cf. also 'la plume délicieuse de sa toque' (*OC*, p. 302), and the 'plume solitaire éperdue' and the 'toque de minuit' of *Un Coup de dés* (*OC*, pp. 468–9). And for the expression 'du geste évoquais', cf. 'Villiers [. . .] évoqua du geste l'Ombre tout silence' (*OC*, p. 531). Villiers was the occasion of the most extraordinary and powerful use of 'histrion' in all Mallarmé's work: 'Histrion véridique, je le fus de moi-même! de celui que nul n'atteint en soi, excepté à des moments de foudre et alors on l'expie sa durée . . .' (*OC*, p. 495).

23 Cf. Jean Starobinski, *Portrait de l'artiste en saltimbanque*, pp. 40–41: '*Trouer dans le mur de toile une fenêtre*: c'est ce qu'accomplit le pitre de Mallarmé, à l'exemple du clown de Banville. Son idéal, il le poursuit non dans l'altitude stellaire, mais dans l'eau limpide d'un regard aimé. Plus dangereusement, il meurt à soi pour tenter de renaître dans l'absolu d'un amour transfigurant. Mais contrairement au vol dans les étoiles, la nage heureuse dans le lac vivant n'est pas un triomphe de l'art. C'en est au contraire la négation coupable. Le pitre mallarméen découvre qu'il a trahi la "Muse"—la poésie—en cherchant à vivre une résurrection

extatique; le génie est inséparable du *fard*. La conscience qu'en prend le pitre est sa punition.'

24 *OC*, p. 300.

25 Georges Poulet admirably brings out the notion of metaphysical death and rebirth in Mallarmé, in *Études sur le temps humain*, II, *La distance intérieure*, Paris, Plon, pp. 324–5. Cf. also J.-P. Richard, *L'Univers imaginaire de Mallarmé*, p. 111, for the liberating and purifying effect of water on the Hamlet-figure in this poem; p. 202, for the equation of love and death ('Il traverse l'amour comme une suite de morts et de résurrections,—à moins qu'il n'éprouve la mort comme une coulée doucement amoureuse'. Richard also affirms: ' "Le Pitre châtié" nous paraît l'écho d'un bain dans l'eau glacée du Rhône' (p. 138).

26 *OC*, p. 368.

27 *L'Art Moderne*, 20 novembre 1887, p. 373.

28 In Mallarmé's day, the word 'hilare' was really 'étranger à la langue'. It is not in Littré. Robert remarks: 'Disparu au XVIe s., *Hilare* renaît au XIXe, mais reste absent des dictionnaires jusqu'à la fin du siècle dernier. Admis ACAD. 1935.'

29 See L.-J. Austin, 'Mallarmé et le réel', in *Modern Miscellany presented to Eugène Vinaver*, Manchester University Press, 1969, p. 17, for a comment on this passage; and 'The Mystery of a Name', in *L'Esprit créateur*, I, 3, Fall 1961, *Stéphane Mallarmé*, pp. 130–8, for the method of evocation followed by designation.

30 *OC*, p. 372. For the word 'sacre', see Walter Naumann, *Der Sprachgebrauch Mallarmés*, pp. 119–20.

31 Jean Starobinski admirably sums up the ultimate significance of the sonnet as he sees it in these terms: 'Selon ce poème hautement allégorique l'artiste, à la fois exclu de la vie et séparé de l'idéal, doit rester le prisonnier d'un espace clos: *histrion*, ou *mauvais Hamlet*, il ne doit pas quitter les tréteaux, l'univers factice où la suie des quinquets sert à représenter la plume ornant la joue de l'acteur. Le sacrilège est de vouloir abandonner le lieu de la figuration métaphorique (à la fois parodique dans ses moyens et grave dans ses effets) pour conquérir les satisfactions de la vie.' (*Portrait de l'artiste en saltimbanque*, p. 41.)

I wish to express my gratitude to Professor Alison Fairlie for having closely read the various drafts of this article and enriched it by many detailed and substantial suggestions.

MALLARMÉ'S USE OF CHRISTIAN IMAGERY FOR POST-CHRISTIAN CONCEPTS

A number of poems, written by Mallarmé during the first fifteen years of his literary career, contain examples of Christian images used to express his conception of the modern poet's quasi-religious post-Christian function. In this essay I propose to examine some of those images from the point of view not of their Christian meaning and status, but of the meaning the poet converts them to. I hope in this way to make some contribution to the understanding of the poems concerned and more generally of Mallarmé's 'theology of letters'.[1]

A very straightforward example of the kind of conversion I refer to occurs in the very poem in which the poet proclaims his renunciation of Christianity, and although the new religion to which he turns is not yet the religion of literature, the example is worth noting. The poem is 'Pan', written in 1859; the 'new' religion is a Hugo-inspired deistic pantheism, and the image takes the following rebellious shape:

> O Pan! fais de ma voix la trompette fidèle
> Qui jette à l'univers au milieu des éclairs
> Un éclat de ta voix, un feu de ta lumière!
> Fais de moi ton archange! . . . une aile dont les airs
> Gardent la trace en feu comme de ton tonnerre!

The immediate source of this first of Mallarmé's archangels in more likely to be literary than visual; for instance, Ithuriel in Lamartine's 'L'Ange' or the 'Poète! . . . Archange!' in Hugo's 'A Madame G. de G'.

The sonnet 'Contre un poète parisien', to Emmanuel des Essarts and against him, was written three years later. It must be given more attention here than it has hitherto received. It opens our series of Christian images with two clear-cut examples, and at the same time provides a convenient approach to the strand in Mallarmé's thought which the rest of the series will help him, at different stages of development, to express. That from this time on the images are fully post-Christian in the sense defined above is certain, for the poet's religious position is now unambiguous. A clear-sighted letter from his step-mother to his grandmother, dated 11 February 1862, states plainly that religious observances *ne sont plus de ses goûts, dans ses idées, malgré les principes qu'il a reçus.*[2] Any Christian imagery in his poems is consciously retained or recalled from his Christian boyhood, and converted to a new piety, his poetic vocation and aspirations. So it is in the poem to Des Essarts:

CONTRE UN POÈTE PARISIEN[3]

A. E. Des E. . . . . .

Souvent la vision du Poète me frappe:
Ange à cuirasse fauve, il a pour volupté
L'éclair du glaive, ou, blanc songeur, il a la chape,
La mitre byzantine et le bâton sculpté.

Dante, au laurier amer, dans un linceul se drape,
Un linceul fait de nuit et de sérénité:
Anacréon, tout nu, rit et baise une grappe
Sans songer que la vigne a des feuilles, l'été.

Pailletés d'astres, fous d'azur, les grands bohèmes,
Dans les éclairs vermeils de leur gai tambourin,
Passent, fantasquement coiffés de romarin.

Mais j'aime peu voir, Muse, ô reine des poèmes,
Dont la toison nimbée a l'air d'un ostensoir,
Un poète qui polke avec un habit noir.

The point of this poem is not mere playful teasing about poets who dress up and go dancing. The sonnet is a document in an argument, one that was to go on for years, between Mallarmé and his friend and counsellor Emmanuel des Essarts. Its subject, like that of the whole argument, and that of so many of Mallarmé's poems from this time on, is the nature and function of poetry. But, like so many other Mallarmé poems also, the sonnet conceals part of its meaning.

It is significant that Des Essarts remembered it long afterwards, to judge by a remark in a not too generous obituary article he wrote on Mallarmé for the *Revue de France* (15 July 1899)[4]. Perhaps it was to placate him that Mallarmé, after publishing his poem under the title 'Contre un poète parisien' called it simply 'Sonnet' on the copy he kept for himself.[5] For the original title contains a hidden barb. 'Poète parisien' refers not simply to Parisian social habits but to something about which the poet would be much more sensitive, his poetry. It sharpens also the sting in the sonnet's tail, for the final antithesis in the tercets, prepared for by the two in the quatrains, does not contrast only two ways of life, but also like the others two conceptions of poetry. All this would be clear to Des Essarts when he read the poem, because he would not have forgotten two reviews that

Mallarmé had written earlier that year, of the collection of poems he had just published under the title *Les Poésies parisiennes*.

Neither of the reviews had been openly critical of Des Essarts, but both had defined with studied precision his kind of lyric poetry, in terms which privately implied a fundamental disagreement between the reviewer and his friend the poet. The author of the *Poésies parisiennes*, the reviewer noted, *prend le Réel au sérieux et le lyrise*,[6] whereas that prince of lyric poets, Théodore de Banville *ce divin maître*, does precisely the opposite:

Dans les Poésies Parisiennes, ce n'est plus cet idéal étincelant et moqueur et harcelant la réalité de sa flèche d'or qui vous enivre dans les vers de cet exquis maître: c'est un idéal sincère s'élevant au-dessus du réel et le prenant au sérieux.

A further remark in the earlier of the two reviews provides confirmation that the polkaing Emmanuel in the last line of the sonnet is an emblem not merely for bourgeois tastes but for a type of poetry to which he was also addicted. One poem is singled out for special comment as representing the essential character of *Les Poésies parisiennes*:

je dirais que la 'Danse Idéale' révèle le mieux le procédé du poète qui s'élève d'une mazurka à des théories platoniciennes.[7]

The emblem which contrasts with the dancing poet in evening dress, and which occupies the first tercet, also refers to a type of poetry as well as to a way of life. Neither in life nor in verse do the bohemian poets 'take reality seriously'. They include Banville, the author of poems like 'Mascarades' and 'Le Saut du tremplin' in *Odes funambulesques*, as well as his bohemian disciples. In his schoolboy poems Mallarmé had claimed to be one of them.

Of the two pairs of emblems in the quatrains (the bishop in his contemplative role and the warrior angel—surely Saint Michael—on the one hand, Dante and Anacreon on the other) which provide a deceptively sober setting for the satirical snapshot at the end, the first pair is clearly dominant. It probably represents two contrasting objects of Mallarmé's present admiration. It does so with symbols which are squarely Christian in their usual meaning and post-Christian in the meaning Mallarmé gives them. The *blanc songeur* could be the Archbishop of Sens on his high altar. On the other hand, in the stone and glass of St Stephen's Cathedral there were numerous depictions of earlier dignitaries, one or other of which the young poet may have had in mind.[8]

Similarly, the Saint Michael who figures on a sixteenth-century tapestry in the same cathedral could well be the *ange à cuirasse fauve* (Plate 1).[9] However, there are innumerable depictions of Saint Michael, and most of those that give him armour and a sword, not a flowing robe and a spear, could support the symbol in the poem. Moreover, Hugo offered literary models, including some that illustrated strikingly Saint Michael's adaptability to other than Christian purposes;[10] Saint Michael and the archbishop might indeed stand for two aspects of Hugo's own literary mission, the champion of freedom and social justice in *Les Châtiments*, and in *Les Contemplations* the seer or the dreamer (*le rêveur sacré*).

Hugo had seen these two aspects of 'the Poet' as capable of living in harmony together.[11] Perhaps Mallarmé had already noted, however, that another poet whom he was also studying attentively declared them incompatible. For in Baudelaire's terms Saint Michael would figure *l'action* and the bishop *le rêve*, and Baudelaire had written:

> —Certes, je sortirai, quant à moi, satisfait
> D'un monde où l'action n'est pas la sœur du rêve;
> Puissé-je user du glaive et périr par le glaive!
> Saint Pierre a renié Jésus . . . Il a bien fait!

Any possibility that Mallarmé, inspired by Hugo, might see in the antithesis between Action and Dream a two-sidedness in his own vocation seems to be promptly and firmly denied by his article 'L'Art pour tous', published on 15 September 1862 in *L'Artiste*. In it he proclaimed, thus early, his belief in the sacredness of art, but also in the need to make of poetry a spiritual domain accessible only to an élite:

L'homme peut être démocrate, l'artiste se dédouble et doit être aristocrate . . . Que les masses lisent la morale, mais de grâce ne leur donnez pas notre poésie à gâter.[12]

Similarly in all the effort of his early manhood, the poet seems firmly to renounce any earlier schoolboy vision of an active warrior-like part in his ambition. When Saint Michael and the bishop return to his poetry, they do so, as we shall see, in a shape that subordinates all action, all living even, to the dream.[13]

This conception will be reached by way of a process of reflexion and experiment which takes him ever further in his idealism and leads ultimately to his doctrine of poetic Transposition: the art of poetry considered as a technique for raising nature *du fait à l'idéal*, through *sa presque disparition selon le jeu de la parole*[14] to the region of pure ideas. Mallarmé's early attempts to seize clearly the principles which might govern such a technique are attested in his correspondence. He confided to Cazalis that *l'art suprême, ici, consiste à laisser voir qu'on est en extase, sans avoir montré comment on s'élevait vers ces cimes;*[15] (could this be a politer version of the lesson to Emmanuel, platonic raptures but no mazurka?). A little later he told him of his new rule: *Peindre, non la chose, mais l'effet qu'elle produit.*[16] In answer to one of his letters, Lefébure wrote:

C'est là, je crois, l'idée qui a dû vous conduire à rejeter de votre œuvre tous les filaments qui lient la beauté à la partie grossière de l'homme, et l'alourdissent de matière. Vous avez coupé les racines chargées de terre de vos fleurs . . . Coupée, la fleur dont vous avez nourri la racine garde sa sève et perd son pied terreux.[17]

Two phases in the development of such ideas as these are symbolized by two poems, 'Sainte' and 'Mes bouquins refermés', one written at the end of 1865 and the other probably at the beginning of 1867.[18] A copy of 'Sainte' was sent to Aubanel and another to Cazalis early in December 1865. To each of his two friends Mallarmé spoke, in an accompanying letter, of his work on 'Hérodiade' as well as of the poem he enclosed. To Aubanel he wrote:

j'ai besoin de la plus silencieuse solitude de l'âme, et d'un *oubli* inconnu, pour entendre chanter en moi certaines notes mystérieuses . . . Je te charge en remettant le billet ci-joint à Brunet de lire à Madame une *Sainte Cécile* que je lui avais promise. C'est un petit poème mélodique et fait surtout en vue de la musique.[19]

The melodic little poem in its first form was entitled *Sainte Cécile jouant sur l'aile d'un chérubin (Chanson et image anciennes)*. In certain details the early text differs from the final version, and the variants are helpful in the interpretation of the whole composition:

A la fenêtre recélant
Le santal vieux qui se dédore
De la Viole étincelant
Jadis parmi flûte ou mandore

Est une Sainte, recélant
Le livre vieux qui se déplie
Du Magnificat ruisselant
Jadis à véprée et complie,

Sainte à vitrage d'ostensoir
Pour clore la harpe par l'ange
Offerte avec son vol du soir
A la délicate phalange

> Du doigt, que, sans le vieux santal
> Ni le vieux livre, elle balance
> Sur le plumage instrumental,
> Musicienne du silence.[20]

A reasonable understanding of this poem, vague it is true but not unduly so in view of the poet's insistence on its 'mainly musical' character, would be to take it as symbolising the poet's mood when listening to the mysterious notes, the siren music 'singing within him'. The description of the *image ancienne* is not vague, however, and the inquisitive reader will wish to identify it among the Saint Cecilias (and there are many) depicted in ecstasy, listening to unheard melodies celestially sweet. Perhaps the poet actually sent one such, on a name-day card to Madame Cécile Brunet on 22 November, St Cecilia's Day, promising that a *chanson ancienne* would follow the *image ancienne*. In later years he was to send innumerable *vers de circonstance* to friends on similar occasions, and Madame Brunet was entitled to very special marks of friendship and respect as his little daughter's godmother.

My own suggestion is that Mignard's very well-known *Sainte Cécile* at the Louvre (Plate 2), reproduced on a greetings-card within a reducing frame to show the upper central part only (including the cherub sculptured at the top of the harp) would fit the description in the poem. The saint, 'with monstrance window enclosing the harp . . .' formed by the angel's evening flight, would be 'at the window'. The lower half of Mignard's picture (which the reader must be presumed to know) would be concealed, and without the viol and the music scores the harp would seem no earthly instrument but a creation of the cherub's wing. This metaphor—of the harp-maker's or the painter's, completed and refined by the poet[21]—would raise the music to an ideal plane. The saintly artist would be shown in ecstasy *sans avoir montré comment on s'élevait vers ces cimes*. The rest, viol, woodwinds, scores, would be mere aids to the ascent, discarded when it is achieved, devices which have served *l'instinct qui dégage, du monde, un chant . . . et rejette, vain, le résidu.*[22]

A little more prying in the correspondence, to trace the private origins of this poem, is rewarded by a vivid impression of the hold that a Christian environment retained over a post-Christian poet who was also a son, a grandson, a husband, a father and a respectable young schoolmaster. The most revealing part of the story is the chapter of Geneviève's christening, from the private baptism (*par sécurité*, saving the infant from all superstitious threat of eternity in limbo and her parents from public disapproval) to the full ceremony with Des Essarts as godfather's proxy, five months later (*enfin!*, wrote grandmother-godmother Desmolins), and the *dragées* taken back by the godmother's proxy Madame Brunet to friends at Avignon. If one notes too that whenever Mallarmé went to Sens he would see around him his step-mother's copies of pictures of the saints (including *une sainte Colombe d'après Mignard*,[23] and who knows what others after the same artist), it appears quite possible that the only way for him to escape from Christian symbolism was to turn it to his own use. By so doing he might also touch his reader's mysticity in the interest of sensitivity to art—an advantage of which his aesthetic did not fail to take account.[24]

'Mes bouquins refermés' is the poem in which Saint Michael and the bishop, first met in 'Contre un poète parisien', return to Mallarmé's imagery in a changed relationship. They have united to form, together, a symbol quite close in meaning to the Saint Cecilia of 'Sainte', but much more sophisticated and rather humorous. Placed at the very end of a sonnet whose subject is transposition, it serves as an emblem of the transposer-poet:

> Le pied sur quelque guivre où notre amour tisonne,
> Je pense plus longtemps peut-être éperdument
> A l'autre, au sein brûlé d'une antique amazone.

We do not know, of course, on which of the many possible medieval tombs Mallarmé may have contemplated the effigy of a bishop teasing with his crozier the wyvern under his feet, as one might stir with a poker the embers of a dying fire. That is the image most likely to have inspired the final tercet of his sonnet. Well might the poet recognise how harmoniously it brings together the antithetical pair of emblems in his earlier poem, to form another which symbolises poetic sublimation as aptly as it did once the church's victory over evil. The merging was perhaps aided by the mediation of other Saint Michaels than the one at Sens, nearer to the *blanc songeur*. A good example of an earlier, gentler conception of the archangel is found in an eleventh-century manuscript at Avranches (Plate 3).[25] United with the contemplative bishop, such a Saint Michael, his spear coinciding with the crozier and his dragon dwindling to a wyvern, would produce the effigy on the tomb.[26] Action and Dream find their right relation when the purpose of all action, life itself and the heart's affections, is to feed the poet's thought.

One such image was well placed to capture Mallarmé's attention while he still had the 'Parisian poet' in mind. When he was in London in 1862–63 a plaster cast of the tomb of Bishop Roger in Salisbury

Cathedral was on show in the Byzantine and Romanesque Court of the Crystal Palace.[27] It illustrates the symbol very adequately (Plate 4).

Mallarmé's subtlest use of Christian imagery is found in 'Toast funèbre', written in 1873 for the collective *Tombeau de Théophile Gautier*. But it is his most secret use also. He seems in the whole poem to follow with special strictness Gautier's precept, that a poet should not provide the vulgar with a ladder to his thoughts.[28] Help in approaching them can be found, fortunately, elsewhere. To begin with, in the circumstances of the poem's composition. A letter from Catulle Mendès to Coppée defines the general convention which presumably all contributors to the *Tombeau* were asked to respect:

Après un prologue . . . où il est dit qu'un certain nombre de poètes sont réunis autour d'un repas funèbre, en l'honneur de Théophile Gautier, tous, l'un après l'autre, se lèvent et célèbrent chacun l'un des côtés du talent de leur maître mort.—Ils s'adressent à une image de Gautier. Donc la forme 'tu' est recommandée, au moins dans la première strophe.[29]

Similar instructions appear to be reflected in a letter that Mallarmé wrote about 'Toast funèbre' but of which only the following fragment is known:

Commençant par *O toi qui* . . ., et finissant par un vers masculin, je veux chanter en rimes plates une des qualités glorieuses de Théophile Gautier: le don mystérieux de voir avec les yeux (ôtez mystérieux). Je chanterai le *voyant* qui, placé dans ce monde, l'a regardé, ce qu'on ne fait pas.[30]

The word *voyant* underlined in the letter, and the play on the word *mystérieux*, are pointers to the theme Mallarmé intended to develop in his poem, and also I believe to a text he had in mind. In an essay by Baudelaire on Gautier, which had contributed a good deal to his early reflexions on poetry (in 'L'Art pour tous' for instance, and 'Symphonie littéraire'), he must have noted the following passage:

Si l'on réfléchit qu'a cette merveilleuse faculté [his command of the French language] Gautier unit une immense intelligence innée de la *correspondance* et du symbolisme universels, ce répertoire de toute *métaphore*, on comprendra qu'il puisse sans cesse, sans fatigue comme sans faute, définir l'attitude mystérieuse que les objets de la création tiennent devant le regard de l'homme.[31]

This praise of Gautier may be one of the sources of 'Toast funèbre', in the sense not that Mallarmé adopts it but that he replies to it. His reply is dictated by the belief that the mystery, the hints of supernal beauty and intimations of immortality, are not in the visible world but in the spirit of man.[32] The mysteriousness of the universe is a projection of what he calls diversely *l'instinct de ciel en chacun*,[33] *la maladie d'idéalité*[34] and *désir et mal de mes vertèbres*.[35] The modern poet, guided by his own imaginative awareness of external nature, and of the meaning which our immortal longings fondly ascribe to it, must seek to find in the supreme human creation, language, a purer mirror of our divinity. By so doing he will pursue the task of isolating the ideal from the real, and thus restoring to the two natures of man, the divine and the natural, their separate homes: recreating heaven and earth. (The new Genesis: *Igitur perfecti sunt cœli et terra.*)

The function of the poet's eye is to inspire his voice: *Le monde est fait pour aboutir à un beau livre.*[36]

> Le Maître, par un œil profond, a, sur ses pas,
> Apaisé de l'éden l'inquiète merveille
> Dont le frisson final, dans sa voix seule, éveille
> Pour la Rose et le Lys le mystère d'un nom.

What his searching eye has enabled him to do is to transfer from nature to language (from roses and lilies to their names) the wonder that speaks of Eden. Expressed by a different metaphor, this conception of the poet's task will provide a clue to the Christian image secretly active in these lines. The Master has used his art to exorcise from our natural life the poison of ideality. Other poets had written of the malady of modern man, a prey to the restless chimaera,[37] and it was with good literary support that Mallarmé, at the beginning of his poem, likened the dutiful disciple drinking the *toast funèbre* (and also the Master himself, as the later lines show) to Saint John the Apostle exorcising the poison cup (Plate 5).[38]

> Ne crois pas qu'au magique espoir du corridor
> J'offre ma coupe vide où souffre un monstre d'or.

It may be noted in passing that this emblem gives to the Master surrounded by younger poets a vague resemblance to Christ appearing to his disciples, but the poisoned cup relates to an event in John's later life. It is succinctly abridged from the Golden Legend by Marcel Pacaut, with an indication of its popularity in Christian iconography:

C'est alors que les prêtres de Diane le font arrêter: leur chef, Aristodème, le force à boire le poison, qui ne lui fait aucun mal, et l'apôtre ressuscite deux esclaves sur lesquels il a été éprouvé (vitraux de Bourges, Chartres, Tours, Troyes, Reims, Sainte-Chapelle, Sant-Julien-du-Sault; bas-reliefs de Reims).[39]

Plate I. Saint Michael, sixteenth-century tapestry, Cathedral of Sens (photo Caisse Nationale des Monuments Historiques).

Souvent la vision du Poète me frappe:
Ange à cuirasse fauve, il a pour volupté
L'éclair du glaive . . .

Plate 2. Saint Cecilia, painting by Mignard, Louvre (photo N. D. Giraudon).

Plate 3. Saint Michael, eleventh-century miniature,
Bibliothèque Municipale d'Avranches.

Plate 4. Plaster cast of Bishop Roger's tomb
in Salisbury Cathedral, Victoria and Albert
Museum.

Le pied sur quelque guivre où notre amour tisonne,
Je pense plus longtemps peut-être éperdument
A l'autre, au sein brûlé d'une antique amazone.

Plate 5. Saint John the Evangelist, lithograph, after Lucas van Leyden (?),
reproduced by courtesy of Glasgow University Library.

Ne crois pas qu'au magique espoir du corridor
J'offre ma coupe vide, où souffre un monstre d'or.

Plate 6. 'The Whore of Babylon', water-colour by William Blake, British Museum. Reproduced by courtesy of the Trustees of the British Museum.

Mais, comme un vil tressaut d'hydre, oyant jadis l'ange
Donner un sens plus pur aux mots de la tribu . . .

Plate 7. Angel at the gate of Paradise, tenth-century manuscript, Bodleian Junius 11.

S'ils sont vaincus, c'est par un Ange très puissant
Qui rougit l'horizon des éclairs de son glaive.

Le Poète suscite avec un glaive nu
Son siècle épouvanté de n'avoir pas connu
Que la mort s'exalt ait dans cette voix étrange.

Plate 8. Drawing of a miniature in a twelfth-century manuscript in the Vatican Library, reproduced by courtesy of Glasgow University Library.

Elle dit ce terme: Anasthase!—
Gravé sur quelque parchemin . . .

How directly Saint John the exorciser figures one side of the post-Christian task Mallarmé himself has undertaken is shown by a passage (which I hope by liberal omissions to make readable) in Mallarmé's letter to Lefébure of 17 May 1867:

> *La Vénus de Milo,* . . . la *Joconde* du Vinci, me semblent, et *sont,* les deux grandes scintillations de la Beauté sur cette terre—et cet Oeuvre, tel qu'il est rêvé, le troisième. La Beauté complète et inconsciente, ou la Vénus de Phidias, la Beauté ayant été mordue au cœur depuis le christianisme par la Chimère, . . . la Beauté, enfin, . . . souriant mystérieusement maintenant, mais de bonheur et avec la quiétude de la Vénus de Milo retrouvée.[40]

Mallarmé does not of course credit Gautier with the achievement which he himself pursues. The Master has inspired by his example disciples who must strive in their turn to bring the art of poetry nearer to the point of perfection which must be reached if a poet is one day to create the Work:

> Le Livre . . . tenté à son insu par quiconque a écrit, même les Génies. L'explication orphique de la Terre, qui est le seul devoir du poète et le jeu littéraire par excellence.[41]

Three years after 'Toast funèbre' Mallarmé wrote his sonnet for a Memorial Volume to Poe. In the well-known later version it is a difficult poem to understand, but exegetists have made good use of the comparative clarity of the earlier text, and of an English rendering of it, with notes, by Mallarmé himself.[42] Nevertheless, it would be a mistake to suppose that it has no more secrets. In particular, the Christian imagery—the struggle between the angel and the 'hydra'—still needs clarification.

'Le Tombeau de Poe', as its title is probably meant to signify, is a poem about the monument unveiled at Baltimore in November 1875,[43] though only the last tercet refers directly to it:

> Sombre bloc à jamais chu d'un désastre obscur,
> Que ce granit du moins montre à jamais sa borne
> Aux vieux vols de blasphème épars dans le futur.[44]

Sombre bloc, indeed, if all the praise the poet can offer it, is to wish it may 'at least' guard Poe in death against the calumnies his compatriots plagued him with in life. But even this praise is ironical. It is a sardonic inversion of the terms of an image used elsewhere by Mallarmé to express with bitter scorn his true opinion of the Baltimore memorial stone. In the 'scolies' he added to his translation of Poe's poems, published in 1889, appears a paragraph written perhaps earlier, at the time of the unveiling:

GHF

Aussi je ne cesserai d'admirer le pratique moyen dont ces gens, incommodés par tant de mystère insoluble, à jamais émanant du coin de terre où gisait depuis un quart de siècle la dépouille abandonnée de Poe, ont, sous le couvert d'un inutile et retardataire tombeau, roulé là une pierre, immense, informe, lourde, déprécatoire, comme pour bien boucher l'endroit d'où s'exhalerait vers le ciel, ainsi qu'une pestilence, la juste revendication d'une existence de Poëte par tous interdite.[45]

The positive message of the poem, replying to the negative character of the monument, asserts that Poe's work is his true memorial and splendid tomb. It takes up the two quatrains. It is expressed in an allegory, in which the combat between an angel and a hydra—surely the blasphemous many-headed beast of the Apocalypse (Plate 6)[46]—represents the idealist's struggle against the materialistic Philistines. The drama is in two acts, the persecution of the angel by the hydra, figuring the poet's unhappy life (second quatrain), the triumph of the angel and discomfiture of the hydra, figuring his glory in death (first quatrain):

> Tel qu'en lui-même enfin l'éternité le change
> Le poète suscite avec un hymne [glaive] nu
> Son siècle épouvanté de n'avoir pas connu
> Que la mort s'exaltait dans cette voix étrange:

> Mais, comme un vil tressaut d'hydre, oyant jadis l'ange
> Donner un sens plus pur aux mots de la tribu,
> Tous pensèrent entre eux le sortilège bu
> Chez le flot sans honneur de quelque noir mélange.[47]

This conception of the life and death, or martyrdom, of a poet, conforms so closely to a judgement expressed by Chateaubriand in *Mémoires d'Outre-tombe*[48] that the resemblance can hardly be accidental. Chateaubriand writes:

Notre espèce se divise en deux parts inégales: les hommes de la mort et aimés d'elle; troupeau choisi qui renaît; les hommes de la vie et oubliés d'elle, multitude de néant qui ne renaît plus. L'existence temporaire de ces derniers, consiste dans le nom, le crédit, la place, la fortune; leur bruit, leur autorité, leur puissance s'évanouissent avec leur personne: clos leur salon et leur cercueil, close est leur destinée.

Whether or not Mallarmé had this passage in mind, it clarifies his allegory considerably. The same idea of a kind of immortality reserved for *les gens d'idéal*[49] dominates the two quatrains, and their paradoxical opposition of light and gloom. The darkness of life for the poet, reality, the opacity of the flesh, *vieux vols de blasphème* and *noir mélange,* all give place to the brightness of death as the work shines out (for *les hommes de la mort*) in its ideality.

It shines, indeed, like an avenging angel's sword and the idea of the poet's revenge is implicit in the comparison. It is not clear, however, in what capacity exactly the poet-angel takes vengeance. There seem to be two possibilities. One is suggested by certain details in Baudelaire's *Edgar Poe, sa vie et son œuvre.* In that essay, Baudelaire presents his hero as one of those *natures spirituelles et angéliques,* to torment whom there exists a special providence. They are the *enguignonnés: L'Ange aveugle de l'expiation . . . les fouette à tour de bras pour l'édification des autres.* Does the poet after death become in Mallarmé's allegory an avenging angel in his turn, punishing the many-headed monster that blasphemed against him, called by Baudelaire *la tyrannie des bêtes, ou zoocratie?*[50] This Baudelaire-inspired notion may well contribute to the idea of Poe's metamorphosis, or glorification of the poet in death, but it does not entirely elucidate it. There is a second explanation.

In a letter to Cazalis, written from Besançon on 5 August 1867, Mallarmé complained of all the people who stood in the way of his transfer to a post in another school, and jokingly cursed them, saying:

Tous ces gens-là me paieront cela, car mes poèmes futurs seront pour eux des fioles empoisonnées, des gouttes terribles. Je les priverai du Paradis comme ils me privent du département de la Lozère.[51]

Is this not tantamount to declaring that on the one hand a poet's work admits the elect to that communion of minds which is the only immortality and the only true paradise, while on the other hand it signifies to the Philistines their exclusion? In Mallarmé's poem similarly, is not the Angel with a hymn that is a sword the Angel at the gate of Paradise? The Christian angel that stood there before, according to Genesis 3.24 (Plate 7) refused entry to all comers, and was the poets' foe; hence in 'Le Guignon':

> S'ils sont vaincus, c'est par un Ange très puissant
> Qui rougit l'horizon des éclairs de son glaive.

The post-Christian Angel on the other hand opens the gate to the men of death, closes it only to the men of life.[52] This would be a nobler, or at least less vulgar role than that of a mere *ange de l'expiation* on the model of Baudelaire's. It is the role that is formally claimed for the poet (though the communion in mysticity is still recognised as an inferior substitute for the communion in poetry) at the end of Mallarmé's article on Léon Dierx, written in 1872:

L'âme, tacite et qui ne se suspend pas aux paroles de l'élu familier, le poète, est, à moins qu'elle ne sacrifie à Dieu l'ensemble impuissant de ses aspirations, vouée irrémédiablement au Néant.[53]

What post-Christian meaning Mallarmé conferred on the protagonists of his unfinished 'mystery', *Les Noces d'Hérodiade*, is too complex to be considered here. So is the question whether there is Christian imagery in 'Prose, pour des Esseintes'. I would simply suggest that in its beginnings 'Hérodiade' probably owed more to Banville's short story 'L'Armoire' (in *Le Boulevard*, January 1863) than to visual depictions, whereas the 'prose' may hide in the lines

> *Elle dit ce terme: Anastase!—*
> Gravé sur quelque parchemin . . .

the most ambitious of all Mallarmé's adaptations of Christian imagery. The fact that the word is given a capital and an exclamation mark suggests that *'anastase'* has for him an exciting meaning. My surmise is that that meaning was perhaps not the Resurrection of Christ, or of all souls on Judgement Day. It was the meaning, traditional in the Eastern Church, of the raising from limbo of Adam and Eve, and John the Baptist and diverse kings, and the just, when Christ harrowed hell between his death and his resurrection. Christian iconography could offer Mallarmé no more dramatic symbol than the traditional depiction of this apocryphal event (Plate 8)[54] to figure the rescue of mankind from limbo by the post-Christian poet to come, the new Messiah. It might seem unlikely *a priori* that the Master of the rue de Rome would directly compare the accomplishment of his own ambition with this majestic manifestation of the divinity of Christ, were it not that the comparison with Christ and his disciples seems to be clearly implied in later statements such as for instance the following, in 'Confrontation':

Surtout qu'on se voua originellement à un miracle préludant avec l'inspiration, achevé par la formation, alentour, d'une élite.[55]

Glasgow   AUSTIN GILL

NOTES

1 The Christian images in 'Le Guignon' and 'Les Fenêtres' do not fall within the group to be studied, though they are related to it. I have said something of them in an article 'Mallarmé on Baudelaire', *Currents of Thought in French Literature, Essays in Memory of G. T. Clapton*, Blackwell, 1965.

2 It is the letter which appears to have overcome the last efforts of the grand-parents to resist their dear but misguided Stéphane's obstinate desire to be a poet and not a civil servant, and as a first step, to go to London and so be qualified to teach English for a livelihood. For the text, see Henri Mondor, *Mallarmé plus intime*, Gallimard, 1944, pp. 118–19.

3 The text is that published in the *Journal des Baigneurs*, 6 July 1862, as reproduced in *OC*, pp. 20–1, but with C. P. Barbier's emendations of spelling and punctuation (*Documents Stéphane Mallarmé*, III, p. 89).

4 'Il évitait les relations mondaines et ne comprenait pas nos ferveurs pour la danse'.

5 See C. P. Barbier, op. cit., p. 90.

6 *Le Sénonais*, 22 March 1862; *OC*, p. 255.

7 *Le Papillon*, 10 January 1862; *OC*, pp. 250 and 251.

8 That unbelief did not keep him out of the cathedral (one of whose pillars is no doubt the one in 'Pan', *Dont l'ombre séculaire abrita plus d'un doute*) is attested in a letter to Marie Gerhard, dated 26 June 1862: 'Vous avez dû voir . . . à la manière dont je vous contemplais dimanche à la Cathé-drale que vous n'étiez pas sans avoir fait sur moi une impression sérieuse'; *Corr.* I, p. 33.

9 The other emblems too seem visual (as the word *vision* gives us to expect). Dante is very like the Dante of Raphael's 'Parnassus', at the Vatican, in some black-and-white reproduction that turned the pink garment into a shroud. (In 1862 *L'Artiste* presented all readers who took out a full subscription with a 'free' copy of an engraving after Raphael's 'Parnassus'. One of them can be seen in the Print Room of the Victoria and Albert Museum. The Dante fits Mallarmé's description nicely). Anacreon and the *grands bohèmes* (though the latter also remind one vaguely of Baude-laire's gypsies) could quite well be contemporary vignettes.

10 In *Les Misérables*, which Mallarmé was reading with such enthusiasm when he published this poem (see *Corr.* I, pp. 34, 38 and 41), the fearful Inspector Javert himself is seen as a lay Saint Michael (I. viii. 3). Perhaps Mallarmé knew also *La Liberté, l'archange des peuples*, in *Napoléon le Petit*.

11 See his preface to *Les Rayons et les Ombres* (1840).

12 *OC*, pp. 259 and 260.

13 See p. 78, above.

14 'Avant-dire au *Traité du Verbe* de René Ghil'; *OC.*, p. 857.

15 To Cazalis, 25 April 1864; *Corr.* I, p. 116.

16 To Cazalis, October or November 1864; *Corr.* I, p. 137.

17 27 May 1867; Henri Mondor, *Eugène Lefébure*, pp. 252–3.

18 For the second date, see A. Gill, 'La Transposition mallarméenne', in *Revue de linguistique romane*, July–December 1968.

19 7 December 1865; *Corr.* I, p. 181.

20 *OC*, p. 1463 (later editions, p. 1468).

21 The suggestion that several important features of Mallarmé's poem are taken from Mignard's *Sainte Cécile* was made, I believe for the first time, by A. Fongaro in *Studi Francesi*, No. 27, Sept.–Dec. 1965. My own exploration of the iconography, including a large collection of greetings-cards for Saint Cecilia's Day in the Cabinet des Estampes of the Biblio-thèque nationale, had led me to the same opinion. Indeed, I attribute to

the painting, or a reproduction of it, an even greater importance as a source for the poem. To my mind, Mallarmé's 'Sainte' is a subjective interpretation of, or feflexion on, Mignard's *Sainte Cécile*. Mallarmé had looked, often no doubt, at 'the concert of angels' in the rose-window of the north transept in Sens Cathedral. He describes it in 'Symphonie littéraire', mentioning angels *blancs comme des hosties* who *chantent leur extase en s'accompagnant de harpes imitant leurs ailes*. Mignard too, however, in his picture, plays on this analogy, relating the wing of the cherub holding the music to the harp that prolongs the sculptured cherub's wing. But also, I have it on good authority that French harps of the sixteenth and seventeenth centuries were often decorated like the one in Mignard's picture, with a cherub carved in the top.

22 Footnote to 'La Musique et les Lettres'; *OC*, p. 655.

23 In *Mallarmé lycéen*, 1954, p. 50, Henri Mondor gives the text of a letter sent by Mallarmé, at the age of fourteen, to his sister Marie. He tells her that 'petite maman m'a conduit chez une dame où elle peignait une sainte Colombe d'après Mignard'. On the same page (note 1) Mondor quotes from a letter he has from a granddaughter of the step-mother. She writes: 'Elle a conservé jusqu'à sa mort des toiles d'études, qui ornaient son atelier. . . . Au décès de notre grand-mère, ses toiles ont été disséminées dans la famille, j'en possède plusieurs: un saint Louis offrant la couronne d'épines, une sainte Colombe dont Mallarmé a parlé dans une lettre. . . . Il y a au Carmel de Sens une sainte Thérèse. . . . Toujours à Sens . . . se trouve une copie d'un Christ en croix de Van Dyck . . .' (and why not somewhere a Saint Cecilia, also *d'après Mignard*?). The glimpses of Sens in the early poems are worth attention. A nice example, confirmed by a corrected title in C. P. Barbier's *Documents*, vol. 3, is the six-line poem '. . . *Mysticis umbraculis* (Prose des fous)'. The three dots indicate a quotation, and the words in brackets its source: the medieval manuscript at Sens known as the 'Prose de l'âne' or 'Prose des fous'.

24 The 'theory of mystery' about which Mallarmé corresponded with Lefébure seems to have recognised that the post-Christian poet might benefit from his familiarity with the Christian sense of mystery. Lefébure wrote, in a letter dated 2 June 1867 (Henri Mondor, *Eugène Lefébure*, pp. 252–3): 'Mais, mon cher ami, . . . pour éprouver le grand frémisse-ment de l'Inconnu, il faut croire qu'on est appelé à le posséder absolu-ment, ou tout au moins l'avoir cru: le Mystère a été votre Dieu, de sorte qu'il peut l'être encore, à présent que vous savez, car une impression profonde résiste à une certitude postérieure.'

25 Reproduced by kind permission of the Librarian, to whom I am obliged for courteous assistance.

26 In Christian iconography there is no lack of wyverns and dragons under-foot, any of which might support the bishop's effigy and Saint Michael in the imagination of the poet. Christ is sometimes represented *le pied sur quelque guivre*. So are various saints. So is the Virgin; writing to Des Essarts on 22 August 1862, Mallarmé told him of one Iboüet, crossed in love, who will not accept consolation, 'craignant sans doute que pour le consoler je ne descende son idole du piédestal sur lequel elle broie son coeur du pied, comme l'Immaculée le serpent'. His famous 'miroir de Venise', according to the prose poem 'Frisson d'hiver', had a frame of carved wyverns.

27 I owe this information, and permission to have the cast photographed, to the Keeper of the Victoria and Albert Museum, where it is now to be seen.

28 In 'Consolation' (España):

> La foule est comme l'eau qui fuit les hauts sommets . . .
> Ne fais pas d'escalier à ta pensée ardue.

29 The letter was published by J. Monval, in 'Deux camarades du Parnasse, Catulle Mendès et François Coppée. Lettres inédites', *Revue de Paris*, March–April 1909. He dates the letter 'en 1872'.

30 In *Corr.* II, p. 37, and *OC*, p. 1465 (later editions, p. 1470), the letter is said to have been written to Coppée, but in Henri Mondor's *Vie de Mallarmé*, p. 345, to either Coppée or Mendès. If Mendès sent to all the contributors a letter similar to the one he sent to Coppée, Mallarmé's could be his reply. In that case, November or December 1872 would be a more likely date than 1873.

31 'Théophile Gautier', published in *L'Artiste* and then as a plaquette, in 1859; included later in *L'Art romantique*.

32 That is the theme of the poem 'Quand l'ombre menaça . . .'

33 'La Musique et les Lettres'; *OC*, p. 654.

34 *Igitur; OC*, p. 440.

35 'Quand l'ombre menaça . . .'

36 *Enquête sur l'évolution littéraire*; *OC*, p. 872.

37 For instance:

> Imparfait ou déchu, l'homme est le grand mystère . . .
> Malheur à qui du fond de l'exil de la vie
> Entendit ces concerts d'un monde qu'il envie! . . .
> Hélas! tel fut mon sort, telle est ma destinée.
> J'ai vidé comme toi la coupe empoisonnée . . .
> > (Lamartine 'L'Homme', in *Méditations poétiques*),

> Mais, ô Nature, hélas! ce n'est point toi qu'on aime: . . .
> Ta coupe toujours pleine est prop près de nos lèvres;
> C'est le calice amer du désir qu'il nous faut!
> > (Leconte de Lisle, 'Ultra cœlos', in *Poèmes barbares*)

> Une jeune Chimère, aux lèvres de ma coupe,
> Dans l'orgie, a donné le baiser le plus doux . . .
> > (Gautier himself, 'La Chimère', in *Poésies diverses*)

38 The photograph is of a lithograph copy of a painting attributed to Lucas van Leyden, (Plate 51 in *Die Sammlung Alt- Nieder- und Ober-Deutscher-Gemälde der Brüder Boisserée und Bertram, lithographirt von I. N. Strixner*. Stuttgart and Munich, 1831–6. An etching figuring St John with the chalice, copied from either this lithograph or the original or some other copy of it, is to be found in Anna Jameson's *Sacred and Legendary Art*, vol. I, 1848; there the original is attributed to Memling.

39 Marcel Pacaut, *L'Iconographie chrétienne*, P.U.F. *Que sais-je?* 1962, p. 104.

40 *Corr.* I, p. 246.

41 'Autobiographie'; *OC*, p. 662. In so far as the poetic art is concerned (and that is only part of the task of writing the Book), the point reached by Gautier would seem from 'Toast funèbre' to be precisely that of which

Mallarmé says, in a letter to Coppée, 'Le hasard n'entame pas un vers, c'est la grande chose. Nous avons, plusieurs, atteint cela' (5 December 1866; *Corr.* I, p. 234). In the same letter, he goes on to say what still remains to be achieved.

42   For both translation and notes, see Charles Chassé, *Les Clefs de Mallarmé* (1954), pp. 103–4.

43   In a letter to Mrs Rice dated 4 April 1876 (*Corr.* II, p. 110), Mallarmé wrote: 'Pieusement, j'accomplirai votre désir pour mon humble part, en vous envoyant, pour l'époque que vous voudrez bien me fixer, quelques vers écrits, Madame, en votre honneur: je veux dire commémoratifs de la grande cérémonie de l'automne dernier'.

44   The original version, less reticent than the later one, is the one quoted here, from *OC*, pp. 1487–8 (p. 1493 in later editions).

45   *OC*, p. 226. An aphoristic version of the same image is found in the *Bibliographie* included in the Deman edition of Mallarmé's poems: 'un bloc de basalte, que l'Amérique appuya sur l'ombre légère du Poëte, pour sa sécurité qu'elle ne ressortît jamais' (*OC*, p. 78.)

46   Revelation, chapters 13 and 17.

47   'In plain prose', explained Mallarmé to his American readers, commenting on this line, 'charged him with always being drunk'.

48   IV, xi. 8.

49   The immortality reserved by Chateaubriand for his *hommes de la mort* is similar to that promised by Renan to *nous autres hommes de l'idée* (Mallarmé's *gens d'idéal*, 'Solitude'; *OC*, p. 408): 'Le règne de l'esprit est l'œuvre propre de l'humanité, Notre vie aura été une partie de la vie infinie. Nous aurons notre place marquée pour l'éternité' ('Lettre à Marcellin Berthelot', 1863).

50   The hydra was a traditional symbol for the populace. Naudé in *Considérations sur les corps d'Etat* (1667) notes that: 'Ceux qui en ont fait la plus entière et la plus particulière description la représentent à bon droit comme une bête à plusieurs têtes'. Baudelaire's criticism, in his life of Poe, of the democratic materialism of the United States is so harsh that Mallarmé's hydra may well be his *zoocratie*. Whether in the apocalyptic context Baudelaire's *barbarie éclairée au gaz* has become the modern Babylon seems doubtful, but it is possible.

51   *Corr.* I, p. 256.

52   Some realisation of their exclusion is attributed to the Philistines. It may, Mallarmé suggests in the *Scolies* to his translation of Poe, *répandre en la sérénité d'un peuple quelque trouble subtil* (*OC*, p. 226.)

53   *OC*, p. 694.

54   This rather crude drawing, of a miniature in a twelfth-century gospel-book at the Vatican, is chosen as an illustration because it was easily accessible, as part of Plate LXI in vol. V of Seroux d'Agincourt's *Histoire de l'art par les monuments*, 1823. Such copies (and much better ones) were not rare in volumes of facsimiles and also in works on Christian iconography by authors like Didron.

55   *OC*, p. 412.

EROS AND POETRY: MALLARMÉ'S DISAPPEARING VISIONS

'J'ai pour devise: *Rien de louche.*'   Letter to Cazalis (s.d.)

Pour les vers je suis fini, je crois: il y a de grandes lacunes dans mon cerveau qui est devenu incapable d'une pensée suivie et d'application. J'expie cruellement, par un réel abrutissement, toi seul le sais, mon ami, le priapisme de ma jeunesse. Oui, je me regarde avec frayeur, comme une ruine: dans toutes mes lettres, je vais mentir à mes amis et leur dire que je travaille—mais cela n'est pas vrai. Un poète doit être uniquement sur cette terre un poète, et moi je suis un cadavre une partie de ma vie. A peine pourrai-je prétendre un jour au titre d'amateur.

La solitude aussi me tue. Je n'ai pas dit un mot à un homme depuis que j'ai quitté Paris: il faut être bien fort pour résister à cela, et je ne le suis pas.

L'ombre de ton;

STÉPHANE[1]

Rare in its explicitness, this famous letter sent from Mallarmé in Tournon to Henri Cazalis in 1864 has been quoted with unfeigned delight by critics eager to find keys to force their way into the secret recesses of the private life of the most private of poets, one who celebrated the *fermoirs d'or* and the *hiéroglyphes inviolés* (*OC*, 257). The exceptionally prudish M. Mondor leaves out the confession of *priapisme*, giving us only paraphrase with commentary: 'Il craint, dans son atonie actuelle, que quelque frénesie génésique de sa jeunesse, dont il semble s'exagérer les excès et à laquelle il fait trop de reproches, ne soit responsable de cet affaiblissement. Que n'accuse-t-il, avec moins d'invraisemblance, la hauteur peu accessible de ses visions d'artiste, la difficulté jamais égalée des vers qu'il rêve, l'usure incessante d'un labeur inhumain'.[2] And M. Charles Chassé, who is the opposite, quotes with approval, and regards as proof, Huret's description of the poet: 'Des oreilles longues et pointues de satyre', and concludes: 'Rien d'étonnant que le poète ait écrit l'*Après-midi d'un faune.*'[3] Both use the letter to move from its unveiling of a secret to biographical documentation which does not exist or, worse, to biological speculation on Mallarmé's supposedly constitutional sensuality. What should interest us, it seems to me, is not the relative accuracy of this confession of adolescent solitary excesses in a projected definitive *Vie de Mallarmé* but its impact, if any, on his poetic vision and on the poetry itself. For we are not prying into a secret after all, merely receiving confirmation of Mallarmé's participation in a universal human phenomenon; he would echo Flaubert's refrain 'O dortoirs de mon collège, vous aviez des mélancolies plus vastes que celles que j'ai trouvées au désert!'[4] And beyond that, his letter reveals his all-too-human participation in a universally shared burden of subsequent guilt and fear of retribution in the form of aboulia or worse, witness another letter of the same dark winter at Tournon: 'Moi, je me traîne comme un vieillard et je passe des heures à observer dans les glaces l'envahissement de la bêtise qui éteint déjà mes yeux aux cils pendants et laisse tomber mes lèvres'.[5]

Since happily we are not in the France of Madame de Gaulle, let us call things by their names without circumlocution. I have quoted Mallarmé's admission that he believes his depression, his fatigue and poetic impotence, his distracted incapacity for work and concentration to be the expiation for excesses of adolescent masturbation. It matters not whether Mondor is correct to dispute Mallarmé's self-prognosis; it matters only that Mallarmé thinks it so, that he attributes poetic sterility to his masturbation, doubtless remembering the threats of dire punishment held out by his mentors in the *pension* or at the Lycée de Sens. It is of little interest, and it would be disturbingly indiscreet, to probe further into Mallarmé's biography. The psychical and literary significance of adolescent auto-eroticism resides not in physical performance but in the fact that phantasms always accompany the ritual, that erotic energy is channelled into the creation of images or visions, which disappear after depletion. To quote Wilhelm Stekel: 'preceded by a sort of ecstasy or intoxication during which the current moment disappears and the phantasy reigns supreme for a few minutes or seconds, the curtain then falls over the secret.' By repeating the gestures, one can renew or resuscitate the phantasm. A moment of presumptuous retrospective omniscience would allow us to say that for the poet-to-be, Stéphane Mallarmé, his adolescent experience was the first, and perhaps ultimately the most important, revelation of the almost physical reality of the purely mental phantasm of 'le péché de voir le Rêve dans sa nudité idéale'[6] long before the *nuit de Tournon*; that he was, in poems of partially veiled eroticism, to be obsessed with the phenomenon of the disappearing vision, and that his attempts to recapture or immobilise it would become the very substance of much of his verse; that his unhappy devotion to the *Muse moderne de l'Impuissance* in a cult of *ennui* and sterility is the inevitable sequel to the ecstatic moment of vision and illumination which fades all too quickly: 'Quoi! de tout cet éclat pas même le lambeau/S'attarde. . . .' In other words, that the physical drive leading to the creation of the phantasm was, for Mallarmé, an adumbration of the very processes of inspiration and poetic creation moving from the fugitive and ephemeral vision to the quest for permanence as artifact: 'soupirer que cette vive nue/L'ignition du feu toujours intérieur/Originellement la seule continue/Dans le joyau de l'oeil véridique ou rieur'.[7]

An indiscreet early version of 'Victorieusement fui le suicide beau', sent interestingly enough to the Paul Verlaine who called *L'Après-midi d'un faune* 'l'adorable poème cochon', provides, I think, some confirmation of my hypothesis.

SONNET

1 Toujours plus souriant au désastre plus beau,
 Soupirs de sang, or meurtrier, pâmoison, fête!
 Une millième fois avec ardeur s'apprête
 Mon solitaire amour à vaincre le tombeau.

5 Quoi! de tout ce coucher, pas même un cher lambeau
 Ne reste, il est minuit, dans la main du poëte
 Excepté qu'un trésor trop folâtre de tête
 Y verse sa lueur diffuse sans flambeau!

 La tienne, si toujours frivole! c'est la tienne,
10 Seul gage qui des soirs évanouis retienne
 Un peu de désolé combat en t'en coiffant

 Avec grâce, quand sur les coussins tu la poses
 Comme un casque guerrier d'impératrice enfant
14 Dont pour te figurer, il tomberait des roses.[8]

15 Victorieusement fui le suicide beau
 Tison de gloire, sang par écume, or, tempête!
 Ô rire si là-bas une pourpre s'apprête
 A ne tendre royal que mon absent tombeau.

 Quoi! de tout cet éclat pas même le lambeau
20 S'attarde, il est minuit, à l'ombre qui nous fête
 Excepté qu'un trésor présomptueux de tête
 Verse son caressé nonchaloir sans flambeau,

 La tienne si toujours le délice! la tienne
 Oui seule qui du ciel évanoui retienne
25 Un peu de puéril triomphe en t'en coiffant

 Avec clarté quand sur les coussins tu la poses
 Comme un casque guerrier d'impératrice enfant
 Dont pour te figurer il tomberait des roses. (*OC*, 68)

The first stanza stresses the repetition of the ritual orgasm (*Toujours une millième fois avec ardeur*) described in the traditional Mallarméan cluster of love, death, sunset and exultation (*Soupirs de sang, or meurtrier, pâmoison, fête*), as well as celestial erotic fireworks in the etymology of *désastre*. It is interesting that Mallarmé's predilection for the word *soupir* combines ecstasy with a musical term, a quarter-rest or crotchet rest, thereby leading to the idea of a music of silence and absence as in *et je bois les soupirs* of *Monologue d'un faune*. The solitary dreamer is preparing once more to conquer death through the orgasmic love-death which allows him to resurrect the image of light and the fetishistic object, the luminous hair of his absent mistress. The explosive *Quoi!* marks the culmination of his ecstasy (more forceful in the *éclat* of the definitive version), for thereafter the poet will lament the disappearance of the phantasm perceived visually as light:

> Quoi! de tout ce coucher, pas même un cher lambeau
> Ne reste, il est minuit, dans la main du poète . . .

One cannot help being shocked by the directness of 'pas même un cher lambeau/ne reste . . . dans la main du poète', though this is attenuated by the bad pun on *ce coucher*, first indication in this version of the sunset image which will dominate the definitive text. But surely Mallarmé's sunset does not take place at midnight! The indication of time seems to me to be the preparation for *excepté que*: as midnight is the moment when night ends and day begins, a transitional moment; as it were, so the disappearance of the luminous phantasm into darkness at the moment of depletion is immediately followed by renewal of the desired image in the mind, though not of desire itself. Thus, the *trésor trop folâtre de tête* which pours its light both into midnight and the hand is *not yet* the imagined head of a woman but the imagining head of the poet-dreamer himself, custodian of the treasure (*trésor* contains its own golden luminosity) secreting its own light which has become diffuse through the *désastre*. The link between *pâmoison* (line 2) and *soirs évanouis* (line 10) moves us out of the poet's mental treasury into his mental image of the fetish, not the head now but the hair—the original source and object of the phantasm it would appear from Mallarmé's many *chevelure* poems (see Camille Soula's pioneering but unsatisfactory discussion, *Essai sur le symbole de la chevelure*,[9] but more especially J.-P. Richard's *L'Univers imaginaire de Mallarmé*, pp. 134ff.).[10] The possibility for renewal comes from the vestiges of light contained in the *chevelure*. But this is not a 'real' scene—there is no woman present, only an imaginary and invisible woman represented by the roses and existing only in the poet's conjuration of the *chevelure*. The verb *figurer* (compare

figurent un souhait de tes sens fabuleux in the *Faune*) is absolutely
central to Mallarmé's phantasmic vision. Here it conveys the very
essence of the mental attitude of the fetishist: an object or fetish is
detached from the body and thereafter stands as surrogate for the
whole woman. What matters above all in this revealing preliminary
version is the time sequence: the poem begins just prior to the orgasm
which, in the second quatrain, has already passed; the two tercets
take us back to the phantasmic origins of the ecstasy of the first
stanza and thus lead partly along the circle of renewal and repetition.

The definitive version is far more hermetic; the poet's secret is
hidden behind wilful abstraction—*dans la main du poète* has become
à l'ombre qui nous fête; lueur diffuse, caressé nonchaloir; coucher, is now
éclat, and the sexual *ardeur* has become descriptive *pourpre*. One is
entitled to ask whether in fact we are dealing with the *same* poem or
whether Mallarmé has created a new entity with a new theme
upon the scaffolding of the discarded original. One key word seems to
me to embody the vestigial essence of what Mallarmé was so successfully disguising in the definitive version: *suicide*. We all know the
Romantic convention, immortalised in Wagner's *Tristan*, of the
orgasm as death, of love as death; and no one was more faithful to this
topos than Mallarmé. In a variant of the early precious poem, 'Placet
futile' we read: 'Et qu'avec moi vous avez succombe';[11] in 'Tristesse
d'Été', where such hints as *breuvage amoureux* tempt me to see
Tristesse as a feminine form of *Tristan*, the poet's beloved laments:
'Nous ne serons jamais une seule momie'.[12] But these are love deaths
à deux, whereas in 'Victorieusement fui', in keeping with the version
sent to Verlaine, the love-death is solitary; and *suicide*, with its
etymology in the reflexive *sui caedere*, expresses the solipsism of that
love-death. Moreover, as most critics now acknowledge, the past
participle *fui* is used intransitively; the poet has not escaped from
suicide, he has triumphantly committed a type of unfortunately
ephemeral suicide whose beauty is then evoked in line 16. And *fui*
might well be read in its most physical sense as a periphrasis for
depletion. That Mallarmé was aware of this tension between two and
one can be seen in the *Improvisation d'un faune* where the Faune's
erotically inspired song is expressed:

> . . . Car son angoisse élut pour confident
> Le jonc vaste et jumeau dont vers l'azur on joue;
> Qui, détournant à soi le trouble de la joue,
> Rêve avec un duo que nous amusions
> La splendour d'alentour par des confusions
> Fausses entre lui-même et notre amour crédule . . .

Which becomes in the definitive version:

> Rêve, dans un solo long, que nous amusions
> La beauté d'alentour par des confusions
> Fausses entre elle-même et notre chant crédule.

Beyond that, I am happy to concede that *priapisme* is not the theme of 'Victorieusement fui'. As I intimated earlier, I am not searching the work of Mallarmé for a theme, nor for hints of his continuing addiction to masturbation even as a means of conjuring visions, but for signs of an essential and formative experience that points the way to a basic imaginative structure in his work: the ecstatic but disappearing vision linked to an original erotic inspiration. Richard, in his magnificent thesis, calls it 'du soleil mourant à la veilleuse' in discussing 'la mort solaire'.[13] It can be found in many poems: 'La Chevelure vol d'une flamme'; 'Tout Orgueil fume-t-il du soir' with its 'affres du passé nécessaires'; 'Une dentelle s'abolit' with its image of dream as the way to rebirth—'Mais, chez qui du rêve se dore/Tristement dort une mandore/Au creux néant musicien'; even in the 'Cantique de saint Jean', the phantasm leading to Hérodiade's adolescence, where the decollation leads to the familiar shudder and fall and then to the ascent to renewed vision in the dream of salvation 'là-haut.'

But the crowning example of the pattern of disappearing vision which I attribute to Mallarmé's adolescent *priapisme* is without doubt *L'Après-midi d'un faune*. Soula has a fine discussion of the Faune as prototypical adolescent 'uniquement occupé à satisfaire des instincts sur la nature vraie desquels sa conscience encore est mal éclairée, mais dont la légitimité lui paraît suffisamment hors de doute, pour qu'il manifeste un étonnement sincère de ne pas voir l'univers conspirer à leur satisfaction'.[14] I would like to approach this poem with some obliquity to avoid any feeling that I am distorting its pattern. André Gide has told us that auto-eroticism was, along with 'beaucoup d'amour, de musique, de métaphysique et de poésie . . . le sujet de mon livre';[15] the book was his first, *Les Cahiers d'André Walter*, and in it Gide shows himself to have been a sensitive reader of Mallarmé's *Faune* when he describes one of Walter's masturbatory visions:

Je jouissais douloureusement de ma solitude et je la peuplais d'êtres aimés;—devant mes yeux se balançaient, d'abord indécises, les formes souples des enfants qui jouaient sur la plage et dont la beauté me poursuit; j'aurais voulu me baigner aussi, près d'eux, et, de mes mains, sentir la douceur des peaux brunes. Mais j'étais tout seul; alors un grand frisson m'a pris, et j'ai pleuré la fuite insaisissable du rêve.

This could almost be a précis of the Faune's pattern of disappearing vision, although Mallarmé, free from Huguenot remorse, celebrates the renewal of the vision through dream phantasm: *Couple, adieu; je vais voir l'ombre que tu devins* is confident in the nourishing power of dream, the real subject of the poem, whereas the original elaboration, *Monologue d'un faune,* focused on the violation of the pure: *Adieu, femmes; duo de vierges quand je vins.* This movement towards preoccupation with the very thought processes of phantasmic creation and the subsequent quest for permanence through art can be found in the modification of the openings of the three versions of the Faune:

Monologue—J'avais des Nymphes!
　　　　　　　　　　　　　Est-ce un songe? Non: . . .
Improvisation—Ces Nymphes, je les veux émerveiller!
　　. . . . . Baisai-je un songe?
L'Après-midi—Ces nymphes, je les veux perpétuer.
　　. . . . . Aimai-je un rêve?

Perpétuer by prolonging or renewing the dream is what the tired Faune contents himself with when he finds renewed phantasm-producing energy in the male world of the sun and decides to make the Orphic pilgrimage of illusion into the world of shades to relive his dream; at the same time *perpétuer,* to make permanent, to perpetuate the species (the link of sexual depletion and art is obvious here) is what the Faune-poet seeks futilely to do in the italicised passages marked CONTEZ and SOUVENIRS.

The pattern of disappearing vision in *L'Après-midi d'un faune* is essentially the same as in the revealing first version of 'Victorieusement fui', though probably at a slightly different point in time, just *after* the orgasm has caused the phantasm to disappear (*Après-midi* clearly links high noon to sexual climax as earlier sunset had led immediately to midnight). The Faune is thus heard initially seeking to prolong his pleasure: *Ces nymphes, je les veux perpétuer,* only to come quickly to the awareness that the vision has faded into illusion: 'Aimai-je un rêve? . . . bien seul je m'offrais/Pour triomphe la faute idéale de roses.' His passion was both a dream and ideal thought. The analytical mind then takes over to attempt in vain to revitalise an apparition: 'les femmes dont tu gloses/figurent un souhait de tes sens fabuleux.' The senses inspire and create the vision and give it symbolic form: *figurer* (in the meaning 'to give shape'), *souhaiter* (with its etymological link of desire and naming), *fabuleux* (with its union of illusion and invented narrative). Interestingly enough, the expression *sens fabuleux* is present in all three versions. Each attempt to renew the vision by conscious effort (Proust would call it *mémoire volontaire*), is characterised by familiar sexual imagery:

> O bords siciliens d'un calme marécage
> Qu'à l'envie de soleils ma vanité saccage,
> Tacite sous les fleurs d'étincelles, CONTEZ

And:

> O nymphes, regonflons des SOUVENIRS divers.

Each ends in admission of failure; this is a poem about the triumph of dream over artful recreation of the dream:

> Inerte, tout brûle dans l'heure fauve
> Sans marquer par quel art ensemble détala
> Trop d'hymen souhaité de qui cherche le *la*:

And:

> Tant pis! vers le bonheur d'autres m'entraîneront

Each admission of failure leads to a hope for sexual replenishment which would allow the senses to become fabulating forces once more in the re-creation of the original phantasm:

> Alors m'éveillerai-je à la ferveur première,
> Droit et seul, sous un flot antique de lumière,
> Lys!

And:

> Tu sais, ma passion, que, pourpre et déjà mûre,
> Chaque grenade éclate et d'abeilles murmure;
> Et notre sang, épris de qui le va saisir,
> Coule pour tout l'essaim éternel du désir.

Finally, the Faune attempts to invent a new fabulation of Etna and Venus, but here too, within the narrative itself, the vision fades— 'Quand tonne un somme triste ou s'épuise la flamme'. Only through sleep can the fabulating senses be revitalised, yet this sleep is itself a form of love-death as the words *succombent* and *gisant*, linked to *midi* in the final paragraph following the final failure of narrative re-creation (marked by *Non*), signify:

> Non, mais l'âme
> De paroles vacante et ce corps alourdi
> Tard succombent au fier silence de midi:
> Sans plus il faut dormir en l'oubli du blasphème,
> Sur le sable gisant et comme j'aime
> Ouvrir ma bouche à l'astre efficace des vins!

Once again light is the image of sexual energy—the sun is, of course, the traditional male force and the Faune's mouth, like the ripening grape, receives its vitality from the sun. The very source of the shadowy phantasm (*l'ombre que tu devins*) is paradoxically light itself.

If the Faune's narrative attempts (*Contez, Souvenirs, Etna*) fail, it is not so with music: the mouth, wine and the Dionysian cult of music are inextricably interwoven here. There is a second continuing line in the poem, that of musical art as being made of the very substance of passion as the flute itself is made of the substance of Syrinx. And yet the flute is also patently phallic and therefore represents the transformation of sexuality into an artifact producing an art that is the embodiment of sexuality: 'Le visible et serein souffle artificiel/De l'inspiration qui regagne le ciel.' Paradoxically, the flute, rather than the more visual attempted narratives, produces the plasticity of the line in an essential pun:

> Et de faire aussi haut que l'amour se module
> Evanouir du songe ordinaire de dos
> Ou de flanc pur suivis avec mes regards clos,
> Une sonore, vaine et monotone ligne.

The total fusion of music and line is made manifest when the notion of escape through Dionysian drunkenness is expressed by the transformation of the grape into a kind of flute when the Faune breathes into it and looks through it in a bizarre ceremony of pagan elevation;

> Rieur, j'élève au ciel d'été la grappe vide
> Et, soufflant dans ses peaux lumineuses, avide
> D'ivresse, jusqu'au soir je regarde au travers.

Until finally the Faune's mouth seems itself to become a flute into which the sun breathes its music of renewed desire leading to resurrection of the phantasm: 'comme j'aime/Ouvrir ma bouche à l'astre efficace des vins!'

'Gloire du long désir, Idées.' That key line from the *Prose pour Des Esseintes* expresses the origins of Mallarmé's poetry of disappearing erotic visions more concisely and accurately even than his confession of *priapisme* in the letter to Cazalis. We are dealing here with the human origins of inspiration, not with biographical or psychological gossip. It seems to me that in treating such a matter honestly, candidly without the leer of indiscretion and, above all, without making excessive claims that we have found a key, not to mention the key, we can gain new insight into the poetic process. And at the same time we will not have violated Mallarmé's credo and caution, expressed in another letter to Cazalis: 'J'ai pour devise: *Rien de louche.*'

Princeton ALBERT SONNENFELD

NOTES

1 *Correspondance* (1862–71) edited by Henri Mondor and J.-P. Richard, Paris, 1959, pp. 144–5.
2 Henri Mondor, *Vie de Mallarmé*, édition complète en un volume, Paris, 1941, p. 150.
3 *Les Clefs de Mallarmé*, Paris, 1954, p. 70.
4 *Corr.* II, Conard, 1926, p. 403.
5 *Corr.* I, p. 142.
6 *Corr.* I, p. 270.
7 *Œuvres complètes*, Bibliothèque de la Pléiade, 1951, p. 53.
8 Ibid., p. 1487.
9 In *Gloses sur Mallarmé*, Paris 1945, pp. 112–65.
10 Editions du Seuil, Paris, 1961, pp. 134ff; see also the fine discussion scattered throughout R. G. Cohn's *Toward the Poems of Mallarmé*, Berkeley and Los Angeles, 1965.
11 *OC*, p. 1415.
12 *OC*, p. 37.
13 Op. cit., pp. 165ff.
14 Op. cit., p. 248.
15 On the first page of his autobiography *Si le grain ne meurt.*

RIMBAUD'S INTERNAL LANDSCAPE

In several poems of the collection called *Derniers Vers* Rimbaud sounds as if he were looking at a broader sweep of outdoor scene than he permits his reader to see, referring to individual features of what can only be a landscape without our having more than the dimmest of notions of their relation to the total picture.[1] Since, despite the immediacy we sometimes feel, he can hardly have recorded his visions on the spot—surely he did not write 'Entends comme brame . . .' by moonlight and in a fog—these landscapes have to be internal, at least in the sense that they are stored in his imagination. Hence the present title. Not even in 'Mémoire,' of course, does he reproduce the whole picture, but he speaks repeatedly as if he saw more than he needs say: where there is a 'vieille cour d'honneur', for example, there must necessarily be other remains of a château.

Doubtless this observation is of only limited interest. Relatively few of Rimbaud's poems are affected by it. But it may not be too much to hope that an awareness of this aspect of his practice may lead to readings of several—including 'Mémoire', 'Larme', 'Michel et Christine', and even the frustrating 'Entends comme brame . . .'—that will satisfy without offending common sense. For such a thing to happen, however, we should have to revise certain notions about the value of an important department of Rimbaud scholarship, namely our unflagging effort to identify allusions.

Not that the poems are not richly allusive. Too many sensitive readers of Rimbaud have testified to the contrary. Thus Jacques Rivière long ago reported the feeling that the poet often addresses not the reader but some real, though to us invisible, companion at his side; and one gathers that C. A. Hackett, who discusses Rivière's intuition very attentively, also shares it.[2] And surely no one who has made the journey to Charleville-Mézières for the single purpose of placing himself at what he imagines to be the scene of 'Mémoire' will deny either the presence of allusions in the poems or the legitimacy of studying them.

And certainly not I, who am persuaded that the old peasants in 'Comédie de la soif' must be the family of Vitalie Cuif Rimbaud, and that 'Honte' alludes to the increasing unpleasantness of the relationship between Verlaine, Rimbaud, and Verlaine's family. One loses nothing by knowing that the colour of the iron-stained water of the Semoy may justify identifying this stream as the 'rivière de Cassis', and there may even be profit in poring over maps to trace back tributaries in the hope of discovering how Rimbaud could think of a rivulet in the Ardennes as 'cette jeune Oise'.

But it may be well to recognise that there are various kinds of allusion, and they are not equally valuable. Some are social and biographical: the 'amis' whom Rimbaud addresses in 'Comédie de la soif' almost have to be the drinking companions he frequented in Paris; 'Bruxelles' and 'Jeune Ménage', as well as 'Honte', must evoke the affair with Verlaine. A failure to recognise allusions of this sort could manifestly end by obscuring connexions between the *Derniers Vers* and *Une Saison en enfer*, or authorise assuming that Rimbaud's references to thirst are consistently allegorical. But another series of allusions is geographical or topographical in nature, and these, I would maintain, are often not only of dubious helpfulness in reading the poems but also could serve at times to deflect us from satisfactory readings.

Both sorts of allusion present themselves in 'Mémoire'—which, if they did not do so, would be a relatively easy poem to interpret. The beginning is almost pure landscape: river, retaining walls, flowers, brilliant light, a predominance of golden yellow, and, in the stream bed below a bridge, the sumptuous body of a woman formed by the shadowy movement of the weeds. But now the eye moves out into the field where the Black Woman, standing too tall, tramples the white flowers; whoever she is, she is a blot on the landscape. Presently someone—a male figure associated with whiteness—will depart over the shoulder of a hill, as if in flight. Then, when the observing eye returns to the stream, the light has changed; so has the season, as I read the poem; there is no more delight in the scene and no more mention of the shadowy woman in the stream; images of melancholy frustration dominate the closing lines.

Once the black female and the white male have appeared in the poem, the need to establish the biographical allusion becomes imperious. By identifying them with the poet's mother in the first case and with his father, his brother, or even himself in the other, most interpretations turn the piece into a sort of family allegory. All is golden harmony until Vitalie invades the scene and drives away who-ever the corresponding male is alleged to be. The action is, quite naturally, taken to motivate the change in the poet's mood. It must be admitted that this interpretation leaves certain subsequent difficulties intact, and does nothing at all to explain why the child in the boat at the end of the poem, unable to reach either the blue or the yellow flower because of the way the boat is tied up, should seem so much more juvenile than the voice in the early strophes.

Were these human figures not in the poem, attention would not be diverted from the fact that 'Mémoire' follows a pattern that appears in Rimbaud's work as early as the 'Bateau ivre'. A first moment of pleasure and of heightened sensual and emotional excitement gives way to one in which the speaker's state has become less euphoric and less satisfactory to him. In most of the instances the change occurs without specific reference to time or place, and the pattern seems almost an archetype. Here, however, some specification is literally forced upon us. The intrusion of the human figures makes identifying allusions mandatory—and somewhat changes the nature of the poem.

For if this black woman has to be Madame Rimbaud, not only does the corresponding male have to be someone connected with her life, but also the scene of the episode must be near Charleville. In other words, biographical allusion must be sustained by geographical allusion also; the river must be the Meuse, and the setting must be located at a point where the stone wall that confines the stream could be momentarily confused by the observing eye with something reminiscent of ancient battlements. No doubt such a reading can be defended, but at the cost of reducing the poem itself to a recital of an anecdote in the life of a family.

I do not reject this reading of this particular poem, but I do experience a feeling that it may lead to too much emphasis upon geographical allusions—real or imputed—in other poems of the *Derniers Vers*. There are, for example, other references to châteaux in this collection, including the indirect one in 'La Rivière de Cassis', the inferential one in 'Michel et Christine' mentioned above, and the sudden, ecstatic (and inexplicable) cry in 'Age d'or',

O joli château![3]

It is noteworthy that in three of the four poems in which these references appear the speaker begins in a euphoric tone which changes abruptly with a change of the lighting, brought about by a change in the weather.

This conjunction of mood and image seems to me more important than the possibility that the mention of a château may place the poet in a given spot at a more or less verifiable time. Even the late Suzanne Bernard, the most circumspect as well as faithful of editors, accepts Delahaye's suggestion that the 'rivière de cassis' is in fact the Semoy because she recalls that there is a château in its valley to which the poem may refer.[4] In her faithfulness she could, of course, do nothing else. But the significance of the reference may be, rather, that it occurs in a poem in which, in spite of his anxiety about the threatening 'paysan matois', the poet takes comfort in the presence of the rooks which will protect him.

I have insisted on references to châteaux in these poems largely for convenience: whoever is following this discussion is likely to remember them. But they are far from being the only fragments of landscape in the *Derniers Vers* whose presence amounts to more than mere geographical allusion. And again I must seem less grateful than I feel to the late Madame Bernard.

She remarks[5] that the references to the mist in the first and second quatrains of 'Larme' may place the scene in the neighbourhood of Roche because several other poems refer to the 'brouillard ardennais'. She adds, in a subsequent note, that the scene changes from 'ardennais' to 'exotique'. That it becomes exotic cannot be contested, and no one is likely to deny that green glades, nut trees green with spring, or even perhaps stretches of grass with no flowers in them, are to be found in the Ardennes. But it would be equally impossible to deny that such scenes occur in many other regions north of the Loire. Or that overcast skies and pleasant mists are characteristic of the same far-flung regions.

The mist—'brouillard d'après-midi tiède et vert'—could figure in the poem for reasons that are not geographical in the least. To the extent that 'Larme' is 'about' anything whatever, it is, like 'Mémoire', about a change in the poet's affective state. He is in an extremely rural setting, so remote that not even cattle find their way into it, and squatting (or kneeling) among briars where he is about to drink something (or perhaps already drinking it). The scene is one of complete calm and peace, until the one event in the poem takes place and changes everything: 'l'orage chassa le ciel . . .'. The warm mist is swept away, and the quiet landscape gives way to a turbulent and chaotic vision of which the elements cannot be present in the imagination simultaneously but must succeed each other; movement replaces stasis, hardness replaces softness, icicles replace tender greens, winter replaces spring. The role of the mist here would seem plain enough: it is part of a scene in which the poet is affected pleasurably; in fact, it may be the controlling element, since when it is blown away the light changes and both mood and scene are disrupted.

In 'Larme', and of course in 'Mémoire', we are dealing with narrative; the event is in the past, and whatever bit of landscape is associated with it is thus part of an emotion recollected in some degree of tranquillity. 'Michel et Christine', on the other hand, is presented dramatically; there is no feeling that the present tense is historical; we are placed beside the poet to watch the event take place. But the difference in time-perspective does not affect the role that the fragments of landscape are called upon to play.

The central happening, in this instance, is again a change of light, although it is brought about not by the dissipating of a mist but by the onset of a shower. The change has begun as the poem opens: clouds have started to block the sun. There is time only for a glimpse of the setting, but the glimpse is enough to reveal its nature: country roads now coming into shadow, the 'cour d'honneur' of the château not otherwise mentioned, willows, briars, and the literally pastoral touch of the flock of lambs with their shepherd.[6] Before our eyes, as the light reddens, these give way to a wild series of images that melt into each other and metamorphose as if obedient only to free association. (Attempts to account for the soldiers, the appearance of Christ at the end, and the names Michel and Christine, have to date been gallant failures.) Much in this poems remains to defeat us. But the fact remains that what we do grasp of the poem comes from our rapid recognition of that first, tranquil landscape.

In other words, I am suggesting that the bits and pieces of landscape in such poems are not merely decorative, not 'nature poetry'. Even less is their importance that they put Rimbaud in a specific place at a specific time. These water courses, fens, evergreens, nut trees, and willows, briar patches, stone parapets, châteaux, soft skies, and mists may in a sense be *ardennais*, but not in a sense useful to us. (And is it not strange that this poet of the Ardennes so rarely mentions hills?) To call these bits of landscape objective correlatives may be to attribute to T. S. Eliot something he did not quite have in mind, but their function is far less to place the poem geographically than to objectify an emotion. If one agrees with C. A. Hackett that the distance from Rimbaud's subconscious to his conscious, poetic mind was exceedingly short, one may wonder how aware the poet was of the use he was making of them.[7] But not question that such was the use he made.

Believing that an awareness of them on our part may help in reading some of Rimbaud's most intractable poems, I propose using 'Entends comme brame . . .' as a test case. Surely the test is a real one: this piece is often dismissed as pure poetic babble or, more charitably, as a failure to *dire l'indicible*, and, to increase the difficulty, the only element associated with landscape and emotion in the other poems to appear here is the mist in which everything else is bathed. My hypothesis is that with this one element, if one keeps in mind other works in which a change in a mood—one objectified in a landscape—is motivated by a change in weather, 'Entends comme brame . . .' can be brought to give up at least an incomplete meaning.

An indulgent reader, aware of the difficulties involved, will regard what follows as a series of suggestions which he is free to accept or reject.

Entends comme brame
près des acacias
en avril la rame
viride du pois!

Dans sa vapeur nette,
vers Phœbé! tu vois
s'agiter la tête
de saints d'autrefois . . .

Loin des claires meules
des caps, des beaux toits,
ces chers anciens veulent
ce philtre sournois . . .

Or ni fériale
ni astrale! n'est
la brume qu'exhale
ce nocturne effet.

Néanmoins ils restent,
—Sicile, Allemagne,
dans ce brouillard triste
et blémi, justement!

The poem presents such a variety of difficulties that one feels true sympathy with interpreters who have preferred the reading 'bois' for 'pois' at the end of the first strophe. The former would be infinitely more convenient: woods are indeed so noisy in spring that 'brame' would then be nothing worse than a disturbing hyperbole, and we could side-step the question whether or not peas would be climbing their supporting sticks, in the Ardennes, during the month of April.[8] Unfortunately, the reading that has survived is 'pois', and meanwhile our attention may have been deflected from the first of three mentions of mist, in the fifth line.

But we should not overlook the obvious: this is a poem about a misty evening and a 'nocturne effet' in which mist plays an important part; and we know that in other poems (see 'Larme') Rimbaud finds mists pleasant. The mist is rising toward the moon, but not thickly enough to obscure it. Indeed, the adjective 'nette', which has baffled readers for good cause, may be understood as the conclusion of a process of perception: something in the air has, after hesitation, been recognised as water vapour. This vapour will thicken. In the second reference it is called 'brume'.

Again the adjectives may baffle us, but fortunately the statement is negative. And if it is neither 'fériale' nor 'astrale', may it not be that the speaker simply recognises that, despite his pleasure and perhaps excitement, this is a quite normal mist and destined, like any quickly formed mist, to continue thickening?

Thus in the third reference, where he calls it a 'brouillard', it is qualified as 'triste/et blémi'. It would seem that something has spoiled the 'nocturne effet': the fog, at first translucent has become opaque. The moonlight (from 'Phœbe') can no longer mix with it. The mist is now no more than an impenetrable, soggy blanket. His joy has not survived the accumulation of moisture in the atmosphere.

But who, or what, are the 'saints d'autrefois', the 'chers anciens' whom he points out with the 'vois-tu' that reminds one of Jacques Rivière's observation about the poet's invisible companion? In 'L'Alchimie du verbe' he will report that, when he was writing *Les Derniers Vers*, he was feeding his fevered imagination from various trivial sources including, enigmatically, 'dessus de portes'. Could not these last refer to *tympans*, those panels over church doors so often ornamented with the heads of Romanesque figures? If this is possible, then it may be worth suggesting that the 'filtre sournois' they would like to share is the mist itself.

This then could be a poem on a familiar pattern: the joyful nocturne has faded. But this time, for once, delight has not departed completely: even when the fog has become sad 'they' somehow remain and 'ils' should refer to the 'chers anciens'. And with them, it would seem, is another source of enchantment—the old legends he mentions in 'L'Alchimie du verbe' he thought of as coming from Germany and, perhaps, Sicily.

Of course it would be folly to force upon such fragile, inchoate poems more meaning than they can hold. But nothing proves that any of them, even this one, is completely meaningless. In short, an awareness of the landscape Rimbaud seems to have kept in his imagination may reveal suggestions in a poetry that we value, above all, for its suggestiveness.

Harvard   W. M. FROHOCK

NOTES

1 I am elaborating here an observation that appeared first in my *Rimbaud's Poetic Practice* (Cambridge, Mass., Harvard University Press, 1963), p. 158. In the intervening years I have become so persuaded of the personal and even idiosyncratic nature of interpretations of Rimbaud that I have abandoned the academic-impersonal mode for the first person, meaning by doing so to emphasise that my views are those of one, necessarily fallible, individual.

2 *Le Lyrisme de Rimbaud* (Paris, Nizet et Bastard, 1938), p. 65. He cites Rivière's *Rimbaud* as published in the NRF of July and August 1914.

3 I have not included the 'château mouillé' in 'Comédie de la soif', the 'tour' in 'Chanson de la plus haute tour', or the mention in 'O saisons, ô châteaux', because not entirely sure, at this writing, about the emotion associated with them.

4 In Rimbaud, *Œuvres*, Paris, Garnier, 1961, p. 430, n. 1.

5 Ibid., p. 429, n. 2. It should be added that Mme Bernard was entirely aware that this poem was much more than a mere evocation of a landscape.

6 I am at a loss to identify the 'aqueducs' in the second stanza, unless, needing three syllables, Rimbaud uses the word for 'canaux'.

7 So, at least, I interpret the argument of both *Le Lyrisme de Rimbaud* and *Rimbaud l'enfant*, Paris, Corti, 1947. I find the argument more persuasive with each re-reading.

8 More geography! The date for planting green peas varies with climate. In almost any latitude, however, this vegetable is among the earliest to be safely planted; the traditional date for planting the first crop in the not unrigorous weather of southern New England is 17 March; I have seen well-developed pea-vines growing in northern France (though not in the Ardennes) in the first week of April. If these in the poem must absolutely be *petits pois ardennais* they can indeed have been climbing their supports before the end of the month, given a decent season, and a farmer willing to risk something for a profitably early *cueillette* might have had them doing so several weeks before. But then again Rimbaud may just possibly have seen peas growing, in a fog, elsewhere than near Roche.

A NOTE ON *CINQ GRANDES ODES:* SOME AMBIGUITIES OF ORDER AND ADVENTURE

Order is an equivocal term, as is to a rather lesser degree adventure. Order may be barren, a mere convention, a timid conformity. Adventure may be only a disruptive breaking away. But order may also be a difficult patterning of a violent movement, the making sense of chaos; and adventure may be the pursuit of the worth-while, the staking of one's all on an activity whose outcome remains unknown, unpredictable. It is this latter sense of order and adventure that we find in *Cinq Grandes Odes*, though not in quite so simple and straightforward a relationship. In Claudel the poetic and the spiritual are indeed inseparable, since it is a basic tenet of the poet that his creative word participates in the creative Word of God:

> Ainsi quand tu parles, ô poëte dans une enumération délectable
>   Proférant de chaque chose le nom.
> Comme un père tu l'appelles mystérieusement dans son principe,
>   et selon que jadis
> Tu participas à sa création, tu coopères à son existence!
> Toute parole une répétition.
> Tel est le chant que tu chantes dans le silence, et telle est la
>   bienheureuse harmonie
> Dont tu nourris en toi-même le rassemblement et la dissolution.
> Et ainsi,

> O poëte, je ne dirai point que tu reçois de la nature aucune leçon,
>   c'est toi qui lui imposes ton ordre . . . (29)[1]

Creation is the ordering of chaos, whether cosmic or verbal. It may be said that all poetic activity is at one and the same time an adventure and the creation of an order. That is true at least of Claudel's odes, but the adventure is at least threefold and the order twofold. There is the human adventure that began on the *Ernest-Simmons* in 1900 and ended, insofar as it ever ended, with the departure of the woman for Belgium in 1904. There is also the adventure that began on Christmas Day, 1886, the discovery of God's existence, and the poetic adventure through which these other two adventures are to be merged to become one. Indeed, the odes reveal the discovery, most thoroughly explored in the fourth ode, that the writing of poetry and spiritual life are inseparably bound together, that is, to be authentic, poetry must express the innermost being of the poet, and that innermost life, to be itself authentic, must always move towards an ever more complete self-emptying. The poet realises that there is only one adventure, the search for and discovery of God and all that is associated with this, the task of redeeming and transforming the world. Ultimately he is to realise that the transformation of the self, the transfiguration which appears with such startling rapidity at the end of *Partage de Midi*, is what is needed of him. As there is fundamentally only one adventure, so is there only one order, that of God's design, which Claudel considers it to be the poet's function to perceive and express. That is the aim of his poetry. There is the verbal order that the poet imposes on the disparate elements that he brings together and there is God's redemptive order for the salvation of the world. The difficulty arises with Claudel's claim that his poetic conferring of order on the world partakes essentially of the divine order, that his creative word is really an extension of the redemptive activity of the creative Word of God. The odes clearly express the notion that the poet's conception of order, the attempted redemption of the world through the ordering of poetry, was purely external, therefore superficial. That conception has to be rejected. Indeed, it was destroyed for him by the encounter with the woman whom we may call Erato or Ysé. In a sense, there was a period of disorder in the poet's life between 1900 and 1905. But this was also an adventure, an adventure fraught with extraordinary ambiguity, an adventure that brought new life to the poet's art. It is certainly not true to say that Claudel's finest poetry coincides necessarily with his most spiritual aspiration. In fact, in the intensely personal poetry of the odes the aspiration of the spirit, the call of a woman now gone, and poetic creativity are closely linked together. The odes bear witness to the painful restoration of order in the poet's life, an order at once spiritual and poetic, since Claudel sees no distinction between the two. Yet, though the order that we see emerging in the later odes may be more authentic than the first rather external notion of order that the poet had, it may not entirely satisfy us. The largely conjugal order of the fifth ode, for instance, may seem not only cold and joyless but also poetically unmoving and spiritually unenlightening.

In a sense, 'Les Muses' is a preparatory ode, the one in which too purely a poetic order is sought and indeed achieved. Certainly, Claudel succeeds in ordering the most violent movements, the intense meaningful activity of all the nine muses brought startlingly to life from their sarcophagus, led by Terpsichore whose arm is 'Tout impatient de la fureur de frapper la première mesure'(17). The whole poem is a violent act of parturition, the mysterious upheaval of the whole being from whom a new life bursts forth:

> La clameur noire de toute la vie nouée par le nombril dans la commotion
> de la base,
> S'ouvre, l'accès
> Faisant sauter la clôture, le souffle de lui-même
> Violentant les mâchoires coupantes,
> Le frémissant Novenaire avec un cri! (19)

One may see in this bursting forth of a new life in parturition almost a prophecy of the adventure to come, the disruptive and yet extra-ordinarily creative appearance of Erato in the final verses, but at first the adventure is solely poetic:

> Toute route perdue! sans relâche pourchassé et secouru
> Par les dieux chauds sur la piste, sans que tu voies rien d'eux que
> parfois
> La nuit un rayon d'or sur la Voile, et dans la splendeur du matin, un
> moment,
> Une face radieuse aux yeux bleus, . . .
> . . . toute route à suivre nous ennuie! toute échelle à escalader!
> . . .
> O mon âme! il ne faut concerter aucun plan! ô mon âme sauvage, il faut
> nous tenir libres et prêts,
> Comme les immenses bandes fragiles d'hirondelles quand sans voix
> retentit l'appel automnal!
> . . .
> Que mon vers ne soit rien d'esclave! mais tel que l'aigle marin qui s'est
> jeté sur un grand poisson,
> Et l'on ne voit rien qu'un éclatant tourbillon d'ailes et l'éclaboussement
> de l'écume! (20-22)

Yet, even in 'Les Muses', the poet recognises his affinity with Divine Wisdom participating in the creation of the cosmos. His poem confers order on the world, making meaningful relationships of the apparently disparate elements. It is at the point when he is claiming that he will reveal the meaning of the created world that the sudden rupture of the poem occurs: '—Je laisse cette tâche à la terre; je refuis vers l'espace ouvert et vide' (30), that brusque change of subject and tone which André Vachon connects with Claudel's discovery of the lack of a monastic vocation.[2] Be that as it may, however, the order we have seen in the earlier part of the ode, the careful categorising of the nine muses and the assignment to each of her rightful role in the birth of

the poem, this skilful renewal of an old mythology in the contained
violence of somewhat triumphal rhetoric, breaks down. Erato comes
to life with a directness, an intensity, a frenetic quality, new to the
poem. The order, it seems, was only provisional; it is now vanished:

> O mon amie! car le monde n'était plus là
> Pour nous assigner notre place dans la combinaison de son mouvement
>   multiplié,
> Mais décollés de la terre, nous étions seuls l'un avec l'autre,
> Habitants de cette noire miette mouvante, noyés,
> Perdus dans le pur Espace, là où le sol même est lumière. (32)

Human contact, her hand on his, has done its work. As a symbol of
the destruction of order, the hair of the woman unwinds and is
loosed in the wind:

> Toi-même, amie, tes grands cheveux blonds dans le vent de la mer,
> Tu n'as pas su les tenir bien serrés sur ta tête; ils s'effondrent! les
>   lourds anneaux
> Roulent sur tes épaules, la grande chose joconde
> S'enlève, tout part dans le clair de la lune! (32)

Before the light of love, the light of Christ, shines again, the poet
plunges through the fire of passion. Images of fire dominate the
closing lines of the poem:

> Et chaque soir, à l'arrière, à la place où nous avions laissé le rivage, vers
>   l'Ouest.
> Nous allions retrouver la même conflagration
> Nourrie de tout le présent bondé, la Troie du monde réel en flammes!
> Et moi, comme la mèche allumée d'une mine sous la terre, ce feu
>   secret me ronge,
> Ne finira-t-il point par flamber dans le vent? qui contiendra la grande
>   flamme humaine?
>   . . .
> Le hourra qui prend en toi de toutes parts comme de l'or, comme du
>   feu dans le fourrage! (32-3)

In this adventure of the flesh and the soul, the poet's known world is
destroyed. All has to be rediscovered in a rediscovered order, though
it does not necessarily follow that every aspect of that order is fully
authentic. Reaction is customarily fraught with a certain extremism.

Adventure is a dominant theme of the second ode, though the
adventure is now lifted from the carnal presence to the invisible
spirit; the ode was written in 1906. The sea, which made its appearance with Erato, 'mon amie sur le navire', in the closing lines of 'Les
Muses', remains in 'L'Esprit et l'eau' a symbol of freedom, but also

of ubiquity: 'Je partage la liberté de la mer omniprésente!' (38). Yet, though the adventure of the spirit in its all-embracing quest is symbolised by the sea, breaking down the material earth, nonetheless, as always with Claudel, the creative spirit of the poet, sharing something of God's creative spirit breathing on the waters, brings order and meaning, limiting therefore the longing for freedom:

> Que m'importe la porte ouverte, si je n'ai la clef?
> Ma liberté, si je n'en suis le propre maître?
> Je regarde toutes choses, et voyez que je n'en suis pas l'esclave, mais le dominateur. (40)

There is a certain contradictoriness in these odes until we reach the last one. The verse-prayer of: 'Je suis libre, délivrez-moi de la liberté!' (40), typifies the poet's dilemma, the difficulty, the seeming impossibility, of being one with God, of sharing perfectly in the god-manhood brought within human reach by the Incarnation:

> Je vois bien des manières de ne pas être, mais il n'y a qu'une manière seule
> D'être, qui est d'être en vous, qui est vous-même! (40)

At this point of time, the poet has not yet seen what he will regard as the solution for himself, but the conclusion of the fifth ode, the containment of the divine within the finite, the presence of the transcendent within four walls, is already foreseen in this second ode:

> O mon Dieu, je la vois, la clef maintenant qui délivre,
> Ce n'est point celle qui ouvre, mais celle-là qui ferme!
> Vous êtes ici avec moi!
> Il est fermé par votre volonté comme par un mur et par votre puissance comme par une très forte enceinte!
> . . .
> Je pourrais aux quatre points cardinaux relever les quatre dimensions de la Cité.
> Il est fermé, et voici soudain que toutes choses à mes yeux
> Ont acquis la proportion et la distance. (42)

Much of 'L'Esprit et l'eau' is a magnificent prayer for a godlike spirituality, for freedom from the contingent, for freedom, as he says, from the weight of this inert matter (46). Through the symbol of water, the water that God separated from the earth in the story of the Creation, the baptismal water that brings with it the life of the Holy Spirit, the figurative water that man desires in order to quench his spiritual thirst, the hypostatic water of the two natures united in Christ, human and divine (48), the poet poignantly expresses his

desire of total life in Christ. Water brings with it, however, the
memory of the mountain side, with the hot spring gushing forth,
where the poet hid his grief in 1905,[3] and of the tears that were shed
at the thought that the beloved woman would never again be seen in
this life (49). In this death of bodily separation, the poet sees in himself the absence of God, the emptiness of all else:

> Maintenant jaillissent
> Les sources profondes, jaillit mon âme salée, éclate en un grand cri la
>   poche profonde de la pureté séminale!
> Maintenant je me suis parfaitement clair, tout
> Amèrement clair, et il n'y a plus rien en moi
> Qu'une parfaite privation de Vous seul! (50)

The symbol of water is here used even of the depths of the inmost
being, uniting in its liquidity, its near-ubiquity, every element in the
poem.

There is evident throughout this second ode too sharp a distinction
between God and man, or in reality woman, between the spirit and
the flesh. The year 1906 is still too close to the pain of loss, the loss
not so much of God as of the woman. The words of Peter at the
Transfiguration of Christ which Claudel makes his own: 'Seigneur, il
fait bon pour nous en ce lieu' (51), like the transformation of Ysé in the
the final act of *Partage de Midi* and the transfiguration which seems to
be implied in the closing lines of the ode, possibly that of the woman
now speaking with the voice of Divine Wisdom (52), occur perhaps
rather too easily in 'L'Esprit et l'eau'. Darkness returns in the final
section of the fourth ode. Yet these fluctuations of mood but
emphasise the personal, human, quality of these poems, the movements of the spirit with the rebellious stirrings of the heart and flesh.
The last twenty verses or so of this second ode clearly reveal that the
one great adventure, the transfiguration of man in the love of Christ,
has at least begun. Whether the verses are to be attributed to the
resurrected Christ or to the woman perceived as the voice of Divine
Wisdom, matters not at all. The voice speaks to the lover as much as
to the poet, for they are one:

> Il y a bien des bruits dans le monde et cependant l'amant au cœur
>   déchiré entend seul au haut de l'arbre le frémissement de la feuille
>   sibylline.
> . . . .
> Pourquoi donc seul l'entends-tu? Parce que seule soumise à une mesure
>   divine
> Parce qu'elle n'est tout entière que mesure même,
> La mesure sainte, libre, toute-puissante, créatrice! (51-2)

It would seem that the heart-rent lover is particularly well-equipped to hear and understand that order which is God's. Erato or Rose, whatever one wish to call her, she who brought disorder, the disorder of adulterous love, has been transformed now into the supreme order, Love itself:

> O ami, je ne suis point un homme ni une femme, je suis l'amour qui est
> au-dessus de toute parole!
> Je vous salue, mon frère bien-aimé.
> Ne me touchez point! ne cherche pas à prendre ma main (52).

She is no longer, for the poet, of this world. Her body is glorified, untouchable. She leads the way for the poet, as Beatrice did for Dante, as Prouhèze was to do for Rodrigue in *Le Soulier de satin*. So does Claudel in this ode ultimately humanise the rather harsh aspiration towards God alone which dominates the poem at one point and at the same time divinise the beloved, making of the earthly adventure a spiritual one, foreseeing already to some degree the order towards which he was moving.

There is no order more definitive, in many ways, at least ideally, than conjugal life, especially conjugal life that flowers into family life. Only Coventry Patmore has celebrated family life in poetry more fully, though in verse much flatter and more trivial, than Claudel. 'Magnificat' is poetically, in the opinion of the writer, one of the finest of the odes, in spite of some bombast and some unpleasant invective, for there is a complete merging of the liturgical and the personal in this hymn of praise and thanksgiving. The verses of the *Magnificat* itself and the birth of the Christ-Child, intermingled with the poet's joy in the birth of his own child and the memory of the birth of the new man in himself, also at Christmas, in 1886, clearly demonstrate that the human adventure, the life to be lived Godwards on earth, and the divine adventure, the taking of the manhood unto God, the life of Christ on earth which the Liturgy brings before us in the theophany of the Eucharist, are one and the same adventure. That the adventure is not purely a personal one, but that of the whole of the material world, for which the Redemption has to be actualised, the poet repeats again and again:

> Car ce n'est pas de ce corps seul qu'il me faut venir à bout, mais de ce
> monde brut tout entier, fournir
> De quoi comprendre et le dissoudre et l'assimiler
> En vous et ne plus voir rien
> Réfractaire à votre lumière en moi! (61-2)

IHF

Yet, in this third ode, as in the earlier ones and in 'La Muse qui est la Grâce', this striving towards pure spirit is inevitably followed by the feeling of acedia, the vanity of all effort. The memory of the woman as she was in her person intervenes, if only to be cast aside, at the level of consciousness: 'Ne me parlez plus de la rose! aucun fruit n'a plus de goût pour moi' (62). In this overharsh conception of divine love, where God is seen apart from mankind, inevitably He is equated, not with warmth, but with cold:

> Voici la rigueur de l'hiver, adieu, ô bel été, la transe et le saisissement de l'immobilité.
> Je préfère l'absolu. Ne me rendez pas à moi-même.
> Voici le froid inexorable, voici Dieu seul! (62)

The freedom of the spirit, likened to the open sea in the second ode, is once more subjected to what the poet takes to be the divine order, God's determining plan: 'Heureux non pas qui est libre, mais celui que vous déterminez comme une flèche dans le carquois!' (64). The poet's new role of father, in which God shares with him his divine fatherhood, brings him irrevocably into an order from which there is no going back, for he is ordained for an end which he does not know (66). 'La passion païenne' has given place to 'la volonté raisonnable et ordonnée' (67).

One of the dominant images in 'Magnificat' is that of the priest. The poet holds his child in his arms, the real, living image of man now raised to the godhead by the Incarnation, just as the priest holds in his hands the bread of the Eucharist, the Body of Christ (65). The image is so dominant that the ode ends with the evocation of the priest raising his eyes to the host in the monstrance at Benediction and the mingling of the *Nunc dimittis* and the *Magnificat*. The final section of the poem, with its images of light, of the sun rising, of refreshing waters gushing forth, in the setting of the basic analogy with Joshua entering the Promised Land, finely expresses once more the poet's function to evangelise the world by his word, to give back what he has received in a spirit of thanksgiving, to make all things new in the poetically creative word.

The familiar symbols of sea, opening doors and opening windows, introduce in 'La Muse qui est la Grâce' the continuing fluctuation of self-offering to God and the poetic evangelisation of the world by the word which we already see in the previous odes, but in this fourth ode these two alternating modes become completely identified. The poet comes to the final realisation that there is no alternative to total consecration to God, an understanding that brings with it a temporary resurgence of the old passion in the closing verses of the poem, which are the most poignantly moving of the ode. The order to which the poet has aspired, purely as a poet bringing creative form to the chaos of the world's diversity, is seen to be his own imperfect conception, to which he desperately clings:

> Laisse-moi être nécessaire! laisse-moi remplir fortement une place reconnue et approuvée,
> Comme un constructeur de chemins de fer, on sait qu'il ne sert pas à rien, comme un fondateur de syndicats! (76)

He would like his adventure to remain poetic, the writing of the poem of mankind freed from chance, assigned his rightful place in the poet's re-created world (78). The light that he has seen in previous odes, the cold absolute of God alone, here he rejects as being beyond his reach:

> Cette lumière qui n'est pas pour les fils de la Terre!
> Cette lumière-ci est pour moi, si faible qu'il lui faut la nuit pour qu'elle m'éclaire, pareille à la lampe de l'habitacle!
> Et au dehors sont les ténèbres et le Chaos qui n'a point reçu l'Evangile. (82)

The image of fire which dominates the closing verses of 'Les Muses' reappears in this ode with a new meaning, the fire not of passion but of the Holy Spirit:

> Que parles-tu de fondation? la pierre seule n'est pas une fondation, la flamme aussi est une fondation,
> La flamme dansante et boiteuse, la flamme biquante et claquante de sa double langue inégale! (85)

The cold absolute here becomes a new warmth. The voice of divine Grace, identified now for all time for the poet with the muse of poetry, in the sense that poetry must be for him the expression of God's grace, tells him that fire alone unites, that fire which burns up all that is self:

> C'est le feu pur et simple qui fait de plusieurs choses une seule.
> Connais ma jalousie qui est plus terrible que la mort!
> C'est la mort qui appelle toutes choses à la vie.
>
> Comme la parole a tiré toutes choses du néant, afin qu'elles meurent,
> C'est ainsi que tu es né afin que tu puisses mourir en moi.
> Comme le soleil appelle à la naissance toutes les choses visibles.
> Ainsi le soleil de l'esprit, ainsi l'esprit pareil à un foudre crucifié
> Appelle toutes choses à la connaissance et voici qu'elles lui sont présentes à la fois. (88-9)

The image of crucified lightning gives a maximised expression to the
intensity of suffering and spiritual coming to life that the action of the
Spirit induces in His life-giving creativity. The image of parturition
so dominant in the first ode in a purely poetic context is here transformed into a spiritual birth-giving, with no less pain and violence.
The final peroration of divine Grace culminates in a blaze of fire
imagery:

> Voici les sceaux de Dieu rompus qui s'en vient juger la terre par le feu!
> Voici que du ciel et de la terre détruite il ne se fait plus qu'un seul nid
> dans la flamme,
> Et l'infatigable cri de la cigale remplit la fournaise assourdissante!
> Ainsi le soleil de l'esprit est comme une cigale dans le soleil de Dieu. (89)

That destruction of the world that took place with the encounter with
Erato, also in a blaze of fire imagery, at the end of 'Les Muses', left
something of the self which has to be destroyed by a more fully
re-creative fire than the passionate love of a companion who seemed
predestined. But, for the moment, the poet takes refuge from the
blaze of the informing Spirit in darkness, the darkness of a purely
earthly memory of a woman's love (90). This is the last time that she
is evoked in the odes and it is also the last time, in the opinion of the
writer, that Claudel succeeds in these poems in moving us deeply and,
except in the final verses of the last ode, in achieving a high degree of
poetic intensity.

The poet's enclosure within a necessary order is firmly asserted by
his wife, his guardian, at the opening of 'La Maison fermée':

> Ce qu'est la clôture pour un moine, est le sacrement pour lui qui fait
> une seule chair de nous deux.
> La poutre de notre maison n'est pas de cèdre, les boiseries de notre
> chambre ne sont pas de cyprès,
> Mais goûte l'ombre, mon mari, de la demeure bénite entre ces murs
> épais qui nous protègent de l'air extérieur et du froid.
> Ton intérêt n'est plus au dehors, mais en toi-même là où n'était aucun
> objet,
> Entends, comme une vie qui souffre division, le battement de notre
> triple cœur.
> Voici que tu n'es plus libre et que tu as fait part à d'autres de ta vie,
> Et que tu es soumis à la nécessité comme un dieu
> Inséparable sans qui l'on ne peut vivre. (93)

Advocates of communal living might see in these verses a certain
indication of a selfish self-sufficiency in the exclusiveness of family
life. However, the poet sees this life of man, wife and first-born child

as a God-willed unity. It is as if, in the new-found domestic safety of marriage, he were anxious to repudiate the woman whose inspiration plays so large a part in these odes as a whole, either positively, in remembered love or the pain of separation, or negatively, in the desire to forget in the love of God alone. The one recollection of his recent past that this ode embodies is cold, abstract, impersonal:

> Jadis j'ai connu la passion, mais maintenant je n'ai plus que celle de la patience et du désir
> De connaître Dieu dans sa fixité et d'acquérir la vérité par l'attention et chaque chose qui est toutes les autres en la recréant avec son nom intelligible dans ma pensée. (94)

His poetic task of bringing God to mankind through his creative word is again developed at length in 'La Maison fermée', though with the emphasis now on the need for enclosure, for communication with God to be established. The open sea of 'L'Esprit et l'eau' seems far away: 'Point de Dieu pour toi sans une église et toute vie commence par la cellule' (99). The poet repeats the Gospel injunction to pray in privacy with an exclusive finality which disconcerts: 'Entends l'Evangile qui conseille de fermer la porte de ta chambre' (100). The adventure is now purely interior, an adventure within the mind and heart of the poet, enclosed within his four-walled house, the abode of his family. Adventure and order are firmly one. God's creation of the world is now entirely seen in terms of conservation and order:

> Elle [temperance] est cela en nous qui nous maintient avec un art secret au milieu de tout changement
> Le même; ouvrière de l'accord imperturbable et cela en nous
> Qui conserve, à la manière de Dieu quand il crée. (103-4)

We are indeed a long way from 'l'esprit liquide et lascif' (36) of the second ode, as from the echo of *Proverbs* in the first ode, where in the creation of the world Divine Wisdom was daily God's delight, rejoicing always before him (28).

Erato, who destroyed the old order, is at least for the moment effectively replaced by the more prosaic voice of the poet's wife. There are no more lyrical flights, no plunges into the carnal past, no lamentations over the spiritual darkness from which the poet is slowly and painfully emerging. All that is finished. *Partage de Midi* has been written and confined to its limited private edition. The poetry of 'La Maison fermée' is indeed largely free from the grandiloquence that mars so much of Claudel's writing; it is more dense and more restrained than in the previous odes, but the violence has departed, the tension has slackened. The poet is calm and self-possessed, within his newly restricted order, his recently established conjugal life, confident that he is giving God to the world:

> Nous avons conquis le monde et nous avons trouvé que Votre Création est finie
> Et que l'imparfait n'a point de place avec Vos œuvres finies, et que notre imagination ne peut pas ajouter
> Un seul chiffre à ce Nombre en extase devant Votre Unité! (106)

A rare complacency is reached with the verse: 'Un peu de lumière est supérieur à beaucoup de ténèbres. Ne nous troublons point de ce qui est hors de nous' (107). Such unshakeable serenity, such Olympian imperviousness, does not please. Yet, the conclusion of the poem, with its fine affirmation of the solidarity of the living and the dead, the mutual interdependency of one with another, has great beauty. Making use once more of the image of the priest which underlies 'Magnificat', in a complex eucharistic imagery where Communion is seen as the foretaste of eternal life, the poet leaves behind his theme of finitude, the order of domestic life within four walls, and opens his ode outwards into the oneness of all life in God, that communion one with another and all with God which the Eucharist brings into being.

It would, I think, be unwise to draw too firm conclusions from the movements through which the odes pass, the grand poetic plan at the outset, the sudden eruption of Erato, the resumption of the poetic plan years later, with overtones of spiritual disquiet, the desire for spiritual rebirth and the apparent transformation of Erato into Divine Wisdom, then the thanksgiving to God for spiritual birth and rebirth as well as for the birth of the poet's daughter, the deepening sense of vocation in fatherhood as well as in poetic creativity, the realisation that God requires the service of the whole self, that the feminine in all its cosmic complexity is in fact the way to God, and ultimately and rather abruptly, in the final ode, that God is contained within the four walls of church or house, that within the family unit God is wholly present, enabling the poet to embrace the living and the dead in one grand eucharistic offering. If we leave out of account certain constant imagery, the imagery of fire, for instance, and the increasingly dominant sacerdotal imagery, we can maintain with some simplification that the corresponding movement of the basic imagery is from opening, violent movement, infinite seas, ubiquity, towards stability, immutability and enclosure in the last of the odes. Adventure and order have become one, the former indeed subsumed in the latter. The impression is of a certain stasis. Carnal passion is put behind and married life appears as a kind of defensive fortress. Too much store is perhaps set on security and stability in the excess of reaction after the four years of passionate love in China. The love of God that is revealed seems as yet to be of the mind rather than of the mind and heart, the latter still bruised no doubt by a sense of betrayal. Disquiet and dissatisfaction are of course uncomfortable companions and the poet seems largely to have dropped them. Few no doubt willingly entertain them.

The *Cinq Grandes Odes* remain a unique achievement in modern French poetry. The rich diversity of these poems has hardly yet been explored. This short essay only touches on one aspect of the odes, the expression of a personal anguish and the search for wisdom and enlightenment, above all, for a unifying harmony. These odes bear witness to a vital phase in the poet's life, both as poet and as man. From 1900 to 1908 the distance travelled is immense; yet certain factors remain constant, the poet's evangelising mission with a new kind of poetry of whose originality he is fully conscious and his fidelity to the experience which took place at Christmas 1886. The various extremes to which his reactions took him in these turbulent years are but the indications of his all too human nature. Even the rock-like affirmations and the cast-iron platitudes reveal that human weakness and fallibility in which Claudel, in common with every one else, participates.

Southampton   E. M. BEAUMONT

NOTES

1 All page references in the text relate to the 1966 printing of the Gallimard edition of *Cinq Grandes Odes*.
2 See André Vachon, *Le Temps et l'espace dans l'œuvre de Paul Claudel*, Seuil, 1965, pp. 250–1.
3 ibid., p. 276, n. 2.

VALÉRY AND PASCAL: ORDER AND ADVENTURE

Personne n'approche de Pascal avec sang-froid

Henri Lefebvre

The second part of Descartes' *Discours de la méthode* includes the following passage:

... les grands chemins, qui tournoient entre les montagnes, deviennent peu à peu si unis et si commodes, à force d'être fréquentés, qu'il est beaucoup meilleur de les suivre, que d'entreprendre d'aller plus droit, en grimpant au-dessus des rochers et descendant jusques au bas des précipices.

This topographical image, characteristic of Descartes' 'spatial' imagination, may serve as an indication of the difference between 'order' and 'adventure' conceived of as two contrasting types of temperamental or intellectual disposition. Indeed, in expressing a preference for smooth and clearly defined paths, and a reluctance to scramble over rocks or climb down precipitous slopes, Descartes formulates—however unconsciously—a fundamental distinction between his own intellectual approach and that of his younger contemporary, Pascal. More than two centuries later Taine was to express the same idea. He describes Descartes as 'modéré en tout, doué d'une curiosité calme, n'ayant point d'angoisse et d'excès dans son amour du savoir, douteur par méthode et non par nature, aimant la science seule, s'occupant moins de morale que de métaphysique et de géométrie . . . ne s'occupant guère du problème de la destinée humaine.' Pascal, on the contrary, is presented as being 'tout passion, tout ardeur, esprit impétueux aux éclats de génie, comprenant le vrai non par une méthode logique et lente, mais par des illuminations d'intelligence . . . âme pleine de douleur, d'anxiétés, de doutes, cherchant la vérité avec gémissements et angoisses.'[1]

In the light of these general distinctions it is significant that Valéry, in his various essays and comments on Descartes and Pascal, shows a deep admiration for the former and a remarkably sustained dislike of the latter. As one who worshipped what he called 'l'idole de l'Intellect', he expresses an instinctive sympathy with the 'rigueur' and 'constructions rationnelles' of Descartes while accusing Pascal of confusion and deviousness, of being 'impur et ambigu'.[2] In fact, Valéry adds a moral dimension to the familiar Descartes/Pascal contrast.

This movement from intellectual differentiation to ethical judgment emphasises Valéry's own status as a proponent of Cartesian order. At the same time it explains, in part at least, his fundamental inability to sympathise with the type of intellectual adventure implicit in the *Pensées* and which claims that non-rationalist positions can and should be arrived at on rationalist grounds. It has sometimes been argued that Valéry's severity towards Pascal can be accounted for by intellectual jealousy or by the promptings of a thoroughly secular temperament. While there may be some truth in both these suggestions, neither leads us very far. The clash between Valéry and Pascal is finally a conflict between two fundamentally different conceptions of true intellectuality. It represents a basic disagreement about what might be called the ethics of intellectualism. It places in opposition the concepts of order and adventure in the sphere of rational discourse.

These opposing casts of mind, represented by an amateur *uomo universale* of the seventeenth century and one of the twentieth, find particularly acute expression in the comments which Valéry wrote on the subject of Pascal's famous fragment: 'Le silence éternel de ces espaces infinis m'effraie.'[3] On the whole, Valéry scholars have paid less attention to these comments then students of Pascal,[4] but both sides have largely ignored an initial difficulty residing in the fact that leading commentators on the *Pensées*—from Michaut and Lafuma to Pol Ernst, but not including Brunschvicg—have attributed the 'silence éternel' phrase to Pascal's putative sceptical opponent. Valéry himself also ignored this problem and was possibly unaware of it. Indeed, he appears to pay no attention to the fact that parts of Pascal's apologia were conceived of in terms of a Christian/sceptic debate and that the whole work remained, in any case, incomplete. Nevertheless, it can be argued that most of his criticisms are unaffected by his direct attribution of the 'silence éternel' reaction to Pascal.

At the simplest level, Valéry uses this fragment as little more than a starting-point for criticisms which rely mainly for their justification on other—undisputed—passages in the *Pensées*. More importantly, it is clear that the 'cosmic fear' to which Pascal refers, while not a part of his own experience at least by the time he wrote the fragment, is a reaction which he understood instinctively and which had a special relationship to a number of his ideas and reactions. It is true that he puts the case against it more than once, in passages where he is undoubtedly speaking in his own voice, by exalting mind and consciousness over size and physical power, e.g. '. . . l'univers me comprend et m'engloutit comme un point; par la pensée, je le comprends'.[5] But there are other passages, one or two of which occur significantly in the *liasse* containing the 'silence éternel' fragment, where he sees fear in the face of infinite space as the reaction one would expect of the secular-minded individual. He writes, for example:

En voyant l'aveuglement et la misère de l'homme, en regardant tout l'univers muet et l'homme sans lumière abandonné à lui-même, et comme égaré dans ce recoin de l'univers sans savoir qui l'y a mis, ce qu'il y est venu faire, ce qu'il deviendra en mourant, incapable de toute connaissance, j'entre en effroi comme un homme qu'on aurait porté endormi dans une île déserte et effroyable, et qui s'éveillerait sans connaître où il est et sans moyen d'en sortir. Et sur cela j'admire comment on n'entre point en désespoir d'un si misérable état.[6]

A passage such as this shows Pascal expressing what is, at the very least, imaginative sympathy with a reaction of fear to cosmic vastness and emptiness. It comes close to the lurking doubt from which few intellectually-minded believers can remain completely free. It may also be connected with Pascal's grappling, in the fields of mathematics and physics, with the concept of infinite quantity[7] and the nature of the vacuum.[8] In this context, therefore, Valéry's attribution of this 'silence éternel' fear to Pascal himself, though formally mistaken, is less misleading than might at first appear. What one can say of Valéry's initial criticism of Pascal as an 'étrange chrétien' who fails to see the glory of God in His creation is that, although this particular fragment does not justify it, arguments to support such a contention are not necessarily lacking in other sections of the *Pensées*.

Valéry's first major charge against Pascal is one of sophistry, though he arrives at it gradually. The opening section of the 'Notes' contains what is, in effect, a brief but penetrating *explication de texte*. The 'silence éternel' statement is analysed as though it were a line by Racine, and Valéry concludes: 'Le poème est *parfait*.' Nevertheless, this initial praise of Pascal is eventually reassessed for purposes of censure. In a passage which has the additional value of illuminating part of his own attitude to poetry Valéry continues: 'Mais le physique des mots et la tactique de leurs arrangements dans les formes grammaticales étant indépendants des valeurs conventionnelles qui leur répondent et qui sont leur *sens, il y a fort peu de chances pour que l'expression immédiate d'une idée vienne à l'esprit dans une condition poétique.'*[9] By combining this statement with his previous analysis of the poetic choice and disposition of words in the 'silence éternel' phrase, Valéry goes on to suggest that what Pascal has written, far from being the formulation of a *thought*, is a deliberately contrived expression of pure *affectivity*—'Car *Éternel* et *Infini* sont des symboles de non-pensée.'

In view of his mathematical knowledge, it is surprising to find Valéry identifying the concept of infinity with 'non-pensée'. His attitude can perhaps be best interpreted as further evidence of the fact that he accepts ordered limits to rationality—'raisonner, c'est ordonner'[10]—whereas Pascal responded to the adventurous call for a means of transcending them. However, one can scarcely disagree with the general conclusion that, in this particular case, Pascal is simply formulating an emotional reaction to the vastness and silence of cosmic space. Indeed, Pascal himself claims nothing else. Valéry therefore creates a false contrast by implying that the 'effroi' masquerades, in a way that is not clear, as an initial expression of thought or rationality. On this basis he goes on to accuse Pascal of verbal manipulation and sophistry with the famous statement made in his original text: 'Je vois trop la main de Pascal.'[11]

While it is clearly true that eloquently formulated despair does not shake the personality with the same force as the original emotion— 'Une détresse qui écrit bien n'est pas si achevée qu'elle n'ait sauvé du naufrage quelque liberté de l'esprit'[12]—Valéry's general charge here is a curious one. It seems to suggest that if analytical criticism can reveal the mechanics of poetic appeal, we should distrust that appeal. It also implies that emotional responses which carry metaphysical overtones are rendered suspect by poetic formulation. At best, Valéry is arguing against much of his own poetic practice. At worst, he is proposing the erection of barriers between poetry and thought— or even encouraging the identification of poetry with sophistry. Whereas much of Pascal's writing depends on the belief that poetry and rhetoric can intensify truths arrived at by reason, Valéry regards 'the sin of poesy' as a temptation to be shunned by the rationalist.

If we accept Valéry's contention that thought formulated with literary skill is tantamount to falsehood, the whole status of literature and of poetic truth is called in question. This was an understandable— though some might say deplorable—attitude in the years of the 'Great Silence' following the 'nuit de Gênes' of 1892. But by the time Valéry wrote the 'Variation sur une "Pensée"' he had already published *La Jeune Parque* (1917) and *Charmes* (1922). The self-contradiction implied is even more striking when one turns to the specific charge of sophistry. Not only does Valéry ignore Pascal's concern to distinguish rhetorical device from sophistical effect (e.g. 'Il faut de l'agréable et du réel; mais il faut que cet agréable soit lui-même pris du vrai');[13] he goes on to criticise polemical writing as such: 'Je ne puis souffrir les apologies. S'il est quelque chose qu'un esprit de grande portée se doive interdire, et ne doive même concevoir, c'est l'intention de *convaincre* les autres et l'emploi de tous les moyens pour y parvenir.'[14] The same idea is expressed succinctly in Vol. XI of the *Cahiers* where Valéry writes: '. . . tout prosélytisme entraîne mauvaise foi.'

Whether or not one agrees with the viewpoint expressed here—and it seems to do less than justice to certain forms of missionary zeal, both political and religious—one is bound to convict Valéry of elementary inconsistency. His own attack on Pascal clearly seeks to convince his readers and is a work of propaganda, within his own meaning of the term, with all that this implies of strength and weakness. The fact that he formulates his objections with such deliberate verbal skill lays him open to the charge of sophistry in the terms in which he levelled it against Pascal. More particularly, he displays a lack of scruple as well as of sympathy in so far as he attempts to belittle Pascal's mathematics (contrasting him with Cavalieri and Saccheri), suggests that Pascal in not to be numbered among 'les hommes véritablement religieux', asserts that in Pascal's view 'tout est vain', and describes him as 'un esprit singulièrement timoré' in the scientific field.

While Valéry's original impulse may have come from a temperamental inability to understand Pascal's mind, his conscious rejection of any pretence of impartiality is suggested in the frequently quoted letter of 1917 to Pierre Louÿs: 'J'ai indiqué à mon cerveau futur les principes directeurs d'un éreintement sauvage des *Pensées* de Pascal.'[15] What we have in this 'Variation', in fact, is an extreme form of criticism based on unrestrained antipathy towards the object of inquiry. The tone of certain passages, as well as the arguments used, makes this clear. One consequence is an intensely personal, even egotistical, form of criticism which Valéry acknowledges when he makes the following comment with its significant final italics: 'Le développement de notre "Variation" nous a conduit naturellement à opposer *l'idée* que Pascal nous donne de soi-même (ou bien, celle que nous présente de lui la tradition), à *l'idée* que nous pouvons nous en faire, *par nous-mêmes.*'[16] This approach (another aspect of Valéry's continuing concern with methodology) amounts to trial by partisanship and is ultimately more revealing about the critic than the object of his criticism. Yet it is only fair to add that Valéry seems to have believed it genuinely possible to obtain special insight into others by means of systematic critical malevolence:

La haine habite l'adversaire, en développe les profondeurs, dissèque les plus délicates racines des desseins qu'il a dans le cœur. Nous le pénétrons mieux que nous-mêmes, et mieux qu'il ne fait soi-même. Il s'oublie, et nous ne l'oublions pas. Car nous le percevons aux moyens d'une blessure, et il n'est pas de sens plus cuisant, qui grandisse et précise plus fortement ce qui le touche, qu'une partie blessée de l'être.[17]

In practice, the gap turns out to be a very wide one between Valéry's theory here and his actual achievement in his 'Variation'.

In addition to its general charges of sophistry and bad faith, Valéry's essay contains a series of attacks on Pascal as thinker, scientist and mathematician. These attacks, made on a broad front, use different types of evidence and demonstration and vary greatly both in their intellectual content and degree of fairmindedness. It is not always easy to distinguish all the different threads in the argument, but the overall nature and shape of the criticism are clear enough. Valéry is concerned to uncover, by all available means, what he considers to be the feebleness and irrelevance of Pascal's thought— his emotionalism, his aversion to a broad scientific synthesis, his readiness to import non-rational considerations into intellectual debate.

Valéry's picture of Pascal in the 'Variation' is of a scientific thinker possessing an intellectually timid disposition and weak synthesising powers compared, for example, with Descartes.[18] Such a view interprets as 'timidity' Pascal's careful and conscientious experimentalism; takes no account of his 'modern' emphasis on experiment rather than authority in science; ignores his demonstration of the existence of the vacuum at a time when Descartes, by accepting the authority of Aristotle's *plenum*, built up a synthesising—but wholly false—theory of vortices. Indeed, if Descartes is to be set against Pascal as a model figure in the history of science, this must be done in terms of his intellectual ambitions rather than his practical achievements. Descartes did attempt, with pioneering courage, to account comprehensively for the physical world along purely mechanical lines, but the immediate scientific conclusions of his theoretical cosmology were mistaken in many cases. It is no service to his reputation to confuse his importance and originality as a rational philosopher with his work as a physicist. However, had Valéry not been so determined to discredit

Pascal and praise Descartes, he might have seen them, more justly, as representing two contrasting approaches which have both proved essential, by their very opposition and difference, to the development of science in terms of observation, theory, and experimental confirmation. Descartes emphasised theory in his attempt to base his scientific ideas on a set of rational, fixed, *a priori* laws. Pascal, distrustful of *a priori* theory, brought an exemplary experimental method to bear on certain precise scientific problems.[19] Scientific knowledge was to advance, in the succeeding centuries, by a fruitful bringing together of the Cartesian and Pascalian approaches.

In addition to the charge of intellectual timidity, Valéry accuses Pascal of intellectual irrelevance—of failing to come to terms with the modern, post-Renaissance world. This reflects a general aggressive modernity expressed, for example, in the *Cahiers* by an entry beginning: 'Montaigne et Pascal ne font presque plus figure de penseurs.'[20] More particularly, in the case of the 'silence éternel' fragment, Valéry ignores Pascal's formulation of the new cosmology and underlines instead his reaction to cosmic space. This facilitates the charge of intellectual irrelevance: 'Ce qu'on pourrait nommer *la réaction de Pascal* peut devenir une rareté et un objet de curiosité pour les psychologues'.[21] Apart from the fact that one form of existentialist sensibility saw Pascal's reaction as both understandable and justified in the decade immediately following Valéry's death, the judgement is extremely one-sided. Valéry, by limiting himself to Pascal's *reaction*, manages to present as an example of archaism what is in fact a succinct formulation of the change from a medieval 'closed' cosmology to a modern 'infinite' one. Whether the speaker is Pascal, as Valéry assumes, or his sceptical opponent, this picture of an infinite cosmos, creating an entirely new intellectual and moral situation for man, breaks completely with the old Aristotelian model of musical spheres rotated by rational intelligences.

Having accused Pascal of intellectual timidity and archaic insignificance, Valéry goes on to tax him briefly, if rather surprisingly, with immodesty and intellectual arrogance.[22] However, he makes clear that his most serious charge is one of intellectual impurity and perversion. Following the 'misanthrope sublime' tradition of Voltaire, he regards Pascal as an enemy of humanity—'une sorte de Héros de la dépréciation totale et amère'[23]—and one who exploits an elaborate intellectual structure (previously dismissed as timid inadequacy) in order to give vent to his ineradicable misanthropy. This charge is clearly bound up with the earlier one of sophistry, but it raises further problems in a passage such as this:

Il use d'un horrible mélange de méthode et de stratagèmes, combine les sentiments et les syllogismes, agite les spectres, prodigue les promesses et les menaces, excite le bestial et l'idéal tour à tour. . . . Le Serpent peut-il faire pire?

Voilà ce que je nomme *impur*, que je ne puis supporter, et que je ressens comme un attentat. S'il existe une Éthique de l'esprit, rien ne l'offense davantage.[24]

These statements are particularly interesting because of the reference to 'impurity' and the suggestion of a possible ethical quality inherent in the reasoning faculties—a morality of knowledge. Valéry is entirely right in suggesting that some kind of ethics of knowledge exists, but he is quite wrong in seeking to identify it with explicit, objective, impersonal truth. In his criticism of Pascal (curiously at odds with his own practice in the 'Variation') he uses the archaic notion, derived from Aristotle's concept of separate mind, that the act of knowing can be purely rational and morally neutral. Quite apart from the more recent blows dealt against this idea by phenomenological and existentialist epistemology, the concept of neutral rationality was exploded earlier, and in different ways, by Nietzsche, Bergson and Freud. Nietzsche, in particular, related his vews to the progress of the natural sciences and believed that a boundless faith in objective truth would result, to the detriment of science, in intellectual confusion and an enfeebling inability to discern any truth in faith. In this connection Erich Heller has written: 'While all his [Nietzsche's] scientific and scholarly contemporaries throve on the comfortable assumptions that, firstly, there was such a thing as "objective", and therefore morally neutral, knowledge, and that, secondly, everything that *can* be known "objectively" is therefore also *worth knowing*, he realised that knowledge, or at least the mode of knowledge predominant at his time and ours, is the subtlest guise of the Will to Power; and that *as a manifestation of the will it is liable to be judged morally*. For him, there can be no knowledge without a compelling urge to acquire it; and he knew that the knowledge thus acquired invariably reflects the nature of the impulse by which the mind was prompted. It is this impulse which creatively partakes in the making of the knowledge. . . .'[25]

It can be shown that this view of knowledge underlay Pascal's epistemology, and partly shaped his *apologia*, more than two hundred years earlier.[26] At the same time, although we may accept its validity and even, in a certain sense, its inevitability, this is not to remove at a stroke the problem of 'impurity' which Valéry raises. The difficult idea of 'une Éthique de l'esprit' remains, but it now takes a different form. A genuine morality of knowledge is no longer identified with (impossibly) neutral statements presented in purely quantifiable or traditionally logical terms. It arises, rather, from the manner in which we handle the natural and inevitable 'impurity' involved in knowing. Because the act of pursuing knowledge is a function of the whole person and involves a range of purposes and presuppositions, moral consequences follow from it. The ethical status of these consequences will depend to a considerable degree on their conscious acceptance, and justification, by the individual thinker. Pascal is fully aware of what he is doing in terms of his epistemology. He sees it neither as sophistry nor impurity, but as realism. Yet it is precisely in terms of sophistry, impurity and unreality that it must appear to Valéry. In fact, we are led at this point to confront a fundamental difference between the two conceptions of reality underlying the attitudes of Valéry and Pascal to the nature of knowledge and of the physical world. While the latter, despite his carefully experimental approach, instinctively adds the question 'why' to the question 'how', the former considers it an essential part of intellectual integrity to limit himself to explaining 'how'. He remains suspicious of all attempts to add a further dimension of meaning. Indeed, he goes so far as to say:

L'homme de science regarde l'ensemble étoilé sans y attacher aucune signification. Il met *hors du circuit* tout le système émotif de son être. Il essaye de se rendre soi-même une manière de machine, qui, recevant des observations, restituerait des formules et des lois, et travaillerait à substituer finalement aux phénomènes leur expression en pouvoirs conscients, volontaires, définis.[27]

Later, in the same spirit, Valéry expresses interest only in 'une idée statistique de l'univers.'[28] Curiously enough, then, it is Valéry, the non-scientist, who claims that the scientist should limit himself to physics and he takes Pascal, the experimental scientist, to task for opening up perspectives beyond physics to metaphysics. Once again, while Valéry remains within the analytical order of the 'how', Pascal moves forward, through analysis, towards the speculative adventure of the 'why'. In this Pascal is surely right. It is neither possible nor desirable to put an intellectual *cordon sanitaire* around science. Scientific inquiry is as much a part of life as are politics or religion. It is a source of moral and philosophical consequences, it prompts emotional reactions, and neither fact can be ignored. Pascal's is the more boldly synthesising mind because he rejects the idea of pure rationality and seeks, at various points in the *Pensées*, to explore the difficult and fascinating territory that lies between rationalism and emotion, knowledge and belief, empiricism and faith.

Valéry's repeated references to Pascal, throughout the whole range of his writings, suggest that the fundamental difference between their two ways of thought—a difference that is partly temperamental and partly historical—can be expressed in more general terms. Whereas Valéry regarded truth as something exact, rational, coherent,[29] Pascal saw it as disconcertingly multi-layered (the break-up of the medieval synthesis) and ultimately discontinuous (the consequence of Renaissance knowledge). Valéry attempted to enclose existence within a uniform order of rationality. Pascal affirmed variety and preserved the claims of intuitive, evaluative knowledge by his three categories— body, mind, spirit[30]—and his distinction between the *esprit de géométrie* and the *esprit de finesse*.[31] Valéry embodied the *esprit de géométrie* both correctly and impressively in his strictly scientific and mathematical ideas. But he applied it wrongly, according to Pascalian criteria, by using it to attack metaphysics, history, religious speculation and the concepts of the good, the beautiful and the true.[32] He regarded intuition and feeling as subordinate, secondary experiences. At best they supply the mind with relevant but negative evidence in its work of arriving at rigorously rational truth. In the case of Pascal, for whom *raison* and *sagesse* were distinct but equally indispensable means of arriving at different kinds of truth,[33] intuitive understanding can overcome those limitations which the strictly rational and positive mind is bound to encounter in such spheres as metaphysics and religion. And a consequence of Pascalian epistemology is the conviction that, while maintaining the efficacy of reason within its own appropriate order of inquiry, a reality exists which is beyond rationality yet accessible to poets, musicians, mystics—and perhaps madmen.

Although Valéry seems to have denied this view, and to have attacked Pascal with it in mind, he was much too perceptive and well-informed to remain blind to the difficulties inherent in his own devotion to the rational intellect. This is clear in at least three ways. Firstly, he was painfully aware that the first World War reflected a crisis in strictly rationalist thought and presented a challenge to certain of its claims. Secondly, he became conscious of the fact that a number of his own intellectual categories had been rendered irrelevant or inapprorpiate by the advances of twentieth-century physics. Thirdly, he went so far, at the beginning of the second World War, as to praise Bergsonian intuitionism. Indeed, in this last case, he came near to the Pascalian position in so far as he praised the

KHF

esprit de finesse as well as the *esprit de géométrie*. Admittedly, what he says on this subject was briefly expressed and perhaps only temporarily held, but it suggests that it is difficult to engage in debate with Pascal's ideas and remain entirely unaffected by them.

The emphasis on abstraction in Valéry's thought resulted from his continual effort to impose the coherence of rational categories on the incoherence of experience. He even argued strongly that abstraction is an indispensable condition of creativity. Nevertheless, during the first World War, his confidence in rational abstraction suffered a reverse. He saw the war as a challenge to a body of rationalist assumptions which he had shared, and as introducing doubt and self-questioning into the very heart of the rationalist enterprise:

L'Esprit est en vérité cruellement atteint; il se plaint dans le cœur des hommes de l'esprit et se juge tristement. Il doute profondément de soi-même.[34]

Significantly, he also saw the application of the scientific and positivist spirit as giving rise to acute moral problems:

Il a fallu, sans doute, beaucoup de science pour tuer tant d'hommes, dissiper tant de biens, anéantir tant de villes en si peu de temps; mais il a fallu non moins des *qualités morales*. Savoir et Devoir, vous êtes donc suspects?[35]

Valéry even seems to have glimpsed the possible dangers of abstraction when he defined 'le métier des intellectuels' as 'remuer toutes choses sous leurs signes, noms ou symboles, sans le contrepoids des actes réels'.[36]

These doubts and questions were part of an inevitable reaction to the circumstances of war. They did not cause any dramatic or permanent change in Valéry's fundamental intellectual position. They called for a reorganisation of some of his ideas but brought about no thoroughgoing reappraisal. In a similar way, his awareness of changes in physics and of the growth of the biological sciences necessitated some adjustment. Within a year of the first publication of his 'Variation' on Pascal, the appearance of his essay, 'Au sujet d'*Eurêka*', made clear his sense of the need to reconstitute his own ideas in the light of the new physics:

L'apparence de la matière est d'une substance morte, d'une *puissance* qui ne passerait à *l'acte* que par une intervention extérieure et tout étrangère à sa nature. De cette définition l'on tirait autrefois des conséquences invincibles. Mais la matière a changé de visage. L'expérience a fait concevoir le contraire de ce que la pure observation faisait voir. Toute la physique moderne, qui a créé, en quelque sorte, des *relais* pour nos sens, nous a persuadés que notre antique définition n'avait aucune valeur absolue, ni spéculative. Elle nous montre que la matière est étrangement diverse et comme indéfiniment surprenante; qu'elle est un assemblage de transformations qui se poursuivent et se perdent dans la petitesse, même dans les abîmes de cette petitesse; on nous dit que se réalise, peut-être, un mouvement perpétuel. Il y a une fièvre éternelle dans les corps.[37]

This is clearly and eloquently stated. It will be noted, too, that in his emphasis on 'la petitesse' and 'les abîmes de cette petitesse' Valéry moves close to one of the two terms—posed with equal clarity and eloquence—in Pascal's 'disproportion de l'homme' fragment.[38] In Pascal's thought this world of the infinitely small, of the submicroscopic, is inseparable from the world of the infinitely great, the intergalactic, and both create an intellectual challenge which Valéry eventually admitted in the case of the former but tried to minimise as regards the latter because of its traditionally religious implications. The possibility of framing adequately in words a reality of which we can conceive, but with which we cannot make immediate and direct contact, breaks down in both cases and presents rational discourse with a major crisis.[39] Pascal said neither more nor less in his comments on 'les deux infinis'. It is in a Pascalian perspective that Valéry sees things, even though he does not draw Pascalian consequences, when he continues:

Nous savons que des propriétés et des puissances inconnues s'exercent dans l'*infra-monde*, puisque nous en avons décelé quelques-unes, que nos sens n'étaient pas faits pour percevoir. Mais nous ne savons ni énumérer ces propriétés, ni même assigner un nombre fini à la pluralité croissante des chapitres de la physique. Nous ne savons même pas si la généralité de nos concepts n'est pas illusoire quand nous les transportons dans ces domaines qui bornent et supportent le nôtre. . . . Quand la discontinuité devient la règle, l'imagination qui jadis s'employait à achever la vérité que les perceptions avaient fait soupçonner, et les raisonnements tissue, se doit déclarer impuissante.[40]

This particular essay ends with a firm rejection by Valéry of what he calls intuition. Nevertheless, he also admits the inadequacy of the traditional logic by which he had been working up to this time: 'Comme l'univers échappe à l'intuition, tout de même il est transcendant à la logique.'[41]

Valéry came nearest to accepting something like intuition—and nearest also to approving a Pascalian form of epistemology—in his *allocution* on Bergson delivered in the Académie Française on 9 January 1941. Two passages are particularly noteworthy. In the first,

Valéry praises Bergson for having helped to free late nineteenth- and early twentieth-century thought from the outmoded habits of analysis connected with Cartesian mechanism: 'Tandis que les philosophes, depuis le XVIIIe siècle, avaient été, pour la plupart, sous l'influence des conceptions physico-mécaniques, notre illustre confrère s'était laissé heureusement séduire aux sciences de la vie. La biologie l'inspirait.'[42] A few lines later he adds: '[Bergson] avait rendu le service essentiel de restaurer et de réhabiliter le goût d'une méditation plus approchée de notre essence que ne peut l'être un développement purement logique des concepts, auxquels, d'ailleurs, il est impossible, en général, de donner des définitions irréprochables. . . . Il osa emprunter à la Poésie ses armes enchantées, dont il combina le pouvoir avec la précision dont un esprit nourri aux sciences ne peut souffrir de s'écarter.'[43]

What Valéry is describing in these lines—with apparent approval— is a comprehensive approach to intellectual inquiry based on a multi-dimensional view of reality. Bergson expressed, in terminology appropriate to his own philosophy, an attitude to knowledge which Pascal fought to defend, which the seventeenth century eventually lost, and which has been revived in our own day. Cartesian order of the kind Valéry admired and embodied with such distinction is increasingly rejected in favour of an epistemological adventurousness which has turned for its models to a tradition stretching from Pascal, through Kierkegaard and Dostoevsky, to Jaspers.

Sussex   JOHN CRUICKSHANK

NOTES

1 Quoted in G. Michaut, *Les Époques de la pensée de Pascal*, Paris, 1902, p. 21.

2 Cf. 'En résumé, je n'ai jamais songé á contester l'extraordinaire puissance intellectuelle de Pascal, ni sa valeur d'écrivain, mais je trouve en lui, plus je le considère, ce que j'appelle son *impureté* et que j'oppose à ce que j'appelle la *pureté cartésienne*. Je trouve chez Pascal la confusion—un désordre tout moderne—entre les divers ordres ou les divers moments de l'être vivant, ordres et moments que la gloire de Descartes aura été de distinguer. . . .' in F. Lefèvre, *Entretiens avec Paul Valéry*, Paris, 1926, pp. 83-4.

3 Pascal, *Pensées* (Brunschvicg 206, Lafuma 201). Further references to the Brunschivicg and Lafuma editions of the *Pensées* are indicated by the letters 'Br' and 'La'.

Valéry's original 'Variation sur une "Pensée" ' appeared in the special Pascal tri-centenary issue of the *Revue Hebdomadaire*, *VII*, 28, 14 July

1923, pp. 161–70. The following year it was reprinted in his *Variété I*, pp. 139–53 and reappeared accompanied by a second set of comments, the so-called 'Notes', in Valéry's *Variation sur une 'Pensée', annotée par l'auteur*, Liège, 1930. The two texts ('Texte' and 'Notes') are printed, mainly on facing pages, in the Pléiade edition of Valéry's *Œuvres I*, Paris, 1957, pp. 458–73. The source of all quotations from Valéry's two texts is indicated below by the letters 'Pl', followed by the appropriate page-reference.

4 Two notable exceptions, in the field of Valéry studies, are M. Bémol, *La Méthode critique de Paul Valéry*, Paris, 1960 and, more particularly, E. Gaède, *Nietzsche et Valéry: essai sur la comédie de l'esprit*, Paris, 1962. Among Pascal scholars, the best discussion of one line of criticism in Valéry's 'Variation' is J.-J. Demorest, 'Pascal's Sophistry and the Sin of Poesy' in J.-J. Demorest (ed.), *Studies in Seventeenth-Century French Literature presented to Morris Bishop*, New York, 1962, pp. 132–52.

5 *Pensées*, Br 348, La 113. Cf. 'Tous les corps, le firmament, les étoiles, la terre et ses royaumes, ne valent pas le moindre des esprits; car il connaît tout cela, et soi; et les corps, rien' (Br 793, La 308).

A specific claim on behalf of consciousness is made in the third sentence of the 'roseau pensant' fragment: 'Mais, quand l'univers l'écraserait, l'homme serait encore plus noble que ce qui le tue, puisqu'il sait qu'il meurt, et l'avantage que l'univers a sur lui; l'univers n'en sait rien' (Br 347, La 200).

6 *Pensées*, Br 693, La 198.

7 In the fifth century B.C. the problem of infinite quantity was formulated by Zeno of Elea in eight celebrated paradoxes including that of the arrow in flight which appears to be both in motion and at rest. Valéry's interest, as a mathematician, in the same problem is reflected in some familiar lines from 'Le Cimetière marin':

> Zénon! Cruel Zénon! Zénon d'Elée!
> M'as-tu percé de cette flèche ailée
> Qui vibre, vole, et qui ne vole pas!

8 It is perhaps significant here that Pascal should have experienced such reluctance in disproving the Aristotelian *horror vacui* assumption. He writes towards the end of his *Récit de la grande expérience de l'équilibre des liqueurs*: 'Ce n'est pas toutefois sans regret, que je me dépars de ces opinion si généralement reçues; je ne le fais qu'en cédant à la force de la vie qui m'y contraint. J'ai résisté à ces sentiments nouveaux tant que j'ai eu quelque prétexte pour suivre les anciens; les maximes que j'ai employées en mon *Abrégé* le témoignent assez.'

9 Pl, pp. 458–9.

10 Valéry, *Cahiers IV*, p. 124.

11 Pl, p. 465. Cf. Valéry, *Cahiers X*, p. 749: 'Le silence éternel . . . m'effraie mais le rythme savant de cette phrase me rassure.'

12 Pl, p. 463.

13 *Pensées*, Br 25, La 667.

14 Pl, p. 468.

15 Valéry, *Lettres à quelques-uns*, Paris, 1952, p. 121.

16 Pl, p. 462.

17 Valéry, *Autres Rhumbs*, Paris, 1934, p. 188.

18 Pl, p. 472: '... les idées de Pascal dans l'ordre physique sont d'un esprit singulièrement timoré. ... Il manquait de cette imagination du mécanisme des phénomènes qui abondait en *Des Cartes*. ...'

19 The distinction between the scientific attitudes of Descartes and Pascal has been neatly expressed as follows: 'Descartes ... voulait refaire la physique à la manière d'Aristote; Pascal ... se contentait comme Archimède d'îlots de vérité contingente, étayée par des expériences nombreuses, précises et bien interprétées,' P. Sergescu, *Coups d'œil sur les origines de la science exacte moderne*, Paris, 1951.

20 Valéry, *Cahiers VII*, p. 622.

21 Pl, p. 473.

22 Pl, p. 468: '... il manque quelque chose ... à tout esprit qui ne discerne pas son faible et son médiocre aussi nettement et curieusement qu'il reconnaît en soi quelques beautés et quelques lumières parfois prodigieuses. En tout ceci, Pascal est digne de Pascal.' This seems particularly outrageous in view of Pascal's own repeated insistence on the paradoxical nature of reason, its strengths and weaknesses.

23 Pl, p. 464. There is a similarity of approach between Valéry and Voltaire in 'Qu'est-ce que nous apprenons aux autres hommes en leur répétant qu'ils ne sont rien' (Pl, p. 463) and 'Il s'acharne à nous peindre tous méchants et malheureux' (Voltaire, *Lettres philosophiques*, introductory remarks to Letter XXV, 'Sur les Pensées de M. Pascal').

24 Pl, p. 468.

25 E. Heller, 'The Importance of Nietzsche', *Encounter*, No. 127, April, 1964, p. 62.

26 See my 'Knowledge and Belief in Pascal's Apology' in J. C. Ireson *et al.* (eds), *Studies in French Literature presented to H. W. Lawton*, Manchester, 1968, pp. 89–103.

27 Pl, p. 466.

28 Pl, p. 471.

29 Hence Valéry's statement in the 'Note et Digression' of 1919: '... je ne croyais pas à la puissance propre du délire, à la nécessité de l'ignorance, aux éclairs de l'absurde, à l'incohérence créatrice'. He adds some pages later: 'Ce sont des instants dérobés à la critique implacable de la durée, ils ne résistent pas au fonctionnement complet de notre être: ou nous périssons, ou ils se dissolvent', Pl, pp. 1207 and 1220–1.

30 See Pascal, *Pensées*, Br 460, La 308.

31 See Pascal, *Pensées*, Br 1–4, La 511–13, 751.

32 See, in particular, Valéry's 'Discours de l'histoire' and his 'Léonard et les philosophes', Pl, pp. 1128–37 and 1234–69.

33 The distinction involved here is put in elliptical form by Pascal when he writes: 'Les curieux et les savants: ils ont pour objet l'esprit. Les sages: ils ont pour objet la justice', *Pensées*, Br 480, La 933.

34 Pl, p. 1001.

35 Pl, p. 989.

36 Valéry, *Rhumbs*, Paris, 1926, pp. 47–8.

37 Pl, p, 859.

38 See Pascal, *Pensées*, Br 72, La 199.

39 This problem, in the case of the infinitely small, has been expressed as follows: 'The laws of physics of bodies of household size can be expressed fairly satisfactorily using words of household origin. We should be surprised if the same words and laws did not also describe the behaviour of bodies a thousand times smaller or bigger than ourselves. We might even hope to manage to talk about bodies a million times smaller than ourselves because we can still see them. But take another step downwards in size by a factor of 100, say to 10^{-6} cm, and we are in a region where no refinement of our own senses can help us. We cannot ourselves be put into touch with things on this scale; they can never make a direct appeal to us and we have therefore no right whatever to suppose that there will not here exist phenomena to which language simply does not apply. . . . In *talking* of the sub-microscopic world we are never doing any more than employing analogies which may or may not be useful and may or may not be misleading. We must thus anticipate that our understanding, if by that we mean our ability to describe things in words, will break down completely or at best involve the simultaneous employment of terms which, in the macroscopic world of our sensory experience, are mutually exclusive', D. H. Wilkinson, 'Towards New Concepts. Elementary Particles' in A. C. Crombie (ed.), *Turning Points in Physics*, Amsterdam, 1959, pp. 155–6.
40 Pl, p. 860.
41 Pl, p. 866.
42 Pl, p. 884.
43 Pl, pp. 884–5.

VALÉRY ON 'BÊTISE ET POÉSIE': BACKGROUND AND IMPLICATIONS

'Un des dadas de Teste, non le moins chimérique, fut de vouloir conserver l'art—*Ars*—tout en exterminant les illusions d'artiste et d'auteur. Il ne pouvait souffrir les prétentions bêtes des poètes' (*Oeuvres*, Pléiade II, 67).[1] Like much else in Valéry that is seminal, the indications of an alleged relation between stupidity and poetry are to be found in Teste, but the connexion is frequently reasserted in the *Cahiers*. 'Bêtise et Poésie. Il y a des relations subtiles entre ces deux ordres. L'ordre de la bêtise et celui de la poésie' (IX, 234).[2] 'Sottise et poésie. Pas de poésie au 18 ème [siècle]—pas assez niais' (X, 167). 'Sottise et Poésie—Si un homme d'esprit actif peut supporter la lecture des poètes?' (X, 439). 'Sottise et Poésie. Comment ne pas dire des niaiseries ou des bizarreries?' (X, 412). 'Sottise et poésie. Niaiseries traditionnelles. Les 9/10 des œuvres des plus grands poètes sont illisibles à un lecteur de grande culture et d'intelligence' (X, 628). 'Sottise et Poésie. L'imagination poétique est par malheur nécessairement grossière' (XI, 228). 'Sottise et poésie. Dans l'époque moderne les rapports de la sottise et de la poésie sont devenus étroits et presque nécessaires' (XI, 505).[3] Many readers may regard such observations as a mixture of *boutades* and arrogant pretentiousness. I wish to show that this view would be superficial, that, on the contrary, the theme *bêtise et poésie* is a very important if not crucial one in Valéry's reflections. It is not my present purpose to look at particular poems or even, at first, to say much about poetry itself at all. I propose to take largely for granted a reasonable acquaintance with Valéry's thought, poetry and aesthetic theories so that I can pursue the implications, for him, of *bêtise et poésie* and sketch in some of the background to this contemptuous association of ideas. So doing, we will see open up a range of speculations that take us into an area of great order and adventure, the adventure (as Valéry sees it) of the human race, the order he thinks it will need to face and, correspondingly, the adventure, order and revaluation in art and poetry which he thinks are called for.

A certain conception of the natural sciences clearly had a deep influence on Valéry's thinking and lies behind his iconoclastic analyses in many spheres of human activity. His general views on philosophy, mathematics, science and language are now well known.[4] He constantly postulates a clear and often sharp rift between the old, traditional ways of thought and behaviour and the new ways that are emerging or that are at least implicit, and for which he is regularly a spokesman. The 'old world' was characterised by fairly fixed, stable ideas, by certain absolutes, by hierarchies in thought and in society, above all by fairly unquestioned fiduciary values in all spheres and by acceptance of the not clearly understood workings of gods, kings, governments, religions and ethical or social values. The pace of existence was unhurried and regular, the future was not seen as likely to be other than approximately a continuation of the past. By the criteria of the modern natural sciences (not to speak of the more recent social 'sciences'), the 'old world' was a confused state of affairs; it functioned and functioned moderately well partly because it was mostly not subjected to those criteria. The energetic exercise of man's analytic powers and their application to the material world have intruded into this muddled life at an increasingly gathering speed with consequences which fascinate Valéry. 'Le "monde" a été saisi par les faits nouveaux. Terre tout occupée; monde fini; accroissement des moyens—Démocratie—Diminution des *rites* et de la magie organisée' (XX, 255). If he had been living today, more recent concepts like environmental pollution and population explosion would doubtless have found their way into such statements.

Precision and verifiability are alleged by Valéry to be the advanced thinkers' new absolutes and, to a considerable extent, it would seem, they are his too. The implications of their full application would or will be enormous. 'Peut-être faudrait-il rejeter presque toutes les idées générales et immémoriales (que nous recevons par le langage et la culture, avec toutes leurs contradictions latentes, leurs in-suffisances, etc.) antérieures à l'époque des faits nouveaux et des vérifications impitoyables?' (XIX, 261). 'La mathématique est une manière de "penser" [...] Reste à savoir si elle peut s'étendre à tout, si on peut tout traiter utilement par voie comme mathématique? c.à.d. tout transformer en *pouvoirs* distincts' (XIX, 493). The highest knowledge of which man was once capable was founded on the general-isation of a basically individual question and answer procedure, with a vague assumption of universal similitude and unity—e.g. the very notion of 'universe' or the ideal of exploring 'gaps' in our knowledge in order eventually to reach the assumed goal of complete understanding. Gradually, the emphasis shifted from the 'why' questions to the 'how' questions (XX, 31). Increasingly, illegitimate and naïvely teleological questions have ceased to be asked. 'Nous avons appris qu'il ne faut pas répondre à des questions que le fait seul peut décider' (XX, 98). Valéry thinks that common sense, what he frequently calls 'la vision commune', has been shown to be quite inadequate to explain or even to understand the complexity of new phenomena revealed by modern thought (XX, 386).

In this process, the actual notion of knowledge (*savoir*) has evolved to the point where it is seen as being strictly dependent on our means (*pouvoir*). 'Aucun *savoir* ne va plus avant que notre *pouvoir*; et s'il le prétend, il est imaginaire' (XXI, 624). By modern standards, *pouvoir* is the only real *savoir*. Valéry thinks this is true at all levels, from the highest, scientific or philosophical, to the lowest and most ordinarily individual.[5] Against all the traditions of the past, we are learning, he alleges, that the concept 'knowledge' means no more than the purely provisional rationalisation of the real powers of action, intervention or control that we can verify: only the verifiable powers count; if they change, our knowledge has to change to catch up. The paradigm is clearly one derived from the natural sciences and from the principle of constantly modifying theories or testing them to possible destruction. 'Ns [nous] avons appris, aux dépens de nos habitudes, de notre bon sens, de nos préférences et de nos espoirs, que même les fondements de notre raison, même ceux de notre langage n'étaient faits que de ce qui était possible ou impossible, à une tout autre époque que la nôtre, et n'étaient en harmonie qu'avec les moyens de ce temps. [//] Ce que ns [nous] pensons aujourd'hui, et qui n'est pas, d'ailleurs, encore en accord avec nos moyens et nos pouvoirs, subira la même épreuve, sans doute. [//] Ce sont ces pouvoirs qui règlent et demeurent, et nos connaissances tendent à être des équations à ces pouvoirs' (XX, 200). Precarious equations indeed! The boldest statement of this line of thought is found in comments like the following: 'Ma doctrine = la "connaissance" est un transit. Elle est passage—figure de transformation—et peut-être n'existe que comme *forme* cf. les ondes, les éclairs, qui n'ont figure que par l'inertie de la rétine' (XX, 532). Knowledge is a transitional and shifting phase. But in any case, although, for Valéry, knowledge implies prediction, it does not at all necessarily imply understanding: the distinction between knowledge and understanding is an important one in this thought (cf. XIX, 218). In his beautiful prose poem *l'Ange*, composed not long before his death, *connaître* and *comprendre* are set in opposition to each other ('Et pendant une éternité, il ne cessa de connaître et de ne pas comprendre', *Oeuvres*, Pléiade I, 206). Transitional and shifting are adjectives that, by Valéry's lights, would have to be applied to much else in modern times. Not only is *savoir* purely transitional and, so to speak, functional, thought itself is to be seen as the same, as no more stable or permanent, being merely a passage from one state to another (cf. XIX, 690 and *Oeuvres*, Pléiade I, 1215–16). Language is equally transitional and provisional. 'Quoi de plus simple, quoi de plus évident que ceci, que tout ce qui est langage est provisoire, transitif par essence, se passe entre deux états d'*énergie*' (XII, 204).[6]

If language, thought and knowledge are so seen by Valéry, one may well wonder what in his view remains fixed, stable or certain about man's nature and man's place in the universe. In brief, very little. For Valéry, the most salient mark of the contemporary world is the realisation that man's destiny is, to use a modern cant word, 'open-ended', or rather, that man has no 'destiny' at all. 'La vie n'a pas d'objet—L'homme a *tel objet*, à *tel moment*' (XIX, 373). 'Ma philosophie—L'Homme sans destin. Tout (ou presque tout) me suggère que l'homme est une aventure— [//] Rien ne permet de penser qu'il ait un 'destin' [. . .] Point de *pourquoi*' (XXI, 623). Opposing the 'why' of former times to the 'how' that, according to him, now predominates, Valéry links the evolution of the concept of knowledge with the transformational openness conferred by present trends: '"Pourquoi" signifie *but*, psychie, partie de l'être, écart. "Comment" signifie *moyens*. [//] Or—ceci est tourné vers une sorte d'explication ou justification de *ce qui est*—c.à.d. de *ce qui fut*. Mais il semble que la tendance (inconsciente) actuelle (à partir des faits nouveaux) est plutôt une volonté de transformation de l'homo,—une aventure indéfinie' (XX, 31). Valéry would no doubt have felt the last words quoted (written in 1937) were strongly predictive if he could have witnessed developments at the present time; for instance, the current predominance of financial and material considerations in Western European society, or, say, the rapid evolution of ideas concerning abortion and the sacredness of human life. It is clear that the adventure in which he sees man as now engaged is largely intellectual in origin. The power of the human mind is transforming the modern world at an increasing pace but, above all, it is transforming man himself, the human mind itself, with unpredictable consequences. 'Je ne trouve en moi au sujet de MOI et de l'homo que cette idée que ns [nous] sommes engagés dans une aventure qui a commencé avec la pensée' (XXI, 81). On this reiterated theme, he is frequently pessimistic: thus he writes of humanity's development as a kind of '*tropisme* de la connaissance et de la volonté d'épuisement' (XX, 877) —through the instinctive and almost blind urgings of his own intellect and as a result of its applications, man will not just exhaust the earth, he will not just pollute his environment irremediably, he will exhaust himself, do himself to death.

But these are projections into a relatively distant future. In the present, in his own time, Valéry is above all struck by the confused co-existence of the new and the old, by the gap which really separates the new outlook implied by 'les faits nouveaux et les vérifications impitoyables' from the large body of ideas, beliefs, conventions and institutions which, by a kind of inertia, still make up our life and society. 'L'accroissement considérable de la différence entre la vision naïve des choses et la vision revisée—(plus grande que celle entre la vision du nouveau-né et la vision de l'homme)—met aussi un intervalle choquant entre les jugements et sentiments littéraires-philosophiques et *politiques* et ceux qui s'imposent aux esprits, *au même esprit,* dans le domaine des parties refaites du savoir. [//] Jamais le problème d'ajuster les parties d'un système qui doit être *Un,* et qui est désaccordé—ne fut si nettement proposé, et jamais l'hiatus plus grand' (XII, 491). Many of the analyses in the *Cahiers* have as their main function to explore this dissociation between old and new.[7] We are encumbered, 'gênés par [. . .] la *diversité incohérente* de nos biens hérités' (XX, 436): we thus need to rid ourselves of past problems that, by the latest standards, are not now ours. The incoherence and confusion to which Valéry points are augmented by the political structures entailed by the pressures of growing populations and the increased speed with which everything, news or industrial development, is now propagated. He concludes: 'incohérence [. . .] surprise—Formes anxieuses. Attente. Trémulation de la lumière mentale—[//] Ne pas omettre la confusion généralisée (radio) ni la présence réelle de *Tout, en tout point, à tout moment*' (XXI, 615). With how much more feeling and force would he have been able to make the point in his last sentence now, in the 1970s! The view often implied is that the present confused co-existence of what, for brevity's sake, we have called the old and the new will last for some time, but not indefinitely.

What then will be the outcome? Valéry seems to presuppose that the new outlook will eventually predominate. He thus depicts with some zest the end of nearly all *fiducia* and *magie,* with the concluding stark choice which will face humanity between naked fact or power and 'pure', self-conscious fiction for fiction's sake: 'Le Poème de la Fin de la Fable—[//] Tous les mythes et fables, croyances de ts [tous] ordres perdant valeur, résonance,—apparaissent enfin dans leur naïveté et formation trop simple de "Phénomènes mentaux" *non traités ni perçus comme tels* [. . . //] Les mythes montrent leur génération—La Fiducia s'évanouit—Les dieux, les idéaux, les entités sociales, le crédit, la "Nature",—Amour, Vie et Mort perdent toute magie—Le "Passé", le "Vrai",—le Savoir—Etc. [//] A la place de tout ceci, demeure ou s'installe le *Ce que l'on peut faire* et la *Combinatoire psychique*—avec ses conventions *explicites*' (XX, 452–3). But he frequently professes that he is unable to envisage how life and society as we have known them until now will accommodate themselves to the victory of the new outlook. We thus find in the following passage a typical open-ended conclusion to a vigorously sweeping denunciation of the old myths still embodied in our lives: '"Sauvages" nos cultes, nos idéaux, nos arts, nos éthiques, nos "grands hommes", nos politiques, nos passions, nos philosophies, nos lois et principes divers, notre Droit, notre Economie—notre "poésie"—la *personnalité* [//] tout ceci Sauvages ou *mélange de Sauvages* [//] Ce dernier point est particulièrement intéressant. Il y a plusieurs luttes dans chacun de nous. [//] Lumière *blanche* d'Europe faite d'une quantité de *spectres*. Problème—de la vie possible si l'on réduit tout ce qui n'est pas vérifiable, superposable— à zéro, à être sans conséquence hors de son domaine de *relais humains*' (XI, 740). 'La conscience' or 'la conscience de soi' is a key concept and value in Valéry and is clearly associable with the new values and outlook in question.[8] It is reasonable to suppose that questions like the following imply the fundamental irreconcilability of the new outlook and life as it has been known until now: 'La politique, les mœurs, la société tout entière sont-elles compatibles avec la variation de la conscience, qui tend à différencier les valeurs, à réduire, sinon à abolir, celles qui sont purement fiduciaires?—Les mœurs et lois sont des habitudes de l'*inertie*, de l'automatisme' (XII, 866). Valéry affirms that he does not know what will become of man when *conscience* and his analytical powers have done their work of elucidation and demystification, when they have been fully incorporated into his style of thinking and living (XXI, 727). 'Peut-on vivre sans blagues?' (XI, 594) is his impatiently laconic conclusion.

If Valéry is interrogative, rhetorically or not, about the future of man, it is understandable that, influenced by the views indicated, he can be even more tentative about the future of literature. He links its existence and nature until now with the mythical and outmoded as already described. 'La littérature est impossible sans une confusion, subie ou consentie,—de l'effet avec l'existence' (IX, 526). Once readers have absorbed the new values, once they become, in Valéry's terminology, not 'passive', but 'active', what will happen to literature? (IX, 758). The man of the future will be 'active' particularly with regard to language; he will not easily succumb to the traditional literary 'superstitions' (IX, 135), he will not forget the verbal nature of all literature. So Valéry asks: 'Quelles conséquences pour la littérature la connaissance et conscience plus profonde du fonctionnement *langage?*' (XXI, 348). His answer is that literature will either die or evolve: 'Si le lecteur était *actif*, ou il n'y aurait plus de littérature, ou elle serait infiniment autre que ce qu'elle est' (IX, 760): 'la litt.[érature] telle qu'elle a été admise, et pratiquée par lecteur et auteur jusqu'ici est *condamnée*' (X, 883—written in 1924).[9] It follows that, for Valéry, a question-mark hangs too over the future of poetry. 'J'avoue que je ne crois pas ts [tous] les jours à l'avenir de la poésie— Les excitations qu'elle peut donner sont aujourd'hui fort distancées. [//] Aux esprits de qualité difficile la Science donne plus' (XII, 29). Poetry is a survival, a tradition inherited from the past and if it did not exist, no one would think now of inventing it (XI, 410). The constant development of human consciousness and analytic awareness is inimical to the nature of poetry as it has hitherto been.[10] The often mystically intuitive vagueness on which poetry has hitherto fed is being replaced by precision.[11] There has already taken place a separation or dissociation which is full of great consequences for poetry: 'Les fonctions ou usages *intelligents* du langage se sont développés loin de sa fonction musicale, et il n'est plus resté concret, synthétique, *poétique* que niaiserie. [//] La forme chantante, humaine—complète, l'accord parfait du langage primitif n'a pu suivre les développements psychiques de la connaissance; il faut pour y demeurer, se mettre dans l'état des primitifs, grecs, persans, latins, etc.—considérer le monde avec les yeux de l'an zéro. [//] d'où petits oiseaux, âme, couchers de soleil, amour, regrets, ébriété, rêves, choses épiques' (XI, 505).

We have come back to our point of departure, to the relationship *bêtise-poésie*, with now a general idea of the larger context in which Valéry sees poetry and a much clearer view of what *bêtise* implies for him: lack of *conscience*, confusion of language with reality, *croyance*, *fiducia*, mythopoeia, passivity, disorder, failure to take for granted the arbitrariness of so much. His aversion for these features of the past is part of his general espousal of many of the values of the new outlook and can find expression at a very personal level of exasperation: 'Si la poésie doit admettre la niaiserie, si elle doit être mesurée sur la capacité des esprits inférieurs, s'il suffit de Musset pour vous satisfaire, si les moyens grossiers lui sont permis, si une mosaïque d'images est un poème, alors au diable la Poésie' (IX, 591). Such impatient reactions are outweighed by the careful examination he makes of the evolution poetry—and, indeed, all art—must, he thinks, undergo if it is to survive. Understandably and no doubt inevitably, such examinations are self-affirming or self-confirming, that is, they are usually descriptions of the kind of poetry Valéry himself wrote or tried to write.

The future cannot do other than arise from the past; the question is how and with what antagonisms and different emphases. Unsurprisingly, Valéry sees all art as having arisen and developed empirically. Painters, prose writers and poets have been mostly concerned with production, not with understanding. 'L'art—entreprise qui jusqu'ici précède la connaissance de son *but "profond"*. Déplacements divers de son but apparent—d'où la diversité des écoles' (XIX, 536). Hence an identification in his thought between art in the past and all we have already seen him associating with the 'old world'. 'La phase idolâtre des arts (et parmi eux la métaphysique) est celle pendant laquelle la pratique des arts est liée à la croyance que *ce qu'ils font naître* (dans les hommes) *les fait naître.* [//] Et cette croyance initiale masque la généralité des possibilités, cache la structure combinatoire, empêche de voir les œuvres comme autant de cas particuliers ou d'applications d'un système de moyens et d'un ensemble d'effets. Les conventions inconscientes se confondent avec des conditions absolues. [//] Cette phase est inévitable chronologiquement.' (XIX, 613). He believes that poetry's present 'état élémentaire embryonnaire' (XII, 163) needs to be improved upon. In poetry, what has been mostly intuitive and instinctive will of necessity become more reasoned and methodical (III, 901). Old-fashioned *vague-à-l'âme* is inevitably doomed and, given the dissociation discussed earlier, the poetry of the future 'a pour objet ou pour matière la composition ou recomposition savante consciente du mélange dont l'intellect et le langage en tant que moyen de l'intellect ont poursuivi l'analyse' (VII, 243). Conscious composition will be in high esteem. Messianic poetry, poetry inspired by proselytising commitment will be replaced by poetry that does not seek to be other than an exploitation of language and man's sensibility. Mystery and transcendence as we have known them will go. 'Qui est poète doit avouer son habileté, parler de versification et non s'attribuer des voix mystérieuses' (IX, 440). Illusion and belief in anything but the intrinsic powers of poetic language will diminish. 'Grand Art = celui qui réduit les conditions de croyance au minimum;—et à la limite, aux conventions explicites fondamentales' (XX, 837). The general aim will be to 'porter la notion de littérature, celle de poésie à un degré de précision, et d'abord, de *séparation* plus conforme à l'exigence moderne [//] non point par le sujet c.à.d. par le vocabulaire, mais par la *conscience*, les objectifs' (XI, 750).

We have seen that, for the total sceptic which Valéry—theoretically —was, almost any belief or commitment is viewed as idolatry. In any context, all that matters is 'form'. 'Le "fond" (par opposition à la "forme") c'est la *crédulité*, la foi, la chose qui enchaîne en soi, ce qui se croit absolu, non relatif [. . .] On croit au *fond* de sa pensée, sans songer que ce fond n'est jamais qu'une forme' (VII, 639). 'Tout est problème de *forme*. Car le reste, l'homme n'y peut rien et n'y connaît rien. Il n'y a pas de *fond*' (IX, 135). Valéry's programme for poetry is a peculiar combination of the negative and the positive, excluding certain things and promoting others. For him, the impression of *bêtise* arises when naïveté and *inconscience* are encountered, in poetry or in prose, when in the light of his modern awareness, all seems false, pretentious and arbitrary. 'Bêtise et Poésie. C'est un grand sujet. Exagération. Fausse voix—Ventriloques—faux désespérés. Faux fous, faux extasiés, faux simples, faux. [//] La volonté de génie [//]— Et puis ils parlent de "génie" [//] Ce n'est pas sérieux' (IX, 281). Hugo's *Eviradnus* is impossible to take seriously. 'L'envie d'étonner, d'écraser, d'en imposer, etc., prédomine et se combine avec l'art et l'artifice—[. . .] Donc il a fallu chercher à sauver *l'art* et *l'être*— donc à *supprimer* tout ce qui éveille la méfiance, la sensation de mettre de la complaisance à croire aux objets trop gros du poème, etc., et d'autre part Reconnaître—l'artifice, le mettre en évidence' (XI, 293). That is Valéry's way of dealing with arbitrariness: reduce it to the minimum and then make a virtue of it. 'Règle—Précepte. Donner l'arbitraire comme tel. L'accuser' (XI, 469). Like Valéry himself, future poets, the poets attuned to the new outlook, will make a virtue of difficulties encountered, will want to make what is crudely called technique their main inspiration, technique freed from illusion and verisimilitude, technique which will exploit 'la *Combinatoire* psychique' of poet and reader. 'Moins idolâtres, les poètes oseraient nommer un poème: Poème pour bien placer le mot X; Poème pour mettre en valeur telle forme ou figure syntaxique' (XII, 752). They will want a theory of language, literature and poetry, a *poétique* and a *rhétorique*.[12] The art of composition will absorb them as it did him.[13] In their own very different domain, poets will be following a procedure comparable with that of the modern natural sciences: 'ces succès heureux (puissance, précision etc)—dans les domaines où les plus grands, les plus certains, les plus constants résultats ont été obtenus— ont été dus dans ts[tous] les cas à l'abandon des notions données—de la vision commune moyenne vague—et à l'institution de notions "pures"' (XI, 834). 'Pure poetry' (different facets of which these various remarks have been adumbrating) is a counterpart to pure science.[14] Poetry and stupidity will part company as the new ethos penetrates and informs art and poetry.

If this picture of the future appears too good or too bad (according to taste) to be true, too simplistic to be credible, this is partly because I have set down and interrelated a number of reflections and speculations that are most certainly and most genuinely Valéry's but only at the expense of leaving out much else—above all, many doubts and hesitations. He is often far from sure that his poetic ideal can ever be realised. 'Poésie. Peut-on conduire la préoccupation poétique à un haut degré de conscience et de précision sans perdre ce qu'il faut de confiance dans le vague et dans l'abandon au mouvement qui semblent nécessaires à l'*état de chant?*' (XI, 502). He is thinking not just of the reader ('les hommes pourraient-ils tolérer la poésie si elle ne se donnait pour une logomancie?', IX, 440), but of the poet. His ideal hits up against his realisation that the poet needs to have incorporated into his whole being, into his beliefs and his body, the conventions—syntactic, metric and others—on which poetry is based: too much analytic awareness would probably impair the poet's power of exaltation and his lyricism. Furthermore, neither poetry nor society showed many signs of following the future course indicated by Valéry,[15] though one can see more clearly now how much the New Novelists and various contemporary *littérateurs* exemplify some of his preoccupations concerning art which shuns the 'realist illusion'.[16] It would be wrong to see Valéry as a naïve science-worshipper. His attachment to the values I have described is definite, but his vision of the future is not rosy. As we have seen, it can be very black. He is disturbed if not horrified by many aspects of the modern world—the tyrannical abuses inherent in the development of man's analytic powers and in the search for 'purity' and the separation of functions, the political, social and ethical consequences (cf. especially *Regards sur le monde actuel, Oeuvres*, Pléiade II). He was anguished by his anticipation of the barbarousness that would result from some aspects of the new outlook, e.g. totalitarianism or the ugly, extravagant waste and inhumanity entailed by mass production. The reality often shocked him. Cultureless technocrats were decidedly not his ideal men of the future. He represented a curious combination of values of the future—as he saw it—and values of the past (with regard to his ideas about art, beauty, craftsmanship, peace and calm, dedication to the notion of the civilised, universal man). His imagination and sensitivity as well as his intelligence were of a superlatively high order, expressed through consummate mastery of language, in poetry and in prose. His poetry particularly—and sometimes despite his poetic theories and expressed intentions—reveals a man constantly at grips with the distressing problems as well as the delights engendered by analytic thought, especially when it was applied to himself.

Valéry's life and thought embody some of the important features of recent times, the adventurous sense of man's capacity for indefinite evolution and the order needed to shape that evolution (in our minds, our society or our poetry). He is a post-Romantic and also an anti-Romantic, a man of deep, complex and resonant feelings, imaginatively open to man's enormous possibilities but resolved, in a manner seen by many as 'Classical', that man should remain in control of himself and cherish that inalienable asset, *la liberté de l'esprit* (cf. *Oeuvres*, Pléiade II, 1077–99).[17] Baudelaire thought that all good poets necessarily become good critics, balance their *volupté* with *analyse* and *connaissance*. For some tastes, Mallarmé already goes too far along a road which leads from Baudelaire through Mallarmé to the tortured dilemmas into which analysis and self-analysis brought their successor Valéry. In this perspective, Valéry can be seen as a kind of paroxysm of order and adventure in poetry and in thought. *Bêtise* as he understood it will not so easily be worked out of the human mind and heart (for which realisation many of us are no doubt immensely thankful); belief, commitment, participatory enjoyment with others of untidy 'life' are too central and too dear to too many of us. One may doubt whether Valéry himself would have been prepared to pay the price that would have to be paid for the disappearance of *bêtise* as he understood it. But he would probably have replied that we would pay the price whether we want to or not.

Southampton   W. N. INCE

NOTES

1 *Oeuvres* will refer to one of the two volumes in the Bibliothèque de la Pléiade edition (Pléiade I, 1957 and Pléiade II, 1960).

2 The roman numerals, in the body of the article and in the notes, refer to the volume of Valéry's *Cahiers*, the arabic to the page.

   Valéry's *Cahiers* present peculiar problems for the transcriber, especially with regard to punctuation. It is often difficult to be sure whether a mark is a full stop, a comma or a dash. It is also hard to be sure when Valéry really intends a new paragraph, that is, what significance to attach to a new line with an indention (often he is adopting what is tantamount to a note form and making points or lists). I have indicated all possible breaks for paragraphs by [/]. Anything between square brackets is mine, not Valéry's. So [. . .] is an indication that I have made an omission from his text.

3 These generalisations are based on personal experience as much as on pure reflection. As early as 1897, he notes: 'J'ai connu bien des poètes. Un seul était ce qu'il faut ou ce qui me plaît [This is undoubtedly a reference to Mallarmé.] Le reste était stupide, ou plat, d'une lâcheté d'esprit inébranlable. Leur impuissance, leur vanité, leur enfantillage, et leur grandiose, dégoûtante répugnance à voir clairement ce qui est. Leur superstition, leur gloire, leur terrible ressemblance à n'importe qui, aussitôt la besogne faite, leur servilité d'esprit. Enfin, ils portent toutes les chaînes du langage ce qui en fait, dans le monde actuel, des villageois, des provinciaux. Tout ceci, indépendamment de ce qu'on appelle le talent littéraire qui vit parfaitement d'accord avec la sottise la plus aiguë' (I, 193).

4 See Judith Robinson, *L'Analyse de l'esprit dans les cahiers de Valéry*, Paris, José Corti, 1963.

5 Cf. 'L'idée des choses et des êtres dans la science moderne est seulement une formation ou production en équilibre mobile avec les moyens' XX, 655): 'Désormais, il faut considérer tout ce que nous "savons" comme un *moyen* et non plus comme une *fin*' (XIX, 218): 'Le mot "Savoir" a pour moi un sens tout "humain" et ne peut être complété que par de l'humain—c.à.d. par de l'instant, du provisoire, du relativable' (XXI, 81).

6 Cf. 'Tout ce qui est verbal est provisoire. Tout langage est moyen' (XII, 673).

7 Cf. 'La grande modif[ication] rapide du monde moderne est donna [*sic*] naissance à l'embarras du nombre des *faits* et pouvoirs nouveaux c.à.d. imprévus—dans un système de conventions incarnées, de langage immémorial—[/] Le nombre des idées renversées, des notions devenues impossibles est extraordinaire. [/] Or en littér[ature], art, phil[osophie], histoire, etc., la terminologie est demeurée la même' (XX, 390).

8 Cf. 'La "conscience de soi" est peu compatible avec la croyance, et la fiducia—lesquelles consistent à percevoir comme *en soi* ce que cette conscience perçoit comme *de moi*' (XIX, 597).

9 As early as 1899, Valéry notes: 'Toute la littérature connue est écrite dans le langage du *sens commun*. Hors Rimbaud. [/] Une littérature à procédés plus recherchés est possible' (I, 616).

10 Cf. 'Des choses qui ne s'accommodent pas de la conscience développée. Merveilleux et poésie. Dupes du beau. Le *merveilleux* est dû à la limitation de la "conscience"—c.à.d. de l'observation et de la question' (XI, 501).

11 Cf. 'Destins de la Poésie. Générations en qui les notions précises— c.à.d. exprimables en actes corporels—Tot acta quot vera—en termes finis—remplacent l'infus de quoi la poésie se nourrissait [/] (Le romantisme, ce qu'il y a de plus vieux,—de plus vieilli par l'ère moderne)—Enfants jouant avec l'électricité' (XII, 488). Cf. also 'Pourquoi certains ne sont pas poètes. [/] L'état-poète est l'état symbolique ou de symbolisme lequel est un état susceptible d'un degré ultérieur de précision—et s'oppose à ce degré de précision—[/] N'être pas poéte c'est souvent être accoutumé à franchir le stade symbole, et à

le tenir pour tâtonnement, ou à ne pas le reconnaître pour ayant quelque prix' (VII, 466).

12 See Gérard Genette, 'La littérature comme telle' in *Figures*, Paris, éd. du Seuil, 1966.

13 If Valéry's attitude is carried to the furthest possible point, the consequence is 'pure poetry' which would have nothing to *say*—'Poésie extrême finit par ne plus rien vouloir *dire*. Car à la fin on ne peut plus dire que sottises' (IV, 908).

14 Cf. 'La poésie pure résulte de l'observation et revient en somme à fonder la notion de poésie uniquement sur des considérations linguistiques *positives*' (XII, 781).

15 Indeed, quite the contrary, as is to some extent shown in my paper 'Paul Valéry et le concept du moderne' (read at the colloquium devoted to *Paul Valéry et la pensée contemporaine* at the C.N.R.S. in Paris on 15 and 16 November 1971 and to be published in the *Cahiers Valéry* of the recently founded *Société Paul Valéry*). Various considerations of the present article are there examined from a different viewpoint, viz. the apparent contrast between Valéry's views on modern thought (seen by him as largely derived from experience of the sciences) and some of his conclusions concerning what modern artists, *littérateurs* and poets have produced.

16 Cf. my article on 'Valéry and the Novel' in the special Valéry number of the *Australian Journal of French Studies*, VIII, 2, 1971.

17 Cf. 'Politique et modernité [//] L'immensité des nombres d'hommes et des intérêts *à toute échelle* (ce qui est la nouveauté) que remue le fait politique "moderne"—coïncide avec l'accroissement, sans doute extrême, indépassable, de la *vitesse de propagation* des informations et de *diffusion* ainsi que de la *fréquence* de production de ces faits—incohérence—[//] Des centaines de millions d'hommes sont soumis en 24 *h*. à des signaux variés qui ne laissent en eux aucune liberté d'esprit (projets, réflexions, station en profondeur) mais régime *de la surprise*' (XXI, 614–15).

REALISM AND FANTASY IN THE WORK OF MAX JACOB: SOME VERSE POEMS

The two strongly marked poles of the work of Max Jacob are represented, on the one hand, by the bizarre and enigmatic prose poems of *Le Cornet à dés*, and, on the other, by the fervent mysticism of the main parts of *La Défense de Tartufe*, *Le Laboratoire central* and many other works. At neither pole is the concept of 'realism' a very relevant critical or exegetical tool. In his poems of spiritual aspiration Jacob turns away from reality and the social situation, sometimes, although not always, with a Christian horror of the world as a place of sin and evil. In his prose poems he departs from it no less radically, although this time to create a strange and bewildering universe which disturbs by its apparently gratuitous nature. Nightmarish visions, dream sequences, satirical sketches, parodies, jokes and puns all follow each other rapidly throughout the book and leave the reader amazed and disorientated.

A desire to transfigure the real, to place the poem at a considerable remove from everyday experience, occupies, indeed, a central position in Jacob's aesthetic. He develops this belief in the preface to *Le Cornet à dés* itself, and in many other writings, using terms like *situation* or *marge* to define the quality of a poem which successfully divorces it from the real. One of the clearest statements is in a letter to Jacques Doucet:

J'admire profondément Mallarmé, non par son lyrisme, mais pour la 'situation divinement géographique' de son œuvre. J'entends par situation de l'œuvre cette espèce de magie qui sépare une œuvre (même picturale ou musicale) de l'amateur, cette espèce de transplantation qui fait que l'œuvre vous met les pieds dans un autre univers. Il n'y a en réalité d'œuvres créées que celles qui ont cela: la marge, et cela est aussi très rare: on le trouve surtout dans certains poèmes japonais et persans: pas tous.[1]

Such a conception of poetry is obviously one which must come close to a complete disaffection for the notion of realism, and it is not surprising to find Jacob, in the same letter, uncompromisingly taking up this position: 'Vous avez déjà compris, cher Monsieur, que j'ai horreur du naturalisme, du réalisme et de toute œuvre qui ne vaut que par la comparaison qu'on peut faire avec le réel?'

Yet, despite this statement and much of his practice, there is a great deal in Jacob's work that testifies to his strong interest in social life and manners, and his considerable powers as an observer of society. A satirical depiction of human behaviour is a predominant feature of his prose fiction, and *Le Cornet à dés* itself contains many sketches and pen-portraits of the life and people of his times. He himself wrote to Jean Cocteau in 1922: 'Je ne me suis jamais senti si cubiste que depuis que je fais du réel. C'était le but cubiste. Arriver au réel par des moyens non réalistes'[2] The emphasis here still falls on the process of transposition, the necessary heightening of reality to achieve an aesthetic illusion. Yet the artistic position taken up is no longer so hostile to the idea of literature reflecting reality. Not only is the poet's initial interest and activity situated in that very field (*depuis que je fais du réel*), his ultimate goal and ideal (*arriver au réel*) are even expressed in terms of truth to external experience.

It might be helpful, therefore, to see Jacob's poetic work as describing an arc between the two poles we have identified. At the two extremes, the subject matter, tone and atmosphere of the poems place them at some distance from reality. At various intermediary points, however, there is a greater approximation to the real, so much so that the poems stimulate a type of interest in social life and every-day experience that is rather rare in modern poetry.

Probably at the centre point of the pendulum swing stands a small group of verse poems, written at various times during Jacob's career, but mainly concentrated in the 1910–20 period. Those that will be considered appear in *La Défense de Tartufe* (1919) in *Le Laboratoire central* (1921) and *Les Pénitents en maillots roses* (1925). The characteristic of these poems is that while they may be 'situated' in Jacob's sense, the transposition is achieved through a fantasy that is much milder in tone than the vigorous burlesque of many of his prose poems. It is a playful fantasy that fuses with observations of life to produce a relationship to reality for which a term like realism does not, on occasion, seem too inappropriate. It is not, of course, a realism like that of the nineteenth-century novel, with its case histories of typical figures, its searching analysis of character and situation, and its deterministic assumptions. It will be a much more intimate and evocative form of realism, concerned with conjuring up the 'ordinary texture of reality', with making us feel the atmosphere of everyday living in a given place at a given time. The expression *réalisme du quotidien*[3] has sometimes been used to describe it, and the term conveys well enough the limited goals that such an aesthetic sets itself, at the same time as it hints at its importance. However vast their general ambitions, all the great realist writers were aware of the peculiar fascination that the *quotidien*—the ordinary unstressed moment of ordinary life—has for all of us and in moments of stasis and insight tried to record it in their works. This is what Jacob also tries to do, although by different means.

The social life and environment that Jacob knew best were those of Paris. This was particularly true between 1904 and 1920 when he was immersed in the avant-garde of painters and writers headed by Apollinaire and Picasso, which, although it was cosmopolitan, was nonetheless the very incarnation of the Parisian spirit. Paris therefore looms large in all his early work, but it is especially in the opening section of *La Défense de Tartufe* that he tries to catch the mood and tempo of Parisian life.

The perspective is not limited to the present, for three poems are entitled '1867', '1889' and '1900'. Jacob seems to have had in mind almost a social history of Paris, past, present and future, as can be seen from a letter to Jacques Doucet in which he defines the theme of a projected volume of verse in terms of a series of *chroniques*—a descriptive label which has strong attachments with the realist tradition:

J'appellerai le second recueil:
Chroniques prophétiques et rétrospectives du nom d'une partie qui contient des prophéties de la guerre écrite en 1909, des poèmes sur la guerre et aussi des tableaux du passé: 1889, 1900, 1867, etc. . . .[4]

In this formulation, however, the theme is wrongly conceived, as Jacob quickly realised. The so-called prophetic poems (in prose) and the *tableaux du passé* (in verse) are works very different in tone, and represent two themes in his literary output rather than one. The first are hallucinatory in style, and belong perfectly to the more hermetic atmosphere of *Le Cornet à dés* where they were finally published. In the second the emphasis falls clearly on an attempt to evoke the social climate and manners of Paris at various points in the recent past. It is understandable, therefore, that they should have been separated off and grouped with other poems in *Tartufe* which have a similar range and ambition, but with reference to the present.

The prevailing mood in the whole group of poems, whether they be contemporary or *tableaux du passé*, is undoubtedly one of gaiety. Two of the contemporary pieces are a humorous evocation of

Fantômas, the celebrated fictional criminal who was all the rage at the time; another paints a satirical picture of auditions at the Conservatoire, contrasting the prestigious nature of the classical theatrical rôles with the banality of the contemporary Parisians who aspire to fill them. The intention is thus to give a light-hearted picture of Parisian life at the grass-roots—an ambition seen again in 'L'Auberge "A l'Escarmouche"'' which is a careful tongue-in-the-cheek description of graffiti on the flaking wall of a café.

In the *tableaux du passé* a similar attitude of humorous indulgence is adopted towards the periods being evoked. What is especially picked out for comment are the fashions in dress, leisure and entertainment peculiar to each age and such an emphasis produces in poet and reader alike a reaction of amused interest. It is enough for Jacob to write (in '1867'):

On est très Véronèse et miroir de Venise

or (in '1889'):

On a bâti un music hall qui coûte huit millions
On y fait du magnétisme, c'est une attraction!
Une danseuse javanaise, on trouve ça exquis.[5]

for it to be clear that it is in the field of *la petite histoire* that the poems operate. Many of the graver issues of each period are in fact alluded to: political repression and social injustice under the Second Empire; Boulanger and anarchism; the Dreyfus case. But in this context these issues lose the impact they have in political history. They are lightly passed over and become only part of the general texture of the age, without disturbing the overall tone of the poem. In their place other aspects of human affairs are highlighted, which are much more important in determining the mood and atmosphere: simple *faits divers*, typical utterances of the *vox populi*, the vogue names of the period. It is through his use of these vivid little particulars that Jacob can create a generalised impression of each age that is essentially light and carefree.

Humour is, therefore, an important characteristic of Jacob's approach to reality. His particular version of realism is one in which life is observed and recorded in a spirit of relaxed enjoyment. That this mood has not featured greatly in the main areas of the realist tradition is not a fact that should blind us to its relevance and value in another context. A *réalisme du quotidien* will often be lighter in tone than more serious forms of the aesthetic, and there is no reason why it should not be compatible with an attitude of warm amusement at human behaviour. When Jacob ends '1889' with the lines:

> Mais!
> Y a la construction en fer
> Qui sauvera l'univers.[6]

his slightly mocking rendering of popular optimism accurately catches the mood generated in France by the exhibition of 1889 and its showpiece, the Eiffel Tower.

No doubt, in such a context, humour must be kept within certain bounds, and it is arguable that in the poems mentioned so far, whether contemporary pieces or *tableaux du passé*, it is allowed too much play. Satirical exuberance is sometimes unrestrained, as at the end of '1867' or the brilliant beginning of '1889' which vividly captures the giddiness of *La Belle Époque*:

> Loïe Fuller, c'est épatant,
> Sur le bi, sur le bout, sur le bi du bout du banc,
> Mais ce Rodin est un salaud,
> C'est zéro!
> Otéro!
> Ah! voilà un numéro![7]

But despite such touches of the burlesque, these poems reveal a genuine interest in the world of human affairs and real powers of outward-going observation. If they do not represent quite the ideal balance between observation and humour, they suggest that, with only a slight adjustment in tone, this balance could be achieved—and this is indeed what happens in the major poem in the section, 'Printemps et cinématographe mêlés'.

Two interrelated themes dictate the whole tone and tempo of this poem and make it the essential statement of Jacob's delighted contemplation of Parisian life *circa* 1914: joy in spring, and pleasure in the urban surroundings and way of life of Paris. If the first theme spreads a note of gaiety through the poem, emanating from all the traditional ingredients of spring poetry, the second theme is no less vital, in that it diverts all these associations towards an urban scene and anchors the poem firmly in a precise milieu. For we do not see spring or nature as they would have been sung by a Romantic poet. It is nature as it is seen in the park of a big city, and spring as it is experienced by a city dweller, who is so typically modern urban man that almost his first spontaneous remark is that he is on a diet:

> Les immeubles sont neufs; les verres d'eau sont clairs.
> J'endure pour guérir un régime sévère.
> Allons au Bois si ça m'amuse;
> J'y recontre parfois la Muse!
> Les bourgeons, c'est amer comme un lit d'hôpital
> Et l'on voit la pelouse au travers d'un cristal.

So it is not merely the sun shining and birds singing that the poet evokes, but also people at windows in the city centre, the bustle of café life, all the sights and sounds of Paris:

> De cafés en cafés, les autos en location
> Reçoivent des pourboires comme une bonne occasion.
> Aux fenêtres, le soir, les gens ont l'air de spectres
> Parce qu'on ne tourne plus les boutons électriques.
> Et, dans le Luxembourg qu'un blanc choral allume,
> Un marchand de corsets joue du cor à la lune.
> Sous les épais rideaux de l'avenue du Bois,
> Un membre du Jockey apprend l'art du hautbois,
> Les pieds de ses valets soulignent les cadences.[8]

It is precisely to the urban preoccupations that the title of the poem relates. Although reference is made to the cinema in only one stanza, it is rightly promoted to a position of prominence because the implication is that it is one of the central features of the new life style of urban man. The exhilaration that spring arouses in the poet naturally prompts a desire to walk in the park. But no less naturally and spontaneously—indeed within the same stanza—it prompts a desire to go to the cinema. For modern man, so the title suggests, one impulse is really inseparable from the other. The joys of spring immediately evoke the joys of new collective forms of pleasure, typical of the urban twentieth century, and both are needed to bring fulfilment to a contemporary poet.

In the second instance, the cinema probably stands for the humorous vision that the poet wants to cultivate. The films he evokes are the madly hectic ones of the early days of film, whose absurdities, both intentional and unintentional, he clearly savours. Among many lines eulogising Paris, the most revealing are those in which he prefers Paris to Brittany because he sees it as a more magical world in which he can give his fantasy free rein. And indeed his picture of Paris, and more particularly its people, is coloured by a playful satire. The whole of bourgeois civilisation of this period seems to be viewed through ironical spectacles. In the corset-seller playing his horn to the moon, the member of the Jockey Club learning the oboe, and, later, *Monsieur le directeur des Nouvelles Galeries* perceiving his guardian angel in a tree, we see the placid bourgeoisie being incongruously touched by spring fever and an uncharacteristic desire for self-expression. A whole restrictingly staid way of life is cast into sharp relief by the poet's humorous vision.

On this occasion, however, a balance is kept between the free play of fantasy and faithfulness to external experience. The poet's enjoyment of spring and the Parisian scene, his sharp eye for sensuous details in the real world—which are caught in vivid little cameos throughout the poem—act as restraining factors on his imagination. His fantasy blends with perceptions of the real world, but does not obliterate them.

Where this balance can best be felt is in the language and rhythm of the poem, where Jacob achieves with great success the kind of effect for which he was obviously striving in the other poems as well. The effect could best be described as that of a feigned casualness. The aim is to defeat expectations of a well-made poem by the use of a colloquial, off-hand style, marked by a certain flatness in both diction and rhythm. The metres used are never more than approximate, the rhyming is often of a stop-gap kind reminiscent of doggerel, and the whole development of the poem seems to follow inconsequential lines. But once the reader adjusts to this style, he finds that it is one nicely attuned to the real texture of sensation and atmosphere. The apparent garrulousness develops into a rhythmic flow which varies subtly to accommodate observations of detail, humorous thoughts and remarks, and small changes in mood.

It is a style which perfectly captures Jacob's approach to reality as he tried to crystallise it in all these Parisian poems. It is an approach that can both be compared and contrasted with a similar attitude to be found in other sectors of the avant-garde of his day. A desire to catch the essence of the twentieth century scene and an urban way of life was common to such poets and groups as Guillaume Apollinaire, the Futurists and the Unanimists. All wanted to break out of the enclosed atmosphere of late Symbolism and create a new poetry for a new age. But whereas others were concerned to reflect the dynamism of the new century, with its rapid means of transport, its instant communications and its energy, the carefree mood and casual spontaneity of Jacob's poem proclaim that he is interested in the more intimate, small-scale texture of modern life. The Paris that emerges from his work is quite different from either the corrupt capital of so much nineteenth-century literature, or the pulsating metropolis of the modernists. The city has become simply the natural habitat of man, providing an environment and a life style in which the poet takes an equable and absorbing pleasure.

By its totally good-humoured acceptance of an environment and way of life, in the way that the tempo and atmosphere of Parisian life in Jacob's day are warmly brought alive, while at the same time being subjected to a degree of ironic distanciation through humour and fantasy, 'Printemps et cinématographe mêlés' is thus one of the best examples of Jacob's type of realism.

The mood it represents, however, soon disappears in *La Défense de Tartufe*. The rest of the volume becomes the poignant, and often anguished record of Jacob's conversion to Catholicism and his meditations on his new faith. The experience of the revelation led him naturally to quite different themes, a wider range of moods, and writing that is generally more highly charged. In the new spiritual atmosphere of the later sections, even his view of Paris begins to change, with the city tending to take on new associations as a place of darkness and sin.

The contrast, indeed, between the very secular nature of the Parisian poems and the rest of the volume is so marked that Jacob tried to rationalise it in a preliminary note to the opening section:

Le poète cache sous l'expression de la joie le désespoir de n'en avoir pas trouvé la réalité.

Yet this seems a contrived explanation, which does not reflect in any sense the real tenor of the early poems. To find a more convincing reason for the juxtaposition within the volume of two apparently very different kinds of inspiration—apart from the drastically simple one of the conveniences of publication—one has to look for another form of continuity.

It can be found in the fact that, although the *mood* of the poems in which Jacob recounts his discovery of Christ is naturally very different from that of the secular pieces, the variation in the *tone* of his writing is not always so marked. His conversion was distinguished by the unpropitious circumstances in which it took place. Christ first appeared to him on the wall of his dingy lodgings in the rue Ravignan, and for the second time in the cheap seats of a Paris cinema. The banality of the context thus offers a striking contrast with the shattering nature of the experience—even more so than was the case with Verlaine in his prison cell. And while Jacob usually leans towards pointing the contrast, and in this respect is in direct descent from much traditional Christian meditation, including Verlaine, he also on occasion stresses the ordinariness of the context and captures the experience in a uniquely low key.

It is in such an infiltration of banality even into a dramatic event that one discerns a deeper continuity between the secular and some of the Christian poems. An instinctive feeling for place, and a spontaneous preference for low-toned aspects of reality still seem to be guiding Jacob. Thus a prose account of the revelation is full of trivial detail amost garrulously narrated:

j'ai mangé dans la rue des pommes frites et deux petits poissons et je ne sais pourquoi je suis allé au cinéma. J'ai oublié de dire ici que le fils D . . m'a donné un poignard dont le manche représente un cadavre foulant au pied un serpent. J'ai pensé de suite que c'était un avertissement du ciel, mais je ne savais pas de quoi. Et voilà qu'au cinéma . . . mais je ne comprends rien à tout cela, je suis trop bête! . . . J'ai beaucoup pleuré, même dans les entr'actes, on me regardait: j'ai fumé; je me suis intéressé à la pièce et je suis parti pour écouter mes voix qui me parlaient et pour pleurer dans la rue.[9]

'Le Christ au cinématographe' is the verse equivalent of this passage, and it has a similar casualness of utterance, irregularly heightened by a more fervent note:

Dryade du Gibet, descends comme hier au soir
Dans la stalle du Ciné, lorsque tu vins t'asseoir
Près de moi. Ta main! mets ta main sur la mienne
Et ta chaleur humaine et ta divine haleine!
Ah! comme j'étais las d'avoir tant réfléchi.
Permets que mon corps sur le tien s'infléchisse.
Eh toi! tu daignais, mes yeux cachés par ton épaule,
Parler du drame et m'expliquer les rôles.
C'était aux places à quatre-vingt-quinze centimes;
Tu parlais charité devant les sombres crimes
Que le Parisien veut tous les soirs en dessert.
. . . .
. . . .
'Bande des habits noirs', drame de Paul Féval;
Le drame est dans mon cœur et non pas sur le film.
Les agents et la gendarmerie à cheval
Encerclent un voleur dans un mortel dilemme,
Une taie sur la foule et des pleurs dans mes yeux!
La tache était un nimbe, le nimbe entourait Dieu.[10]

In many contexts, the situation and the setting, as well as certain details of these passages—the familiar *Ciné*, Christ explaining the film—would have seemed incongruous and produced an effect of bathos. If this does not happen here, it is not—as one might at first be tempted to think—because Jacob's 'sincerity' surmounts inadequacies of style. Sincerity is a function of style, and the poem's success is due rather to the persistence of the simple colloquial methods of expression of the earlier poems. We have seen that it is the characteristic of this colloquial style to be extremely flexible, so that it can absorb the most trivial details and turn them to account in the creation of a mood. In this case, the way in which banal items of the cinema or the film are integrated into the expression of a spiritual vision creates a stylistic texture of great suppleness, which is a tacit guarantee of the poet's truthful reaction to his experience.

Within the play of light and shade peculiar to this style, there has been a considerable change of emphasis. The humour and fantasy have not entirely disappeared, but they occupy a less prominent position. Features of Parisian life survive, but are no longer celebrated in and for themselves. The light falls on a drama potentially more vivid than the modest life style that Jacob was content to evoke earlier. Nevertheless, for a brief space of time, the drama is contained within the same chromatic range as in the earlier poems. The tone of voice still conjures up a picture of a man who is inseparable from a certain urban context. The grain of life in a big city can be felt in the language, rhythm and colour of the verse, underlying and giving particular substance to the drama it presents. To this extent, one can feel that an extra dimension is added to many of the poems of spiritual meditation in *Tartufe*. No matter that Jacob ultimately develops quite different themes and registers, 'Le Christ au cinématographe' and similar poems demonstrate that the pull of reality on his imagination, while it lasted, was powerful and fruitful.

It must be added, briefly, that while Paris is the main environment that attracted Jacob's sympathetic interest, it is not the only one. A number of poems, which can be grouped under the title of *poèmes de voyage* show a similar reaction to other places that he visited. Of course, a delight in observation and a desire to catch the essence of a local atmosphere are not unusual features of travel poems. But Jacob brings to the genre powers of empathy and a capacity to identify with the observed scene which go well beyond simple *couleur locale*.

'Honneur de la Sardane et de la Tenora'[11] in *Le Laboratoire central*, has a place among the travel poems equivalent to that of 'Printemps et cinématographe mêlés' among the Parisian poems, in that it shows his sympathy with another environment at its fullest and most untroubled. It was inspired by a holiday in Catalonia, in the summer of 1913, in the company of Picasso, and evokes Spain and the

Spanish way of life, particularly as it is revealed through the dance called the sardana.

The poem is original in form, falling into three parts which are each different in style. The first part describes the Spanish scene in a mode of humorous reportage similar to that of the Parisian poems; the second, evoking one of the instruments that accompany the dance, the tenora, is, surprisingly, in a controlled and careful prose; the third, expressing the pleasure that the poet takes in the dance, assumes a more lyrical form, with humorous undertones.

While the poem moves in the direction of lyricism, the progression is carefully restrained and moderated by the contrasting styles of the earlier parts, and by the all-pervasive humour. The medley of styles is not intended to produce the effect either of a virtuoso exercise or of a sudden lyric climax. On the contrary, it suggests an attentive involvement in the local scene, making itself felt through conscious variations in the tone, form and texture of the writing. Though stylistically more complex and wide-ranging than other pieces, therefore, 'Honneur de la Sardane' is no less concerned than they with appreciation of external reality. It is certainly one of the major expressions of Jacob's delight in the world around him.

It is true, however, that the impact of religious belief tended to produce in the travel poems the same change of attitude that affected the Parisian poems. In slightly later works we find the beginnings of a disenchantment with the ordinary ways of the world setting in.

Three poems from *Les Pénitents en maillots roses*,[12] 'Voyages', 'Nice' and 'Dimanche à Marseille' show the mood beginning to change. All have passages in the deliberately free and easy-going style with which we are now familiar. In 'Nice' there is particularly deft use of casual observations and reflexions which are blended together by discreet repetition to form a smooth impressionistic flow:

> Un jardin disparaît, des statues: c'est de l'art
> nous portons beaucoup de coutil jaune cette année
> et des cols blancs tombant ainsi qu'un lys fané.
> Le long d'un quai sans eau poissons et fleurs embaument.
> Oui! nous portons beaucoup de coutil jaune.
> Ciné, Cinémata domine en ce pays
> et l'on annonce un gala du génie.
> C'est l'Opéra d'un belge! Opéra! opéra.
> Car on chante sur ces bords à gorge déployée.

But 'Voyages' alone maintains to the end this equable note, heightening it in the last lines with a touch of burlesque humour. In the other two the mood threatens to turn sour. A disgust with the selfish opulence he saw around him on the Côte d'Azur, and with the whole materialistic bias of contemporary civilisation, emerges in both poems, springing clearly from the poet's Christian convictions. The vision in 'Dimanche à Marseille' has particularly sombre moments, yielding a black and striking picture of the dockland area. Wandering through this shabby district, the poet represents himself in ambivalent terms as *l'enfant perdu des cités magnifiques*, as an *orphelin fatigué* and again as *l'enfant des villes scientifiques*. Here, obviously we are nearer to the Baudelairean image of the poet as an exile in the modern city than to Jacob's earlier picture of urban man happily adjusted to his milieu.

However, the revulsion is not total. In both poems, despite the sombre moments, Jacob continues to note small details of the scene with the light quiet touch of the amused observer. 'Dimanche à Marseille' ends on a positively frivolous note:

> Or les monts bleus flottaient comme un aéroplane
> et les gens à binocles appuyés sur leurs cannes
> regardaient l'ouvrier manger des poissons crus
> les chauffeurs du tramway galants avec les femmes
> œil d'onyx et peau couleur de miel
> Les marchands mêlaient la grâce avec le flegme
> 'Ici l'on paie d'avance!'
> Le nègre et le japon mangent dans la faïence
> un refrain d'opéra s'élance de l'office
> Ici l'on flirte avec la fille de service.

As with 'Le Christ au cinématographe', therefore, these poems generate a tension, both thematically and stylistically, between two contrasting attitudes. Against the more powerful images and rhythms expressing horror at the godlessness of the contemporary world, we find a less powerful but pervasive impressionism working to capture the atmosphere of a given place and inviting poet and reader to immerse themselves in it. Although from 1921 onwards, with Jacob's retreat from the world to a life of meditation, the pendulum will swing markedly towards the more forceful spiritual vision, it is possible to say, here again, that in the equilibrium it establishes with a conflicting principle, the impulse towards the real in Jacob's imagination proves itself to be tenacious and genuine.

In conclusion, one cannot claim that the kind of atmospheric realism we have been discussing is a major aspect of Jacob's work in either a temporal or a quantitative sense. It produced relatively few poems in a prolific writing career, and, while these may be found episodically in later periods, the best examples seem concentrated in the 1910–20 decade. But some of these poems are among the most attractive that Jacob ever wrote, and for this reason alone deserve to survive. They throw light on an unexpected and under-appreciated aspect of a poet whose whole work has, anyway, not yet been properly assessed, and they provide a basic point of reference from which to investigate the many other ways in which Jacob comments on his society and his age.

Stirling   S. I. LOCKERBIE

NOTES

1 Letter of 30 January 1917. F. Garnier, *Correspondance de Max Jacob*, Tome I, Paris, 1953, p. 132.
2 ibid. Tome II, Paris, 1955, p. 83. The reference is to a book of short stories, *Le Roi de Béotie*.
3 S. J. Collier, one of the few commentators to give proper emphasis to this aspect of Jacob, uses the term *poésie de lieux communs*, in: 'Max Jacob's *Cornet à dés*', *French Studies XI*, April 1957, p. 165.
4 Letter of 6 February 1917. *Correspondance de Max Jacob*, p. 136.
5 *La Défense de Tartufe*. Nouvelle édition. Introduction et notes par André Blanchet. Paris, 1964, pp. 82, 85.
6 ibid. p. 86.
7 ibid. p. 84.
8 ibid. pp. 79, 80.
9 ibid. pp. 124–5.
10 ibid. pp. 127, 129.
11 *Le Laboratoire central, poèmes*. Préface d'Yvon Belaval. Paris, 1960, pp. 49–55.
12 In *Ballades, suivi de Visions infernales, Fond de l'eau, Sacrifice impérial, Rivage, Les Pénitents en maillots roses*. Préface de Claude Roy. Paris, 1970, pp. 208–9, 225–7, 254–5. These poems were written in 1920 during a convalescent holiday in the south of France. Cf. *Correspondance de Max Jacob*, Tome I, pp. 209–11, 214–17.

GUILLAUME APOLLINAIRE AND THE SEARCH FOR IDENTITY

Car si je suis partout à cette heure il n'y a cependant
que moi suis en moi

A dominant theme of twentieth-century French literature has been the search for the understanding of the self within the context of *la condition humaine.* Whether it be through the memory as in Proust, through the unstable moral universe of Gide, the analysis of the creative mind in Valéry, the exploration of the subconscious in Surrealism or the philosophical implications of confrontations between men in the novels of Malraux, Sartre and Camus, the urge to define and discriminate is very clear. The phenomenon of alienation, already hinted at in Chateaubriand's *René,* becomes an obsession. One of the earliest twentieth-century explorers in this field is Guillaume Apollinaire using not moral or philosophical tools but the gifts of a natural poet seeking a 'lyrisme neuf et humaniste'. His own confession that 'chacun de mes poèmes est la commémoration d'un événement de ma vie'[1] is an encouragement to begin a search for the origins of Apollinaire's preoccupations with identity in the circumstances of his birth.

There is enough here, at first sight, to furnish sufficient explanation for the most demanding critic. Born in Rome, the illegitimate son of an Italian father of Swiss descent and a Russo-Polish mother, Angelica de Kostrowitzky, Apollinaire's parenthood remained a mystery to his friends and those Picasso drawings showing him wearing a high-ranking ecclesiastical hat refer directly to the discreet rumour that his father was an important official in the Vatican. It was not until the publication of Marcel Adéma's authoritative biography, *Guillaume Apollinaire le mal-aimé,* in 1952 that this and many other problems were solved, problems which had been encouraged by Apollinaire himself partly as a deliberate mystification and partly because of a considerable personal reticence, surprising in one so apparently *abordable.* After seven years in Rome, the family of mother and two sons born outside wedlock moved to the Riviera and from thence eventually to Paris. Their life was chequered; when, in 1899, Apollinaire and his brother Albert returned to Paris after absconding without paying their three-month bill from a *pension* in Stavelot, their mother changed her name to Olga Karpoff and described her sons as her nephews.[2] Numerous incidents and influences of this unusual childhood and adolescence are referred to in *Le Poète assassiné*; Croniamantal has, as André Rouveyre noted, many of the characteristics of Apollinaire himself. From this time dates his abiding interest in different ethnic groups and above all in Jews and *tziganes*, the perpetual *émigrants* who people his prose and his poetry. It is tempting to speculate on the rootless nature of this upbringing and on the Gidean *produit de croisement* who is this child of two races inheriting a Northern and a Southern culture. This Tainean approach could lead to the construction of interesting hypotheses but Guillaume's brother Albert, the respectable bank clerk who shared these excitements, experienced no similar reactions. This is how Apollinaire described him in a letter to Lou:

Tu sais, j'aime beaucoup mon petit Albert, esprit si droit, intelligence fine, plein de bon sens, travailleur, volontaire et très doux. Très pieux, il avait voulu se faire prêtre et très joli garçon, il était tant que je l'ai connu aussi chaste que St Louis de Gonzague ou St Stanislas Kostka qui fit pénitence toute sa vie pour avoir regardé une femme avec plaisir.[3]

As so often happens, two brothers go their different ways from the same starting point and we must conclude that whatever influence Apollinaire's upbringing may have had on his development, there are other and more significant causes to be found. Yet there is something of vital importance to be retained from the circumstances of birth. Apollinaire is stateless; although France is his *pays adoptif*, the country to which he gives his admiration, his aspirations and even his love, he is not a French citizen. His arrest in 1911 after the theft of the Mona Lisa from the Louvre exposed his precarious situation and, even before this shattering event, André Salmon had noted in his *Souvenirs sans fin* how Apollinaire had talked to him of his 'soucis d'apatride'.[4] Whatever else may be found later, there are certain administrative and political foundations to Apollinaire's insecurities.

What records remain of Apollinaire's early days reveal his voracious interest in the widest possible range of reading; disconnected, undirected, it depends on the hazards of chance for its material. From medieval literature to the present day, his eclectic tastes found subjects for pleasure and for wonder which his remarkable memory will revive for illustrative image in later poetry. André Breton in an essay of as early as 1917 remarked on Apollinaire's 'don prodigieux d'émerveillement'[5] and Apollinaire's own choice of the *devise*

'J'émerveille' as *marque d'éditeur* for the limited edition of *Le Bestiaire* (1911) illustrated by Raoul Dufy, is significant. It seems clear that from his earliest days Apollinaire knew that he was going to be a writer; his wide eclectic reading represents not only a search for masters but, above all, a means of satisfying a ceaseless curiosity about the nature of man. The wide and unexpected range of allusion which runs through his work derives, at least in part, from the need of assurance that Apollinaire is like other men and that the experience of sadness and suffering has, as recompense, an increased sense of identification. Jottings from the notebook of the nineteen-year-old poet in Stavelot reveal something of the self-questioning common to those of his age:

Pourquoi ne suis-je pas né riche comme tant d'autres. Pourquoi mon avenir se présente-t-il mystérieux, hermétique alors que les autres, fils de famille, riches, ne voient dans l'avenir qu'une succession de fêtes, de noces, avec le gâtisme final à l'heure du mariage, tandis que moi. . . .[6]

It is strange to see Flaubert, at the age of eighteen, uttering a similar cry of despair to a friend:

O que je donnerais bien de l'argent pour être ou plus bête ou plus spirituel, athée ou mystique, mais enfin quelque chose de complet, d'entier, une identité, quelque chose en un mot![7]

Whilst in Stavelot he began to write *L'Enchanteur pourrissant* which was not to be published until 1909. This was his first published work and Miss Margaret Davies has well described the essential centre of this evocation of Merlin. She argues that Apollinaire's major preoccupation in this work is:

the conception of himself as the creator, ubiquitous in time and space, a magician able to conjure up a whole turning world from his still centre. This is one of his most important and constant ideas; throughout his whole life he never ceases to grapple with the problem of portraying it most effectively.[8]

The poem 'Merlin et la vieille femme', although first published in 1912, dates from this period. The personage of Merlin fascinated Apollinaire. Son of a devil and a mortal woman, Merlin has God-given powers of prophecy and can foretell the future. This paradoxical figure, half devil and half man, the enchanter who was baptised, the dead man who speaks, the prophet who fails to use his own powers to avoid his death through love, has something of Apollinaire himself. The rôle of memory and the sense of an emerging world against which Merlin is set add to the personal relevance of the poem. In an important article,[9] S. I. Lockerbie has demonstrated convincingly how Apollinaire had taken themes of *errance* and quest from Symbolist sources. They fit naturally with his growing preoccupations in the field of self-knowledge and aesthetic discovery.

Apollinaire's stay in the Rhineland from 1901–2 proved to be an important stage in his development. The picturesque autumn of the forests set off deep resonances in the poet whose 'saison mentale' it was; dormant atavisms were awakened by its abundant legends; the *dramatis personae* of his poems was enriched by the strange figures he saw; his poetry began to flow with the emergence of his own distinctive tone and his love-affair with Annie Playden deepened immeasurably his register of emotion. His happiness in love brought with it a warming comfort and, in a curious way, even the eventual end of his relationship culminating in the bitterness of *La Chanson du mal-aimé* seemed to strengthen his tenuous links with a suffering humanity, a need also displayed by the impulsion he shows in the poem to compare his own experience with that of a great list of characters drawn from history or legend. The poetic climate of the *Rhénanes* bears witness to the fertile ambiguity which enriches so much of his later work. Here are juxtaposed life and death, legend and reality, the supernatural and the ordinary, the trivial and the solemn, the real and the imaginary in a series of brief, tense poetic structures where humour often neutralises sentimentality. The self-confidence is only superficial and, not far below, lie real doubts. The brightly-lit interior of the house in which 'Les Femmes' carry on their touching daily tasks is set against the darkly menacing forest where tricks of light turn the uneven snow into sinister shapes:

> La nuit tombait Les vignobles aux ceps tordus
> Devenaient dans l'obscurité des ossuaires
> En neige et repliés gisaient là des suaires.

The shadow of death lies over all. In 'Mai' the flaws are more concealed. The opening lines mislead the reader by presenting an idyllic scene:

> Le mai le joli mai en barque sur le Rhin
> Des dames regardaient du haut de la montagne

but immediately the sweep of time bears the poet irrevocably away from the possibility of happiness:

> Vous êtes si jolies mais la barque s'éloigne
> Qui donc a fait pleurer les saules riverains.

The inability to make a lasting contact with the world becomes an increasingly important theme of the poet—sometimes as in the lines quoted above, because time drives him away from happiness, sometimes, as in 'Le Pont Mirabeau', by a reversed vision in which he remains static, unable to move into the flux of life:

> Vienne la nuit sonne l'heure
> Les jours s'en vont je demeure.

In 'Mai' even the Spring is flawed for the *pétales* are *flétris* and the permanence of ruin lies under the transitory colours of the season:

> Le mai le joli mai a paré les ruines.

The theme of the passing of time makes its appearance in *Rhénanes* with all the melancholy it brings throughout Apollinaire's life. He wrote to his *marraine* on 4 August 1916:

Rien ne détermine plus de mélancolie chez moi que cette fuite du temps. Elle est en désaccord si formel avec mon sentiment, mon identité, qu'elle est la source même de ma poésie.[10]

The passing of time makes even sharper the sense of isolation he experiences and more poignant his need to impose a sense of continuity on a world he can only perceive as discontinuous. Michel Butor well observes:

[. . .] pour lui, tous les noms, tous les objets flottent; il faut les saisir, les mettre en place, les dénombrer, découvrir leurs coordonnées.[11]

One of the permanent Apollinairean dichotomies is the contrast between transience and permanence, the first strongly felt, the second vainly desired. Yet in these poems of private experience there is a marked sense of direction. If Apollinaire sees himself in the traditional poetical situation of poet-emotion-nature, the circle of obsession is never completely closed. At a point when the confession is about to become too intimate and the passion too intense, the private universe of grief is invaded by strangers. In 'Les Colchiques' it is the noisy irruption of school-children:

> Les enfants de l'école viennent avec fracas
> Vêtus de hoquetons et jouant de l'harmonica.

In 'Mai' it is the tziganes and a martial music:

> Sur le chemin du bord du fleuve lentement
> Un ours un singe un chien menés par des tziganes
> Suivaient une roulotte traînée par un âne
> Tandis que s'éloignait dans les vignes rhénanes
> Sur un fifre lointain un air de régiment.

Sometimes the relief is provided by an incongruous image as in the lines from *La Chanson du mal-aimé*:

> Et moi j'ai le cœur aussi gros
> Qu'un cul de dame damascène.

The Apollinaire of *Rhénanes* has his own *pudeur* which is partly due to a natural sense of privacy unusual in a lyric poet and partly to inner uncertainties which prevent total self-exposure.

The ending of his love-affair with Annie Playden, as described in its great epitaph *La Chanson du mal-aimé*, ushered in a period of moral depression for Apollinaire in which he found himself unable to work. All seemed once more to be in question and it required the revelation of Cubism and his growing friendship with Picasso to provide the jolt which set him in motion again. His meeting with Marie Laurencin in 1907 soon developed into a close attachment with all the easements and imaginative flights that love always provoked in him. To talk of a Cubist poetry is unhelpful and indeed, in the last year of his life, Apollinaire expressly stated that 'il n'existe pas de relations entre le cubisme et la nouvelle orientation littéraire'. Cubism, he argued, was an art of analysis whilst poetry, being essentially lyrical, was an art of synthesis.[12] What is important to Apollinaire is the climate of fermenting experiment. In 'La Jolie Rousse', the last poem of *Calligrammes*, he set up three pairs of aesthetic opposites which he proudly claimed to have reconciled: *ancien* is opposed to *nouveau, tradition* to *invention* and *Ordre* to *Aventure*. This does not imply a conscious *dosage* of such elements in all his poetry or even that Apollinaire always achieved this difficult marriage of contrasts. It does, however, indicate an unstable aesthetic belief which is itself a symptom of Apollinaire's self-questioning. The end of his period of poetic silence is signalled by the appearance of the important poems 'Le Brasier' and 'Les Fiançailles' which is dedicated to Picasso. These poems he himself commended, with 'Vendémiaire', as his own preferences amongst the poems of *Alcools* because they were new, profound and lyrical. In 'Le Brasier', he wrote confidently of:

> Ce Passé ces têtes de morts

and asked with equally confident expectation of answer:

> Où sont ces têtes que j'avais
> Où est le Dieu de ma jeunesse.

In this poem as in 'Les Fiançailles' he stresses the rôle of the poet as creator, often employing a vocabulary with marked religious overtones. Experience and sensation are recreated in the flame of art for, as he wrote in a contemporary article, 'les miracles lyriques sont quotidiens'. The new-found confidence in the joy and mystery of poetry is strongly to be seen in these poems as it is in 'Vendémiaire'. This poem, published in 1912 but dated by Michel Décaudin from 1909 or 1910, has an almost apocalyptic vision of the poet as the centre of the universe as he cries:

> Je suis ivre d'avoir bu tout l'univers.

Yet, in spite of these triumphs 'JE est un autre'. The poem tells us little about Apollinaire and, although he has a satisfying aesthetic triumph, nothing is solved. The plaintive lines of 'La Souris' in *Le Bestiaire* may be answered in the field of poetic achievement:

> Belles journées, souris du temps,
> Vous rongez peu à peu ma vie.
> Dieu! Je vais avoir vingt-huit ans,
> Et mal vécus, à mon envie

but the poet's own identity remains in doubt.

He soon received a blow which could have had disastrous results. The theft of the Mona Lisa from the Louvre in 1911 resulted in his incarceration in the prison of La Santé for four days on suspicion of complicity. The comedy of errors which Apollinaire described as 'cette histoire singulière, incroyable, tragique et plaisante' has been recounted in a letter.[13] *Plaisante* it may have been in retrospect but it had a very serious side for Apollinaire which did not escape him. As a stateless person such an incrimination might have led to deportation and the consequent deprivation for Apollinaire of his livelihood, his friends and his country. This blow was soon to be followed by another. His relationship with Marie Laurencin had become increasingly stormy and ended in 1912. It is from this time that date poems like 'Le Voyageur', 'Cortège' and 'Zone' in which the torments of the search for identity are expressed in some of Apollinaire's finest verse. In all three poems, personal crisis becomes involved in a new aesthetic.

In 'Cortège', first published in 1912 but with some anterior lines, Apollinaire wrote:

> Un jour
> Un jour je m'attendais moi-même
> Je me disais Guillaume il est temps que tu viennes
> Pour que je sache enfin celui-là que je suis
> Moi qui connais les autres.

Enfin he writes with some anguish, for the knowledge of other men which he has absorbed does not mask the central void in his own self-knowledge. Philippe Renaud has an interesting commentary on this passage in which he analyses the *ignorance de soi* and *connaissance des autres* theme.[14] The great procession of humanity, 'mille peuplades blanches', come to Apollinaire, all having contributed in some way to his creation, for:

> On me bâtit peu à peu comme on élève une tour.

But the central question of what he is remains without an answer. We must however note at this point that the failure of Apollinaire's self-questioning does not lead him to bitterness although in 'Zone' (1912) the tone becomes harsher and more terrifying. The poem is of great complexity and reveals a masterly control not only of a flowing, varied verse form but also of a discontinuous autobiographical meditation which ranges freely over time and space. Like Leopold Bloom wandering through the streets of Dublin in Joyce's *Ulysses*, Apollinaire quarters Paris in a walk which lasts for almost twenty-four hours. Chronologically the poem begins in the sunlight of a pleasant morning and moves through the lurid Paris night to an uncertain dawn; geographically, the scene is Paris, ending in Auteuil where Apollinaire then lived, but the poem spans a life-time and follows Apollinaire through Europe in brief flashes of remembrance. Themes of aesthetic change elbow a private meditation which expresses a desperate grief embodied in the revealing line:

> Je me sens abandonné sur terre depuis mon plus jeune âge

which, typically enough, remains in a manuscript *ébauche*. Apollinaire's loss of religious faith is contrasted sharply with the pious beliefs of his youth so that the sense of abandonment is double. The sadness mixed with nostalgia and the pointless *errance* are powerfully reinforced by the 'point of view' adopted in the poem. Apollinaire had previously used more than one grammatical person in a single poem and even in the early 'Merlin et la vieille femme' had employed *je* and *tu* in an unsystematic way. In 'Zone' however the use is constant and the poem is in large part a dialogue between *Je*, representing the poet, humble and penitent, and his *alter ego*, interlocutor or confessor who addresses him as *Tu*. The *alter ego* takes the poet through his life explaining, reminding, exhorting and accusing. The alternating dialogue is rapid and even breaks into the construction of single lines. Here is an example in which I have used italics to differentiate the voices:

Tu as souffert de l'amour à vingt et à trente ans
J'ai vécu comme un fou et j'ai perdu mon temps
Tu n'oses plus regarder tes mains *et à tous moments je voudrais sangloter*
Sur toi *sur celle que j'aime* sur tout ce qui t'a épouvanté.

The poem conveys with great technical brilliance the deep alienation in which the two voices talk but never fuse into one.

The acute depression which inspires 'Zone' is shortlived for soon after this poem was finished he had written 'Les Fenêtres' as a preface to the *album-catalogue* of the exhibition of paintings by R. Delaunay held in Germany in 1913. This year saw the publication not only of *Alcools* but also of *Les Peintres cubistes: méditations esthétiques*. These two volumes, together with Apollinaire's popularity as art critic, journalist and occasional lecturer, established his position as a leader of *les jeunes* with especial leanings towards the modern. Once again aesthetic excitements compensate for the bleak answers his self-questioning had provided. He was now preoccupied by the theory of Simultanism which was something he felt he had been groping for all his life. 'Les Femmes' of 1901 had sought to represent time as the apprehension of simultaneous sensations rather than as the presentation of successive states. *L'Enchanteur pourrissant* had also contained examples of this technique. Apollinaire had already seen in the Cubist representations of different aspects of an object simultaneously (a face seen both in full and in profile) another justification for the attack on representationalism and ultimately on time itself. It brought with it the possibility of a poetry which would be the opposite of narration. In 1912, he wrote thus:

La simultanéité [. . .] seule, est création. Le reste n'est que notation, contemplation, étude. La simultanéité, c'est la vie même et quelle que soit la succession d'éléments dans une œuvre elle mène à une fin inéluctable, la mort, tandis que le créateur ne connaît que l'éternité. L'artiste s'est trop longtemps efforcé vers la mort en assemblant des éléments stériles de l'art et il est temps qu'il arrive à la fécondité, à la trinité, à la simultanéité.[15]

It is not my concern at present to explore these aspects of Apollinaire's work. As we have seen before, his new literary directions provide a great compensation and he can write with pleasure in 'Le Musicien de Saint-Merry':

Je ne chante pas ce monde ni les autres astres
Je chante toutes les possibilités de moi-même hors de ce monde et des astres
Je chante la joie d'errer et le plaisir d'en mourir.

The outbreak of the 1914–18 war is at hand and this had a crucial effect on Apollinaire's personality and his way of life. As a stateless person he was not involved in the *mobilisation générale* but he volunteered immediately for the Armed Forces and was eventually enrolled as a gunner on 5 December 1914. In 1915 he was promoted *sous-lieutenant* in an Infantry Regiment and naturalised French on 9 March 1916. His severe head wound was sustained at the front only a few days later.

'La Petite Auto' (*Calligrammes*) relates Apollinaire's immediate reactions to the outbreak of war as he returned by car from Deauville with André Rouveyre. Above all he seems to have realised instantly that a world was ending:

> Nous dîmes adieu à toute une époque

and that in the trials to come, men would come to grips with themselves and emerge, as from the *brasier*, in a new mould. The poem ends thus:

> Nous arrivâmes à Paris
> Au moment où l'on affichait la mobilisation
> Nous comprîmes mon camarade et moi
> Que la petite auto nous avait conduits dans une époque
> Nouvelle
> Et bien qu'étant tous deux des hommes mûrs
> Nous venions cependant de naître.

We are well documented on Apollinaire's years from 1914 to his death in 1918. His poetry and prose reflect with great authenticity his war experience; with the gradual re-awakening of literary life, his *chroniques* were resumed and he began a vast correspondence. A number of points stand out. Apollinaire saw the war as a challenge to himself and, from the simple act of becoming a soldier, derived a most profound satisfaction. His reactions build up into a complex picture of attitudes towards war which contrast sharply with those of many of his contemporaries on both sides. There is firstly the sense of honour that he has been chosen to fight:

Je suis heureux au possible qu'on m'ait trouvé digne d'être soldat dans cette bagarre titanique et je ne céderais pas ma place pour un empire, surtout celui d'Allemagne.[16]

His action is caused by a feeling of gratitude to France; Louise Faure-Favier records that Apollinaire told her he had joined the Army because 'je dois tout à la France, c'est bien le moins que je me batte pour elle'.[17] Primitive atavisms are aroused in Apollinaire and a simple feeling of personal and racial honour:

Un soldat est un soldat. Faut partir, on a besoin de toutes les énergies. Les énergies polonaises surtout. C'est le pays qui a le plus souffert de cette guerre, ma Pologne. Si mon sacrifice peut le sauver, me servirai avec joie de mon grand fouet de conducteur. Sommes la race la plus noble et la plus malheureuse du monde, mais la plus brave. Il faut pas mentir à son sang. Me sens l'âme des chevaliers d'autrefois.[18]

There is the joy of self-realisation, of finding an identity in companionship:

> Me voici libre et fier parmi mes compagnons
> ('2e Cannonier conducteur')

and, more, the identification of the poet with the world of war:

> Je suis seul sur le champ de bataille
> Je suis la tranchée blanche et le bois vert et roux
> ('Chant d'horizon en Champagne')

From this turmoil will emerge not only self-knowledge but that deeper understanding of man which is to be the aim of poetry as expressed in 'Les Collines' and 'La Jolie Rousse':

> Ne pleurez donc pas sur les horreurs de la guerre
> Avant elle nous n'avions que la surface
> De la terre et des mers
> Après elle nous aurons les abîmes   ('Guerre').

The visual effects of war impress him and recur in the war poems. In a poem aptly entitled 'Fête', he writes:

> Feu d'artifice en acier
> Qu'il est charmant cet éclairage
> Artifice d'artificier
> Mêler quelque grâce au courage

and the poem goes on into the erotic imagery which is never far from his thoughts at this time:

> Deux fusants
> Rose éclatement
> Comme deux seins que l'on dégrafe
> Tendent leurs bouts insolemment
> IL SUT AIMER
>   quelle épitaphe.

'Ah Dieu! que la guerre est jolie' he can write in 'L'Adieu du cavalier' and it is this reaction[19] which brought down the wrath of the young Surrealists who were deeply imbued with what André Breton described as 'le défaitisme de guerre'. This is to miss the total significance of war in Apollinaire's life. Now, at last, he could affirm his identity firmly in his own eyes and in the eyes of the world. Now he knew who he was and what his role was in the world of change. The voice is different, more solemn; surer of himself, grave and direct, he can now write in 'Merveille de la guerre' (dated 19 décembre 1915):

> Je lègue à l'avenir l'histoire de Guillaume Apollinaire
> Qui fut à la guerre et sut être partout

as in 'La Jolie Rousse' he can set out before his readers his qualifications for being their voice:

> Me voici devant tous un homme plein de sens
> Connaissant la vie et de la mort ce qu'un vivant peut connaître
> Ayant éprouvé les douleurs et les joies de l'amour
> Ayant su quelquefois imposer ses idées
> Connaissant plusieurs langages
> Ayant pas mal voyagé
> Ayant vu la guerre dans l'Artillerie et l'Infanterie [. . .]

The voice of the poet is no longer hesitant and ambiguous; his eyes turn to the future, to the *bonté* and *volonté* of the poet-creator. The statement of 'Le Brasier' takes on a new meaning:

> Je flambe dans le brasier à l'ardeur multiple

and the poet, like the phoenix, rises again, transformed and yet the same.

The sense of alienation and the search for identity in Apollinaire's work have a peculiar flavour which sets him apart from other writers who have treated the same theme. When he writes in 'Zone' of 'la grâce de cette rue industrielle' he is unselfconsciously celebrating the joys and pleasures of being alive which never deserted him, even in his blackest moments. In accordance with his belief of *L'Esprit nouveau et les poètes* his aim is to 'exalter la vie sous quelque forme qu'elle se présente' so that even the noise and smoke of the city as seen in 'le bar crapuleux' do not excite his disgust. For Apollinaire the world is good and it is he, the 'poète maudit', who cannot share its pleasures. There is none of the horror of the society, environment and institutions which one finds in *La Nausée*. Apollinaire does not wish to change the world but rather to make its joys and mysteries available to all. The lines of W. B. Yeats in 'The Second Coming' are as far as it is possible to be from Apollinaire's view:

Things fall apart; the centre cannot hold;
Mere anarchy is loosed upon the world,
The blood-dimmed tide is loosed, and everywhere
The ceremony of innocence is drowned.

Apollinaire keeps his own kind of battered innocence. He seeks himself in others yet uses introspection to this end; in a world of flux, he embraces change and yet seeks for permanence; he recognises the incoherence of the world, and yet finds a curious comfort in this very incoherence. By the end of his life his aesthetic and personal quests had coincided in their solution and 'La Victoire' (1917) celebrates more than a feat of arms:

La Victoire avant tout sera
De bien voir au loin
De tout voir
De près
Et que tout ait un nom nouveau.

Hull   GARNET REES

NOTES

All quotations from the poems are taken from:
Œuvres poétiques de Guillaume Apollinaire, ed. Adéma and Décaudin, Paris, Bibliothèque de la Pléiade, 1956.
Other material is quoted from:
Œuvres complètes de Guillaume Apollinaire [abbreviated to *OC*], Paris, 4 vols, 1965–66.
Lettres à Lou, ed. Décaudin, Paris, 1969.

1 Letter to Henri Martineau, 19 juillet 1913, *OC*, 4, p. 768.
2 Marcel Adéma, *Apollinaire le mal-aimé*, Paris, 1952, p. 32.
3 *Lettres à Lou*, 2 février 1915, p. 154.
4 Paris, 1955, vol. I, p. 116.
5 'Guillaume Apollinaire', reprinted in *Les Pas perdus*, Paris, 1924, p. 28.
6 J. R. Lawler, 'Apollinaire inédit: le séjour à Stavelot', *Mercure de France*, 323, 1955, p. 297.
7 Letter to Ernest Chevalier, 19 novembre 1839, *Correspondance*, Paris, 1926, vol. I, p. 61.
8 *Apollinaire*, Edinburgh, 1964, p. 56.
9 '*Alcools* et le Symbolisme', *Guillaume Apollinaire*, 2, Paris, *Revue des Lettres modernes*, 85–9, 1963.
10 *Lettres à sa marraine*, *OC*, 4, p. 686.
11 'Monument de rien pour Apollinaire', *Nouvelle Revue française*, May, 1965, p. 505.

12 'Une interview d'Apollinaire en juillet 1918', *Guillaume Apollinaire*, 7, Paris, *Revue des Lettres modernes*, 183–8, 1968, pp. 179–87. For a discussion of Apollinaire and Cubism, see M.-J. Durry, *Alcools*, Paris, 1964, vol. 2, pp. 177 *et seq.* and L. C. Breunig, 'Apollinaire et le Cubisme', *Guillaume Apollinaire*, 2, Paris, *Revue des Lettres modernes*, 85–9, 1963.

13 *Tendre comme le souvenir*, 30 juillet 1915, *OC*, 4, pp. 491–5.

14 *Lecture d'Apollinaire*, Lausanne, 1969, p. 153.

15 *OC*, 4, p. 279.

16 Letter to Alfred Vallette, 19 octobre 1914, *OC*, 4, p. 818.

17 *Souvenirs sur Apollinaire*, Paris, 1945, p. 121.

18 *Lettres à Lou*, 4 avril 1915, pp. 242–3.

19 See Norma Rinsler, 'Guillaume Apollinaire's War Poems', *French Studies*, XXV, 2, April, 1971.

POETRY AS THE RECONCILIATION OF CONTRADICTIONS IN APOLLINAIRE

In 1917 Apollinaire described Picasso's contribution to *Parade* in these words: 'Il s'agit avant tout de traduire la réalité. Toutefois le motif n'est plus reproduit mais seulement représenté et plutôt que représenté il voudrait être suggéré par une sorte d'analyse-synthèse embrassant tous les éléments visibles et quelque chose de plus, si possible, une schématisation intégrale qui chercherait à concilier les contradictions en renonçant parfois déliberément à rendre l'aspect immédiat de l'objet.'[1]

Two points strike the attention here; one is that the grandiose stated aims could well apply to Apollinaire's own in every detail; the other that the conditionals 'voudrait être', 'chercherait', and the putative 'si possible' imply that this vision of reconciling opposites is in the nature of a mirage still trembling on the horizon. The implications in this description could well prove to be revealing about Apollinaire's own work.

There the existence of powerful contradictions is always in evidence. It is by now a commonplace to say that the world of his imagination is built out of antitheses, but like all commonplaces this is an over-simplification, for what the rational mind in its linear way perceives as opposites can in the world of poetry lie coiled inextricably one inside the other.

Another confusing factor is the distinction between the creative and the empirical selves.[2] In Apollinaire it is primarily the empirical self which is set in polarised motion, so that the swing between opposites goes endlessly up and down, to and fro. But the creative self is quite different, and Apollinaire makes no bones about this fact.

> La joie venait toujours après la peine
> Vienne la nuit sonne l'heure
> Les jours s'en vont je demeure[3]

Tensing itself against the opposing pulls, the *je* which transcends conflicting emotions and the passage of time walks the perilous tightrope of the words it spins out of itself, must in fact do so if poetry is to be poetry and not inarticulate notations. This equilibrium maintained through tension, this balance held at the still point of the turning world could in fact well be Apollinaire's 'schématisation intégrale qui chercherait à concilier les contradictions'.

The great problem, however, for Apollinaire more than for many another poet, was that because of the extremely polarised nature of his empirical self, the tension was so great that the balance was particularly difficult to obtain, and once kept so quiveringly poised. It needs only a verbal shift as delicate as a hair's breadth to turn the exquisite awareness of the delicious bitterness of life into an excruciating perception of madness and death. The most fascinating example of the extreme pull on both sides is the changing of one word in 'La Porte' during the process of composition. The line which originally read 'D'être cet employé pour qui seul tout existe'[4] was switched to the opposite: 'Pour qui seul rien n'existe', an alternative determined finally by purely aesthetic considerations such as the general tone pattern: 'terriblement, profonde eau triste, mourir et remourir' as well as that of the sounds: the predominant 'i' and the nasals emphasised by the rhymes: 'hier matin' 'chant lointain'.

In *Le Bestiaire* Apollinaire himself characterised his poetry as dynamic form maintained in tension.

> Mes durs rêves formels sauront te chevaucher,
> Mon destin au char d'or sera ton beau cocher
> Qui pour rênes tiendra tendus à frénésie,
> Mes vers, les parangons de toute poésie.[5]

In the choice of a single word here he reveals one of the most characteristic ways in which he keeps his balance: frenzy—madness or divine inspiration from the god, or both? The word itself in its ambiguous nature contains and reconciles contradictions. Ambiguity is in fact an essential spring in the workings of his poetry.

Sometimes the tension and reconciliation are effected not merely by juxtaposition or fusion of alternate meanings, but by juxtaposition and fusion of sounds which are normally associated with opposite meanings. To take a much quoted example, there is the whole sequence of the association of *amour* and *mourir*, seen at its pitch in 'un amour à mourir'.[6] To unite two totally opposed forces in a game of homophony is another way in which the creative self asserts: 'Je demeure'.

Ambiguity, verbal play, sound play, the whole of what Ezra Pound called 'logopeia', or 'the dance of the intellect among words',[7] such marked characteristics in Apollinaire are associated with the essentially double-faced nature of irony. Psychologically irony springs from the same stance as that which leads to creation, the self being similarly split into two, and the mockery which results is indeed often an integral part of the creative act. Certainly with Apollinaire the irony often manifested in word play plays an important part in the process of 'schématisation intégrale'.

From the vantage point which permits him not only to see the dichotomies in his empirical self but also to attempt to resolve them, he can at the same time perceive and try to reconcile the dichotomies and contradictions in the whole world of nature. Apollinaire's images are simple enough, but they are all markedly double-faced. More particularly the poet's own favourite avatars incorporate the most fundamental of dichotomies, that between life and death. Some are semi-mortals, like Orpheus, Amphion, Merlin and Pan, who also embodies the opposition man/animal. Icarus represents god-like aspiration and man-like fall, Merlin magic powers but the weakness of dependence on a woman. Even Christ whose presence can be felt in Apollinaire's poetry more than it is explicitly stated, was God made man, and had to die like the Phœnix before he was resurrected.

Apollinaire's early works show him struggling towards a resolution of this basic opposition between life and death by means of poetry. The Enchanter pinned down in his tomb, witnessing everything, but incapable of action, can be seen as a symbol not merely of the conflicting emotions of the empirical self, but at another level of the poet, uneasily aware of the conflicts inherent in multiplicity and overwhelmed by his inability to impose the unique force of his unifying will. In La Chanson du mal-aimé, the refrain which first makes it clear that the poem is really a 'chanson' is significantly an evocation of what ideally for Apollinaire poetry should be and do. The voie lactée refrain is in fact a vision, couched in the most mellifluous of language, of a beautiful synthesis of those irreconcilables love and death, in which life and love triumph with difficulty after death in a sort of cosmic simultaneous transcendence. It is clear that here on the threshold of his career Apollinaire is already animated by the vision of poetry as a transcendental synthesis far distant in actual realisation, but nevertheless able to be encompassed by the imagination.

It is however in the 1908 period that he becomes much more self-consciously aware, not only of his aims as a poet, but of the means which he can adopt to bring them about. Love which had worked for the forces of death in both L'Enchanteur pourrissant and in La Chanson du mal-aimé now moves over to reinforce the whole creative process of poetry. Onirocritique sets up a new pattern in which the coupling of opposites (dissemblables) punctuates and provokes each new stage of creation. From now onwards love is increasingly seen as part of the general life forces whose most intense manifestation is poetic inspiration.

More specifically, at this time Apollinaire begins to focus on a range of symbols, which in the event opened up a way of actually miming the process of the reconciliation of opposites. In his repeated choice of the sun, or of the brazier where the flames die down and leap up again, or of the Phœnix who is reborn from his ashes, as symbols of his own creativity, Apollinaire has lit upon a natural and highly significant means of embodying the desired synthesis. Implicit in the cyclical course of the sun is a constant, dynamic resolution of opposites, zenith and nadir being united in the circular trajectory. From this year onward Apollinaire clearly becomes aware that the schematisation represented by the cyclical pattern, be it in the choice of images or in the overall structure of the poem, is one of the methods by which he can reconcile the contradictions which, seen in any linear fashion, appear irreconcilable.

I have elsewhere[8] developed some of the reasons why I consider that 'Lul de Faltenin' is a composite myth, relating various doubles of the poet himself to the central figure of the sun reaching its zenith and full opposition to night in the centre of the poem with the poet's assertion of his own creative powers, and its nadir—the poet's failure for he has not vanquished the sirens by his own song—when it rejoins the sun of the previous day as it sinks under the sea. Nevertheless, even here, the last line is contrived so as to point forward to the continuation of the eternal cycle: the hero is in the nest of the Sirens, sign of birth; and even in the denial, 'loin du troupeau des étoiles oblongues' there still hovers a vision of the sky.

In the same way at the end of 'Le Brasier' when the flames of inspiration have died down, and the poet's imagination seems to have been stretched beyond its limits into immobility, there is a fall back to the earth, and a dependence on women, time and mortality. But even here firmly expressed is still the desire to know the secret that will reconcile all contradictions and thus enable him to die: 'Vouloir savoir pour qu'enfin on m'y dévorât'. I would in this context agree with J. C. Chevalier[9] who equates *savoir* with the particular 'science' of the poet. Here it is attempting to impose itself even on death.

This dichotomy between life and death, the greatest of all the irreconcilables, is the final problem which presents itself at the end of 'Les Fiançailles'. Even the creative self which is born out of flames from the immolation of his empirical half has to die. Apollinaire resolves this here first by the characteristic play of the intellect among words and sounds: 'Je mire de ma mort la gloire et le malheur', exploiting both passive (to reflect) and active (to aim at) meanings of *mirer*, and by placing this verb first, drawing the similar sounds in *ma mort* under its influence and thus subjugating death. Out of the fall of the *incertitude* which is the painted mask of his empirical self, emerge all the characteristics that he would like to associate with his own creation; sun, a joyous love, the dance, procreation, ambiguity (*bien ou mal habillés*), which finally enable him to transcend the basic death/life opposition, aesthetically at least, in the image of the Phœnix and the choice of words that make the source of death, *bûcher*, also *le nid*, the source of life.

It seems to me significant that the two big poems which give a symmetry to the framework of *Alcools* have themselves as framework a cyclical structure. At the end of 'Zone,' despite the image of death applied to the sun itself, a morning is being born. This fusion of death and birth is again reflected through the poet's consciousness, at the close of 'Vendémiaire', although pitched at the opposing end of the emotional scale: 'Les étoiles mouraient le jour naissait à peine'.

These closing passages of 'Vendémiaire' also reveal, for the first time in explicit form, another process of the imagination by which it can bring all the perceptible, warring manifestations of the universe within its compass.

After stretching out to contemplate:

> Actions belles journées sommeils terribles
> Végétation accouplements musiques éternelles . . .

the creative self distils the overwhelming multiplicity into a concentrated essence: 'L'univers tout entier concentré dans ce vin', and characteristically expresses it by means of a refined, ephemeral sense perception: 'Je sus alors quelle saveur a l'univers'. A similar reduction and stylisation of conflicting opposites could also be seen as an integral part of the workings of poetry in the sixth section of 'Les Fiançailles' when the laurel leaves, initially the signs of Apollo's failure as a lover, become universally known as the symbol of glory. They are then whittled down by the de-realising process of schematisation into the same exquisite sense perception: 'la saveur du laurier', and here it is possible that this is further refined by piquant punning on *laurier* and Laurencin.

However conscious this process of reduction had been before 1912, it now definitely and increasingly asserts itself along with the general cyclical structure and images, and the pirouettes of word play that transform the poet into a sort of *rose des vents*, as a constant line of force in Apollinaire's imagination.

'La Cravate et la montre' has recourse to all three of these processes in a totally self-conscious fashion. It is the most schematic of all Apollinaire's representations of life's cycle. There is the full circle of the hours and particularly those of the poet's imagination, embracing his senses, his occult beliefs, the pastoral past, philosophy, love and eroticism, adventure, and finally poetry which contains both light and death: 'le vers dantesque luisant et cadavérique'. This complete circle inevitably contains death at its centre: 'tout va finir', but significantly is in its turn encompassed on one side by the words: 'La beauté de la vie passe la douleur de mourir', which asserts the dominance of poetry. The whole circular mechanism, a microcosmic version of the way poetry transcends the life/death opposition, dangles from the watch-chain which is figured by: 'Comme l'on s'amuse bien'. The creative, unifying dance of the intellect among words here finds actual pictorial notation.

'Un Fantôme de nuées' beautifully shows how the cyclical structure, here seen in variations of the form of the circle, can fuse and work with a gradual process of refinement and vaporisation into otherworldly fantasy. The poet takes his position in a circle of people; at its centre are repeated patterns of circles, halters, weights, balls. The fact that this is a perfectly harmonious form is underlined by accompanying references to the harmony of music. Again by a process of schematisation, colour is reduced to a single melodic line: 'un air de musique', the future to the thin lament of the barrel-organ. Parallel with this is developed a series of images which reduce the opposition of life and death to an impalpable essence, be it the smoke of a cigarette: 'Doigts roulant une cigarette amère et déliceuse comme la vie', or the rose-blush which is the sign of death in life, or the headless phantom which was a man.

The little acrobat describes a circular movement as he salutes the four cardinal points, then proves his own domination of the circular shapes by walking on the ball. Thus he accomplishes a trick of balance similar to that of the poet-artist who imposes his skill upon the circular patterns of words and shapes, and eventually brings about the fusion of music and the circle in a music of forms. In a gradual process of stylisation and etherealisation, the music becomes a barely audible music of the spheres, the miraculous child disappears like a puff of smoke, time and the world are merely clouds.

But there are witnesses who remain. Here it is interesting to see that it is no longer merely the 'je' of the poet who stays and observes, but all the spectators who had formed the circle, a fact which, in the event, is highly significant. The miraculous operation is felt as actually existing in germ within each spectator in the circle; I think that this is already a tentative, perhaps barely conscious appearance of that extended notion of a moral synthesis, in which the poetic, creative spirit in all men will eventually unite them, that so markedly becomes the main theme of Apollinaire's last works.

He is still, however, at this stage concerned to include and unite all the contradictory elements in his own perception. From 1913 onwards this endeavour can ever more clearly be seen to be directed along the two opposed axes which have already begun to be apparent, the one in a centrifugal movement out to embrace infinite variety, the other centripetally to affect the reduction of multiplicity into the unity of a refined, stylised quintessence. Too far either way, that is beyond the limits where the finite mind can conceive both of the infinitely large and the infinitely small, lie silence, immobility, lack of form and colour. In 'La Petite Auto' the grandiose vision of the future takes the shape of gigantic beings who eat up words. Later, in *Vitam Impendere Amori*, as poetry works its alchemical changes on the raw stuff of life, complexity is whittled down until it becomes an indefinable thread of sound: 'Un air qu'on ne peut définir'. The larger the ambitions, the more explicit is the obsession with silence.

One of the ways of cutting down the infinite variety to more manageable proportions is to limit it to what the senses can actually perceive of the present. This is in fact what Apollinaire attempted to do in his efforts to capture the 'ambiant lyricism'[10] of life in 'Lettre Océan', 'Lundi rue Christine', 'Les Fenêtres'. But despite his craving to plant himself fair and square in the centre of modernity like the Eiffel Tower receiving radio signals from all over the world, it is clear that he was also firmly earthed into the past. He may no longer have clung wholly to the old Platonic belief that imagination *is* memory, but he was perceptive and honest enough to know that the present, however dynamic, is constantly 'lined' with the past, that the structures of the imagination are perched, like the characters at the end of Proust's novel on the stilts of their past selves, upon the scaffolding of 'le temps perdu'. To be faithful to the movements of his own sensibility, he had somehow both to trace out his explorations into the opposite directions of the past and the future-laden present, and yet to keep them both under his control. Poems like 'Arbre', 'Le Musicien de Saint-Merry', 'A Travers l'Europe' are evidences of his attempts to do this and show signs of the sadness and the tension that the opposing pulls engendered.

'Arbre', which with its references to the prophetic powers of the Dodonian grove is turned to the future that is to be born out of speed and simultaneity, is nevertheless interspersed with snapshots from the poet's own past, and significantly at its centre contains the figure of Dame Abonde, ostensibly the fairy of medieval legend, but also, as the reference to 'une chasse' makes clear, used in a similar way as in Heine's *Atta Troll* as a symbol of the ideal for the 'chasseurs maudits'. In my opinion she is another version of the lady at the window in Orkenise (*L'Enchanteur pourrissant*) and in 'Les Fiançailles', of the lady who wears the colours of France in 1909, and would seem to be closely associated with poetry: and here this antique fairy Dame of poetry appears in the modern vehicle of the time, a tram. The past finally inserts itself into every interstice of the present, but the poet remains firmly and centrally enough in control for his voice to be the echo of the whole universe and for new trinities of beings to spring up.

'Le Musicien de Saint-Merry' clearly states initially that however divergent are the paths the creative self explores, nevertheless it can encompass all these wanderings within its own unity, and perdurance. The whole trajectory of the poem as well as of Apollinaire's desires is contained in the lines:

> Je chante toutes les possibilités de moi-même hors de ce monde et des astres
> Je chante la joie d'errer et le plaisir d'en mourir

where the lyrical 'je' reduces the wanderings of its own multiplicity to the unique joy of creation that transforms even death. The crucial fact at the end of the poem is that the 'je' remains, witnessing everything, even the disappearance of his double and the death of the note of music to which his flock of women have been reduced. 'J'entends mourir le son d'une flûte lointaine'.

The experience of the war wrought many changes in Apollinaire, but I consider that it only deepened and strengthened his desire to hold all disparate things within the one circle of his poet's mouth: 'ma bouche pleine de disparates', as he puts it in 'Chef de section'. Perhaps due to lack of time or energy he had increasingly recourse to mechanical, superficial devices like the long accumulations and the repeated 'il y a', which seems dangerously like cheating.

In the earlier period, however, before he was too hard-pressed, 'La Nuit d'avril 1915' bears witness to the fact that he could translate even war and death into a 'pur effet de l'art'. 'La Nuit d'avril' sets the battlefield immediately in a totally fictional decor, composed of fairy-tale, adventure-story, legend and history. The rattle of gun-fire is stylised into a jolly music. One marvellous metaphor, recalling the cluster of images in the *Voie lactée* refrain of *La Chanson du mal-aimé*, exploits the full power of language to unite love which is life (*cœur*) with death (*obus éclaté*) and to transmute them into a cosmic life after death: 'comme un astre éperdu qui cherche ses saisons', which finally produces poetry: 'tu sifflais ta romance'. One of the rounds in the wrestling match between language and death is won by sheer homophony:

> Les obus miaulaient un amour à mourir
> Un amour qui se meurt est plus doux que les autres.

Another is wrested out of the now familiar process of distillation and vaporisation. Dying love becomes a mere breath: 'Ton souffle nage au fleuve où le sang va tarir'. In an inverse movement, the actual rain-drops are dead eyes. The way in which Apollinaire wants poetry to come into being and then to work is seen clearly in the extraordinary lines:

> Couche-toi sur la paille et songe un beau remords
> Qui pur effet de l'art soit aphrodisiaque.

Imagination working on the real present (*la paille*) and memory (for the past always seems to evoke the emotion of remorse), creates beauty which in its turn can create life (the erotic being the most powerful of life forces). Swelling out of this then is the glorious music of a future which is seen as Paradise.

The little sequence of seven poems which begins 'Lueurs des Tirs' is, I think, along with 'La Nuit d'avril' and *Vitam Impendere Amori* and 'Les Collines', a perfect example of the way in which Apollinaire can succeed in reconciling contradictions in 'une schématisation intégrale'. Quite explicitly and self-consciously it mimes the process by which real life is turned into poetry: so much the worse for the real woman if she still hankers for the past to be revived. Not only has she been turned into a symbol, 'la colombé poignardée', but even that has been stripped down to its skeleton of an idea:

> J'en plume les ailes l'idée
> Et le poème que tu fus.

The process of transforming a painful reality into poetry can be seen at work from the beginning. The real woman is magicked into a rain-bow and then wafted away on the wind. The disappearance and death of love is caught up into a sequence of circular shapes, the rainbow, the curl of hair, and then led into rebirth with eyes, mouths and the sun. The heart-rending rift between life and death is bridged by an exquisite play on words. The false Annunciation led to a crucifixion instead of a birth—and Passion here looks in two directions, the passion of love, the suffering of Christ—but to the creative self it is now merely the source of poetry: 'Et qu'elle était charmante et sade/ Cette renonciation'. Similarly the seemingly light-hearted pun on Grenade, exploiting its triple meanings, extends this role to the terrible instrument of death:

> Et que la grenade est touchante
> Dans nos effroyables jardins

where even the word *touchante* is equivocal. Is it in fact the touch of death, or the touch of the poet's song?

The structure of the seven pieces taken as a whole is cyclical, moving from death to life, then to death again, born from the wind 'au vent de bise', returning to the wind 'le vent se mêle à vos soupirs', arising out of disappearance of the woman and ending with the disappearance of the man. The past dies, is made poem, the present flowers in love and sunshine, those symbols of poetry:

> Comme ils cueillaient la rose ardente
> Leurs yeux tout à coup ont fleuri
> Mais quel soleil la bouche errante
> A qui la bouche avait souri.

The image of life in the midst of death which is 'cette flotte à Mytilène'[11] veers by that slightest hair-breadth shift, which here Apollinaire effects as miraculously as his own little boy acrobat, into that of death in the midst of the laughter and life, the adventure and wonderment which is poetry: 'Et mourut là-bas tandis qu'elle/Riait au destin surprenant'. The much abused quotation: 'Ah Dieu! que la guerre est jolie' is the simple statement that the poet has transformed even that monstrosity by his verbal spells. If there is any doubt that Apollinaire managed to achieve the so tantalising synthesis, to walk his self-appointed tightrope between yawning contradictions, these poems along with those of *Vitam* should dispel it.

There are undoubted changes in the Apollinaire of 1917 as indeed there were in all those who took part in the particular experience of the war. To my mind the major modification is that the creative self takes upon it certain moral assignments which had not come before within its scope. The word *volonté*, not surprisingly after such a testing, comes to the fore, and the sense of the need for universal solidarity becomes more pronounced. The concept of 'eros', passionate, self-centred, subjective, seems to give way to that of the communal 'agape'. But in all these changes, the poet retains his firm belief in the order that poetry must impose upon life.

'La Victoire' reveals, explores and conquers a major difficulty for the creative self which changing circumstances have thrown up. The conflict, which gives rise to the tensions and indeed the bitterness of the poem, is between an order—that of a language that Apollinaire had learned to master and impose upon the disparate stuff of experience—and the need for change and renewal which at certain moments demands the break-up of all established order, even that of language. Here I am in complete agreement with Claude Touradre's percipient remarks[12] about the bitter references to the total destruction and anarchy inherent in the Dadaïst experiments of the 'poètes bruitistes'. The fact that critics have not been quite sure whether Apollinaire is really advocating a new language made out of the most rudimentary of noises, or whether he is mocking such an idea, is a clear indication that his reactions are mixed. The Victory is in fact the way in which Apollinaire manages imaginatively to win the war within himself between an intellectual recognition for growth and change even if needs be by revolution, and an occasional, nostalgic, yearning for the known past.

It is quite clear at the beginning of 'La Victoire' that the creative self is in conflict. *Je rêve* leads to tormented visions of the most miserable of doubles of the poet, *les aveugles*, who in their turn are doubles of the false Icarus in his fall into the sea. At the opposite pole are superb images which connote the flowering of poetry: light, air, jewels, flowers, all, however, situated in the past. The present hinges on the one stable feature which he hopes will help him through to victory, namely the new love in his life.

The problem itself is introduced characteristically by the irony of the derisive rhyme which associates the ideal *bouquet* with *hoquet*, one of the involuntary noises he is going to advocate later on as a new language. The simple fact is stated simply: 'L'homme est à la recherche d'un nouveau langage'. It is, however, prefaced by a backward-looking, regretful: 'O bouches', and followed by a clause of total negation: 'Auquel le grammairien d'aucune langue n'aura rien à dire' which obviously envisages a void of silence. The danger is that without renewal, language will die. Silence, even the mutism of the silent films, is a rival.

The remedy he now tries out is imposed by sheer will-power. In a series of commands, as much to himself as to others, he mimes the whole process of starting from scratch, from sheer animal noises. His own instinctive reaction to this, his reluctance and bitterness about such experiments, can be seen from the harsh assonances and ironical repetitions:

On veut de nouveaux sons de nouveaux sons
On veut des consonnes sans voyelles.

The interruption of the splendid and sonorous line, 'Et quelle lettre grave comme un son de cloche à travers nos mémoires', the music amongst sheer noise inserts instead the totally other sound out of the past, and sets up a pattern where the conflict is played out by the alternation between a series of exhortations to set off into the future with the minimum baggage, and wistful invocations to the defeated words, and the myrtle groves of past creations. Eros and Anteros as well as representing all forms of love and dissimilarity in similarity (for they were brothers, if opponents), could also stand for the order of the past, for in primitive times Eros was considered to be the force which imposes harmonious order on the universe.

The sudden announcement, 'Je suis le ciel de la cité', is disconcerting, using the principle of surprise to bring the whole picture within a synoptic view. With a movement like that in 'Le Musicien'[13] and at the same place in the poem's structure, he rises above the conflicts within himself so that he can reconcile them in a god-like vision. The immediate development too follows the same pattern. Here it is the variations of the living sea which he hears, and which he wants to incorporate in his own voice. One of these variations is in fact the poetry from out of his own past. It is the admirable line which announces the advent of poetic inspiration: 'La parole est soudaine et c'est un Dieu qui tremble' where the trembling seems to unite both poet and God, that leads into the fusion of a present, past and future dominated by the poet, but trailing off into the characteristic 'incertitude':

> Qui sait si demain
> La rue devenait immobile
> Qui sait où serait mon chemin.

The whole conflict is thus set into a cyclical motion which, despite its rotations, has inevitably to draw towards the future. The Victory simply stated for the future and not yet imaginatively bodied into imagery, will be to stretch out in time and in space, 'de loin' 'de près', and to create not merely new sounds but a proper, appropriate language 'Et que tout ait un nom nouveau'.

The necessity for the poet to accept the inevitable and eternal cycle of nature is the dominating theme of 'Les Collines'. The sharp war within the poet's self between his attachment to a familiar past and the need to conquer the future is immediately won, and then set into the general cyclical pattern of nature: 'Ainsi la nuit contre le jour'.

The poem itself is what emerges after this conflict has been fought
and resolved: and now the song which in *La Chanson du mal-aimé*
had been the song of one individual, is the song of a whole city, and,
moreover, a city which for the poet was the centre of the modern
world. The bid for universal synthesis is clear:

> Sache que je parle aujourd'hui
> Pour annoncer au monde entier
> Qu'enfin est né l'art de prédire

It would now seem that after this claim the poet is able to dominate
the inevitable cycle of time. The lines which I take as applying to the
poet:

> Ornement des temps et des routes
> Passe et dure sans t'arrêter

echo the *Je demeure* refrain and are further developed in the image of
the Aphrodite-bearing foam which will always fertilise the future even
in a world made of machines. *L'écume*, undoubtedly the source of love
and beauty, is yet another version of the impalable, ideal quintessence
(*une saveur, un parfum*) of poetry, or rather as it becomes clear in the
following verses, the enlarged conception of poetry which informs
'L'Esprit nouveau et les poètes', namely the eternal creative spirit in
man. Of necessity this depends on the moral qualities which Apollinaire is increasingly concerned with, and with which he punctuates this
programme for the future: 'le désir', 'la souffrance', 'la volonté'.

The cyclical pattern of time is repeated: 'Rien n'y finit rien n'y
commence', and it is by means of the circular shape which is its
concrete symbol, 'la bague à ton doigt' that the transition is made
from the universal order of all things to the order of his own life, in
which he once again vindicates his poet's claims to immortality, and
accepts the death of the empirical self with equanimity: 'Je peux
mourir en souriant'. The process of *dédoublement* which will allow
this to happen, just as it allows him to transform his own youth into
'musique douceur harmonies', finds striking expressions in the image
of the serpent: 'Qui suis la flûte dont je joue/Et le fouet qui châtie les
autres'.

Again, it is noticeable that the lyrical musician *je* has identified
itself with a stern moraliser who sees suffering as crucial to the
totally new concept of *bonté* which is to transform the very nature of
man. Lyricism, as Apollinaire states in 'L'Esprit nouveau', is only
one of the domains of the new spirit. It is, nevertheless, the one which
he himself is qualified to explore, and which he proceeds to reproduce,

first by means of his own ready-made images from the past, 'un vaisseau', 'une flamme', the 'abîme' of 'Dans l'abri-caverne'; and then, acting out the moment when inspiration strikes like love: 'Il neige et je brûle et je tremble', by virtue of his own visions of the future.

These glimpses which now take shape have often been seen by critics as an anticlimax to his splendid claims. In fact, if they are taken as visual realisations, they are rather thin and insubstantial. They are more significant if they are seen as symbols for his own past efforts and for what he is now trying to do with his poetry, in fact as a real 'schématisation intégrale' which reconciles the past and future of his own work. It is perhaps no accident that in the article on *Parade* where he formulates this phrase, he also writes of 'une sorte de sur-réalisme' which has resulted, for these images belong in no way to the real world, but are created totally by the poet's sur-real imagination. The influence and interaction of the visual arts, of music and of friends is clear; but the crucial point is that they are all dead, 'au fond du temps'. What remains out of the death of past moments is the *saveur* of the orange, the unreal champagne which foams like a poet's brain, and the song of a rose. This surely underlines once again the ways of poetry, which acts on the real, distilling out of it its own elixir, as heady and frothing as the poet's brain.

The future is now revealed in a new trinity of beings, which here, as opposed to those of 'Arbre', have actually taken shape. The first symbolises the necessary destruction which Apollinaire found so hard to bear in 'La Victoire', but which he now manages to face in his imagination: 'Et chaque fois qu'elle s'abaisse/Un univers est éventré/ Dont il sort des mondes nouveaux'. The second figures the centrifugal force which takes the poet's imagination endlessly out into speed and space: 'Il paraît à perte de vue/Un univers encore vierge'. The third, perhaps invoked by that very adjective, is Our Lady of poetry, yet another transformation of Dame Abonde in the tram or the lady of Orkenise. In the same way in which Apollinaire made Christ into a modern aviator, so this Madonna-like figure mounts to Heaven in a super-lift. It is a naïve and touching and splendid assumption for poetry, and it may well be the religious associations in the final trans-figuration which lead him back into the moral preoccupation that is now so pressingly linked with creation. The ideal of human solidarity and brotherhood envisaged in:

> Et feront de vous cent morceaux
> A la pensée toujours unique

is in fact perhaps what he had already had an intuition of in 'Merveille de la guerre': 'C'est moi qui commence cette chose des siècles à venir'. Born out of the community of the war experience, but also indissolubly linked with his recognition of the need for renewal, for fraternity is always part of any revolutionary ideology, is this faith that it is the new, creative spirit in men which will achieve the supreme synthesis of uniting them into one thought.

The poem ends with a repetition of the basic pattern in yet another development that harmonises man's changing experiences with the cycles of nature, and finally and, as it would now seem, following inevitably a basic structure of Apollinaire's imagination, reduces both man and the whole order of nature into the Apollinairean quintessence of poetry, in images of gold and flame and speed and flowers and love that distil to the very last their own synthetic, exquisite scent.

It is profoundly significant that so many of Apollinaire's greatest poems end finally with poetry itself. This is strikingly the case with all the later poems where the *chanson*, the *hymne*, the desire to *savoir* have been refined to 'un parfum exquis', 'le pollen parfumé', the new name, the indefinable air. Indeed, I would suggest that the growth of the obsession with images and structures which embody the concept of synthesis is in direct proportion to the growth of Apollinaire's awareness of the way in which the creative self functions. In earlier works the choice of double-faced images, of ambiguous words and sounds, the verbal play, the ironical twists, may well have been semi-conscious. From 1908 onwards two major innovations, namely the adoption of images and structures which represent a cyclical pattern, and the reduction of the complexity of life into the unity of a single exquisite form, reflect the increasingly conscious concern to reconcile all contradictions. The technical experiments with the *idéogrammes* even attempt to foist this concern on to the reader so that he too can share in the poet's bird's-eye view. It is, however, in the last poems that the yearning towards unity and reconciliation on all levels, moral and social as well as purely aesthetic, becomes the one obsessive theme, and at the same time that the double register of the poet's voice, telling of the creative process itself, swells out in full diapason.

If, nevertheless, this yearning is always expressed in terms of anguish and amorous longing, as something so evanescent and exquisite and indefinable as still to be out of grasp, that is because the victory is never won once and for all time, but is always in the future. Whatever the past triumphs of the creative self in synthesising all antitheses by its domination of the real, it is only in the actual process of accomplishing the 'schématisation intégrale' which is each separate and particular poem that the creative spirit can prove itself. The miraculous balancing act has to be repeated endlessly: and even Apollinaire and his little boy acrobat must have known that miracles do not always happen.

Reading   MARGARET DAVIES

NOTES

1 Cf. *Chroniques d'Art*, ed. L.-C. Breunig, Paris, 1960, p. 427.
2 I use the terms employed by Michael Hamburger in *The Truth of Poetry*, London, 1969.
3 'Le Pont Mirabeau'.
4 Cf. M. Décaudin, *Le Dossier d'Alcools*, Genève, Paris, 1960, p. 142.
5 'Le Cheval', in *Le Bestairie ou le Cortège d'Orphée*.
6 'La Nuit d'avril'.
7 Ezra Pound, *Literary Essays*, London, 1960, p. 25.
8 A note on 'Lul de Faltenin' to appear in *Guillaume Apollinaire*, 11, Bibliothèque des Lettres Modernes.
9 In *Alcools d'Apollinaire*, Paris, p. 38.
10 Cf. 'Simultanisme-librettisme', *Les Soirées de Paris*, juin 1914.
11 In BC 427 there was a revocation of a decree by the Athenians that all the citizens of Mytilene, which had revolted against Athens, should be massacred. A special fleet arrived with news of the reprieve just when the sentence was about to be carried out.
12 In a paper given on 'La Victoire' at the Colloque Apollinaire in Stavelot, August 1971.
13 Cf. 'Nous allons plus haut maintenanent et ne touchons plus le sol/Et tandis que le monde vivait et variait'.

PIERRE JEAN JOUVE: THE IDEA
OF POETRY

The aesthetic principles that have dominated Pierre Jean Jouve's mature artistic life have not varied greatly since the late 1920s when the first hints of their nature emerged. However, different aspects have been developed and emphasised, both in poems and in theoretical writings, according to differing stimuli. They have been used to test the work of others as well as to guide his own. They have been applied to painting and music almost as much as to poetry, and they form a remarkably comprehensive and stable group.

At the moment when in 1925 Jouve published *Les Mystérieuses Noces* he was in fact putting behind him the diverse, chequered literary affiliations of his earlier career, but the finality of this metamorphosis was only given overt expression in 1928, in a brief postface to *Noces*. Although Jouve has subsequently[1] commented a little ironically on the tone of this declaration, it plunges directly into the central assertions of his whole aesthetic thinking in both their negative and their positive aspects. If it is to be at all authentic, poetry is seen as directly related to an imperious spiritual reality, and can be assessed only in this Christian context:

... la plus grande poésie et la véritable est celle que le rayon de la Révélation est venu toucher.[2]

This definition implies exclusivity, and indeed Jouve felt at this period a strong revulsion from what he saw as 'un ahurissant désordre des choses de l'art'.[3] But if he judged the literary values of his contemporaries harshly, he was even more uncompromising in his condemnation of his own previous publications—'le poète renonce à son premier œuvre' is how his note ends.

The poems of Jouve's 'vita nuova' all exhibit the same rigorous self-scrutiny, the attrition, the difficulty-defined and beleaguered religious faith, spiritual illuminations, stifling sense of the omnipresence of original sin, and the conditions that apply to the man must apply also to the poet. It is difficult, at least in the earlier books, to discriminate between what Jouve is saying about his personal switch of direction and its attendant rejections, and what he is suggesting as a necessary experience for the artist in any case. But it becomes clear that he sees his own as in fact an exaggerated example of a common pattern in which the search for regeneration and for vocation must be related. Until the second World War Jouve made few pronouncements about his own work; his views have to be inferred from his poetry and from occasional pieces about the writing, music and painting of others. His most developed statements concerned the impact of Freudian concepts and material, and their potentialities for the artist. But the events of the war, particularly in France, convinced him that as a parallel to his poetic treatment of these events he could contribute most effectively by stating and defending artistic values. A profusion of texts attempted to define the relation of an artist to his country, to assess his role as 'témoin' of a national catastrophe, to reinterpret the work of artists of the past and present.

Subsequently Jouve has never ceased, although with less urgency and less expectation of touching an immediate chord, to develop and scrutinise his aesthetic ideas, and the often more expansive and speculative tones of this later poetry have allowed him to pursue a broader meditation on the identity and autonomy of language, on its power to consolidate, perhaps even to create, a spiritual reality.

Poetry, then, is 'une affaire de transcendance'.[4] But for Jouve this means not so much defining the invisible as scrutinising the Pascalian 'misère de l'homme sans Dieu' and attempting a dialogue of which only one half can ever be spoken. For poetry partakes of the human condition, and language is not a neutral instrument but is composed of

> ces mots universels menteurs
> Et formés faux par le sang de naissance.[5]

How then can it tell even a limited truth, how describe even the familiar reality of sin? From beginning to end of his work Jouve is haunted by the terrible sense that his words are not only inadequate but distinctly false, and it is in this form that he carries on and lives out Mallarmé's linguistic dilemma. The cry in *Les Nouvelles Noces* was 'J'ai peur de mentir',[6] and some thirty years later he is still assessing failures in the same terms:

> Quand je t'aspire dans les rocs, éternité ravie et verte,
> Ce n'est pas sans un faux nom de mes langages de prison[7]

Jouve's poetry is not, however, permeated with defeatism and despair. His very strong belief in the artist as a 'dépositaire spirituel'[8] leads him to a tenacious search for areas of validity, which will have to be meticulously tested and verified. One characteristic device is to

OHF

suggest awareness of spiritual ambivalence by using words like 'vrai' and 'réel' with different meanings within the same phrase; and if familiar aesthetic criteria are applied to art these are rigorously redefined. It is inevitable that Jouve should be suspicious of the seduction and the implicit arrogance of formal aesthetic beauty, and he makes it clear that when he says of a painter 'il veut élever continuellement les images les plus obscures à un niveau de beauté et de lucidité',[9] this beauty is to be an essentially spiritual quality—'je n'ai aucun goût pour la beauté formelle et d'harmonie, j'aime la beauté de forme, d'essence'.[10] Once dissociated from trivial, static and limitedly sensuous identifications beauty can be released for a dynamic rôle in the 'coup de dés divin'[11] that is the poem. It can hold together warring opposites and release their energies into a new harmony:

> Un seul accord, Beauté! si ton immense jeu
> Marie le ciel avec l'enfer[12]

—a hypothesis, perhaps, but strongly stated; elsewhere, and with a reference to Baudelaire, the optative is used, again emphatically:

> Que la beauté non plus comme un rêve de pierre
> Jaillisse désormais du laid de notre horreur
> Redoutable . . .
> Et que cette beauté aux mille rayons vive
> Traverse la machine du temps[13]

A similar analysis could be made of the way in which 'lucidité' is given a special interpretation, related on the one hand to visionary illumination and on the other to the poet's rôle as vigilant witness to a world of sin, at once 'voyant' and 'voyeur'.[14]

It is perhaps because of these exigencies that Jouve has elevated music to pride of place in his aesthetics. It was his earliest artistic preoccupation, as he has often stated, and is a continuing dominant influence. He has written studies of Mozart and Berg, and some of his strongest assertions of confidence in the power and validity of art have appeared in his comments on music and musicians. He continues the late nineteenth-century tradition of seeing music as the purest of the media, and adds a peculiarly Christian sense of revelation; music is for him 'avant tout autre art sur la voie d'accomplissement parfait dans la Promesse'.[15] It is, however, through opera, which some people would see as a hybrid and therefore 'impure' art, that Jouve can most satisfactorily demonstrate the religious function of music. One of his own books of poems is entitled *Mélodrame*, and he sees as a privileged form of expression this particular mixture of drama and music, of orchestral and human sound. Whatever Mozart's conception or inspiration, his *Don Giovanni* is for Jouve 'essentiellement chrétien',[16] demonstrating as it does the 'domination sur la Mort exercée par l'esprit de raison, qu'éclaire la Foi et selon la règle d'or de la beauté'.[17] This last quotation contains in fact a precise formulation of all that Jouve hopes for from art, and a definition of the precarious but positive balancing of elements at a point of tension which he sees as necessary if art is to have a transcendental dimension.

But when Jouve speaks at this level of certainty he is commenting on a few works that he considers unique and exemplary. For his own poetry there is no short cut to spiritual transmutation, and the tainted words have to follow the same weary path as the poet. Jouve does not believe only in a single incontrovertible revelation, giving subsequent spiritual stability, but in an endless series of grim initiatives from an apparently desperate position. He subscribes to the paradox of 'He that loseth his life for my sake shall find it', but the process of abnegation, the extinction of pride and desire, the renunciation of all that can be achieved and possessed, even of art itself, all this is an exhausting and absorbing discipline. We see Jouve attempting various modes of detachment, propounding models of negation. A sacrifice of identity: the heroine of his novel *Paulina 1880* changes her name twice, and in his translations from Hölderlin attention is drawn to the poet's signature to his poems of madness, 'Avec humilité, Scardinelli', and to his cutting all but a few of the wires of his piano and then improvising on the remaining notes. A sacrifice of function: when Orpheus is evoked it is a torn and dying body whose severed hands still touch the lute.[18] A sacrifice of formal beauty: many of Jouve's poems are abrupt truncated exclamations, and even in his more rhetorical constructions the syntax is wrenched away from its expected pattern; a similar reorientation of language is seen by him not only in Mallarmé but also in Baudelaire whose distinction is to 'briser en un certain sens l'instinct logistique de la langue française'.[19] These manœuvres have complex aesthetic implications, of course, but are also seen by Jouve, certainly in his own case, as part of a spiritual struggle. Finally there is the paradoxical sacrifice of all the accepted positive qualities of poetry, its material texture, its vision, its harmony, its autonomy.

A critic has described Jouve as an Abraham-poet,[20] another sees his poetry as 'née sous le signe de Niobé',[21] and certainly the disciplines that Jouve lists in *La Vierge de Paris* as 'oublier', 'briser', 'accepter' dictate a poetic pattern based on negative concepts, 'néant', 'vide', 'rien', 'Nada', and call for new definitions:

> Ce sont des livres nus que je rêve d'accomplir
> A présent sans odeur et sans voix.[22]

It is in terms of sensual 'dénuement' that Jouve undertakes the purification of

> ces livres qui regardent vers l'extérieur avec les yeux crevés[23]

and which are to acquiesce in their own mutilation

> Gratias
> Ou le chant d'asphodèle et de dépossession![24]

—this line, which recalls the Eliot of *East Coker*, crystallises the inexorable internal logic that leads Jouve to the apparent artistic suicide of

> Mon silence est le verbe nu que tu désires.[25]

Or this would be so if the 'Nada' concept did not also signify an overwhelmingly rich spiritual possibility. Only within or upon the idea of total self-abandonment does Jouve dare to envisage fulfilment or possession, and this has the quality of revelation. If we return to the image of voluntary blinding we find the poet as Oedipus:

> Absolument dévasté et comme Oedipe l'œil crevé mais clair rebandé
> en esprit.[26]

The vital 'mais' of this phrase introduces a different dimension of being, and it is here that a great flowering of certainty can take place:

> Le Rien contient croyances et ombrages
> Musique de l'église et langues et vaisseaux
> De chair et de voyage et des douceurs superbes
> Le Rien a les tableaux parfaits de liberté.[27]

Jouve cannot move from the immanent to the transcendent, but must reverse the sequence. And just as he can only envisage the sexual act liberated from its association with original sin in rare and miraculous-seeming circumstances, so the creative act may exceptionally be released into spiritual significance. It represents 'la vie même du grand Eros morte et par là survivante'.[28]

Jouve may very well seem to have appropriated poetry in a peculiarly personal quest for salvation, and indeed ultimately this is how his position may perhaps be interpreted, in spite of all that he has to say about the aesthetic validity of art. But at least it is clear that this quest is not exclusively self-centred. His view of the poet's rôle includes a preoccupation with contemporary problems and a sense of mission. His responsibility is to 'placer le trésor mystique bien près de l'humanité',[29] and to engage with other men of good will in a stand against 'le démoniaque contemporain'.[30] This 'démoniaque' takes many forms, from triviality to sadism; but its most public identification is with elements of German aggression in the second World War. In seeing the poet as 'le créateur des valeurs de la vie'[31] Jouve is following the Romantic tradition, and for him this suggests a combination of Baudelaire's 'phares' and his 'intercesseurs'. He expects estrangement and solitude, though he may sometimes complain at what Pierre Emmanuel calls his 'fatalité salutaire'.[32] This makes him particularly appreciative of the few artists whom he sees as sustaining kindred spirits. The names of these 'guérisseurs' appear often in his poetry as well as in his aesthetic comments, and, as with Eliot, quotations from their work are embedded in the texture of the poems. These parallel the 'objets de lumière',[33] the 'dorures de pensée contre un beau ciel de peur'[34] which initiate a re-spiritualisation of the world.

Jouve is exclusive in his artistic affinities; but, in addition to a group of mystical writers, these range from Dante and Shakespeare through Blake and Hölderlin to Segalen and Emmanuel; his musicians are Mozart, Beethoven, Mahler, Bartok, Berg; painters include Meryon, Delacroix, Courbet and Balthus. There is a special place for Nerval, Rimbaud and Mallarmé, but the most permanent presence in the poetry is perhaps what Jouve calls 'le réconfort Baudelaire',[35] clarifying for him his own dualism, his sensuality, his spiritual sense, his aesthetics. Such affinities seem predestined to Jouve, and 'Quand on est très enfermé dans son monde, on n'accepte que les nourritures pour ce monde-là;[36] the rest is rejected, undifferentiated but disturbing. In the context of such a position, intransigent because intuitive, a late capitulation to Racine takes on an unexpected and moving quality. It might have been assumed that Jouve would have felt a special link with Racine, but in fact until the chance experience of a performance of *Phèdre*[37] he had always considered seventeenth-century drama to be alien and artificial.

With this elective support to draw on Jouve found it easier to define the poet's function in a time of national disaster. He saw the second World War as specifically 'une guerre de la foi'[38] and the French as recapturing the high moments of their Catholic and Revolutionary past. Such an apocalyptic view of history demands prophetic treatment, and here artists become the 'témoins' whose 'lucidité terrible'[39] not only records the violence and suffering but reveals their inner significance of chastisement and purification. It is in this sense that Rimbaud appears as 'l'œil de la catastrophe',[40] and that certain texts—Danton's speeches or Revolutionary popular songs—assume a special relevance. This was a period when Jouve could feel confidence in the immediate efficacy of art, since he saw its rôle as positive and unambiguous—'La Poésie a dû lutter pour la Liberté les armes à la main'[41]—and since, particularly during the Occupation, poetry did in fact become a much-prized mode of communication, the short-hand of fraternity, pity and resistance. He could broaden his canons to take in a number of his contemporaries— Claudel, Aragon, Saint-John Perse—since he felt that they shared his patriotic sense of mission or had contributed to defining the true spirit of France. For him there was no clash between the Christian and the Revolutionary elements in the national identity. In a tribute to de Gaulle he wrote:

Les deux principes civilisateurs de la France—le christianisme hiérarchique du Moyen Age, la force insurrectionnelle des Droits de l'Homme —se retrouvent enfin coalisés, et obligés par des accords réciproques de retrouver qu'ils sont une seule et même puissance de liberté et d'honneur.[42]

So he can reject as equally irrelevant the Catholicism of the Restoration and nineteenth-century anti-clericalism. Hence for him 'Courbet, qu'il l'ait su ou non, était homme de foi'.[43] This sense that there is an inner coherence to a major artist's work, often imperceptible to contemporaries, is an important tenet of Jouve's aesthetics, and he has applied it when revising his own poems and novels for republication. Speaking of the volume of poems covering the war period,[44] and the most circumstantial in his eyes, he has said 'J'ai essayé de retrouver pour ce livre sa règle d'or'.[45] This autonomy of judgment reflects clearly some of the processes of aesthetic thinking in an essentially religious temperament.

Another area in which Jouve could feel certain of the ultimate justification and immediate benefit of his artistic activity was in his championship and adaptation of Freudian psychological findings. It was for him of the utmost importance that artists should identify and assimilate the potentially dangerous new material, should be the pioneers who would prevent its misappropriation, for they, just as much as the psychologists, are the 'spéléologues'[46] the 'scaphandriers'[47] of the human mind. The fact that Freudian ideas continued and confirmed at all points Jouve's existing religious conviction and image pattern made him all the more sure that artists are the only people aware enough to be able to fit the new concepts into a wider system of values. And they would immediately gain an aesthetic advantage, the 'incalculable accroissement du tragique que nous

donne la métapsychologie'.[43] Furthermore, the Freudian concept of
sublimation is not just applied generally to the notion of artistic
creation; there is a more precise parallel in that Jouve sees the
necessity for art to be a charge of energy so powerfully directed that it
can reverse the usual concentrations of man's psychological forces. In
his poetry Jouve's imagery habitually suggests random explosions of
energy and the mechanically repetitive play of erotic forces, all
trapped within the static power of the death-wish. But just as the
libido can transcend itself so art can suggest a quickening of the dead
weight of evil, and in this context 'Le péché devient mouvement'[49]
and death is out-manœuvred:

. . . l'artiste est celui qui pense la mort de façon active et sait l'utiliser,
complètement différent sur ce point de la majorité des hommes. L'artiste
est celui qui met sa mort en valeur.[50]

There is an exuberance, a buoyancy in Jouve's welcoming of this
challenge which is only matched by his excitement at finding in
artists of the past anticipations of contemporary developments. One
of his criteria of assessment is how far they are able to reveal to
modern man something new about himself, and at the same time to
offer a 'true' image of their own time. Thus one of the distinguishing
marks of Baudelaire is that for Jouve he should be 'découvreur de son
temps',[51] and as for Shakespeare,

. . . avec stupeur, nous regardons Shakespeare inventer, créer, nommer,
tout à fait près mais aussi tout à fait loin de la réalité (par une vue anticipée
prodigieuse) les terribles structures de l'homme, qui commencent d'appa-
raître, montagnes de noirceur et de lumière.[52]

It is partly because of this sense of a startling relevance that Jouve has
felt justified in devoting considerable effort to the translating of *Romeo
and Juliet*, *Othello*, *Macbeth* and the complete sonnets, while also
being a translator of Hölderlin, Gongora, Ungaretti and Wedekind.

But the discussion of some details of Jouve's literary activities, the
definition of certain terms in his aesthetic vocabulary, may obscure
what is perhaps the most crucial question that his poetry poses: the
relationship between the mystic and the poet, whether their aims can
be at all compatible, what difference there is between the mystic's
account of his quest and the poet's. In a sense Jouve is asking that his
poetry should give him spiritual certainty by breaking through the
barriers of the finite and the material, and achieving the desired
contact with a divine principle. If the mystic can feel that he has
experienced this it will, however, have been a moment of essentially

mute ecstasy and a denial of the material that a subsequent description can only hint at. Jouve is in fact well aware of this problem and its dangers, although the comment he makes on it may still seem ambiguous:

la mystique commence par nier ce qui est le plus important pour l'art: l'orde suprêmement sensuel qui revêt la chose de la beauté. Et cependant tout 'grand' art doit *par paradoxe* contenir une fin mystique.[53]

It is the maintaining of this paradox that produces much of the tension, the energy and the anguish in Jouve's own poetry.

He is at pains to specify, then, that

Il est d'autre part absurde de vouloir que l'expérience de la sainteté se transpose dans la Poésie[54]

but when he is considering, for instance, the 'Nada' idea he makes it clear that this is so intimately identified with forms of artistic expression as to be virtually inconceivable without them:

Nada fut une vérité intime, une vérité à travers laquelle on aspire, une idée qui veut devenir être. Elle était aussi, je demande de ne pas l'oublier, une idée de Poésie. Elle ne peut être maniée que dans la substance, par le jeu contradictoire de l'image à l'intérieur du poème même.[55]

Even if the highest form of spiritual expression is seen to be negative it may very well seem necessary to evoke some remembrance of the material so as to define that negative, and for this images are necessary. The absolute is

la région splendide des hommes sans hommes et des ciels sans ciels;[56]

the immaterial is perceived in terms of a degree beyond the possible:

Ah! le poète écrit pour le vide des cieux
Pur bleu que l'hiver ne parvient plus à voir! il
    écrit dans la conjuration des silences de neige
Des étouffements de fêtes fallacieuses![57]

Jouve has a particularly thorough knowledge of a number of mystical texts, and he is very familiar with Saint Theresa's 'mourir de ne pas mourir' paradox. He is aware that the next logical step is

. . . et voilà qu'il s'agit, pour être l'art en Dieu,
De n'être jamais né . . .
Et dans la non-naissance était la joie, la pure
Joie! la jamais connue de nos peuples sincères, de nos courages nés, de nos visages vieux, de toute notre chair si longtemps survécue.[58]

Yet this is not within human power, even aided by grace, and must remain a suspended paradox. This is one of the contexts in which Jouve uses the word absurd—'la fleur absurde où le parfum est art'[59] —since the poem can perhaps ultimately be only 'une interrogation lancée dans l'inconnu'.[60]

Even when Jouve puts his whole trust in his Claudelian-sounding concept of the 'Seigneur encre de la maison'[61] the tension is not resolved, so strongly does he believe in the spiritual responsibility of each human being. Jean Starobinski has praised Jouve's integrity in that his is a 'parole . . . trop véridique pour s'offrir sous l'aspect d'un itinéraire aboutissant à la vision certaine de l'absolu'.[62] But because his art is built up on the paradox or 'pari' system Jouve has to behave as though a poem *could* achieve this end. For this he uses two main poetic modes, a ubiquitous ambivalence in which, at its simplest, the 'parole humaine abolie'[63] can also be the 'verbe'—

> Je me disais que le Verbe est d'essence absolue,
> péremptoire, et de nature invincible,[64]

and a substitution of the poem for its creator in the spiritual initiative. It is of course only a matter of degree, but the difference can appear decisive, especially when the poem is seen to thrust out and seize upon the mystical presence in a reversal of the traditional 'bride-groom' image:

> le poème est la création
> Quand d'un acte de viol amoureux son extase
> Fait toucher l'invisible immédiatement,[65]

and in a further extension of the erotic metaphor:

> L'art qui voit! plus futur encore que même l'éternel . . .
> Il prend la personne Divine évanouissante à la vue
> Il s'épuise à elle sans voir et dans l'accouplement pur
> Nous avons vu à grandes trombes se refermer les eaux de la joie.[66]

It is this substitution that allows for a new form of hope, since a fresh antithesis can be set up that is ultimately to the poet's advantage—

> . . . et son cœur qui ne meurt
> Remplace en respirant ce corps pesant d'ennui.[67]

This phrase, however, and others like it, have caused Ursula Schneider,[68] for instance, to see this as the most negative and despairing side of Jouve's poetry, reinforcing the idea of the prison of the self, and accepting a prospect of endless 'rechutes'. But other critics have stressed the resilience, power and incandescent quality of this area of the poetry, and find in it, on the contrary 'la lueur d'une invincible espérance'.[69] This divergence of opinion is a measure of the ambivalence of Jouve's position; but an overall impression is certainly likely to be that the idea of the autonomy of language offers Jouve a strong ground for confidence, and is presented in such a way as to suggest a cumulative effect, each statement reinforcing the others.

But what exactly does Jouve understand by the autonomy of language? His attitude is clearest, perhaps, when he is dealing with Mallarmé, with whom he does not expect to share a religious faith, but with whose aesthetic beliefs he is in close sympathy. Here the autonomy is unambiguous—'Les mots sont triomphants et esclaves de la seule Poésie'[70]—and their release is seen as Mallarmé's outstanding achievement. With Baudelaire, a temperament more akin to his own and with perhaps more complex needs, the emphasis is still the same:

Dans ses mots, le Poète se sauve, et point autrement. Dans *l'acte des mots* du Poète est sa mystique. . . . Et j'entends prouver que la souffrance énorme de Baudelaire devait, plus que toute autre nature poétique, comporter le sacrifice du poète, et déposer avec lenteur, dans les poèmes, le contenu de son contenu.[71]

A very similar remark is made by Guy Dumur about Jouve himself:

Chez Jouve, la confiance en l'acte poétique est telle qu'il lui tient lieu de réponse et de salut.[72]

Statements about Jouve's view of poetry are the more confusing because critics bring to it preconceptions about what constitutes a mystical experience, what is its purpose and indeed value. It is really only possible to assess the effect of the poetry and to be guided by its emphases. There is no doubt that Jouve is committed to the idea of the supremacy of poetry and sees himself as first and foremost a poet. When he stresses the dissociation of author and poem this can be seen as a natural speculation about the relationship:

Quand, le poème ayant créé un monde
Seul, réel, franchissant la mort d'un seul trait,
La lumiére éternelle et des monts bleus sur l'onde
En serai-je maître indifférent défait
Qui regarde à la porte de Dieu? et ne tremble.[73]

Certainly, also, Jouve feels committed to the world, 'invinciblement lié au destin de la matière', as Marc Eigeldinger[74] has put it. It would be misleading to see his attitude as one of revulsion and rejection, primarily, for there is very much more of compassion and involvement. While Jouve might well feel that Roger Bastide is laying too great a responsibility on him—

Ce que nous réclamons de Jouve c'est de sauver la matière à l'intérieur même de l'Esprit le plus absolu[75]

the strength of his poetry is certainly its ability to suggest areas of matter being released from their own dark weight and transmuted into a glowing transparent buoyancy. This is the 'matière céleste', the sanctified flesh, the irradiated landscape, that is such a characteristic feature of Jouve's poetry, and by stressing its transmutation through art he is able to bring out all the pathos of the human associations but see them in a specific perspective. Again it is music that best conveys this poignant quality for him when it is

. . . douce de ses oiseaux déchirants, un soleil
Dans les pleurs, et le chant raisonnable des anges,[76]

but this quality is diffused throughout his own poetry and represents the point of balance between not so much the mystical and the aesthetic as the mystical and universally human. It is on this basis that Jouve is justified in describing his poetry as

. . . notre art d'amour . . .
Qui à l'envers de vie humaine est éther de révélation
Tout éternel, exsultate, œuvre et déification.[77]

Birmingham   MARGARET CALLANDER

NOTES

Quotations are taken mainly from the four-volume edition of Jouve's poetry by the *Mercure de France*, 1964–67. Jouve's writings on art are grouped in *Défense et Illustration*, Fribourg, 1943, Paris, 1945; *Apologie du poète*, Paris, 1947; *Commentaires*, Neuchâtel, 1950; *En Miroir, journal sans date*, Paris, 1954.

1 *En Miroir*, Paris, 1954, p. 35.
2 *Commentaires*, Neuchâtel, 1950, p. 23.
3 *En Miroir*, p. 29.
4 *Apologie du poète*, Paris, 1947, p. 8.
5 *Mélodrame*, Paris, 1957, p. 31.
6 *Poésie*, vol. I, p. 54.
7 *Poésie*, vol. IV, p. 26.
8 *Apologie du poète*, p. 53.
9 'Les Portraits de Sima', *NRF*, March 1931.
10 *Apologie du poète*, p. 13.

11 *Poésie*, vol. IV, p. 131.
12 *Poésie*, vol. II, p. 190.
13 *Poésie*, vol. IV, p. 143.
14 v. *Poésie*, vol. I, p. 168, 'Et lui le voyeur des chairs bouleversantes'.
15 *Commentaires*, p. 122.
16 *Le Don Juan de Mozart*, Fribourg, 1942, p. 25.
17 *Le Don Juan de Mozart*, p. 20.
18 v. *Poésie*, vol. I, pp. 272–6.
19 *Défense et Illustration*, Paris, 1945, p. 74.
20 P. de Boisdeffre, *Les Nouvelles littéraires*, 16 October 1958.
21 G. Ungaretti, *NRF*, March 1968.
22 *Poésie*, vol. I, p. 249.
23 *Poésie*, vol. III, p. 200.
24 *Poésie*, vol. III, p. 141.
25 *Poésie*, vol. II, p. 73.
26 *Poésie*, vol. III, p. 225.
27 *Poésie*, vol. II, p. 185.
28 *Commentaires*, p. 34.
29 *Apologie du poète*, p. 52.
30 *Commentaires*, p. 12.
31 *Commentaires*, p. 34.
32 'Pierre Jean Jouve, architecte de l'âme', *Figaro littéraire*, 24 November 1962.
33 *Poésie*, vol. II, p. 46.
34 *Poésie*, vol. III, p. 61.
35 *Proses*, Paris, 1960, p. 76.
36 Interview with H. Fouras, *Figaro littéraire*, 30 June 1956.
37 'La Leçon de Phèdre', *Mercure de France*, February 1960.
38 Preface to Jules Roy, *La Vallée heureuse*, Paris, 1946.
39 *Poésie*, vol. II, p. 55.
40 *Défense et Illustration*, p. 175.
41 *Apologie du poète*, p. 33.
42 *L'Homme du 18 juin*, Fribourg, 1945, pp. 44–5.
43 *Défense et Illustration*, p. 190.
44 *Poésie*, vol. II.
45 Interview with J.-P. Gorin, *Le Monde*, 29 January 1966.
46 *En Miroir*, p. 71.
47 *Commentaires*, p. 65.
48 *Commentaires*, p. 29.
49 *Commentaires*, p. 69.
50 *En Miroir*, pp. 102–3.
51 Preface to Baudelaire, *Critique*, Fribourg, 1944, p. 10.
52 Preface to a translation, with G. Pitoëff, *La Tragédie de Roméo et Juliette*, Paris, 1937, pp. ix–x.
53 *Commentaires*, p. 121.
54 *Apologie du poète*, p. 51.
55 *En Miroir*, p. 125.
56 *Poésie*, vol. III, p. 195.
57 *Poésie*, vol. III, p. 208.
58 *Poésie*, vol. III, p. 215.

59 *Poésie*, vol. IV, p. 47.
60 A. Béguin, *Poésie de la présence*, Neuchâtel, 1957, p. 28.
61 *Poésie*, vol. III, p. 37.
62 *NRF*, March 1968.
63 *Poésie*, vol. II, p. 80.
64 *Proses*, p. 14.
65 *Poésie*, vol. II, p. 213.
66 *Poésie*, vol. III, pp. 165–6.
67 *Poésie*, vol. III, p. 166.
68 *La Quête du Nada dans l'œuvre de Pierre Jean Jouve*, Zurich, 1968.
69 H. Amer, *NRF*, March 1968.
70 *Défense et Illustration*, Neuchâtel, 1943, p. 183.
71 *Défense et Illustration*, 1945, pp. 33–5.
72 *Mercure de France*, July 1959.
73 *Poésie*, vol. III, p. 52.
74 *Pierre Jean Jouve, poète et romancier*, Neuchâtel, 1946, p. 99.
75 *Cahiers du Sud*, March 1934.
76 *Poésie*, vol. IV, p. 101.
77 *Poésie*, vol. IV, p. 51.

PIERRE REVERDY AND THE REALITY OF SIGNS

The highly conceptual, anti-naturalistic art of cubist painters such as Braque and Gris exists on a static plane whose ties with three-dimensional reality are extremely tenuous. Their guitars, table-tops and bottles have been stripped of all substance and connotation: released from the obligation to represent actual things, they become independent forms invested with a purely plastic significance, and relate only to each other within the pictorial area strictly delimited by the frame. If there is such a thing as 'cubist poetry', it would be legitimate to expect it to correspond to this model, and draw its aesthetic validity from a perfect interior balance uncompromised by outside connexions.

If one is looking for cubist poetry in the work of Pierre Reverdy, one will turn to such collections as *Les Ardoises du toit* (1918), in the expectation of finding work reflecting the cubist ideal announced by the poet in various manifestos of the *Nord-Sud* years. At first, one may feel confident of having found something akin to the work of the painters. Each short, lean piece does indeed appear to rely on an interior logic of assemblage and one may well feel inclined to accept the argument that the *raison d'être* of any given part lies in its relation to all other parts. Such poems cannot be un-soldered; their unity is not subject to natural laws, for, according to cubist theory, the poem is an autonomous object that rivals actual external objects, along the lines laid down when Reverdy, at his most dogmatic, demanded 'l'œuvre d'art qui ait sa vie indépendante, sa réalité et qui soit son propre but'.[1] In such poetry, the boundaries of the poetic space need to be rigorously defined. Julia Husson has suggested that 'Reverdy is always conscious of an invisible framework outside of which the poem never extends—it never opens on to anything else', and has drawn attention to the characteristic 'reversal' in the last section or even the last line of a Reverdy poem, whereby the poem turns back on itself or closes itself off.[2] The comment seems relevant to pieces such as 'Soleil', which is so slight and lacking in momentum that it may truly be said to float as an empty, anchorless object, a self-defining aesthetic structure.

SOLEIL

Quelqu'un vient de partir
Dans la chambre
            Il reste un soupir
La vie déserte

    La rue
        Et la fenêtre ouverte
Un rayon de soleil
Sur la pelouse verte[3]

Here there is certainly a veto on motion and substance. There remain but minimal traces of presence: someone has been in the room, for a sigh lingers, and a window has been left open. But there is no encouragement to press for more tangible evidence. The ray of sunlight on the lawn casts a pure light over the carefully selected particles of the poem and summons them into perspective as a constellation of poised signs directed at nothing but a timeless moment of perfect, incorporeal being.

But is Reverdy's poetry really so Mallarmean, so hygienic? I believe that the reticence of his cubist work, the careful trimming of extraneous matter, the neutralising of each dry sign, in fact led to a curiously 'impure' result. That is, where the truncation of clauses and the ban on adjectives and verbs might have been expected to produce a monchrome poetry of quasi-abstract harmonies, something akin to Braque's brown and white still-lifes, the laws of censorship that Reverdy followed seem, paradoxically, to have *provoked* certain vibrations and emotions. I am not referring to structural patterns or 'pure' aesthetic emotion. I am saying simply that the frozen artifact that one might assume to be typical of Reverdy's cubist manner actually has, when one looks into it, an oddly palpitating life.[4] The disposition of carefully sifted 'signes blancs'[5] tends to articulate unsuspected meanings, in a way that adulterates the purity of the cubist ideal. Seen superficially, the poem is hard and self-sufficient; under closer examination, it becomes porous and yielding.

The following poem can help to test this claim (though one might coax a rather different meaning from 'Soleil' if one tried).

SECRET

La cloche vide
Les oiseaux morts
Dans la maison où tout s'endort
Neuf heures

La terre se tient immobile
On dirait que quelqu'un soupire
Les arbres ont l'air de sourire
L'eau tremble au bout de chaque feuille
Un nuage traverse la nuit

Devant la porte un homme chante

La fenêtre s'ouvre sans bruit.[6]

At first, the signs appear to be the familiar, rather monotonous stock-in-trade typical of Reverdy. Yet are they so familiar? Can they ever be truly familiar? The unpretentious sequence of colourless data in fact adds up to rather more than a sum of non-statements. It is perhaps in the sixth line that the poem begins to 'tremble' and the picture to forfeit its even clarity. 'On dirait que quelqu'un soupire.' Of course, Reverdy repeats the expression *quelqu'un* with such deadening frequency in *Ardoises* that it is finally drained of connotations. Yet the neutral word can reveal itself as a sign of life, perhaps the more exciting for being practically extinguished. Who is it that sighs? One may pass over 'on dirait' with its Mallarmean indirection and near-negation; yet one senses at least a minimal mystery here. After registering one uncertain clue, one begins to pick up other hints. Water at each leaf-tip, a nocturnal cloud slipping past—these edge towards a sense of expectancy. Then a man suddenly sings: the effect is of an irruption of sound that one cannot actually hear. The song can only be imagined, abstractly. Louder yet seems the silence that throbs about the shreds of information we have been allowed. The last line enters to re-affirm total absence of sound. 'La fenêtre s'ouvre sans bruit.' This is the sign we have waited for—and it is of silence. It ensures a hermetic closure in that we revert to the silence of the opening line ('La cloche vide'); yet it leaves us uneasy since we know that it represents, *must* represent a response to the song the man sings. The connexions are not made any clearer than this, and the sign remains indecipherable. Yet the poem, simple to the point of naïveté, does embody a secret, the same secret that everyday objects offer when focused upon in an obsessional way. The analogy one wants to draw is no longer with a still life by Juan Gris, but with a photograph of a doorway by Bill Brandt, of something banal seen as a disquieting enigma.

While it is fairly obvious that a poet, in using words rather than lines, cannot expect to strip his statement of each last connotative vestige, it is surprising to discover that the attempt to do so calls forth such subtle mysteries. Where exactly does mystery gain a pur-chase? The answer may be sought in Reverdy's pronouncements on the relation of the poet to external reality, which take us a long way from cubist intellectualism. An ardent observer of nature who sees the poet as 'le réceptacle idéal de toutes les manifestations extérieures', Reverdy conceives of reality as a Baudelairean network of correspondences such that when one looks at a given thing 'ce n'est plus une chose isolée qui l'on perçoit, mais ses rapports avec les autres choses, et ces rapports des choses entre elles et avec nous sont la trame extrêmement ténue et solide à la fois de l'immense, de la profonde, de la savoureuse réalité'.[7] Reality is sustained by an analogical armature compounded of tangible and visible points of reference, the connexions between these, and finally the connexions between them and the receptive consciousness. The problem to be faced is that the latter connexions are not always in evidence. What Novalis called the *Chiffernschrift* of nature, its coded message, cannot always be deciphered by the poet. Phenomena can be obscure, and elude interpretation. Perceptions are often clouded by an awareness of a distance between consciousness and its object. For Reverdy, the evasiveness of reality is a central theme. The world frequently hovers at a remove from him, as though he were suspended in a sensory void:

> Loin
> Rien derrière moi et rien devant
> Dans le vide où je descends
> Quelques vifs courants d'air
> Vont autour de moi
> Cruels et froids.[8]

Cold winds cut the poet off from any intimacy with things, a denial of proper contact which can make him voice bitter feelings of disorientation and existential loneliness.

> Un rayon sur le bord du verre
> Ma main déçue n'attrape rien
> Enfin tout seul j'aurai vécu
> Jusqu'au dernier matin
>
> Sans qu'un mot m'indiquât quel fut le bon chemin.[9]

The ancillary problem is that language is defective. Whilst Reverdy would like to believe that 'grâce aux mots, . . . grâce au langage . . . l'homme s'*approprie* le monde extérieur', he often has to admit the incapacity of words to 'fixer le lyrisme . . . de la réalité'.[10] The maintenance of relations is far from easy for the poet: 'Ces rapports, il est constamment obligé de les créer, de les renouveler, de les contrôler, de les régler et de les maintenir. La réalité extérieure le presse et le menace sans cesse.'[11] The activity of naming and registering connexions through the medium of linguistic signs is accompanied by a gnawing sense of insufficiency. Life must remain 'la vie scellée, inexprimable' so long as there are gaps in the continuity between objects, language and mind. The world will slip away from the poet whenever perception and expression fail to pin it down.

> Le monde s'efface
> . . . .
> Il n'y a même plus de place
> Pour les mots que je laisserai.[12]

It seems hopeless to believe in any final understanding when reality escapes cognition so utterly.

> Toutes les raisons de ne plus croire à rien
> Les mots se sont perdus tout le long du chemin
> Il n'y a plus rien à dire
> Le vent est arrivé
> Le monde se retire.[13]

Yet, despondent and despairing as some of these hollow responses sound, they represent moments that sigh with virtual meaning. The absence of the world, of things, the evasiveness of that which the poet wishes to put a word to, becomes in turn something real, in the way that a gap takes on an element of solidity if one contemplates the continuous wall on either side of it for long enough. The enigmatic gap in reality does begin to signify. It is possible to compare this passage from loss and emptiness to an anguished though optimistic belief in potential meaning to Reverdy's religious experience in the twenties. At that time, he seems to have read with clarity what he calls 'les traits du ciel', a mysterious 'extra' meaning adhering to phenomena.[14] As far as poetic apprehension is concerned, there are important implications. The poetic sign (either the thing seen or its verbal equivalent) may be so envisaged as to apparently transmit an extra measure of suggestive energy: it not only denotes the clearly identifiable idea, but also points to something else. Furthermore, emptiness itself may be taken as a signal of a 'something else'. The unexpected quotient of supplementary meaning that engages the poet's creative attention may be connected to the latent mystery of all existence. Though one cannot hope to be more specific than this, one would like to define more closely the quality of the mystery born of emptiness. Would it be appropriate to speak of 'mysticism'? The word might suggest itself to the casual reader of *Le Gant de crin* (1927), where Reverdy's early *art poétique* appears alongside extensive meditations on his relation to God. However, the point must be made that the poetic theories were composed and indeed published earlier than this, and do not properly belong to the religious context. Not that the theme of spiritual questing is foreign to the poetry. My point is that its lasting tenor is not Christian (Reverdy remained a Catholic for only about two years), and that the poetic quest should be seen in less transcendental terms than those adopted by the poet at that particular time. Undoubtedly there is mystery about the world: all is not explicable in life, the secrets of existence are not spelled out for us. As for poetry, its nature is to allude, to beckon, rather than to capture outright. Nonetheless, Reverdy seems to be saying in his poems, there *are* revelations to hand: one can pick up a few 'épaves du ciel' if one looks about. Basically, I would maintain, Reverdy's 'mysticism' (if one calls it that) is closely associated with a nostalgia for immanence. David Grossvogel has argued that for Reverdy spirituality is closely tied to 'the material quiddity of each thing', a link also stressed by Anna Balakian in her essay on Reverdy's 'materio-mysticism'.[15] There is a certain obscurity on this point, partly due to Reverdy's involvement with Cubism and Catholicism; my contention is that these did not deeply affect the more permanent levels of his poetic sensibility. Admittedly Reverdy occasionally took an idealist line, proclaiming for instance that 'la poésie est dans ce qui n'est pas. Dans ce qui nous manque.'[16] But something prevented him from becoming a complete Neo-platonist or a believer in a perfect world beyond the one which presently eludes him. His 'angelism' stops short a step or so beyond the gap in the wall. He gropes his way back to that wall, rather, in the belief that poetry cannot afford to lose touch with what Rimbaud called 'la rugueuse réalité.'[17] He keeps

> Un poing sur la réalité bien pleine.

This line was once quoted by André Breton as though to do honour to Reverdy as a poet of the tangible, a tough boxer[18] rather than a vapid transcendentalist. However, for accuracy's sake, the stress requires adjustment even here. Had Breton looked to the next line in the poem he was quoting from, he would have found this:

> Un poing sur la réalité bien pleine
> Hélas que tout est loin.[19]

—which is surely a statement of despair at the evasiveness of things. In the last analysis, Reverdy was less confident than Breton would have liked him to be, though no less admirable for being honest about his anguish. Reverdy is ultimately neither symbolist mystic nor rugged materialist, but one who felt called to maintain an obscure but consistent position, 'une position difficile et souvent périlleuse, à l'intersection de deux plans au tranchant cruellement acéré, celui du rêve et celui de la réalité'[20]—that is, on the sharp border-line between subjective and concrete fact, a border-line that is alternately hazy and clear, and which determines switches in mood between a kind of paralysing horror and ecstasy.

The vacillations are brought out in the contrast between fogginess and brightness in Reverdy, a man as it were lost in the fog, yet occasionally reassured by visions of clear light. At dark moments, the 'rêveur parmi les murailles' ventures beyond the solidity of his walls into a dim landscape where things evaporate:

> Les maisons disparaissent
> Les arbes s'évaporent
> Derrière le remblai le claquement des mains
> On entend tous les bruits mais les yeux sont éteints.[21]

A few sounds are of little comfort when one stumbles through these dank zones of experience. Elsewhere, words like *peut-être* and *à peu près* betray the poet's misgivings, even in poems that otherwise seem 'well lit'.[22] This fog-bound hesitancy is a keynote of Reverdy's, and many signs in his inventory are attuned to it: shadows, clouds, smoke, misted outlines that suggest presences of uncertain import. But what of the bright moments? These often reverse the effect of blurriness. Light floods in, something shines with peculiar distinctness in the gloom:

> Une cigarette qui scintille
> Dans la nuit,

or else a precise outline delineates a positive presence:

> Les voyageurs se promènent en noir
> Sur la jetée
> Sous le reflet luisant qui entoure leur tête.[23]

—the background whiteness creates a halo. Sometimes the silhouette, clear-cut, stands out against the fog itself, and will under these privileged conditions reveal its inner meaning or reality:

> Cette figure précise plus fine et plus réelle qui se détache en clair
> Sur le brouillard.[24]

Clear lines seen under abnormally bright conditions are a phenomenon to which Reverdy responds with marked fervour. One passage in *Le Livre de mon bord* strikes a peculiarly ecstatic note, as though it bore a meaning far in excess of its straightforward statement of pleasure in the transformation of a familiar view by frost:

Hier, je me suis enfermé, à la nuit, par un temps doux malgré le vent violent qui avait, toute la journée, brossé les landes. Et ce matin, j'ouvre sur un calme parfait—toute l'étendue poudrée de gelée blanche. Magnifique spectacle, sans nuances, qui m'émerveille et m'enchante et dont je ne me lasse jamais. Comme la gelée est très forte, le décor est d'une remarquable dureté, déjà tout scintillant, bien que le soleil ne soit pas encore levé et qu'un léger brouillard moutonne au ras du sol. Féerie poignante de l'hiver. Éclatante marge de glace qui précise la solitude, la dureté de vivre et resserre la zone de vie humaine et de chaleur.[25]

Out of the night and the lingering mist, the landscape stretches up like a white page. All lines and edges seem to glitter, hard and sharp. The scene is rendered in a simple, forceful way, without hesitation or nuance. The landscape embodies the absolute text, a perfect white page imprinted with a few simple, majestically hard signs that spell out the harsh truth: loneliness, suffering, a minimum of human comfort. For once the signs held out by reality are utterly legible, and although they are sharp with the sense of solitude, though they bear little warmth or hope, a genuine exhilaration seems to derive from the reading of their message. It is salutary because it is clear-cut: for once harshness is acceptable, since haziness and doubt are banished. The signs are unequivocally real.

It now becomes evident that clarity and precision have in fact been Reverdy's principal virtues all along. In many of his most revealing moments, his is a tautness of line, a sharpness of edge that makes the tentative illumination come across with a strangely incisive authority. It is, I feel, his greatest poetic achievement to transmit states of extreme mistiness and mystery through signs that are dry, bare and incontrovertible. He can conjure up a land of hazy gloom, yet he will give it the clarity of an etching, drawing out with eerie sharpness what he calls the 'arêtes dures et précises du réel'.[26] The emotional landscape is subjected to quasi-cubist rules of terse understatement, yet it reverberates with a secret life.

> Sur le mur découvert
> Les volets refermés
> Les ornières du sol se joignent
> Le pont plus près
> Les carrés tout autour
> Les formes
> Les objets
> On franchit l'émotion qui barre le chemin.[27]

All the same, there remains something frightening about Reverdy's refusal to indicate dimensions and colours. His settings usually seem untrustworthy, full of malaise. Hidden meanings lie in wait to confront us: perhaps our reaction will be terror. There are indications that Reverdy himself well knew what panic was like. In a letter written in 1951, he confessed 'En tout cas, la terreur du monde réel n'a jamais cessé de peser dans ma destinée. Je crois qu'on n'a jamais vu, dans mes poèmes, que la terre n'a jamais été solide sous mes pieds —elle chavire, je la sens chavirer, sombrer, s'effondrer en moi-même.'[28] This undertone of mute desperation, this shifting of the ground underfoot, can be felt as a distinctive pulse in his work. Premonition, and unspoken menace. The photographer and sculptor Brassaï records that he expected the 'arêtes dures et précises' of Reverdy's poetry to produce an atmosphere of airy wonder; instead the effect was one of suffocation and oppression. The poet's world, says Brassaï, became 'un monde plein de menaces indéfinissables, de barrières infranchissables, de trappes invisibles. . . .'[29] This evocation of a gloomy Gothic labyrinth is close to the truth. We are almost into Kafka country.

> On entend venir quelqu'un qui ne se montre pas
> On entend parler
> On entend rire et on entend pleurer
> Une ombre passe
>
> Les mots qu'on dit derrière le volet sont une menace.[30]

These lines might read like a scenario for a gangster movie, all in menacing silhouettes and horrifying shadow play against frosted glass. Or perhaps one might prefer to think of the metaphysical paintings of Giorgio de Chirico, with their unexplained items of décor, their painted shadows, their exact arcades and staring windows, their mysterious plume of smoke on the horizon-line. On reflection, the coincidence of mood appears almost complete, the quality of 'metaphysical' enigma almost exactly similar.[31]

If my reading of the signs is correct, Reverdy's poetic world is one of solitude and objective menace. This is to draw well away from the view that he achieved peaceful, balanced word-pictures, the counterparts of cubist *natures mortes*—Reverdy's nature is very much alive. 'Les murs sont au courant.' 'Et la montagne siffle.'[32] His world bristles with signs of a disquieting complicity. The poet's decoding of these signs alerts him to his precarious position: he is a nervous spy in an alien land.

> On ne peut plus
> dormir tranquille
> quand on a une fois
> ouvert les yeux

he warns himself grimly.[33] And once the urgency of the poetic message is recognised, the reader cannot revert to the notion that he is being offered cosy formal patterns; instead he will attend to the dark shadow that falls across the street or the table-cloth.

Having once begun his surveillance of the signs of this reality, Reverdy felt obliged to keep on marking them out. His unfailing vigilance propelled a constant output of poems in basically the same key. No artifice or subjective mystery-mongering could have kept this going: the enigma must have been external and a very real solicitation. The reality of signs demanded the poet's unflinching attention, just in case, by some lucky chance, he might spot the miraculous light shining across the wintry fog. The tension of desperate expectancy is almost unbearable in the finest poems, where the interrogation of the slenderest clues is carried out under conditions of near collapse. In 'La Langue sèche' (the last poem of *Cravates de chanvre*, 1922), the protagonist could be a lover, or possibly a soldier left to defend an evacuated town, or simply the poet. His strained expectancy is sorely tried by the restriction on signs of life; there is only the cruel motion of an ill-adjusted clock, the inhuman flow of the river, and the tantalising echo of a train that will not stop. The waiting goes on indefinitely, in the hope that a positive sign will eventually appear in clear outline against the bleached whiteness of the De Chirico square.

> Pas de goutte de pluie
> Pas une feuille d'arbre
> Ni l'ombre d'un habit
> J'attends
> la gare est loin
> Pourtant le fleuve coule des quais en remontant
> la terre se dessèche
> tout est nu tout est blanc
> Avec le seul mouvement déréglé de l'horloge
> le bruit du train passé
> J'attends.[34]

Marked by tensions and failed connexions, such poetry articulates a tight-lipped defiance of meaninglessness. In Reverdy's world, blank signs never cease to strain towards significance.

Kent   ROGER CARDINAL

NOTES

1 'Essai d'esthétique littéraire', *Nord-Sud*, No. 4/5 (1917); quoted in Robert W. Greene: *The Poetic Theory of Pierre Reverdy*, University of California Press, 1967, a book which deals thoroughly with the poet's theoretical pronouncements.

2 See Julia Husson: 'Pierre Reverdy and the *poème-objet*', *Australian Journal of French Studies* vol. V, No. 1 (1968), pp. 30–1. In the article referred to in note 15, David Grossvogel speaks of the 'disjunctive terminal chord' at the end of a Reverdy poem, a contrapuntal rejoinder to what has gone before.

3 *Plupart du temps*, Flammarion, 1967, p. 206.

4 Gaëtan Picon refers to the 'vibration secrète' of even the most static poems of Reverdy (*L'Usage de la lecture*, I, Mercure de France, 1960, p. 250).

5 *Main d'œuvre*, Mercure de France, 1949, p. 367.

6 *Plupart du temps*, p. 197.

7 *Le Gant de crin* (1927), Flammarion, 1968, pp. 43 and 52.

8 *Plupart du temps*, p. 146.

9 ibid., p. 214.

10 *Le Livre de mon bord*, Mercure de France, 1948, p. 152, and *Le Gant de crin*, p. 15.

11 *Le Livre de mon bord*, p. 153.

12 *Main d'œuvre*, p. 231.

13 *Plupart du temps*, p. 386.

14 cf. *Main d'œuvre*, p. 90.

15 cf. David I. Grossvogel: 'Pierre Reverdy: the fabric of reality', *Yale French Studies*, No. 21 (1958), p. 99, and Anna Balakian, *Surrealism: the Road to the Absolute*, Noonday Press, 1959.

16 *En vrac*, Edns du Rocher, Monaco, 1956, p. 139. Both Mortimer Guiney (*La Poésie de Pierre Reverdy*, Geneva 1966, p. 22) and Gabriel Bounoure (in *Hommage à Pierre Reverdy*, Rodez n.d. (1961), p. 46) insist on the long-term relevance of Reverdy's *néoplatonisme*.

17 cf. Jean-Pierre Richard's argument for Reverdy's 'fidélité terrestre' in *Onze études sur la poésie moderne*, Edns du Seuil 1964, pp. 19–20.

18 In his notes on poetry, Reverdy often draws analogies from boxing, as in the title of his text *Self-Defence* (1919).

19 The lines are from *Plupart du temps*, p. 279. Breton quotes from memory in *L'Amour fou*, Gallimard, 1966, p. 74.

20 *Le Gant de crin*, p. 18.

21 *Plupart du temps*, p. 360.

22 Peter Brunner stresses the doubt and uncertainty integral to Reverdy's manner (*Pierre Reverdy: de la solitude au mystère*, Juris Verlag, Zurich, 1966, pp. 84–5).

23 *Plupart du temps*, pp. 73 and 361.

24 ibid., p. 303.

25 *Le Livre de mon bord*, pp. 13–14.

26 ibid., p. 103. Here I am asking for a reading exactly contrary to that argued for by J.-P. Richard, who holds that Reverdy detests sharp edges, and prefers dreamy penumbrae and Verlainean vagueness (op. cit. p. 27).

27 *Plupart du temps*, p. 343.
28 Letter to Jean Rousselot, 16 May 1951, in *Hommage à Pierre Reverdy*, p. 16.
29 Brassaï, 'Reverdy dans son labyrinthe', *Mercure de France*, Jan.–April 1962, p. 161.
30 *Plupart du temps*, p. 88.
31 While Marcel Raymond writes of Reverdy's poetry that 'tout fait pressentir la menace imminente d'un événement métaphysique' (*De Baudelaire au surréalisme*, Corrêa, 1934, p. 319), Michel Manoll draws the explicit analogy with De Chirico (*Pierre Reverdy*, Seghers, 1951, p. 66). To my knowledge, Reverdy and De Chirico were not acquainted, though they could have met, the latter being in Paris during 1911–15 and 1925–*c.* 1930. Both Apollinaire and the surrealists were potential intermediaries.
32 *Plupart du temps*, pp. 355 and 360.
33 ibid., p. 126.
34 ibid., p. 393.

ARAGON: TRADITION AND INVENTION

In 1942 André Breton, surveying the development of Surrealism between the wars, affirmed that the first concern of the Surrealists had always been 'la quête passionnée de la liberté'; he criticised those who had betrayed this ideal, either by adherence to a party, 'ce parti fût-il à vos yeux celui de la liberté', or by a return to traditional forms in poetry.[1] The combined criticism strikes hardest at Breton's friend and former colleague Aragon, although Breton refers only to 'certains des anciens surréalistes'.[2] Breton pursued his 'quête passionnée' with the single-minded faith that quests require, never doubting the existence or the nature of liberty. For Aragon, however, liberty was always a problem.

The immense upheaval of the War of 1914–18 led to a general re-examination of established values; in the field of literature this concerned not only ideas but also traditional forms, which had proved inadequate to express the experience of the War. The Dadaists, seeing the world as diseased and literature and art as merely symptoms of the sickness, were ready to risk the death of art; others felt that if poetry was to survive, it would at least have to find a new voice. The *enquête* conducted by *Sic* in 1916 confirms the prevalence of this feeling; but there was uncertainty about how the new voice was to be achieved. The most obvious course of action was to reject, along with past attitudes, those forms which were associated with them. Thus Pierre Albert-Birot, the editor of *Sic*, begins by denying the importance of technique: 'La technique en Art me fait un peu l'effet de la raison dans l'amour' (January 1916). This statement implicitly rejects rational thinking; and indeed Albert-Birot adds that 'L'Art a des raisons que la raison ne connaît pas' (February 1916), and describes syntax as a strait-jacket (June 1916). Exclaiming 'SOYONS MODERNES' (February 1916) and 'Le "Style" au Musée' (March 1916), he ingeniously stands respect for tradition on its head: 'la tradition française C'EST NIER LA TRADITION. Suivons la tradition' (April 1916). This assurance did not last. The final issue of *Sic* (June 1919) rather sadly remarks that nowadays 'tout le monde fait partie de l'avant-garde'. The precariousness of the avant-garde position is well known; and a voluntary abdication of total freedom is foreshadowed in Gabriel Boissy's letter from the Front (April 1916): 'Le sens de la limite et du relatif, père des arts, nous revient . . .'. It is against this background that Aragon, in a review of Reverdy's *Les Ardoises du toit* (*Sic*, May 1918), praises not only Reverdy's effort towards 'une discipline personnelle' but also his technical skill, his 'science d'orchestration'.

The first number of Reverdy's own journal, *Nord-Sud* (March 1917), commended Apollinaire's pioneering of 'des routes neuves'; but in the same issue Paul Dermée insisted that Symbolism being dead, what was needed was 'une période d'organisation . . . un âge classique'. Dermée does not define classicism by outward forms: 'il y a classicisme dès que l'auteur domine son objet . . .'. Complete freedom is useless, but so is external constraint: 'La contrainte doit être intérieure'—in Aragon's words, 'une discipline personnelle'. In 'Les Mots en liberté' (*Nord-Sud*, November 1917), Max Jacob pointed out that the writer's freedom vis-à-vis the reader could only be maintained by a constant control, that the Romantics attain greatness only when they are 'classical' in their methods. Finally, Dermée denied that poetry could be a 'sténographie d'associations inconscientes', which he calls 'le type le plus pur du Romantisme' ('Un prochain âge classique', January 1918). The *Nord-Sud* group were by no means unadventurous. Certain freedoms had been won by Apollinaire which they meant to preserve: typographical arrangement as a substitute for traditional syntax,[3] the absence of punctuation. But typically, Reverdy says of this last device that it is not a freedom at all, but constitutes 'un ordre supérieur', only possible in 'des œuvres simples et d'une grande pureté' (October 1917); he echoes Dermée, who in March 1917 had stated: 'Notre esthétique . . . est faite de concentration, de composition, de pureté'.

As early as 1908, the English and American Imagists declared that poetry should 'render particulars exactly' and be 'hard and clear', and that 'concentration is of the very essence of poetry'.[4] Beyond this superficial Parnassianism, they were also concerned to establish that poetry was not definable by metrical standards. The poet was 'to compose in sequence of the musical phrase, not in sequence of a metronome'.[5] In the retrospective *Imagist Anthology 1930*, Ford Madox Ford states that 'all creative prose like all imaginative verse is Poetry'. There is nothing new in this (Shelley, in *A Defence of Poetry*, likewise defines poetry as 'the expression of the imagination' and states that 'the popular division into prose and verse is inadmissible in accurate philosophy'); but such a conception was particularly useful at this period. By rejecting traditional distinctions between prose and verse, both the Imagists and their French contemporaries were able (indeed, they were obliged) to propose a definition of poetry which centred on the artist's activity.

For the *Nord-Sud* group, such activity included both reason and imagination. André Breton, however, found in Freud's studies of the unconscious a theoretical basis for that rejection of rational structure which Albert-Birot had been unable to defend. The voice of the unconscious, he claims, is truer than the voice of reason: 'Automatisme psychique pur par lequel on se propose d'exprimer . . . le fonctionnement réel de la pensée'.[6] In practice, the effect of this dislocation of rational structure is to blur the pattern of the whole poem and magnify the individual word. A similar shift resulted from Reverdy's definition of the mode of action of the image (*Nord-Sud*, March 1918): 'L'Image . . . ne peut naître d'une comparaison mais du rapprochement de deux réalités plus ou moins éloignées. Plus les rapports des deux réalités rapprochées seront lointains et justes, plus l'image sera forte . . .'. The Surrealists, unlike Reverdy, tended to emphasise the distance between the terms of the image, so that their poems were often mere descriptive catalogues of nouns. As Humpty Dumpty remarked to Alice: 'They've a temper, some of them—particularly verbs, they're the proudest—adjectives you can do anything with, but not verbs. . . .' That is, the poet can easily modify things, but not the *relations between* things, which verbs define and express. 'Modernist' poetry often avoids this problem by concentrating on things, allowing the reader to invent the relations between them; the poet builds up a mosaic of nouns by what Ezra Pound called 'a kind of super-position', and deliberately avoids establishing meaningful relations. Early examples of this kind of avoidance of logical structure can be seen in Rimbaud, in Lautréamont, and in Apollinaire's *poèmes-conversations*, the acknowledged models of the Surrealists. A poem such as 'Les Sentiments sont gratuits', the combined work of Breton and Soupault,[7] contains nothing but nouns, some qualified, some not:

> Trace odeur de soufre
> Marais des salubrités publiques
> Rouge des lèvres criminelles
> Marche des deux temps saumure
> Caprice des singes
> Horloge couleur du jour

There is no doubt that the reader is liberated: he is as free as if he had been set down in the middle of the Sahara.

In view of Aragon's links with *Sic* and *Nord-Sud*, one is not surprised to find that his own early verse does not show such fragmentation (indeed, even his attempts at automatic writing are structured and emotionally coherent).[8] In *Feu de joie* (1920), the syntax establishes clear relations in time and space, and the poems often make their effect by reference to traditional forms: thus in 'Soifs de l'Ouest', the echo of a folk-song underlines the melancholy of an urban landscape:

> Dans ce bar dont la porte
> Sans cesse bat au vent
> une affiche écarlate
> vante un autre savon
> Dansez dansez ma chère
> nous avons des banjos

The poems are further structured by Aragon's use of alliteration and assonance, end-rhyme and internal rhyme. One of the most haunting, 'Casino des lumières crues', is a four-line rhymed stanza in alexandrines:

> Un soir des plages à la mode on joue un air
> Qui fait prendre aux petits chevaux un train d'enfer
> Et la fille se pâme et murmure Weber
> Moi je prononce Wèbre et regarde la mer

The sense of *dépaysement* is increased by the familiarity of the form, and by what seems to be an allusion to Nerval's 'Fantaisie'.[9]

Aragon's speciality is a kind of internal *rime-calembour*, a device which he has never abandoned. The echoes have sometimes a largely musical value, but they often produce a comic juxtaposition which has the opposite effect to Reverdy's 'rapprochement de deux réalités . . . éloignées'; instead of charging the words with mysterious significances, it makes them parody and deflate each other, as in 'Parti-pris':

> Je danse au *mi*lieu des *mi*racles
> *Mille* soleils peints sur le sol
> *Mille* a*mis Mille* yeux ou monocles
> *m'illumi*nent de leurs regards

This kind of dislocation requires a sense of location: in *Feu de joie* we find not an absence of logical structure but a parody of structure, as well as an acute verbal intelligence which revitalises both meaning and form.

It would appear so far that by choosing to renew the familiar

instead of destroying it, Aragon has taken in his stride the reconciliation of liberty and tradition. However, in *Le Libertinage* (1924),
Aragon's preface seems ready to equate liberty with anarchy. He
affirms his belief in a love which is destructive of social and intellectual norms and of order, being entirely non-rational: 'Le plus complet abandon règne dans l'amour . . . la meilleure machine à abêtir . . .
une sorte de disqualification de l'esprit' (pp. 11–13). The central
theme of his book is 'le scandale': 'Dans tous les pays du monde
l'enfantillage est maître et l'on nomme *scandale* l'infraction publique
aux lois qu'il a forgées' (p. 17). Aragon hastens to insist that *le
scandale* has no moral aims; it is a gratuitous explosion like anger or
love, *le scandale pour le scandale*. Moreover, 'tout au monde' (there
follows a long and scabrous list) 'n'a jamais été pour moi que
l'occasion du scandale', so that he has even played at defending,
'contre Dada', literature, poetry and art, 'ces saint-sulpiceries
délirantes' (pp. 18–19). His rejection of moral aims is evidently a
way of preserving his freedom; so is his refusal to be defined, even as
'écrivain' (p. 22). He ends by dissociating himself from 'l'intelligence,
ce bien commun, pauvreté de l'esprit' (p. 27), apparently uninhibited
by the fact that his rejection of intelligence, if not rational, is certainly
reasoned. Moreover, the shock tactics of *Le Libertinage* are based on a
controlled use of parody; the pieces in this volume are formal
variations on traditional themes and genres: *conte*, epistolary novel,
memoirs, and so on.

In case anyone should doubt that Aragon is turning his back on the
whole Cartesian universe, the preface to *Le Paysan de Paris* (1926)[10]
explicitly condemns 'la fameuse doctrine cartésienne de l'évidence',
along with 'la raison' and the 'fausse dualité de l'homme', preferring
'l'imagination des sens' to 'l'imagination de la raison'. In fine,
Aragon rejects 'la certitude', choosing neither black nor white, but to
live 'dans la zone où se heurtent le blanc et le noir' (*Paysan*, p. 15).
That is, he chooses a state of pure freedom, a perpetual becoming.
There is an essential paradox both here and in *Le Libertinage*: for *le
scandale* depends for its effect on the *enfantillage* which it opposes,
just as our apprehension of *le merveilleux quotidien* which *Le Paysan
de Paris* creates is only possible against the background of *le quotidien*
itself. Aragon was quite aware of this paradox. In a note on *Les
Aventures de Télémaque* (1923), he comments on 'l'impossibilité du
blasphème chez celui qui ne croit pas en Dieu'.[11] In the same way,
only a lingering attachment to the bourgeois world gives meaning to
le scandale.

Freedom in *Le Paysan de Paris* is clearly not anarchy, but a continuous dialectical play of opposites—and the volume of poems which Aragon published in this same year is called *Le Mouvement perpétuel*. Perpetual motion is an excellent way of avoiding the threat to individual freedom which comes from definition: for what is defined is, by definition, limited. But the distance which perpetual motion maintains between subject and object can lead to a perilous sense of alienation ('Sommeil de plomb'):

> A la voir on ne croirait pas la ville en carton ni le soir
> Faux comme les prunelles des femmes et des amis les meilleurs
> Quel danger je cours Immobile contre le parapet de l'univers

There are moments of hesitant tenderness in this volume: 'Or il fut sur le point/Or il se mit/il chantait' ('Bouée'); but the poet is afraid of committing himself. He chooses liberty, even at the cost of alienation ('Les débuts du fugitif'): 'Je m'échappe indéfiniment sous le chapeau de l'infini/Qu'on ne m'attende jamais à mes rendez-vous illusoires'. The dissolution which seems to threaten the poet is nowhere reflected in the form of these poems. This volume uses *vers libres* and even *prose poétique*, but the poet's control of his material is everywhere apparent, in the carefully orchestrated rhythms, and especially in rhyme and assonance. Compared with *Feu de joie*, however, *Le Mouvement perpétuel* seems less relaxed, more self-conscious in its manipulation of language. There are parodies which rely explicitly on literary models: 'Pastorale', 'Le Dernier des Madrigaux', 'Villanelle'; and a comic use of alexandrines and not-quite-alexandrines in 'La Force'. There is a negative demonstration of the necessity of syntax, as well as a comment on meaning, in 'Persiennes', where the single noun 'persienne' is repeated until it becomes 'Persienne?'. In 'Suicide', the letters of the alphabet are arranged in neat rows, with a final line in which 'X Y Z' are spaced more widely than the letters in the preceding lines, to form a 'dying fall': it is a whole life story *sans paroles*, and a perfect example of what Reverdy meant by the syntax of typography. One might say that this poem and 'Persiennes' are extreme statements of the 'magical' use of form, in which the poet is shown to be lord of language; and Aragon clearly sees formal control as a further guarantee of his freedom. Télémaque's thoughts on language provide a commentary on 'Persiennes': 'Le langage quoiqu'il en paraisse se réduit au seul Je et si je répète un mot quelconque, celui-ci se dépouille de tout ce qui n'est pas moi jusqu'à devenir un bruit organique par lequel ma vie se manifeste . . .'[12] Perpetual motion does not of itself prove that the poet is free; he must, as Jacob remarked, control his movements. When Télémaque defines himself as 'un homme: libre mouvement lâché sur la terre, pouvoir d'aller et venir', Mentor replies: 'On jurerait entendre une boule de billard' (*Télémaque*, p. 98). Paradoxically, if the poet is to show that he need submit to no order but the one which he can create for himself, he is *obliged* to create his own order.

The tension between the desire for liberty and the need for order is patent in Aragon's *Traité du style* (1928). The emphasis in this work is again on the artist's control of his activity. An example of Aragon's position is his attitude to 'l'écriture automatique'. With his usual logic, he maintains that it is not possible, or if possible not genuine: no amount of conscious abdication of reason will take the poet beyond his waking vocabulary, which is full of other men's poetry, to a genuinely 'unconscious' language.[13] Aragon points out that we record our dreams by translating them into words, and 'ce récit, que ma mémoire rêve éveillée, est une simple traduction dans le langage de la veille, de faits peut-être entièrement différents' (pp. 185–6); one can even, he notes, detect a changing fashion in written accounts of dreams. It is not merely perverse wit which makes him declare 'J'exige que les rêves qu'on me fait lire soient écrits en bon français' (p. 183), for the absence of a coherent style will lead to a betrayal of the objective reality even of dreams. Thus Aragon's definition of Surrealism includes a marked degree of conscious intervention: 'Le surréalisme est l'inspiration reconnue, acceptée, et pratiquée. Non plus comme une visitation inexplicable, mais comme une faculté qui s'exerce . . .' (p. 187). True *surréalité* is not reached by passive automatism, but by the artist's active ordering of experience; only thus can he reveal 'cette ligne réelle qui relie toutes les images virtuelles qui nous entourent' (*La Peinture au défi*, 1930, p. 10)—a concept nearer to Reverdy's 'rapprochement' than to Breton's choice of 'le degré d'arbitraire le plus élevé'.[14]

Style is the outward sign of the writer's uniqueness. Without style, says Aragon, one can only produce 'de la littérature': 'La littérature, aux divers sens du mot, se nomme recette. Le style, qu'ici je défends, est ce qui ne peut se réduire en recettes' (*Traité*, p. 193). Aragon recognises that any method, surrealist or otherwise, can be imitated: 'Tout le monde croyait jadis écrire en vers, c'est facile mon bonnet rime avec petit déjeuner, et maintenant tout le monde, après avoir dit un poème dada, rien de plus simple, tenez seau à charbon bonbons confiture, s'écrie le surréalisme j'en suis . . .' (p. 194). (It will be noted that his *poème dada* consists of three nouns). Aragon refuses what belongs to 'tout le monde'. That is why he rejected 'l'intelligence, ce bien commun', preferring his unique 'sottise': 'Il n'y a que ma sottise qui m'appartienne, et j'y tiens' (*Le Libertinage*, p. 27).

The 'langage de la veille' is composed, of course, of words which are common property. The function of style is to enable the poet to make them his own. Aragon ingeniously turns the theory of the unconscious to his own account: the substrate of past literatures in the poet's (and the reader's) mind provides the counters with which the poet plays with his reader, the elements of a language consisting not merely of colourless words, but of highly charged images and associated emotions. In *La Peinture au défi*, Aragon likens the 'ready-made' materials used in *collage*, or the *objets trouvés* of Marcel Duchamp, to 'les expressions toutes faites', which become an 'élément lyrique' in poetry. In *Sic*, style was finally equated with the achievement of order by a willed intervention of the artist—a process which Albert-Birot more succinctly describes (May 1916) as '(Style =ordre)=volonté'; in *Traité du style*, Aragon defines style as the order which the writer imposes on language, as *collage* imposes a new coherence on materials torn from their original contexts, or Duchamp, by merely choosing an object and changing its spatial context, gives it a meaning of his own and makes it his. The poet thus recharges with active life those 'mots d'ordre' with which we normally do our thinking (*Traité*, pp. 67, 71). There is, of course, an element of revolt in this activity: 'le merveilleux est toujours la matérialisation d'un symbole morale en opposition violente avec la morale du monde au milieu duquel il surgit' (*La Peinture au défi*, p. 6); but again, the revolt depends for its existence on the second term of this dialectic, 'la morale'.

In *Traité du style* Aragon returns to the problem of freedom and disposes, with inexorable logic, of some currently accepted false notions of liberty. First, 'l'aventure Dada': we have freed ourselves from the 'idées reçues' of our fathers, Aragon says, only to fall under the domination of 'des images reçues' (p. 48). Second, 'l'aventure rimbaldienne' (p. 58): Rimbaud the hero of disaffected bourgeois adolescents has become an argument against poetry; some of these pseudo-Rimbauds think it enough to travel.[15] The third false freedom is simply 'l'aventure', to be found in 'n'importe quelle rencontre'; Aragon dismisses its adepts as 'une race d'optimistes à tous crins' (p. 82). In his fourth category, 'le départ, l'aventure, le voyage, se sont déconcrétisés . . . C'est l'évasion . . . la forme contemporaine du vague à l'âme'; 'l'évasion' is an excuse for inaction, an abdication of responsibility; if it were actually possible, no one would dream of it. Aragon points out that the nearest the reader is likely to get to a

QHF

perfect *évasion* is a spell in prison (p. 84). In *Anicet* (1921) he had shown his hero, in a Stendhalian mode, enjoying the experience of imprisonment: 'D'un seul coup, les soucis s'étaient évanouis: la tête libre, sinon le corps . . .' (p. 169).

There is only one logical conclusion: 'Il n'y a de paradis d'aucune espèce' (*Traité*, p. 85). Aragon glances at the idea of suicide, the ultimate freedom; but if there is no reason for living there is equally none for dying. Moreover, even suicide is not a demonstration of freedom; when Télémaque throws himself from the cliff-top to prove that he is not determined but free, Mentor comments: 'Télémaque, fils d'Ulysse, est mort dérisoirement pour se montrer libre et sa mort déterminée par les sarcasmes et la pesanteur est la négative de ce hasard même qu'il voulut consacrer au prix de sa vie' (p. 100). Aragon proceeds to review all the *paradis artificiels* which we imagine will bring us release. Religion, happiness, drugs, are all evasions; we must face with dignity the fact that there is no escape: 'Ce n'est pas une raison parce qu'il fait sombre pour manquer si élémentairement de tenue' (*Traité*, p. 114). It is a sombre conclusion indeed, but not a melancholy one. Freedom, as Aragon pointed out in 1925, is the condition of personal morality,[16] and conversely, the individual who accepts full moral responsibility for himself achieves the only possible freedom.

The first corollary of responsibility for oneself is isolation. The alienation which we have seen in *Le Mouvement perpétuel* is even more clearly evident in *La Grande Gaîté* (1929). The 'gaiety' of its title is the fierce joy of destruction, and the volume contains a number of violently provocative poems. The violence is again chiefly directed at bourgeois standards, and at all forms of authority, including the rules of prosody; it polarises around two main themes: the family (sometimes symbolised by 'la nourrice'),[17] and sex. In the family group the poet is the child, protesting at the repressive régime that keeps him clean, tidy and well-behaved; in the sexual context he is deliberately and triumphantly unclean, untidy and aggressive. Reviewing this volume in 1929, Gabriel Bounoure remarked that Aragon's campaign of destruction was 'si visiblement conduit par l'intelligence et le sens satirique des choses de la cité, que le livre . . . garde un accent un peu bourgeois':[18] an astute observation, for as usual the protest indicates how passionately Aragon is still involved with his bourgeois origins. His fury is as near to tears as that of a rebellious child, and as self-destructive: in rejecting the bourgeois admiration for 'la maîtrise', he is even led to add 'De soi particulièrement' ('Ramo dei Morti'). When his sense of humour re-establishes itself (that sense of humour which is defined in *Traité du style* as the negative condition of poetry and of freedom),[19] he can detach himself from the monsters which fascinate him; but then he is soon regarding himself with the same dispassionate eye, and admitting that he is 'Terriblement triste' ('Voyages'). The difficulty is that adventure is not the only alternative to order: there is also chaos. Aragon's art in *La Grande Gaîté* is not so continuously controlled as in the earlier volumes. There is very little use of traditional forms and of rhyme; assonance and repetition strive to hold together lines which constantly threaten to become a rhythmical prose and which frequently tail off in deliberate banality, as in 'Maladroit':

> Je t'aime énormément
> Je fais ce que je peux pour le dire
> Avec l'élégance désirable
> Je n'ai jamais su le moins du monde
> Inspirer le désir
> Quand j'aurais voulu l'inspirer
> Un exhibitionnisme naïf en matière de sentiment
> Me caractérise au moral comme au physique
> Nom de Dieu tout ça n'est guère amusant
> Comme attraction c'est zéro

Here the echo *dire/désir* is muted by the *enjambement, désir* is mocked by *désirable*, and the rhyme *sentiment/amusant* is entirely abolished by the final line which fails to complete the quatrain.

The final pages of *Le Paysan de Paris* offer an uneasy statement of the poet's position in the face of those two abstractions, order and disorder; fragmentary propositions reflect the fragmented state of his universe, and end, like Télémaque's meditations on language, in solipsism (p.249): 'Toute métaphysique est à la première personne du singulier. Toute poésie aussi. La seconde personne, c'est encore la première'. The poet claims to be king of his solitude: 'Je ne m'égare pas, je me domine'. This logically implies the domination also of 'la seconde personne'. But translated in *La Grande Gaîté* into frenzied sensuality, it reduces his contacts with the world to compulsive gestures, himself to a 'cadavre ensorcelé' ('Réponse aux flaireurs de bidet'): he has lost both humanity and freedom. The same loss of identity occurs in *Les Plaisirs de la capitale* (1923). Night in Paris is a kind of hell where men and women pass in the darkness, touching each other with mounting intoxication: 'Chacun devenait dans ce chaos le lieu géométrique de quelques plaisirs partiels. . . . Le difficile semblait être de se retrouver soi-même'.[20] The consciousness of chaos, in which liberty is meaningless, brings the sexual adventure to an end.

Aragon's early aggressiveness is not only self-defence; it is a movement of despair which comes from his growing awareness that there
is no freedom which cannot become a form of slavery: 'Je ne suis
plus mon maître tellement j'éprouve ma liberté' (Paysan, pp. 11–12).
The final irony is that even the writer's control of his art may not be
real. In 1931 Aragon transformed Breton's notion of automatisme by
including the action of thought on the outside world: 'méthode de la
connaissance du mécanisme réel de la pensée, des rapports réels de
l'expression et de la pensée, et des rapports réels de la pensée expri-
mée et du monde sur lequel elle agit réellement'.[21] The young
Aragon was incapable of the submission which Breton's conception
implies. But he had too much intelligence not to be aware that the
writer's action cannot 'circonscrire l'infini'; it gives him only 'l'illusion d'une puissance infinie sur le monde' (Le Libertinage, pp. 20–2);
it is the same illusion that others seek in opium, and leads to the same
drug-dependence. The charlatan Imagination in Le Paysan de Paris
remarks that 'Le vice appelé Surréalisme est l'emploi déréglé et
passionnel du stupéfiant image, ou plutôt de la provocation sans
contrôle de l'image pour elle-même . . .' (p. 83): the control, that is,
has passed to the image; and ultimately writing of any kind takes
control of the writer: 'Par le signe magique de l'encre, je limite ma
pensée dans ses conséquences . . .' (Le Libertinage, p. 20). The
inescapable paradox is that whatever we try to control or absorb ends
by controlling or absorbing us, arrests our free flight and fixes us.

The solution, once again, lies in accepting limitation. In La
Défense de l'Infini (1926) Aragon creates a woman called Blanche,
whose distinctive quality is that 'elle ne se pliait pas à mon imagination'.[22] For the first time, he conceives of a woman who resists his
control, and discovers, without much surprise, that what his strength
has failed to give him can be achieved by his 'impuissance': 'J'ai
aimé . . . Jusque là tout encore était possible. Rien dans la vie
n'était décisif, puis je suis tombé sur le destin. J'ai aimé'. Aragon is
not the first to discover that freedom lies in the willing acceptance of
destiny. His 'conversion' seems all the more genuine in that it was not
effected smoothly or without pain. In Le Mouvement perpétuel he had
written: 'La main prise dans la porte/Trop engagé mon ami trop
engagé' ('Serrure de sûreté'). In Persécuté persécuteur (1931)[23] he
describes himself as 'Les deux mains/prises dans deux portes/l'amour
la mort' ('Lycanthropie contemporaine'). Death has become a reality
precisely because he has learned to love. In La Défense de l'Infini he
notes: 'Il me semble que j'apprends désormais à mourir. . . . Ainsi le
temps prend sa ravageuse origine dans l'essence même des passions.

Dans le silence, il se forme une idée extravagante et terrible. Alors vous commencez à vieillir'. What Gabriel Boissy called 'Le sens de la limite et du relatif, père des arts', finally helped the arch-evader to become willingly *engagé*.

But despite his long emotional attachment to the idea of infinite freedom, Aragon never tried to 'circonscrire l'infini' in his writings. He directed his finite means to finite ends, and 'la liberté' never presented itself to him as a *technical* problem. He has operated comfortably within traditional forms, innovating, as Shelley says every great poet must, 'upon the example of his predecessors'. His critical work has constantly stressed the need for tradition and order in poetry; but like Reverdy he sees tradition as a base-camp for exploration, and he borrows Apollinaire's words to describe his aim: 'l'alliance . . . de la tradition et de l'invention'.[24] Only in ordered activity can the poet find real freedom: 'La liberté dont le nom fut usurpé par le vers libre reprend aujourd'hui ses droits, non dans le laisser-aller, mais dans le travail de l'invention'.[25]

London   NORMA RINSLER

NOTES

1 André Breton, *La Clé des champs*, Paris, 1953, p. 68.
2 Other passages are strongly critical of Aragon, e.g. *La Clé des champs*, p. 280.
3 Cf. Reverdy, 'Syntaxe', *Nord-Sud*, April 1918: 'La syntaxe est . . . une disposition de mots—et une disposition typographique est légitime'.
4 *Some Imagist Poets* (London, Boston and New York), 1915, Preface, p. vii. This unsigned preface is generally considered to be the work of Amy Lowell.
5 F. S. Flint, 'Imagisme', *Poetry* (Chicago), I, 6, March 1913, p. 199. Flint does not name the 'imagiste' he quotes, but Pound used this term in preference to 'imagist', and his own 'A Few Don'ts by an Imagiste' follows Flint's article, and refers back to it. In 'A Stray Document' (*Make it New*, London, 1934) Pound states that the 'three principles' were decided upon by himself, 'H.D.', and Richard Aldington.
6 A. Breton, *Manifeste du surréalisme* (1924); in *Manifestes du surréalisme*, Paris, 1962, p. 40.
7 In *Les Champs magnétiques*, Paris, 1967, p. 109 (first pub. 1920).
8 In *Le Mouvement perpétuel précédé de Feu de joie*, Collection Poésie, Paris, 1970, pp. 141–52. References to *Feu de joie* and to *Le Mouvement perpétuel* are to this edition. All other references to works by Aragon are, except where otherwise stated, to the original editions published in Paris; dates of original publication are given in the text.
9 'Il est un air pour qui je donnerais/Tout Rossini, tout Mozart et tout Weber,/Un air très vieux, languissant et funèbre . . .'; Nerval's own note

reads 'On prononce *Wèbre*' (see e.g. *Œuvres choisies de Gérard de Nerval*, ed. Gauthier-Ferrières, Paris, 1913, p. 218).

10 I have used the recent edition of *Le Paysan de Paris* in the Livre de Poche series (1966), which shows some variants and appears to be an improved text.

11 These Notes were written, according to Aragon, in 1922. They are reproduced in the recent edition of *Les Aventures de Télémaque* (1966), to which I have referred throughout. The note on blasphemy is discussed on p. 129 of this edition, in a footnote dated 1966.

12 *Les Aventures de Télémaque*, p. 29. This passage was first published as one of the '23 Manifestes du Mouvement Dada', *Littérature*, No. 13, May 1920.

13 This argument is developed by Jean Cazaux in *Surréalisme et psychologie*, Paris, 1938, especially with regard to the 'langage intérieur' (p. 9). Leslie Fiedler (*Waiting for the End*, London, 1965, pp. 226–7) discusses American resistance to surrealism: the likeliest candidates were 'too involved with *culture* . . . their madhouses are inhabited by the ghosts of books . . .'.

14 Breton, *Manifestes*, p. 53.

15 Aragon returns to this question in *Chroniques du Bel Canto* (Genève, 1947): 'Il est triste qu'on ait à le dire, mais si Rimbaud est peut-être le plus grand poète des temps modernes, c'est pour avoir écrit des poèmes, il faut s'en persuader' (p. 189).

16 'Sciences morales: *Libre à vous!*', *La Révolution surréaliste*, No. 2, January 1925, p. 23.

17 Cf. the first paragraph of *Le Libertinage* (p. 7): 'J'ai laissé parler ma nourrice pendant vingt-cinq années. C'est au bout de cette patience perpétuée que je vais enfin lui montrer de quoi je me sens capable'.

18 G. Bounoure, review of Aragon, *La Grande Gaieté* [*sic*], *NRF*, No. 210, March 1931, pp. 455–6.

19 Cf. *Traité*: 'Pour qu'il y ait poésie il faut que l'humour fasse d'abord abstraction de l'anti-poésie' (p. 138); 'la brioche de nos contemporains, leur nourriture de mots d'ordre, s'effrite menu sous les doigts de l'humour' (p. 140).

20 *Les Plaisirs de la capitale*, Berlin, n.d. (1923), pp. 14–15. Reprinted with the title of *Paris la nuit* in *Le Libertinage* (pp. 187–205).

21 'Le Surréalisme et le Devenir révolutionnaire', *Le Surréalisme au service de la Révolution*, No. 3, December 1931, p. 4.

22 'Le Cahier Noir: extrait d'un roman à paraître: *La Défense de l'Infini*', *La Revue Européenne*, No. 36, February 1926, pp. 1–17; No. 37, March 1926, pp. 28–38. Aragon destroyed the MS. of this novel in 1928, shortly before he met Elsa Triolet.

23 This volume is generally noted for the violent revolutionary prophecies of 'Prélude au temps des cerises' and 'Front rouge'. Most of these poems, however, are unhappily obsessed with love and death.

24 *Journal d'une poésie nationale*, Paris, 1954, p. 72.

25 *La Rime en 1940*, Post-face to *Le Crève-cœur*, 1946, p. 76. This edition was the first revised by the author; the London edition (1944) does not contain this essay, which was first published in *Poètes casqués 40*, 20 April 1940.

LOVE AND THE 'ACCESSOIRE POÉTIQUE' IN THE POETRY OF ROBERT DESNOS[1]

Those of us who survived German captivity have not forgotten the friends 'qui sont restés là-bas'; and the 'voix de Robert Desnos' reverberates in the memory of many who shared to a greater or lesser extent in his nightmare. Yet, quite apart from this bond and indeed from whatever historical role Desnos may have played in the Surrealist venture, his voice has its own timbre and utterance that distinguish it from his contemporaries—and especially in the expression of love sensed so often as the interval that separates dream and attainment. When he writes

Toi qui es à la base de mes rêves et qui secoues mon esprit plein de métamorphoses et qui me laisses ton gant quand je baise ta main (*CB*, 93)

Desnos offers us a point of entry into his poetic world; and elsewhere he explicitly asserts a correlation between his feelings and the countries of the mind in which he confers upon them a literary existence.

More often than not, Desnos' poetry expresses the frustrations of a love that is unable to coincide with its object. Like Chateaubriand, he experiences a generalised yearning seeking satisfaction in some real, individual vessel; but the *sylphide* either eludes him or does not exist. If and when it does, we read of lovers who meet only once, whose dream belongs to past or future, in whom *je* and *tu* cannot blend into a *nous* (*DD*, 130), who undergo 'rêves parallèles' (*F*, 44), and the theme of the might-have-been persists:

Marche nuptiale de nos reflets oubliés dans une glace quand la femme que nous devrions rencontrer et que nous ne rencontrerons jamais vient s'y mirer (*DD*, 153).

The mirror is associated with time that stands between possibility and realisation; but it also skirts the problems of illusion and identity, and reinforces the preoccupation with the dream which no less than reality holds the *innamorata* at a distance (*CB*, 93). Desnos' conception of love is woven into a fabric of absence, dream and mirage; but the sense of illusion may spread from the relationship that cannot be fulfilled into a disconcerting attitude towards the identity of both lover and loved, an attitude that may show itself in fanciful and humorous fashion as in the more solemn register:

> Oui, je t'ai rencontrée, c'était bien toi.
> Mais quand je me suis approché et que je t'ai appelée et que je t'ai parlè,
> C'est une autre femme qui m'a répondu . . . (*F*, 21).

And the poet goes on to talk of the 'deux visages de mon amour'. When he turns his gaze upon himself, he edges towards similar uncertainties: 'Si j'ai l'air d'être ailleurs si j'ai l'air d'être un autre' (*CB*, 159), and a question mark hangs over the symbolic Satyr: 'Est-ce bien lui-même, ou se confond-il parmi la multitude de personnages qui l'environnent?' (*F*, 139). In more comic vein, Desnos tells of the woman who discovers she has been loving a pair of twins (*DP*, 368); and this blurring of identities seems to underlie 'Au Mocassin le verbe' (*CB*, 79). Desnos looks into himself and perceives distance (*CB*, 116); a while later, he moves in and out of the image he sees as a projection of his own predicament, and things may come to the point where 'Ton être se dissout dans sa propre légende' (*DP*, 394). Desire, dream, absence, oblivion, illusion, metamorphosis, all form a close-knit cluster in his poetic world of love; but above all, love tends to be felt in terms of obstacle, cruelty, frustration, solitude, suffering and even death, at all events *ténèbres*. In a world fraught with the 'mille obstacles que le monde apporte à mon amour' (*DP*, 357), the lack of mutual response prompts a sense of ir-reality in the lovers, and as often a taste of the dream turned sour in the aftermath of next morning. Even so, love on such terms appears less baneful than the 'loveless night'; there is always the lingering hope that the 'douteux' will make way for fidelity, and Desnos accepts all the suffering involved. Indeed dream and catastrophe are intermingled in his symbolic language:

Plein d'algues, le palais qui abrite mes rêves est un récif et aussi un territoire du ciel d'orage et non du ciel trop pâle de la mélancolique divinité (*CB*, 113).

Nevertheless, the gap between dream and authentic love needs filling by poetic means; the greater the tension generated in this space, the more urgent the need to people it with a fabulous country and denizens able to give shape and substance to his yearning. For it is the world of dreams that will sustain him, even though these poetic fictions are, in proportion to their substance, a measure of his existential failure or void.

Desnos himself was fully aware of the compensatory nature of his poetic activity, and his Satyr confesses that 'Ma solitude se peuple des fantômes et des créatures de ma sexualité' (*F*, 138; cf. 'Comme', *F*, 80). The poet fashions a fairy world, highly stylised and highly mobile, in which his 'amour fatal, exclusif et meurtrier' (*LA*, 22) can find expression and resonance. 'Les accessoires de la mythologie poétique' (*CB*, 95; cf. *LA*, 34) are the means of perpetuating, perhaps even of creating the *sylphide* ('Tu naquis de ce mirage', *CB*, 154). Many features of his poetic geography go back to youthful memories, fairy tales, Jules Verne, though with the grimmer tones of Hans Andersen; and to these are joined aspects of Parisian, urban existence. In this kaleidoscope where space and time, as we ordinarily understand them, are often warped, we find a recurring pattern of symbols, animate or not, that might be described as elemental or archetypal. Though Desnos eschews a firm *symbolique* in favour of a more flexible symbolism, there often occurs a repeated correlation between symbol and feeling or within the imagic clusters, as he himself suggests:

> Et puis, voici les champs, les fleurs, les steppes, les déserts, les plaines, les sources, les fleuves, les abîmes, les montagnes
> Et tout cela peut se comparer à nos deux cœurs (*F*, 23).

These associations between land and sea, fairy tale and urban life, are found not only in the poems but in *LA*, especially pp. 102–3. Desnos likes to bring sea and forest together, either at the level of fanciful geography or in symbolic collocation (*CB*, 113, quoted above; *F*, 14 and 172); but more commonly the two cover separate areas of meaning and emotion.

Desnos' fascination with the sea goes back to his childhood:

> Je jouais seul, mes six ans vivaient en rêve. L'imagination nourrie de catastrophes maritimes, je naviguais sur de beaux navires vers des pays ravissants (*Confession d'un enfant du siècle*).

Later these imaginings were enriched by Hugo, Baudelaire, Lautré-amont, Rimbaud and Apollinaire, but clearly the main features of his poetic world were developed in early youth; the 'Fard des Argonautes' or 'L'ode à Coco' (1919), for all their discordant variations upon a theme, contain major elements of the universe evoked in later poems. The sea, with its rich bunch of associations, forms a vital part of his symbolism, even though once he denied such significance, only to affirm that 'la mer n'existe pas car la mer n'est qu'un rêve' (*CB*, 175), thereby restoring its symbolic function. It symbolises life, as does swimming ('Nous nageons, nous vivons', *F*, 132); even if the latter has depressing associations with the siren (*CB*, 153), elsewhere it is mentioned in the hope that love and freedom might be reconciled (*LA*, 18). At all events, the sea is immersing and enwrapping, but also purity, as the Satyr suggests. It is the symbol of love, usually attracting the idea of reflection, mirrors, iridescence, illusion and therefore solitude, sometimes even death (*F*, 13). Such amorous harmonics reappear in contexts where, as in Baudelaire, the *chevelure* is likened to the waves of the sea; and even without these additions, 'Voici l'Océan semblable à notre cœur' (*F*, 23).

Three marine themes form constants in Desnos' world. The first is sea-weed, which has its place in the Surrealist scheme of things; its symbolism often overlaps with that of the sea, but it is related imagically to other features, in themselves important: the stars, the staircase or rocks such as granite. Then there is the shipwreck: storm and jetsam haunt the poet's mind. In the shadow of Rimbaud, Desnos may develop the theme of the outward bound voyage (towards freedom and possibility), and sometimes the cognate topic of safe return to harbour may be broached, but these pale into insignificance compared with the shipwreck. Boats, drifting over the 'flots illusoires', turn into carcasses: 'Un navire de chair s'enlise sur une petite plage' (*DP*, 344), or we may be offered a broader sketch in which shipwreck forms part of a large cluster of images expressing love (*CB*, 154). Night is thought of as shipwreck (*CB*, 156); and Fantomas evokes the same image, a link that shows how deep-seated this motif lies in Desnos' imagination. Often this marine imagery gives off a feeling of despair; if the lover leaves for distant lands, he goes alone, and if he is close at hand, he risks either shipwreck and rocks or is enslaved by the siren; and yet more complex reactions crowd in. In *LA* Desnos asked why men should 'trouver le naufrage moins logique que la navigation'; another text is even more explicit:

J'attends depuis des années le naufrage du beau navire dont je suis amoureux . . . J'aspire à ce naufrage, j'aspire à la fin tragique de ma patience (*PA*, 50–1).

The other symbol is foam, often present to suggest vitality and promise. It recurs very frequently and is one of the key images that Desnos, in accordance with his practice, uses not only to touch off a certain group of responses in the reader but as a link image that brings other images simultaneously into play.

The landscape has its own chart of symbolic reference, and Desnos' imaginative needs tend to concentrate attention on a limited number of *lieux symboliques*. To begin with, there is the desert theme, not as prominent as some, but persistent for all that: Desnos invokes the 'muses du désert, ô muses exigeantes' and in *LA*, 100 he also relates the desert to the creation of illusion. More normally we have the fairy-tale forest (perhaps with castle), denoting obstacle or barrier, though a different meaning is conferred on the trees that make up wood or forest. The symbolism of childhood stories is doubtless reinforced by the example of Apollinaire, in whose poetry the forest develops its own thematic abundance. The fairy-forest appears in an early poem which also dwells on night, dream and sleep ('Les Espaces du sommeil', *CB*, 92); later the poet imagines himself as 'le bûcheron de la forêt d'acier'; in 'Jamais d'autre que toi' (*CB*, 142), a poem of faith and fidelity, he introduces images that suggest the passage from despair to hope:

> Jamais d'autre que toi ne saluera la mer à l'aube quand fatigué d'errer
> moi sorti des forêts ténébreuses et des buissons d'orties je marcherai
> vers l'écume

but the forest image can occur in a context of exclusion (*CB*, 144). Corsaire Sanglot also 'suivait une piste au cœur d'une forêt vierge' (*LA*, 28), and here the link between the wood and another key-theme, the journey, becomes clear. The castle or tower of legend, reminiscent of the sleeping Beauty, may be brought into the land-scape:

> De longues avenues entre des frondaisons
> S'allongent vers la tour où sommeille une dame
> Dont la beauté résiste aux baisers, aux saisons,
> Comme une étoile au vent, comme un rocher aux lames (*F*, 70)

but more usually the castle develops as a variation on the prison or cage ('Tu revois la prison, c'est le château sans âge', *F*, 127). Inciden-tally, birds play only a modest role in Desnos' symbolism, but when they appear, it is often as prisoners in a cage. And in Desnos, the prison-motif, so dominant, denotes the denial of freedom but also adds harmonics to the theme of the criminal. Most of the buildings described by the poet are symbols of exclusion; only rarely do we see the inside of a house, and when we do, we see it from outside, not by entering this or that room. Either the door is being shut or is already locked ('La porte se ferme sur l'idole de plomb', *CB*, 144) or the windows, behind which Desnos suggests lovers or an empty space, are viewed from the street by the solitary passer-by:

Voici venir le temps des croisades,
Par la fenêtre fermée les oiseaux s'obstinent à parler
    Comme les poissons d'aquarium.
A la devanture d'une boutique
    Une jolie femme sourit.
Bonheur tu n'es que cire à cacheter
    Et je passe tel un feu follet ('Destinée arbitraire', *DP*, 341).

Furthermore, the house is the fabric that surrounds staircases and corridors, symbols of unfulfilled and sometimes unending aspiration which recur with impressive insistency and are related to his symbolic figures, Don Juan descending the stairs or the siren standing on the staircase of the castle. The sense of futility is sometimes made more explicit and we are given the feeling of vainly seeking a way through a maze ('Nuit de chemin perdu parmi les escaliers', *F*, 54). The theme of the staircase is associated several times with Corsaire Sanglot (*LA*, 30, 67, etc.) and is obviously linked with the broader symbol of the journey, itself a usually fruitless venture. In this context, two other symbols may be mentioned: the railway line, and the mine which combines the motifs of the corridor, darkness and mineral substance (e.g. *DD*, 122). And the importance certain symbols hold for Desnos is revealed by his tendency to turn them into animate figures: 'Les mines du nord de la France et les mines du Cap et les mines du Baïkal conversent' (*DD*, 147).

Into this landscape Desnos introduces a number of denizens: the central figures of *LA*, Corsaire Sanglot and Louise Lame with their symbolic names and strange *avatars*, lead the column of characters who are nearly all endowed with a cluster of common traits. The men are haunted by their amorous dream, whether it looks to past or to future, and the intense feelings aroused between dream and fruition take us into a world of cruelty and sadism:

Le pirate avait eu des chagrins d'amour
C'était une espèce de chevalier au cœur de pierre
Qui violait les captives en rêvant à son amour
Versons un pleur sur le pirate (*PA*, 96).

The phantom appears as a wanderer along an endless road, solitary, alienated from society and often assuming the guise of a criminal. In *LA*, 45 the lover is described as a 'jeune bagnard', but the association is rather with imprisonment suffered by any man in love, and Desnos adds two other harmonics: the link between love and shipwreck and that between captivity and liberty in the realm of love (*LA*, 46). The anti-social exploration of crime, in unsatisfied love, is a constant in Desnos' sketches; significantly crime and love mingle in the dark ('L'Assassinat, fidèle amant de la nuit', *DD*, 147), and the poet evokes 'le voyageur de la nuit' who makes his way on in the hope that the 'ténèbres bavardes' might bring response to his love. He is above all a *passant*; among the variations on this basic theme, we have the deprived, the blind, and also Don Juan in Spain and the Satyr. The poles of Desnos' projection are Corsaire Sanglot and Fantomas—so beloved of the Surrealists and whose name brings together the themes of love, impishness merging into crime, solitude, metamorphosis and mirage. The female figures are all sirens in one shape or another, elusive, pitiless, and like the males are 'vagabondes' (*CB*, 132) or *passantes*; on one occasion the siren is called 'la Fantomas' (*F*, 15). Their identity may assume various forms, corresponding to Desnos' perplexity about the 'visage de l'amour'; but the *innamorata*'s face is never described, what fascinates the poet are the *chevelure*, the eyes, the hands especially, but also *l'ombre*. These amorous pairs thread their way through Desnos' mythological countryside, though in *NLN* he also uses the persona of the first person singular to express his feelings. In this world animals play a minor part; apart from the caged birds, we find the horse, closely linked in *CB*, 116–19 with the theme of love, and the various marine fauna acquire a modest symbolic value, the crab, the lobster, above all the *hippocampe* which in 'Siramour' is a projection of the poet himself.

Other features enrich the character and tonality of this world; some set the keys in which Desnos develops his themes, others attract to themselves a rather denser symbolism than usual, yet others create a pool of images that serve to bring into recognisable pattern the various elements of Desnos' world. In the first category, perhaps the most prominent are the journey, sound and darkness. His characters are forever on a journey, whether it be a sea-voyage, penetration of a forest or advancing along a corridor. The poet also apprehends his world along the axis sound/silence; one of his finest poems is 'La voix de Robert Desnos' that can conquer the universe except for his love. A world without *la parole* is a dead one, but silence can have two meanings: it may be simply the realm of death or oblivion, or it stands for suspended time that allows experience to reverberate in the memory ('plus silencieuse encore parce que je t'imagine sans cesse', *CB*, 95). More pervasive is the theme of night: Desnos' world of love sought is nocturnal and his characters often make their way down the 'corridor de minuit'. This may also be the world of the abyss and there are references to the sky crumbling down; we are moreover in a world where the sun makes a very wan appearance ('Désespoir du soleil'). Night and its stars are far more prominent:

> Dans la nuit il y a naturellement les sept merveilles du monde et la grandeur et le tragique et le charme (*CB*, 92)

and the links between night and Desnos' world are laid out with extreme lucidity; much of his most anguished poetry appears under the titles *Ténèbres* and *NLN*. Midnight, a fateful moment, is 'si semblable à tout au bonheur et à la tristesse' (*CB*, 105), though the latter state will predominate for obvious reasons. Darkness also allows him to feel nearer the loved one, to 'se glisser dans ton ombre à la faveur de la nuit' (*CB*, 102); but normally it is described in the minor and acrid key, and in very bitter tones in *F*, 54.

The stars, contrasted once with the corruption of the world (*DP*, 357), possess wide-ranging meaning but are seen as essentially mobile—the *étoile filante* is more in evidence than the fixed star. They may take flight through the universe, only perhaps to end up in some shipwreck or they may plunge earthward; but whatever their activity, they are symbols of love. In *DD*, Desnos talked of 'les femmes, étoiles de rêve penchées sur leur propre image'; the hair of the beloved may be described in terms of falling stars, which elsewhere stand for the love to which the poet aspires and are equivalents of the siren or the 'belle dame sans merci'. In different keys the stars, like the night, symbolise love as hope, illusion, *retombée*. The moon and the wind play lesser roles, even though Desnos asserts that 'je méprise ceux qui ignorent jusqu'à l'existence du vent'.

Among more circumscribed phenomena that acquire poetic importance for Desnos flowers occupy a privileged place. Sometimes their symbolic connotations are more relevant than their identity ('fleur d'amour', *CB*, 116ff.), but more usually Desnos evokes particular flowers, especially roses and anenomes. They may be signs of *épanouissement* and *jaillissement*, as in 'Le Bœuf et la Rose' (*F*, 77–8) or used in comparisons to suggest those states (*CB*, 95); in such contexts they overlap symbolically with the fire and the flame, but they also mark a stage of decay and here they resemble the stars which Desnos may use to express an *élan* that is already spent. So the flowers are shown losing their leaves or the poet may choose plants suggestive of the sere and rotting (mushrooms, ferns); but whatever their context the flora are almost always associated with love and therefore retain a certain polyvalency. If the poet talks of rotting ferns, he also admires 'la fleur qui triomphe du temps'.

One striking image that has a wide range of reference for Desnos is the bottle:

Qu'est-ce qui monte plus haut que le soleil et descend plus bas que le feu, qui est plus liquide que le vent et plus dur que le granit?

This text (*LA*, 54) also reveals some of the categories within which Desnos' imagination likes to function; in the same book he alludes to the sexual meaning of the bottle (*LA*, 64), but it is also the means whereby the poet can 'go catch a falling star' and imprison the siren: 'Loin de moi, une étoile filante choit dans la bouteille nocturne du poète' (*CB*, 96). In contrast, it may signify solitude (*PA*, 102) and a recurring image is that of the broken bottle: either we see water flowing from its cracked shape or, more commonly, broken glass in the dawn of the morning after (e.g. *LA*, 32, where it is related to the theme of the journey).[2] In other words it plays a useful rôle in the pattern of failure. Close by are images of glass and crystal and especially of mineral substances, often used to describe the heart of the sirens: coal, basalt, granite, marble, phosphorus and the cognate images of the mines and the volcano. The inner life of the 'Aveugle' (*CB*, 164) is pictured with the imagery of granite, 'cristaux', 'spectres minéraux'; Desnos composes a poem on 'Paroles des rochers', yet another is a train of associations about coal. Often these images are related to cruel, sadistic indifference in love, but further analysis would probably reveal flexibility in the way Desnos utilises them. Steel, for instance, is brought in for imagic effect and may be correlated with the idea of desire (*F*, 36).

What has emerged so far, I believe, is that Desnos' poetic world contains a number of major features that tend to recur, whether they concern landscape, 'character' or smaller object or category. Heterogeneous in their origins and 'normal' context, they achieve a kaleidoscopic effect by the manner in which Desnos throws them together in varying patterns. He removes them from their everyday associations and he may personalise certain elements (flowers, rocks, mines). He subjects them to divers metamorphoses, as he himself has mentioned on occasion; this is intimately connected with the 'protée insaisissable' that constitutes his dream of love, for movement, mirage and metamorphosis inevitably go together. He talks of the 'décor mobile de mes rêves' (*LA*, 62) and is well aware that his intimations of experience require unusual means of expression:

Tu viens au labyrinthe, où les ombres s'égarent,
Graver sur les parois la frise d'un passé
Où la vie et le rêve et l'oubli, espacés
Par les nuits, revivront en symboles bizarres
(Extr. de 'Calisto', *DP*, 394).

However, though Desnos achieves his poetic effect in great measure by this series of imagic patterns, much depends also on his use of verbs and his exploration of counter-syntax which received stimulus from his surrealist days but correspond to the deep-seated needs of his poetic vision. Moreover, some of these disconcerting exercises reveal their links with the categories through which Desnos apprehends experience and of which the most important seem to me to be: illusion; liquidity/hardness; sound/silence; iridescence/darkness; solitude; journey and ascent/fall. On the last there is an interesting aside in *LA*, 47: 'Chaque mot se précipite vers la catastrophe ou vers l'apothéose', but no more than shipwreck is fall associated simply with failure: 'Joyeuse encore comme l'heure en forme de cigogne qui tombe de haut' (*CB*, 95), and 'A présent' (*CB*, 74) winds itself over a trellis of themes such as rise and fall, *épanouissement*, melting and utilises some of the elements examined earlier. Nevertheless, a cursory glance does confirm the impression described by Desnos himself of a 'bouleversement de paysages' (*CB*, 132), and it is later that we become fully aware of the imagic mechanisms operated by the poet. Though we have rejected the presence of too rigid a *symbolique* within his imagic framework, it does seem that for Desnos certain phenomena are more or less closely bound up with certain qualities, states of mind, values, and when he seeks to express these, his mind tends to bring together these associations which in the everyday world would hardly bear one another company. This mechanism we have seen working at the level of landscape, but it also operates in the way images and properties are associated with objects and feelings (e.g. 'la forêt d'acier', *CB*, 112, the 'rose de marbre' also described as 'la reine de la solitude', *CB*, 147, and in *NLN* the links between metals and desire). Two sets (or more) of phenomena are brought into relation with one another, not only by individual linking at one level, but by imagic cross-reference, so that meaning passes like an electric arc from one element to another. Desnos, only too conscious of 'les vides qui séparent les mots retentissants' (*DD*, 124), concentrates much attention on techniques used as linking devices of meaning, especially at imagic level. He wishes to bring about that 'phénomène magique de l'écriture en tant que manifestation organique et optique du merveilleux'. These imagic clusters will come to appear less fortuitous than one thought at first blush, and some of his best poetry is characterised by their dense network:

> Et vous mes yeux fougères presque charbon
> Et toi fougère pourrissante mon cœur
> presque flamme presque flot
> Je parle en vain de la fleur mais de moi (*CB*, 116–17).

'Apparition', *F*, 59–60 should be read in this way too; it has a fairly clear backbone in that the main theme is contained in the first and last lines, but in between Desnos has inserted a vast number of his familiar motifs where accumulation, repetition, individual associations and metamorphosed syntax combine to bring the poem to a triumphant conclusion. It is moreover a poem which reminds us that not all Desnos' poetry is a meditation on disillusioned love. Even in his more despondent moments he still accepts 'douleurs', solitude and the closeness of despair to enthusiasm (*LA*, 98); and he always hoped that the ideal would become reality and that beyond the world of his dream there lay a promised land:

> Je ne veux plus être qu'une voile emportée au gré des
> moussons vers des continents inconnus où je ne trouverai
> qu'une seule personne ('Tour de la Tombe', *DP*, 356).

and significantly, the realm of pure love would be shorn of all the 'accessoire poétique' he had constructed and exploited to preserve the existence of his dream:

> Etre aimé par elle
> Non pas une nuit de toutes les nuits
> Mais à jamais pour l'éternel présent
> Sans paysage et sans lumière
> (*F*, 46) cf. also *DP*, 355).

The lineaments of Desnos' ideal love begin to take shape: removed from the orbit of time (*DP*, 356), she has ceased to be the *passante*:

Tu n'es pas la passante, mais celle qui demeure. La notion d'éternité est liée à mon amour pour toi. Non, tu n'es pas la passante ni le pilote étrange qui guide l'aventurier à travers le dédale du désir . . . Tu n'es pas la passante, mais la perpétuelle amante et que tu le veuilles ou non (*LA*, 114).

Love involves the total absorption of the lover in the beloved and its expression is reduced to an intense statement bare of imagery or oblique formulation. And yet we are still in an area of uncertainty: does the poet see dream simply as dream or does it become reality?

RHF

(*DP*, 347), Does the *innamorata* serve as more than a peg on which the poet may hang his love? In 'Siramour', *F*, 21, he suggested that only *his* love and *his* memory could keep *her* alive. Does there come a moment when the lover is so immersed in the object of his love that he ceases to be aware of her objective reality? Several poems hint that the dream has acquired a measure of self-sufficiency ('acceptons de rêver', *CB*, 132) and even *NLN* allows the expression of his mood:

> Car le plus sincère amant s'il n'est pas aimé par celle qu'il aime
> Peu lui importe, il l'aimera
> Eternellement désirera d'être aimé
> Et d'aimer sans espoir deviendra pur comme un diamant (*F*, 46).

More than once Desnos touches on the theme of the sleeping Beauty who must not be awakened ('Craignez de réveiller la furtive endormie', *F*, 74); and on the neighbouring theme of trying not to see beyond the curtain for fear reality should cancel dream. One cannot, I think, assume a sort of chronological progression from the frustrations expressed by the 'accessoire poétique' to the love of 'une seule personne'; and in a strange manner these two extremes of Desnos' love are found at different periods in his poetry. There is the extremely moving 'Dernier Poème':

> J'ai rêvé tellement fort de toi,
> J'ai tellement marché, tellement parlé,
> Tellement aimé ton ombre,
> Qu'il ne me restera plus rien de toi.
> Il me reste d'être l'ombre parmi les ombres
> D'être cent fois plus l'ombre que l'ombre
> D'être l'ombre qui viendra et reviendra dans ta vie ensoleillée
>   (*DP*, 408; also *PA*, 216),

a poem that achieves startling effects by the incantatory power of intense, accumulated repetition and, rare feature, brings sunshine into the text. It also develops a theme that deserves proper analysis—the shadow which is bound up with the problem of identity and also seems to imply the denial of solitude. But the 'last' poem echoes verbally two earlier compositions. This total absorption of the self into a state of being where time is suspended and the shadow becomes as it were the substance, was expressed in *almost the same terms* in 'A la mystérieuse' in 1926 (*CB*, 91), including the solar reference; and the motif recurs as a partial descant in 'L'homme qui a perdu son ombre' (*F*, 147–8). The final poem, therefore, seems to indicate not the end-game of Desnos' amorous journey, but rather a deep-seated element of his attitude to love which, in its poetic manifestations, is both more varied in its range and less varying in development than one might have thought. What is certain is that for Desnos the immersion of the self in the dream—or reality—of one's love leads to a stripping of the 'accessoire poétique', whereas love experienced as gap between dream and reality urges the poet to the creation of a more formally structured and imagically rich world; but the 'voix de Robert Desnos' sounds at both ends of the range with unmistakable individuality and equal success.

Oxford   I. D. McFARLANE

NOTES

1 The following abbreviations are used: *CB* = *Corps et biens*, Gallimard, 1969; *DP* = *Domaine public*, 7e éd., Gallimard, 1953; *F* = *Fortunes*, Gallimard, 1969; *LA* = *La Liberté ou l'amour*, which includes *DD* = *Deuil pour deuil*, Gallimard, 1962; *PA* = *Robert Desnos*, ed. Pierre Berger in series *Poètes d'Aujourd'hui*, Seghers, 1949; *NLN* = *The Night of loveless Nights* (*F*). I am grateful to my friend Garnet Rees for his patient scrutiny of the draft.
2 cf. another example in *CB*, 139, which passage also illustrates excellently Desnos' technique of imagic convergence ('Un escalier se déroule . . .').

UT PICTURA POESIS: AN ELEMENT OF ORDER IN THE ADVENTURE OF THE POÈME EN PROSE

Si ce que [le poète] rapporte de *là-bas* a forme, il donne forme; si c'est informe, il donne de l'informe.

Rimbaud: Lettre du Voyant.

Whatever *a priori* attitudes poets and critics have had towards the 'robuste hybride'[1] of prose poetry, stressing affinities now with prose and now with poetry, its emergence as a new and flexible form is undoubtedly one of the most remarkable developments in poetry since the Romantics. Suzanne Bernard summarises the twofold allegiances of the genre as follows: 'A la base même de toute tentative de poème en prose il y a une volonté de trouver une forme neuve, individuelle, *à la fois* anarchique par rapport aux formes établies, et artistique dans son organisation de prose en poème.'[2] The present investigation aims at exploring a particular aspect of form which suggests that the *shaping* of the prose poem is as demanding for the poet and as potentially stimulating for the reader as is ever the case with poetry written within the traditional moulds.

Put briefly, what is under consideration is the verbal mimesis of visual sources. Those sources may be existing paintings, etc., or views of natural phenomena as if in a framed picture, which simply offer the poet his narrative structure based on pictorial elements. Or there may be a closer imitation of plastic form in the typographical presentation of a text: such is the case in calligrammatic and related poetry. Or again, more intimately still, and more profoundly, there may be a re-presentation in words of the visual stimulus, far removed both from 'pictorial' writing and from 'picture-poems', in which verbal techniques re-enact the source in the very texture of the poem. The history of the *poème en prose* since Aloysius Bertrand suggests a gradual development from the first to the last of these types of mimesis: one might point in general terms to the narrative interest in pictures shown by Bertrand, to the calligrammes of the Cubist period, and to the highly wrought re-enactments of such a contemporary as Francis Ponge. But the three types overlap, and the weighting seems to change more with the aesthetics of each poet than with his position in the time sequence. Since the historical approach offers in detail so many exceptions to the apparently neat pattern, therefore, it seems more appropriate to consider rather the feature of verbal mimesis of visual sources as such and ascertain as it were the focal apparatus of different poets. When they use visual material, how closely do they assimilate it into the language of their poems, how do they use it to structure their work? None of the answers will provide an immediate value judgment, but it is hoped that they may help towards one by throwing light on the poet's techniques and attitudes.

The first type of writing under review is too well known to do other than recall it briefly: the use by prose poets of pictorial material. Bertrand's *Gaspard de la Nuit* is subtitled *Fantaisies à la manière de Rembrandt et de Callot*, and Baudelaire was inspired by his reading of the work to 'appliquer à la description de la vie moderne, ou plutôt d'*une* vie moderne et plus abstraite, le procédé qu'il avait appliqué à la peinture de la vie ancienne, si étrangement pittoresque'.[3] 'Pictur-esque' is exactly the right word, for however much a turning-point in literary history, Bertrand's poems in no way sought to reflect in their form the shapes presented by the paintings and engravings which inspired him. They are all written in a similar mould, and if this happens on occasion to represent the subject in hand, it is uninten-tional. In 'Les cinq doigts de la main', for example, each finger is allocated a stanza, but the little finger is largest of all on the page, and a sixth stanza is added so that it becomes clear there is no mimetic intention. In 'Le soir sur l'eau' one may detect the very shape of a gondola in the carved prow and curved aft snaking upwards from the long low midships, but it is the narrative interest that remains upper-most. The bravo sets out for, and finally returns from, some dark adventure: the first stanza is repeated with slight variations to close the poem, giving it symmetry, but as the repetition of stanzas occurs elsewhere in the 'fantaisies' to no mimetic effect, one must conclude that Betrand did not construct his poem in conscious imitation of a gondola. His aim, here as in the other poems, is to evoke an atmo-sphere, and his reactions are impressionistic. The tone of the whole volume and the kind of use to be made of visual sources, is established in the first poem, 'Harlem', which begins: 'Harlem, cette admirable bambochade qui résume l'école flamande, Harlem peint par Jean-Breughel, Peeter-Neef, David-Téniers et Paul-Rembrandt'.[4]

Baudelaire was also right in claiming greater abstraction for his own prose poems. His description of an engraving in 'Les Projets' in *Le Spleen de Paris* is different in essence only in that he openly admits that his interest lies not so much in the picture of the hut in a tropical paradise as in the reverie it provokes: 'Pourquoi contraindre mon corps à changer de place, puisque mon âme voyage si lestement? Et à quoi bon exécuter des projets, puisque le projet est en lui-même une jouissance suffisante?'[5] The principal interest here is psychological. It is Rimbaud's elliptical style that by suppressing the false but traditional distinction between inner and outer life makes it impossible to say, in respect of many of his *Illuminations*, whether his starting point is direct experience of the world around him or that already distilled by some other artist. 'Ornières' is a case in point. Delahaye's assurance that Rimbaud saw the circus parade in Charleville in 1886[6] is both inconclusive and ultimately unimportant. The scene is framed, particular features situated (as in 'Mystique') to left and right. The picture comes to life. Its colourful movement could derive from an imaginative reaction (sparked off by the vision of the 'mille rapides ornières') either to a real procession or to the picture of one. Max Jacob finds one of his word paintings so real that he dashes to the rescue of a child in imminent danger, a willing fool of his own illusion.[7]

In this first category, then, visual sources including paintings are one type of subject among many. They are inherent in the poem only as narrative elements, though like other narrative elements they may also serve loftier ends. If we focus now on the second type of relationship between poem and picture, we find the equally well-studied area of the calligramme, where literal shape is given to the object evoked and the meaning of the words made immediately apparent. The calligramme highlights an important consideration underlying the relationship of poetry and the visual arts: that of time. A painting is two-dimensional and can, in one sense, be taken in at a glance; it exists as an object in time but only statically. A poem takes time to be read; it exists through duration in time. The sense of timelessness that a fine painting or scene stimulates in the spectator, capturing eternity in an instant, is a provocation and a challenge to the poet. There is also a challenge in the quality of illusion of a painting which exists effectively in two dimensions but suggests the third by its presentation of perspective and totality according to the conventions of its cultural origins.

One way of making a poem stand outside duration is by so shaping it on the page that its narrative content is assimilated at a glance. Familiarity with Lewis Carroll's mouse's tail/tale might suggest that the picture-poem is little more than a doodle, witty but lightweight. If Rabelais's 'dive bouteille' or Apollinaire's calligrammes do little to dispel this view, our opinion is necessarily modified when Mallarmé brings all his high seriousness to bear on *Un coup de dés*. He wrote to Gide: 'Le rythme d'une phrase au sujet d'un acte, ou même d'un objet, n'a de sens que s'il les imite, et figuré sur le papier, repris par la lettre à l'estampe originelle, n'en sait rendre, malgré tout, quelque chose.'[8] Mimesis is essential, and the 'malgré tout' a wise recognition of the radical difference between 'l'estampe' and 'la lettre'. And Mallarmé puts his finger on the one sure method of conquering time through time in poetry, namely through rhythm. If a calligramme fails rhythmically, it falls between two stools, and fails altogether as poetry; if, as André Billy suggested, calligrammes are 'privées de toute audition possible',[9] then their attempt to straddle the two media leaves them in limbo. What is true of Apollinaire's response to Marinetti's 'parole in libertà' and to the idea of simultaneism is no less true of kinetic, concrete and spatialist poetry, where there is even more concentration of energy and emphasis on the physical substance of words. The hyphenation of key words by Pierre Garnier is no guarantee against falling between verbal and visual: 'signes-éclairs', 'voyelles-lumière', 'cris-soleils'.[10]

The reconciliation of 'l'inéluctable écoulement du temps réel et l'éternel présent de l'art, le successif et le simultané' may be achieved, to continue quoting Suzanne Bernard, in one of two ways: 'Le premier consiste, par des procédés comparables à ceux de la versification, à maîtriser le temps, à le ressaisir, à lui imposer forme et structure par le rythme; le second à se libérer du temps, à le nier, à sortir des catégories temporelles.'[11] The second of these procedures is anarchic. The first characterises the third type of mimesis under consideration, an appropriate term for which might be: 'assimilated calligramme.'[12] This both militates against anarchy and relies on methods appropriate to literature while remaining responsive to the visual experience. Certain writers have consciously striven to cultivate adequate verbal forms and formulations equivalent to their visual inspiration. They are as aware as Apollinaire that, as Souriau put it, 'dans typographique il y a graphique'.[13] They use visual effects on the page as an integral part (but only a part) on their technical armoury. Even Bertrand (*pace* Jacob in his *Art poétique*) was scrupulous about the printer's presentation of his poems,[14] and one appreciates the typographer's patience when he comes to satisfy the requirements of a calligramme, or of a construction by Isidore Isou or Pierre Garnier. But the material presentation of *Un coup de dés* is no more and no less intrinsic to its being than that of poems by Ponge or Saint-John Perse.

In his preface to *Le Cornet à dés*, Max Jacob elaborates on the application of the will to the structuring and style of the prose poem, which should aim at being 'un bijou'. As he writes elsewhere, 'le sujet n'y a pas d'importance et le pittoresque non plus. On n'y est préoccupé que du poème lui-même, c'est-à-dire de l'accord des mots, des images et de leur appel mutuel et constant.'[15] But while the theory, despite its omission of any mention of rhythm, tallies with traditional poetic attitudes towards the crystallisation of material in a closed form, in practice, *Le Cornet à dés* offers precisely the kind of 'historiette' that Jacob condemned in Bertrand. But the recognition that perfect appropriateness of construction is good style is an important element in the assimilated calligrammes of later poets.

Saint-John Perse stresses that 'les mots ne sauraient, pour le poète, tenir l'office de simples signes médiateurs sans intérêt plastique'.[16] It is a cornerstone of his poetics that there should be 'identité parfaite et . . . unité entre le sujet et l'objet, entre le poète et le poème'.[17] But for him movement is essential both in life and in poetic rhythms: 'l'inertie seule est menaçante'.[18] So to the idea of identity we find him adding the necessary ingredient of rhythm, thus presenting in a readable and inherently literary form (as calligrammes are not) his perceptions of the visible world. His insistence on italic type for his poetry underlines its driving force. Writing of modern French poetry in general, but having his own practice clearly to the fore in his mind, he specifies his meaning:

Faisant plus que témoigner ou figurer, elle *devient* la chose même qu'elle 'appréhende', qu'elle évoque ou suscite; faisant plus que mimer, elle *est*, finalement, cette chose elle-même, dans son mouvement et sa durée; elle la vit et 'l'agit', unanimement, et se doit donc, fidèlement, de la suivre, avec diversité, dans sa mesure propre et dans son rythme propre: largement et longuement, s'il s'agit de la mer ou du vent; étroitement et promptement s'il s'agit de l'éclair.[19]

Such a theory is more demanding than any we have seen so far, and *Vents* and *Amers* are ample illustrations of it; his four-line poem on a Zen painting of a kite might be considered an essay on the transcription of lightning.[20] A plain example of the total fusion of the poem's form and its subject in Perse is *Pluies* where as the torrential downpour increases so does the length of *verset* in the three-line *laisses*.[21] Cantos V and VI lead clearly up to the climactic cloudburst of canto VII in which the *verset* pattern also bursts its formal bounds and the page is blackened for the height of the storm. As the clouds pass, the basic ternary pattern is restored. Compared with Apollinaire's

'Il pleut', Perse's poem is a deluge beside a drizzle, but while remaining more legible and more directly literary it shares the concern for plastic form of the calligramme. Beside both of these poems, Bertrand's 'La Pluie', Louÿs's and Jacob's poems of the same name, and Ponge's 'Pluie' are 'paraboles' and 'fables', to use the terms of contempt which Jacob applied to the prose poems of Baudelaire and Mallarmé.[22] That is to say, such poems show no structural attempt to master or deny duration.

René Char's attempt to do this may be summed up in his aphorism 'L'éclair me dure'.[23] His writings satisfy Perse's requirement that one should write 'étroitement et promptement s'il s'agit de l'éclair', and the light pervading his work seems to derive from an inner source illuminating each poem. The very consistency of attitude is none the less something of a restriction where structure is concerned. There seems in fact to be some danger of another 'mould' replacing the one which Bertrand used for his first prose poems or indeed into which verse poetry is poured. It limits the appropriateness of form to content which is a major potential of free verse and so restricts the poet's range.

It is Ponge who continues Perse's approach and who, because he is much readier to discuss theories and write about his own texts, provides valuable material on the nature of the prose poem. He confirms the necessity both of appropriateness and of flexibility: 'Il faudrait non point même une rhétorique par auteur mais une rhétorique par poème.'[24] Later, in 'My Creative Method', he expands the idea, concurring with Perse on the way in which the plastic qualities of the object may be integrated into the form of the poem in a direct but not ideogrammatic way. The passage is of sufficient importance to the present theme to quote *in extenso*:

D'une forme rhétorique par objet (c.-à-d. par poème). . . . Chaque objet doit imposer au poème une forme rhétorique particulière. Plus de sonnets, d'odes, d'épigrammes: la forme même du poème soit en quelque sorte déterminée par son sujet.

Pas grand-chose de commun entre cela et les calligrammes (d'Apollinaire): il s'agit d'une forme beaucoup plus cachée.

. . . Et je ne dis pas que je n'emploie, parfois, certains artifices de l'ordre typographique. . . .

Tout cela doit rester caché, être très dans le squelette, jamais apparent; ou même parfois dans l'intention, dans la conception, dans le fœtus seulement: dans la façon dont est prise la parole, conservée—puis quittée.

Point de règles à cela: puisque justement elles changent (selon chaque sujet).[25]

Thus in *Le Parti pris des choses*, for example, one finds texts which reflect the overall shape of their subject (e.g. 'Le Pain', where the stanzas are fatter in the middle than at the ends, and the whole thing symmetrically elongated), others where sounds mimic the subject in some way ('Le Papillon' flits from plosive to fricative, 'L'Huître' imposes a pattern of plosive + r sounds, 'L'Orange' is rounded on nasalised vowels), and others again where the very shape of the printed letter is used pictorially to descriptive ends (as the first letters of 'Gymnaste' determine the acrobat's appearance and anatomy, or the snails' excelsior is '*Go on*', where the *G* is the shell trailing behind an extended body).

That the assimilated calligramme need not be mere facile play is amply proved by the seriousness of many of its practitioners. Such seriousness has allowed so intellectual a writer as Michel Deguy to adopt the notion governing calligrammes and extend it to his own ends. Professor Hackett has written of them: 'These are not calligrammes like Apollinaire's visual lyricism where words fill predetermined shapes . . . or follow fixed contours; but are metaphysical calligrammes, which are the "configuration secrète de notre existence" and represent or "figure" our very being.'[26] This seems to be nearer the Aristotelian sense of art as imitation, such as expressed in Auden's 'New Year Letter' ('Art in intention is mimesis/But, realised, the resemblance ceases'), than is meant by the present study: only when the resemblance does *not* cease can the reader detect an assimilated calligramme.

To give complete coverage to the question of such assimilation with full examples would take volumes; for the present study a single figure will be traced in a limited number of poems. No claim is made for the examples being representative of their authors nor, more particularly, for the list being anywhere near complete. The figure is a simple one: the parabola. Its literary expression cannot pretend (except through the calligramme) to reproduce, only to re-present its curvature. A poem or section of a poem will use all or some of the following features to re-enact a parabola: a pivotal point representing the axis and the zenith or nadir of the curve, and elements mirroring each other to either side of that centre, either repeated phrases or stanzas, reflected ideas, or sounds arranged in palindromic form.

In such figures, it is clear that the pivotal point will take on particular significance, since it articulates the structure in a crucial way, both in the sense that it is central to the structure and in that it pinpoints the imagery or meaning of the passage. The figure seems to be used in two quite different ways, the first of which reflects the logic of the passage, shaping the movement of the ideas, and the second where there is a more literal mirroring of the parabolic form or movement observed through the text. A first example drawn from traditional prosody will illustrate the pivotal articulation of logic around key phrases.

In Phèdre's confrontation with Hippolyte (*Phèdre*, II, 5), three of her principal speeches have almost exactly at their centres terse questions which give a jolt to the progressive avowal of her passion: 'Que dis-je?' (ll. 627, 693) and 'Que faisiez-vous alors?' (l. 645). There is a shift, particularly apparent on the first occasion, but present also on the other two, from a direct factual account to the unreal world of Phèdre's obsessive delusion. The mirror-image of reality is different in quality from that reality. The world through the looking-glass has, as Alice discovered, a topsy-turvy logic of its own. The glass is a threshold, equivalent to the mediating pivotal words at the heart of the poetic figure, to the unreality or surreality of the reflection. But Mabille reminds us that in these 'états psychologiques limites' (which he describes), 'on n'est pas d'un seul côté du miroir, mais des deux côtés à la fois'.[27] This important observation has multiple ramifications; for present purposes it recalls acutely the question of the temporal dimension in literature. Here is a figure which escapes from duration while retaining complete allegiance to the literary medium.

When the technique is used in free verse, particularly if it structures the whole text, it assumes great importance as a means of avoiding anarchy. The following example shows the classical tradition at work beneath the surface; it is the first in date of Perse's collected poems, 'Les Cloches' in *Images à Crusoé*:[28]

> Vieil homme aux mains nues,
> remis entre les hommes, Crusoé!
> tu pleurais, j'imagine, quand des tours de l'Abbaye,
> comme un flux, s'épanchait le sanglot des cloches sur la
> Ville . . .
> Ô Dépouillé!
> Tu pleurais de songer aux brisants sous la lune; aux
> sifflements de rives plus lointaines; aux musiques étranges
> qui naissent et s'assourdissent sous l'aile close de la nuit,
> pareilles aux cercles enchaînés que sont les ondes d'une
> conque, à l'amplification de clameurs sous la mer . . .

That the text is untypical of Perse in many respects is clear. What matters for our purpose is the crucial position of 'Ô Dépouillé!', the repetition of 'tu pleurais' on either side of it, and the interplay of time and tense. Crusoe is imagined back in London, 'remis entre les hommes', after his island solitude. Yet present events are related in the imperfect. Recollections are more vivid and present to him, and so the tense switches to the present in defiance of the grammatical 'concordance des temps'. 'Ô Dépouillé!' is the hinge at the heart of the poem in more ways than one: physically central, it also underscores the idea that back in civilised society the archetypal 'dépouillé' Robinson Crusoe has an even greater sense of deprivation and exile. The two panels of the diptych act as the two sides of the looking-glass; yet there is a progression, that from reality to unreality, from immediate present to remembered past, from distaste to affection, from past tense to present. At the same time, the poem may be read without difficulty, and its images and rhythms appreciated.

In Perse's poem, there is little repetition as such to hold the balance around the fulcrum or trace a shape. Other poets use repetition to help towards structural unity, and in the *poème en prose* it assumes particular importance just because certain other devices are denied the genre. Even a word for word repetition within a poem offers extra and different resonances by virtue of its being a repetition. More often slight changes are made to the pattern of the initial phrase or stanza to indicate some development. The sense of equilibrium is retained, but the world in the mirror throws into relief some aspect or aspects of the (ultimate) reality explored.

Repetition is not only of ideas and phrases, of course, and a study of what Philippe Bonnefis has called 'l'activité littérale'[29] reveals details of the poet's art relevant to parabolic mimesis. Again an example from traditional prosody may serve to introduce the feature. Mallarmé's 'Brise marine' seems to rock between phonetic extremes of vowel-sound. The title itself sets the pattern: [i—a—i] which is continued in 'Fuir! là-bas fuir!' and in other more loosely woven textures, with [ɥ] providing a variant on [i]. One finds a similar preoccupation with the balancing of individual sounds in a less well integrated but no less fascinating way in Ponge's observations on the word 'verre': 'j'aime assez que dans VERRE, après la forme (donnée par le V), soit donnée la matière par les deux syllabes ER RE, parfaitement symétriques comme si, placeés de part et d'autre de la paroi du verre, l'une à l'intérieur, l'autre à l'extérieur, elles se reflétaient l'une en l'autre.'[30] The mirror-image holds an appeal for poets looking for structural forms for their work, and seems to be applied at every level of literary—and literal—activity.

Reference to two last examples, analysed in greater detail elsewhere,[31] will indicate the variety of parabolic elements which may be brought to bear crucially on individual poems. One of Supervielle's rare excursions into the world of the *poème en prose*, 'Vertige' in *Gravitations*, comprises two stanzas of three sentences each and hinges on the key words 'Joie rocheuse'. The poem opens on the words 'Le granit' and ends on 'les pierres', tracing a curve between them appropriate to the cross-section of the 'ravin' evoked. From 'le paysage' of the first paragraph we shift to the psychological 'intime paysage' of the second. The technique guards against the loss of poetry in a prose presentation and puts a brake on the loose or discursive by replacing the rigour of rhyme. More extraordinary still is the case of a poem to which the word 'vertige' has justifiably been applied.[32] In the closing stanza of Rimbaud's 'Mystique', the symmetry of the poem is underlined by a series of palindromic elements pivoting around the word 'panier', itself suggestive of the curvature involved:

La douceur fleurie des étoiles et du ciel et du reste descend en face du talus, comme un panier,—contre notre face, et fait l'abîme fleurant et bleu là-dessous.

Difficult to establish in all the above examples is the measure of conscious shaping brought to the work. Where a prosodic pattern of some kind is imposed on a series of poems, it seems reasonable to suppose that the idea of 'une rhétorique par poème' may be discounted. Where, on the contrary, there is flexibility of form, the problem remains. To what extent did Rimbaud, in 'Mystique', aim at constructing something as near a palindrome as the French language and aesthetic desirability allow? To what extent did the young Saint-John Perse or Supervielle consciously aim at a balance of reality and unreality around a crucial pair of words? The answers may only be deduced, and then not with absolute certainty, from their other writings.

It remains true, however, that whether visual stimuli from paintings or natural phenomena are used as a basis for narrative, in the form of calligrammes or in that of assimilated calligrammes, they represent an important element in the structure and coherence of a poem. It would of course be wrong to assume that such figures are restricted to the prose poem and to the post-Romantic period. They do however assume greater importance when rigid prosodic armatures are dispensed with. Voltaire's rhetorical question: 'qu'est-ce qu'un poème en prose, sinon un aveu d'impuissance?'[33] could be given the intended assent only by those equating verse with poetry. The fallacy of the equation has been recognised by its perpetrators being consigned to poetic oblivion: the *siècle des lumières* shed little light in the realm of poetry. George Steiner has summarised the necessary distinction: 'The poetic is an attribute; verse is a technique.'[34]

The examples chosen to illustrate a particular point do not necessarily achieve the high state of poetry: a verbal parabola is not a new passport to excellence. But in almost all of the poems selected for discussion, we are presented, so to speak, with both sides of the mirror, and the polarities or dualisms depicted are in miniature both those of poetry, a mediating art working intrinsically in the realm of ambiguity, and of man's nature which is no less ambivalent. These poems manage to transcend the sum of their component parts. They are in fact a further expression of 'l'expérience du seuil', the pivotal phrase being the threshold of the mirror.[35] The relationship between modes of perception, visual and verbal, leads to an intriguing interplay of time passing and time standing still, and it remains demonstrably true that 'the basic material of poetry is active mimicry'.[36] Riffaterre's conclusion to a penetrating study of the poem as representation—'l'efficacité de la mimésis poétique n'a rien à voir avec une adéquation des signes aux choses'[37]—is too extreme. The technique of verbal mimesis of visual stimuli, an example of just such an 'adéquation', is available to all poets. It remains especially valuable in giving structural and aesthetic unity to free verse and prose poems and underlines the importance of recognising the generic continuum within literature and the consequent aptness of the less ambiguous title proposed by Perse for the *poème en prose*:[38] 'poème non versifié'.

Southampton   ROGER LITTLE

NOTES

1 Maurice Chapelan, *Anthologie du poème en prose*, Paris, 1946, p. vii. Cf. Suzanne Bernard, *Le Poème en prose de Baudelaire jusqu'à nos jours*, Paris, 1959, p. 444: 'La polarité du poème en prose se retrouve à tous les degrés de son organisation', and pp. 434–65, *passim*.
2 Bernard, op. cit., p. 462.
3 Preface to *Le Spleen de Paris* in *Œuvres complètes*, Paris (Bibliothèque de la Pléiade), 1954, p. 281.
4 Aloysius Bertrand, *Gaspard de la Nuit*, ed. B. Guégan, Paris, 1925, p. 33.
5 Baudelaire, op. cit., p. 318.
6 Ernest Delahaye, *Les Illuminations et Une saison en enfer d'Arthur Rimbaud*, Paris, 1927, p. 48.
7 Max Jacob, *Le Cornet à dés*, 6e édition Paris, 1945, p. 165 ('Le Fond du tableau'). Étienne Souriau recalls a very similar Chinese anecdote and discusses Segalen's *Peintures* in this vein in *La Poésie française et la peinture*, London, 1966, pp. 42–3.

8 Mallarmé, *Œuvres complètes*, Paris (Bibl. de la Pléiade), 1945 (1956 printing), p. 1582.

9 André Billy, Preface to Apollinaire, *Œuvres poétiques*, Paris (Bibl. de la Pléiade), 1965, p. xliii.

10 Quoted by C. A. Hackett, 'Seven Young French Poets: A New Trend in French Poetry', *Mosaic*, II, 4 (Summer 1969), 109.

11 Bernard, op. cit., p. 443.

12 Jean-Paul Weber's word 'cryptogramme' ('le cryptogramme miroitant en filigrane sous le calligramme', *La Psychologie de l'art*, Paris, 3rd edn, 1965, p. 43) is given pseudo-Freudian overtones unacceptable in the present context.

13 Souriau, *La Correspondance des arts*, Paris, 2nd edn, 1969, pp. 170–1.

14 Bertrand, op. cit., pp. 270–1.

15 Jacob, *Art poétique*, Paris, 1922, p. 66.

16 Saint-John Perse, 'Léon-Paul Fargue, poète', in Fargue, *Poésies*, Paris, 1963, pp. 24–5.

17 Perse, Letter to George Huppert, *Honneur à Saint-John Perse*, ed. Jean Paulhan, Paris, 1965, p. 656.

18 Perse, *Poésie: Allocution au Banquet Nobel du 10 décembre 1960*, Paris, 1961, unnumbered pages.

19 Perse, Letter to George Huppert, p. 656.

20 Perse, in *Honneur à Saint-John Perse*, p. 809.

21 Perse, *Œuvre poétique*, Paris, 1960, I, pp. 190–210.

22 Jacob, Preface to *Le Cornet à dés*, p. 17.

23 René Char, 'La Bibliothèque est en feu', *La Parole en archipel*, Paris, 1962, p. 72.

24 Francis Ponge, 'Raisons de vivre heureux', in *Proêmes*, in *Tome premier*, Paris, 1965, p. 190.

25 Ponge, *Le Grand Recueil: Méthodes*, Paris, 1961, pp. 36–7. Ponge obviously goes too far in rejecting the sonnet, ode and epigram, since they may themselves be the most appropriate form for a given topic.

26 Hackett, op. cit., p. 100, quoting from Michel Deguy, *Actes*, Paris, 1966, p. 73.

27 Pierre Mabille, *Le Miroir du merveilleux*, Paris, 1962, pp. 68–9.

28 Perse, *Œuvre poétique*, I, 63. The original text (*NRF*, August 1909, p. 22) differs in some details.

29 Philippe Bonnefis, 'L'Activité littérale', *Revue des Sciences Humaines*, 142 (Apr.–June 1971), pp. 157–84.

30 Ponge, *Le Grand Recueil: Méthodes*, p. 127.

31 Roger Little, 'Jules Supervielle: "Vertige" ', in *The Poem Within*, ed. Georges Lannois, Irish University Press, forthcoming, and 'Rimbaud's "Mystique": Some Observations', *French Studies*, XXVI, 3 (July 1972), pp. 285–8.

32 Albert Py, ed., *Illuminations*, Geneva, 1967, p. 152.

33 Quoted by Chapelan, op. cit., p. xi.

34 George Steiner, *The Death of Tragedy*, London, 1961, p. 238.

35 See Little, 'The Image of the Threshold in the Poetry of Saint-John Perse', *Modern Language Review*, LXIV, 4 (October 1969), pp. 777–92. The phrase 'l'expérience du seuil' is borrowed from Janine Carrel, *L'Expérience du seuil dans l'œuvre de Julien Green*, Zurich, 1967.

36 P. N. Furbank, *Reflections on the Word 'Image'*, London, 1970, p. 104. On the following page, Furbank offers a very interesting example from English poetry: 'Consider the delicacy with which, in the last lines of Book 4 of *Paradise Lost*

> The Fiend lookt up and knew
> His mounted scale aloft: nor more; but fled
> Murmuring, and with him fled the shades of night.

the motion of a pair of scales is suggested, with "nor more" as its fulcrum. It is a definitive piece of mimicry. . . .' The very repetition of sound in 'nor more' intensifies our awareness of its pivotal effect.

37 Michael Riffaterre, 'Le Poème comme représentation', *Poétique*, 4 (1970), p. 416.

38 Perse, 'Léon-Paul Fargue, poète', p. 18.

IMAGINATION AS ORDER AND AS ADVENTURE

In the 1846 *Salon* Baudelaire defended Delacroix against the charge that his pictures lacked composition, that they were haphazard. His effects are premeditated, Baudelaire maintains, though the reasoning which has led to them may have been elliptical. His earlier copies of work by other artists show that he could have composed like them had he wanted; he has 'passé alternativement sous le joug secoué de tous les grands maîtres'. Through them, Baudelaire implies in a quotation from Heine, he must have become aware of the fundamental structuring principles of art; principles not found in nature, but generated by the human soul. And his technical mastery is such that he can work at a great rate.

For Baudelaire, everything the artist does is eventually in the service of imagination. A thorough-going devotee of the imaginative theory of art would object to the intervention of reasoning in the process. Coleridge would have objected; Schelling, so closely followed by Coleridge, would have objected. Reason, yes; reasoning, no. Coleridge wanted the *noũs* of Neoplatonism to be translated by 'reason' rather than 'intellect', as it was in his day, because 'intellect' suggested a kind of reasoning which, in his view, had no part in the 'esemplastic' functioning of imagination. Baudelaire's notion of 'reasoning out' the way to achieve an effect is bound, now, to make us think of Poe's *Philosophy of Composition*. There is no evidence that Baudelaire knew Poe before 1847. The absence of evidence is never, of course, a proof; Baudelaire *may* have had wind of Poe's ideas by 1846. But I do not wish to re-explore the immediate possible sources of Baudelaire's ideas; rather some general tendencies in thinking about art. The *ultimate* source of the belief that effects can be 'reasoned out' is Aristotle; the *Philosophy of Composition* can be seen as a Romantic parody of the *Poetics*, with the beauty of sadness replacing the purging of the passions. The 'divine logician' of the Middle Ages became the apostle of reason for the aesthetics of classicism; not the mystical or imaginative reason of the Neoplatonist *noũs*, but reason arrived at through logical thinking and the exercise of true judgment which in French classicism, as Antoine Adam tells us, amounted to observing the prejudices of the age; or, if an Englishman may put it more tactfully, the values of the prevailing culture.

Baudelaire, like most French thinkers, is marked by the rationalism of his tradition as, later, are Mallarmé and Valéry. The influence of Poe in France coincides with attempts to rationalise states of mind associated with the operations of imagination. But the dominant influence, the directing ideas come from Neoplatonism, indirectly or directly. Notice that the 'reasoning' Baudelaire ascribes to Delacroix may be elliptical. 'Une chose heureusement trouvée est la simple conséquence d'un bon raisonnement, dont on a quelquefois sauté les déductions intermédiaires. . . .' Reasoning in which we are not consciously aware of the steps approaches intuition.

If we take all Baudelaire's pronouncements about imagination together, we get the following set of ideas. Art is an imaginative adventure contingent upon the imaginative discovery of a transcendent order or structure. Every artist must in the last issue see the transcendent order for himself and embark on his own adventure. But he may be helped to look for the right kind of structure and to set the right direction for his imaginative voyage by responding to the works of earlier artists and inspecting *their* imaginative structures. Thereafter he may use his reason—or that short-circuited reasoning which is one kind of intuition—to create structures that are new and original but of the same nature. Order as Apollinaire means it—learned through imaginative response to tradition—is a help towards new and original order; order grasped afresh, independently not only of conventional norms but of the visions of others. Reasoning and technical know-how intervene to order the artist's materials towards the imaginatively apprehended end.

When Baudelaire is most faithful to his theory of correspondences, composition, structuring are effects of the imagination engaged upon its own spiritual adventures. The more his own imagination is carried away by the notion of imagination itself, the more he seems to forget the careful empirical observations he made about Delacroix in 1846. The earlier implication that the painter intuits structural types from the work of his predecessors has disappeared from the *Exposition universelle de 1855*. 'Dans l'ordre poétique et artistique, tout révélateur a rarement un précurseur. Toute floraison est spontanée, individuelle.' The suspicion that this might need qualifying is dissipated in carefully formulated rhetorical questions, though the paragraph which follows, referring to the growth and decline of artistic fruitfulness in the life of nations and cultures, implies that *something* valuable may be transmitted, at periods of growth, from one artist to another. And in 1859 'la reine des facultés' not only dictates the purposes of artistic creation but creates the forms through which it is realised. Imagination, here, has all the powers and functions which Valéry was later to attribute to his *moi pur*. With this substitution, indeed, Valéry might have written: 'L'imagination est la reine du vrai, et le *possible* est une des provinces du vrai. Elle est positivement apparentée avec l'infini.' Imagining is the adventure of perceiving true order, an order inherent in the mind's potential, which is the infinite in mind—whether derived from a transcendent mind or human evolutionary success.

Valéry and Baudelaire gave very different specific meanings to 'infinite', of course. For Baudelaire, at least in theory, it is divine transcendence; for Valéry, the non-finite, the quasi-divine transcendence of mind itself. Valéry would never have written that 'l'art est la mnémotechnie du beau' or that genius is the recovery of childhood or any of the other indications that Baudelaire's *aspiration vers l'infini* was partly nostalgia for imaginatively transfigured memories of his perceptual world; though the sense of beauty in much of Valéry's poetry is obviously derived in different ways from his own perceptual world. The directions of imaginative adventures can vary greatly from one poet to another while some quality remains common —the adventurousness itself, the pursuit of some dimly perceived ideal. This is what so many post-Romantic sensibilities have in common, and in common with the noetic lyricism in Neoplatonism.

It is a commonplace now to hold that imagination has supplanted imitation in our view of art; and in general the notion of imagination as a creative power of mind has become detached from its Neoplatonist origins. It has not thereby much gained in clarity. Imitation itself is an obscure notion in Plato and Aristotle, and subsequent clarifications often resulted in a naïve view of copying to which neither would have subscribed. If the naïve view lasted longer in connexion with painting than with the other arts, it was because the Renaissance discoveries of colour-space, chiaroscuro and perspective were thought of as means of copying rather than techniques of illusion. But imagination came into the foreground of men's thinking about art, and particularly about literature, at the time of the Renaissance. It existed in happy ambiguity with imitation in the Renaissance notion of invention. The subsequent competition between imitation and imagination seems to be related to the competition between reason and imagination, or between the reason of rationalism and the reason of *noûs*.

What we can see, historically, it seems to me, is that the notion of imagination as adventure into some kind of 'surreality' and as a kind of order which distinguishes that 'surreality' from mere fantasy is to be traced to origins in mysticism, magic and alchemy.

Neither Plato nor Aristotle credits imagination (*phantasia*) with any powers of insight, visionary or scientific. Between Plato and Cicero the notion is established that art imitates, not the objects of the senses, but the ideal vision of what it portrays. The earliest text I have been able to find which connects imagination both with art and with transcendent insight is the 'Life of Apollonius of Tyana' by Flavius Philostratus, who wrote of the powers of imagination as lyrically as Baudelaire. Late Alexandrian Neoplatonism recognised two approaches to transcendent reason (*noŭs*)—reasoning, corresponding to Platonic dialectic and Aristotelian logic, and imagination. We can see this kind of thinking on its way into the climate of the New Aristotle of the early Renaissance in Al-Fārābi's theory of prophecy and divination as set out by Walzer;[2] this medieval Muslim Neo-platonist is 'rationalising' the mysticism of his own religious tradition much as Plato had rationalised the Orphic element in the Pythagorean tradition, replacing the notion of divine 'possession' of the seer's mind by a psychological account of how such a mind can grasp divine truth through the exercise of its own inherent powers.

In the Florentine Academy alchemy and magic come into the picture and the *vis imaginativa* is associated with power *over* the mind—one's own and others—as well as power over astrological forces. But henceforward imagination has to compete for prestige, not with what is thought of as the intellectual apprehension of the same object, the same reality, in a continuous tradition centred on *noŭs*, but with Western rationalism; the persisting theological rationalism of the Middle Ages, Cartesian rationalism, Baconian empiricism and the aesthetic rationalism of the 'Poetics'. In some areas it is ignored, in others combated. Bacon knows all about the *vis imaginativa* but has little use for it. In Hobbes and Locke imagination is trivially treated; the notion either loses its specific meaning through being identified with thought itself, all that goes on in the mind, or shrinks to its humblest beginnings as the power of the mind to produce those ghosts of perceptions called images. But in England, comparatively sheltered from the Counter-Reformation and the Classical separation of Neoplatonist and Aristotelian aesthetics, the Neoplatonist current still flows fairly strongly, mingling the two rivers of the Italian Renaissance and the Northern. In Germany, too, there is a mystical eddy centred on Boehme.

Already in Boehme imagination and the senses are brought together in protest against the kind of abstraction that tends to the purely cognitive awareness of the world and to a conceptual account of transcendent truth. In the Divine Being there is sensuousness as well as spirituality, and God is to be known through the senses as much as through the reasoning mind. God is not only all-knowing, but, like us, has a sensorium, and is all-seeing, all-hearing, all-tasting, all-feeling and all-smelling. In England, the Neoplatonism which comes to the fore again after the temporary classicism of the Restoration takes into itself lessons learned from the sensationalist tradition with which it had earlier clashed. Henceforward the poets who cultivate imagination are less inclined to fix their gaze on transcendence, picking up the stray sensibles which happen into the line of vision, and more intent upon sensibles with a view to 'imagining' their transcendent qualities. There are, of course, variations and exceptions: Shelley is one.

Addison is a great synthesiser of ideas, and his views on imagination combine notions taken from Hobbes, Locke and Shaftesbury as well as contemporary poets. Imagination is reinvested with mystery and power; sensation is as much a matter of feeling—important feeling—as of knowing, and those secondary qualities of perception, like colour, through which things are felt as well as recognised, are attributed by Addison to imagination.

Imagination depends on culture; it is not simply *native*, even in the poet. All the same, the power to feel beauty comes from God, and the sense of beauty can include the sense of the infinite. For Rousseau and the Romantics this becomes: 'Whatever my soul appears to yearn after, the true object of its yearning is God.' Yearning and imagination henceforward go together, and yearning can vary from a gentle nostalgia to a violent passion for *l'idéal*, which often seems to be the infinite projection of impulses and longings recognisably finite.

Familiar are the ambiguities of interpretation which result, in Rousseau's case, from imaginative freedom and the moral imperative. Kant put more system into some of Rousseau's insights and patterned the relations between imagination, reason and morality. Imagination has a part to play in perception itself, in synthesising the mass of sensations into an interpretation, an appearance; but the rightness of this interpretation is judged by reason. The role of imagination in Kant's thinking is important, but always circumscribed. Schelling freed it, and made claims for imagination as knowledge similar to those of the Alexandrian Neoplatonists and of Boehme; Coleridge found in Schelling's religion based on subjective idealism the goal towards which he had himself been tending in his Neoplatonist speculations. And Baudelaire's 1859 *Salon* is written in the same spirit, though without Schelling's and Coleridge's attempts at analytical thought.

When one looks at the detail of all the thinking that has gone on about imagination, so briefly sketched here, one might decide at first that the notion is a sort of rag-bag for odd aspects of experience that do not fit under more definable heads, reason as logical thinking being the most easily definable in a way to elicit common consent. It is not surprising that psychologists handle the notion gingerly and that many philosophers think that such a wide-open concept is not a proper theme for philosophising at all. But, in addition to historical constants within a tradition, like the association of imagination and mysticism, or, later, of imagination with the enjoyment of sensuous vividness, we find some notions which significantly interrelate superficially different kinds of introspective insights.

Primarily imagining is having images, mostly seeing images; and imagination becomes associated with inner fantasies, dreams, hallucinations and illusions of all kinds. When we choose to imagine what is not really there, we find from Aristotle onwards the realisation that we are following our wishes. The animal imagines the goal of its hunger, of its biological drives as *we* might say. Man imagines other kinds of 'goods'; imagination pursues value, as we might now say, leaping across the centuries to phenomenology and Sartre.

Aristotle is still working within a moral order. 'Mind is always right, but appetite and imagination may be either right or wrong—the object may be the real or the apparent good.'[3] Imagination is a way of exploring order, but is itself subject to some higher judgment —as it is later in Bacon and Kant. When, with Sartre, moral order and reasoned judgment disappear, imagination is identified not only with valuing but with the positing of value itself: yet ethical judgment creeps back inside the notion of authenticity.

But to go back to images; some seem to be willed, others to come unbidden. What we choose to bring to consciousness is likely to have a nice, familiar, docile feeling about it; what seems to come unbidden may be strange, exciting and even frightening. Within Alexandrian Neoplatonism there arose the conviction that these 'visions' had a supernatural, thrilling, awesome message to convey. They said things that reason could not say. But it was realised also—as Al Fārābi shows—that they might be seen to convey meanings that *could* be apprehended in another way. Dreams could express bodily sensations and deep affects where 'feeling' as emotional tone is hardly distinct from 'feeling' as sensation. So in modern times these two notions fuse; the 'surreality' which images express either works through or is generated by the unconscious. From Romanticism to Sartre the unconscious changes from a realm of discovery and adventure into a storehouse where we rediscover past choices to reconsider them. Those images which *seemed* to come unbidden have, according to Sartre, been called into being by those buried choices; the schizophrenic *wants* to see images which will justify his fear and hatred. These are the aspects of imaginative literature that *la critique thématique* explores with the help of Freud, Bachelard and Sartre.

So far we have spoken of imagination as the maker of images and of structures of images, things happening in the mind and not immediately dependent on happenings in the outside world. Another group of introspective observations connected with imagination concerns the immediate interraction between mind and world, concerns perception itself. In Plato, *phantasía* is appearance. 'That is a man', it says, of sensations deriving from what may turn out to be a man or a tree. Kant takes this over and completes the account of *true* perception with reference to the mind's logic; the *possible* appearances are judged and the true appearance selected by something other than imagination. Imagination may also *play* with appearances, knowing them to be perceptually false. Philostratus makes Apollonius speak of seeing cloud-shapes as animals and of filling out perceptually incomplete schemata, such as line-drawings, with meaning. This filling-out may be itself part cognitive, part imaginative. Through the shape of a jaw, the curl of the hair, the shape of a nose we *recognise* an Indian, and Apollonius credits this to intelligence. But we then *supply* the missing perceptual features, including colour; and this is the work of imagination.

This basic observation we can link, across the centuries, with the promotion of perceptually erroneous 'impressions' over true perceptions, over those which involve true recognition of the source of the sensations; in Ruskin and Proust, for instance. Recognition, in the case of Apollonius's line-drawing, both directs and limits imagination. It would be eccentric to imagine a blue Indian—or even, in this case, a red one. Indians are swarthy. But the less 'recognisable' the schema, the more play for imagination. The free play of imagination carries with it the sense of enjoyment of freedom as long as this is not inhibited by puzzlement. Moreover, if we read carefully the passages where Proust introspectively explores this sense of inner revelation through mis-perceived sensations, we can surmise that as long as recognition does not terminate the free play by 'labelling' the schema of sensations, the schema can be filled by irrational associations, associations not governed by understanding; so that the meaning spontaneously read into the schema by the mind reveals the mind's deepest affective concerns, its unconscious values; selection of meaning by the mind's logic gives way to selection of meaning by those values which reason may attempt to describe but cannot express. Sensations, before the reason locks them into a percept, can themselves unlock other areas of meaning, and bring awareness of structures in the mind other than conceptual structures.

Our post-Romantic poets—and in this respect Proust is one—prefer the imaginative distortion to the clear percept. Rimbaud deliberately hallucinated—at least he says so in a work which is itself imaginative. Mallarmé seems to have spent some of his midnights gazing at the furniture and projecting himself into it. Valéry explores a similar situation in that curious passage of the first Leonardo essay in which the table comes to life—presumably as Valéry switches to 'seeing' it through energy-physics—and the curtains flow like water.[4] The element of subjective idealism in the post-Romantic mentality sees perception primarily as the exploration of mind rather than of the world through mind.

Addison, Coleridge and Bachelard, with their variously detailed accounts of 'primary' imagination, suggest that the separation between the 'recognising' element in perception and the element which consists of reading affective meaning into sensations need not be absolute. When we reflect on the act of knowing, we concentrate on the aspect of recognition, the ordering of our sensations within a conceptual world. We must do this to reason at all. But in our immediate experience of the world meaning includes something else; it is variously described by those who take account of it as coalescence of subject and object, intentionality, introjection, participation. At one end of a scale it is interpreted as mystical, distinguished from rational 'knowledge'; at the other end, for modern Structuralists, it is relative, culture-dependent and ultimately insignificant. It can be an important element in poetic feeling.

The difference between this perceptual situation and that described in the previous paragraph is that here the mind's non-rational response itself depends on recognition. The object is apprehended as an object, not as the source of sensations which, while still unrecognised, unlock *purely* subjective affects. When such experiences are brought into art, there is still an element of imitation: we are expected or invited not just to feel in this way, but to feel in this way about certain recognisable things. When the concept of imagination excludes imitation altogether, art may become the invitation, not to feel in this way about certain recognisable things, nor even to feel in *this* way, but to feel in any way our own imagination pleases. There are many examples nowadays of such do-it-yourself art, where the art form becomes an empty schema like Apollonius's clouds or Rorschach ink-blots. Form is then significant only as the potentiality of private meanings. And some critics treat in this way art-forms that are patently more than clouds, ink-blots or empty schemata.

Among the mental functionings associated with imagination in the Neoplatonist tradition, the creation of order, 'knowledge' of structure and form, appear. 'Comprendre', wrote Camus, 'c'est avant tout unifier.' Science unifies by establishing general principles which explain perceptually heterogeneous phenomena; only recently has imagination come into play as part of the explanation of how it is done, to the resentment of many scientists. And often it is allowed into play only as the freedom to run through possible hypotheses—the selection of the *likely* hypothesis is due to something else; the hypothesis once chosen, the rest is experimental testing of the logical consequences of the hypothesis. If imagination comes into play here, it is again as the freedom to run through possible experiments to find those which will apply the necessary tests—the choice of the right experiments is due to something else. Insight, for instance. But what is insight? Among our historical collection of ideas about imagination, insight is itself claimed for imagination; imagination directly sees kinds of interrelations which are not given in perception.

In the kind of thinking which we know to have been part of the background of post-Romantic French poetry, insight into inter-relations is mystical. The mystic claims to see the unity of all things in God, and to see that even contradictions only appear to be contra-dictions. In many cases we can see poets taking over these notions of mystical unifying and interpreting them in their own way, with varying degrees of belief in the correspondence between the artistic order they achieve and some divine order. Coleridge does believe in this, and his notebooks show him picking out the contradictory elements in his perceptual world and making a conscious effort to 'imagine' their reconciliation. Dr Davies's essay in this volume shows Apollinaire preoccupied with the unifying of opposites as a principle of 'vision'.

Baudelaire did his best to believe in it, and maintained the belief in his critical writings, though in his own self-doubts the belief seems often to have broken down with respect to his own work; finally, perhaps, altogether.

Mallarmé came to base his technique of suggestion, of evocation of the 'idea', on his own interpretation of Hegel's logic, in which affirmation and negation are complementary and not mutually exclusive. But, in the main, his escape from the rational logic which individuates perceptions into separates and contradictories was not into another kind of logic, but into another way of ordering words. Hegel's idea orders our imagination of the real world; Mallarmé's orders only itself.

Valéry rejected the belief that there is any order to be discovered other than the mind's power to create order, and was convinced that there is no fundamental difference between the practically effective abstract patterns of scientific thinking and the aesthetically effective forms of art. The unity of *le moi pur* in all its conscious manifestations is like the unity of *noûs* in its rational and imaginative manifestations before the forward movement of modern science drove a wedge between the two. The difference, of course, is that *noûs* claims two ways of knowing ultimate truth and Valéry claims that both are illusory; that the only ultimate truth is that of the mind's own nature.

Claudel's imagining was an attempt to order the world as he perceived it, and to show that even evil is part of the good. But for his order he leaned heavily on traditional imaginative patterns, and the acceptance of his order depends on the acceptance of what is traditional in it, on an authority that is not his. Yet many readers who reject his order accept the adventure, the liberation of violent emotion, the heightening of sensuous perception, the enlarging of a spiritual space which seems filled with oxygen.

As Symbolism wanes, the claim that the order of poetry reflects some kind of supernatural order is less constant and has less influence on poetic experiment. Surrealism saw the imaginative adventure less as the substitution of a mystical for a rational order than as the destruction of rational order in favour of the liberation of everything other than order which imagination had stood for—dreams, the lyricism of the irrational, the pursuit of intuited value outside the reach of reason as reasoning, reason as accepted norms, reason as common sense. One can see Surrealism, at its best, as the promotion of uninhibited love of life, including that love between human beings which had become so bloodlessly rarefied by the idealist tendency in the Symbolists or so exclusively sexualised by the ultra-sensual tendency in the Decadents.

Since Surrealism poetry seems to have become less ambitious and to re-connect with the real world in simple and direct ways. With Bachelard's emphasis on imaginative *perception* goes the imaginative exploration of simple things and simple happenings; the hyper-conscious and often lyrical notation of the humblest events. This is adventure not away from the everyday world but into it. There are as many adventures as poets, of course, and some seem to me to be still rather aimlessly fumbling round with the tools fashioned by their predecessors for their own special adventures rather than looking at the world with their own gaze. Even the most imaginative kind of poetry can create its *poncifs*.

Baudelaire wrote of Delacroix as having 'passé alternativement sous le joug secoué de tous les grands maîtres'. *Le joug secoué*—order and adventure as Apollinaire referred to them; tradition and experi-ment. Even the most adventurous poetic spirits of the post-Romantic era went back to tradition to learn from the 'structural types' of earlier poets. And if it proved to be an era nevertheless of daring experiment, of startling technical innovation and adventurousness in the handling of language, the direction of these adventures was suggested to a great extent by ideas about the imaginative functioning of mind derived from the Neoplatonist tradition. When we speak of the move from imitation to imagination as the centre of thinking about art we are usually pointing to notions directly or indirectly derived from this tradition. We are inclined to think that 'modernism' means 'imagination' and that 'modernism' is right. The promotion of imagination meant enrichment of the world of poetry in some ways, but perhaps impoverishment in others. As long as the notion of 'imitation' allows for imaginative freedom and imagined order, it means imaginative awareness within art of the real world and the consequent investment of our real world with imagination directed to some extent by art. As long as the aesthetics of Aristotle's *Poetics* combines with the imagination of Neoplatonism art can include among its ambitions not simply subjective lyrical states of mind but imaginative interpretation of the world and human relations in which reason, judgment, knowledge have as important a part to play as the Neoplatonic functions of imagination itself.

Imagination is not a concept which explains art, even post-Romantic art, but a myth which sustains it; a myth rich in possible interpretations. In general, it embodies the intuitions of artists that human consciousness has been impoverished by the abstractions of rationalism and particularly of science. It can spur the artist to escape from Aristotelian logic into the logic of mysticism or of the uncon-scious; from analytical thinking into synthetic experience where the coherence may imply a claim to insight into features of the perceptual world or to autonomous form from which the perceptual is as far as possible excluded. It can insist that sensations are not merely the bases for conceptual recognition but important elements of experience in their own right; and that the richness and lyricism and drama of every inner experience depends on the myths we build up for ourselves, the images we invest with particular meanings and the way these images cluster—myths and images which usually include some of the rags of the tattered but still surviving collective myths of our cultural past.

In the case of most of the artists of the post-Romantic era, the freedom of imagination can be shown to be subject to criteria which cannot be subsumed under imagination conceived *simply* as freedom, as adventure. There is the notion of 'significant' order, which *can* be subsumed under imagination as mystical awareness—though other kinds of explanations can be offered. There is the notion of formal order—the rules of prosody, the calculation of effects, the 'intuiting' of aesthetically effective structures from the work of earlier artists. There is the notion of the faithfulness of imagined form to perceived experience, or to insights into perceived experience—which brings back the discarded notion of imitation.

But rich and vital notions tend, as they spread, to grow thin and etiolated; ideas spread most easily as simplified abstractions. The myth of imagination is producing some strange results; Valéry's ideal of empty schemata to be filled with private meanings is coming to pass in a way which he would have found surprising. He believed that the schemata had to correspond in some way to the nature of mind to be fillable with meaning at all; the schemata proposed in some areas of contemporary art depend on pure chance, or the chance development of algorithms by computer. Perhaps this will open up a way forward; perhaps it is a dead end. Perhaps the myth of imagination has to give way to another. Of national traditions Baudelaire wrote in 1855: 'Souvent il arrive que c'est le principe même qui a fait leur force et leur développement qui amène leur décadence, surtout quand ce principe, vivifié jadis par une ardeur conquérante, est devenu pour la majorité une espèce de routine.' Too often, in our own day, imagination itself becomes a routine; the spirit of 'L'Invitation au voyage' becomes the small beer of the travel-agent's ad-man.

London   J. M. COCKING

NOTES

1 The distinction between science, in which there is progress because knowledge is cumulative, and art in which genius always starts from scratch goes back to the Querelle des Anciens et des Modernes. Baudelaire is, of course, attacking the notion of science-based progress itself; the only real progress would be in the world of moral value. Proust picked up this two-century-old distinction between progressive science and non-progressive art in *Le Temps retrouvé*, but modified it in a passage of *A l'ombre des jeunes filles en fleurs*, probably in a late addition which took account of his own quasi-scientific ambition to demonstrate *vérités de l'intelligence* as well as 'impressions', or *vérités poétiques*. In Fontenelle the sense of the distinction is concessive to the tradition of art; in the nineteenth century it becomes an aggressive claim for the complete freedom of imagination.

2 R. Walzer 'Al-Fārābi's Theory of Prophecy and Divination', *Journal of Hellenic Studies*, 77, 1957, pp. 142–8.

3 *De Anima*, tr. Ross, 433a 20.

4 *Pléiade I*, p. 1170.

LIST OF SUBSCRIBERS

Mrs. R. Adamson
Mrs. Marion Appéré
K. R. Aspley
Prof. L. J. Austin
Prof. C. P. Barbier
G. Bedser
Bristol University Library
Mrs. Carol Britton
Peter Broome
Dr. David Brown
Mrs. Elizabeth Brown
Harcourt Brown
Ms. Virginia A. La Charité
Prof. Donald G. Charlton
Ms. Vivien A. Coates
P. W. M. Cogman
Prof. Norman Cohn
Mrs. Dorothy Coleman
Ms. Diane C. Cornil
Dr. Christine M. Crow
Dr. M. C. Davies
Ms. Linda Dubock
Prof. P. A. Evans
A. G. Falconer
Dr. Brian Foster
Prof. W. M. Frohock
Prof. O. N. V. Glendinning
Dr. J. A. Hiddleston
I. Higgins
Peter C. Hoy
Jesus College, Cambridge
Prof. Hunter Kellenberger

Prof. Jean E. L. Launay
Wynn Lee
Joseph Long
Merton College, Oxford
Prof. Robert L. Mitchell
Modern and Medieval
   Languages Libraries,
   Cambridge
Modern Languages Library,
   Winchester College
Miss Yvonne Orchard
Malachy J. O'Rourke
Michael Pakenham
Stevan K. Pavlowitch
Dr. A. W. Raitt
Warren Ramsay
Ms. Joanna E. Rapf
L. J. Russon
Dr. J. W. Scott
Ms. Marjorie Shaw
Sheffield University Library
Southampton University Library
St. Andrews University Library
St. Catherine's College Library,
   Cambridge
Dr. Bernard C. Swift
Ms. Margaret G. Tillett
Utica College Library, New
   York
Mrs. Nancy Wilson
W. L. Wilson

NOTE: The above are those who subscribed at the time of going to press. Apologies are due to those too late to be included in the list.